THE PSYCHOLOGY OF ENVIRONMENTAL LAW

PSYCHOLOGY AND THE LAW
General Editor: Linda J. Demaine

The Psychology of Tort Law
Jennifer K. Robbennolt and Valerie P. Hans

The Psychological Foundations of Evidence Law
Michael J. Saks and Barbara A. Spellman

The Psychology of Family Law
Eve M. Brank

The Psychology of Property Law
Stephanie M. Stern and Daphna Lewinsohn-Zamir

The Psychology of Environmental Law
Arden Rowell and Kenworthey Bilz

The Psychology of Environmental Law

Arden Rowell

Kenworthey Bilz

With a Preface by Linda J. Demaine

NEW YORK UNIVERSITY PRESS

New York

NEW YORK UNIVERSITY PRESS
New York
www.nyupress.org

References to internet websites (URLs) were accurate at the time of writing. Neither the authors nor New York University Press are responsible for URLs that may have expired or changed since the manuscript was prepared.

Library of Congress Cataloging-in-Publication Data
Names: Rowell, Arden, author. | Bilz, Kenworthey, author.
Title: The psychology of environmental law / Arden Rowell, Kenworthey Bilz;
with a preface by Linda J. Demaine.
Description: New York : New York University Press, [2021] | Series: Psychology and the law |
Includes bibliographical references and index.
Identifiers: LCCN 2020016959 (print) | LCCN 2020016960 (ebook) |
ISBN 9781479812301 (cloth) | ISBN 9781479891863 (paperback) |
ISBN 9781479835515 (ebook) | ISBN 9781479807574 (ebook)
Subjects: LCSH: Environmental law—Psychological aspects.
Classification: LCC K3585 .R69 2021 (print) | LCC K3585 (ebook) | DDC 344.04/6—dc23
LC record available at https://lccn.loc.gov/2020016959
LC ebook record available at https://lccn.loc.gov/2020016960

New York University Press books are printed on acid-free paper, and their binding materials are chosen for strength and durability. We strive to use environmentally responsible suppliers and materials to the greatest extent possible in publishing our books.

Manufactured in the United States of America

10 9 8 7 6 5 4 3 2 1

Also available as an ebook

For Graham—I hope this helps. —A.R.

For my husband, Dan, with whom I spend as much time as I can enjoying the natural world. —K.B.

CONTENTS

PREFACE

LINDA J. DEMAINE

The NYU Press Psychology and the Law book series addresses an intriguing state of affairs in legal scholarship. Although law and legal process are inherently psychological in nature, traditionally, relatively few law professors, judges, or legal practitioners have drawn on empirical psychological research to inform their perspectives and decisions. In recent years, the legal community has increasingly recognized that both substantive law and legal procedure rest on a multitude of testable assumptions about human behavior that can be informed by psychological research. Without formal training in psychology, however, it can be challenging for legal experts to identify relevant and informative psychological research, evaluate its methodological rigor, and interpret the empirical results. Consequently, in the absence of trusted resources to translate findings from psychological studies and apply them to core legal issues, psychology's potential to inform legal doctrine and practice will remain unfulfilled. Lawyers, in particular, will lack the tools that would enable them to better understand the law's effects on human behavior and how the law might be better constructed to achieve its goals.

Three important exceptions to psychology's peripheral status in legal scholarship are eyewitness testimony, false confessions, and jury decision making. In each of these realms, insights from psychological research have entered legal discussions and debates, resulting in marked improvements in the legal system's functioning. These exceptions, which developed precisely because lawyers communicated the fundamental legal issues to psychologists and psychologists introduced lawyers to informative research findings, demonstrate the potential of psychology to inform the law.

The Psychology and the Law book series is intended to help make the exceptions into the rule by expanding and strengthening the intersection of law and psychology. To achieve this goal, the series applies psychology to subjects covered in the core law school curriculum. The books are designed to facilitate exchanges between lawyers and psychologists about these fundamental legal issues by introducing lawyers to the most pertinent research methods and findings and introducing psychologists to the most central and generally complex legal issues. The books are valuable assets for law professors who desire to incorporate psychological science into their classes. To facilitate their adoption in law classrooms, the books map onto popular casebooks and are relatively brief and practical. The books are also prime resources for participants in psychology-law graduate programs, professors who teach undergraduate law and psychology courses, and mainstream psychologists who study legal issues. The books' expansive coverage of psychological research on core legal topics and their identification of areas in need of further research will provide these audiences with current knowledge and a roadmap to inspire empirical study. Finally, the books will be useful to legal practitioners whose work in particular areas of law can benefit from an understanding of psychology. All volumes are authored by eminent scholars who are conversant in both psychology and the law and possess the expertise necessary to identify and articulate legal issues of import, apply psychological theory and research findings to them, and identify areas of future research for psychologists.

In *The Psychology of Environmental Law*, Rowell and Bilz employ psychological science to explain and critique key facets of environmental law. Since its inception, environmental legal analysis has been dominated by an economic perspective. Although informative, economics provides an incomplete understanding of environmental law's goals, processes, and consequences, as these are inherently psychological in important respects. Rowell and Bilz thus take a groundbreaking approach to environmental law in this volume, elevating the field through a more nuanced, realistic view of environmentally impactive human behavior and its driving forces.

The first part of the book is designed to equip readers to engage in independent psychological analysis of environmental law. To this end, Rowell and Bilz initially identify three defining features of the psychology of environmental injuries: 1) diffusion through time and space unseen in other types of legally recognized injuries; 2) complexity in terms of their interactions with other human behaviors, their nonlinearity in impacts, and their multicausality; and 3) an important nonhuman element insofar as environmental injuries interact with nonhuman natural processes and implicate nonhuman stakeholders. These features are essential to considering how human behaviors are likely to affect the environment and to the law's ability to use humans as intermediaries to shape the environment in desired ways. After explaining the relevance of each defining feature, Rowell and Bilz discuss several empirically tested psychological concepts—including cognitive dissonance, loss aversion, the endowment effect, the status quo bias, and the availability heuristic—that underlie them. These studies investigate the concepts in a variety of settings with resulting, sometimes counterintuitive, changes to participants' behavior. In the aggregate, the studies provide versatile, powerful tools for understanding the causes of harmful human environmental impacts and fostering positive change.

Rowell and Bilz then illustrate how such a psychologically driven environmental analysis might be carried out, describing applications to classic problems in environmental law in the subfields of pollution control, ecosystem management, and climate change. Such problems, they argue, can be more effectively addressed with an understanding of the motivations, biases, and other psychological phenomena that underlie people's interactions with the environment and their evaluations of environmental injury.

By drawing upon the rich offerings of psychology, Rowell and Bilz expertly inform government efforts to regulate the most far-reaching aspects of human behavior—those that impact the natural environment in which we live and on which we rely so greatly for sustenance. They end the volume by forging a promising path for future psychological analysis of environmental law.

Introduction

At first glance, environmental law may seem a strange space in which to seek insights from psychology. Psychology, after all, aims to illuminate the interior of the human mind, while environmental law is fundamentally concerned with the exterior surroundings—the environment—in which people live. Yet those surroundings are constantly affected by human behavior, and as we will explain in this book, psychology can often help in explaining, describing, evaluating, and predicting behaviors with environmental impacts. This can prove helpful in predicting the real-world effects of environmental laws and in constructing environmental policies that are more effective at shaping human behavior toward desired ends. Indeed, in many cases, failing to address psychology can impoverish or even undermine the operation of environmental law.

Yet notably, as we write these words, the field of environmental law and psychology does not exist—though we believe it could and should. In the remainder of this introduction, we explain what we think psychology can offer environmental law—and why we think a psychological approach to environmental law is valuable enough that you should read this book.

Thus far, psychology has lagged behind other social science disciplines in finding purchase within environmental law. Economics, in particular, has long been a dominant force in environmental law, both in developing theories of individual and organizational behaviors and in affecting on-the-ground policy makers. It has been particularly influential through its focus on incentive structures and how they affect decision making in environmental law. Although less pervasive than economics, political science has also made important contributions, particularly in understanding how institutions and institutional actors function in their roles as policy makers and interpreters, and in illuminating how regulators choose particular instruments to pursue environmental goals. Sociology has contributed as well, especially in the area of environmental justice and in addressing how environmental regulation may affect different sectors of society in different ways.

So what does a *psychology* of environmental law contribute, and how does it differ from the perspectives offered by these other social science disciplines? First and foremost, psychology illuminates the internal, mental processes that shape people—who in turn may shape institutions and laws. Some mental processes are rational and thus amenable to classical economic modeling; others, such as many emotional and motivational processes, are not. Often, plural values exist simultaneously within the same human mind; such values may change, conflict, compete, and exist in some contexts but not others. Psychology seeks to be richly descriptive of all these mental processes—including those grounded in emotion, motivation, and social interaction—in a way that is based in empirical (often experimental) observation, rather than in a unified theory of human behavior (such as rational choice theory).

Second, because of its historical emphasis on *experimental* research, psychology offers a different set of insights on human behavior than other social science disciplines, such as sociology and economics, that have developed primarily in observational soil. Psychology emphasizes controlled experiments, often conducted in laboratories, because of their usefulness in generating clean, testable models in which causes versus effects are clear. Because the specific details of an experiment can be tightly controlled, this structure of empirical research is particularly well suited to measuring and evaluating mental processes—whether cognitive, emotional, or motivational—that may flow from multiple causes, values, or influences. Its downside is that it requires extrapolation from experimental settings to real-world contexts. Observational studies, by contrast, excel at describing how people are actually behaving—though they are not well structured for teasing out *why* they are behaving that way; for accounting for plural or context-dependent causes, values, or influences; or for predicting how changes in information, perception, or context might result in changes to behavior. (Of course, some psychologists do observational work, and other social scientists—especially behavioral economists, who have been so influenced by psychology—do experimental work.) Yet experimental research can be used to inform understanding of human behavior in ways that cannot be effectively reached through observational research alone.

To be clear, environmental law and policy may be valuably informed by both experimental and observational empirical research. But as we showcase in this book, the trove of experimental research that psychology has developed offers particular utility in a world pervaded by ever-increasing social and environmental change—though to date what psychology offers in this realm has been underused in comparison to research in other social science disciplines such as economics. As a result, we believe that the core dependence of psychology on experimental research should be seen as a feature and not a bug—and a feature that, particularly when combined with research from observational social science disciplines, can aid law and policy in painting a richer and more predictive account of human behavior and environmental change.

Finally—and we think valuably—psychology strives to be nonnormative. It is interested in understanding human mental processes and using that understanding to predict behavior. It is also interested in understanding and predicting how people will respond to a panoply of situational influences—including not just incentives, but also other people. But psychology is not interested in—or more specifically, is not capable of—deciding what people's goals should be. There is no guiding light of, say, "efficiency" or "justice" integral to the discipline. Thus, a psychology of environmental law will take no position on what the goals of environmental law should be, either in the grand scheme or in particular cases. This is a drawback for those seeking approaches that identify normative ends—for those purposes, philosophy or economics may be more helpful. Yet for those who have already selected normative ends that they wish to serve—to maximize social welfare, create just distributions of environmental goods, or establish environmental quality that is sustainable into the future—psychology's agnosticism is a decided advantage. It makes psychology "friendly," for want of a better word: Those in environmental law can use it to help them effect whatever ends they think appropriate.

So this is what psychology can offer environmental law: a rich, experimentally informed account of why, when, and how people act in ways that affect the environment—which can then be used to more effectively pursue whichever policy ends are desired.

Here, a specific example of how a psychological approach can inform environmental law may be in order. Consider the operation of the En-

dangered Species Act (1973), one of the most comprehensive and important pieces of legislation in the field. As we discuss further in Chapter
7, the ESA describes a procedure by which a species—any species—can
qualify as "endangered." A species can be listed either via agency action
or as the result of citizens petitioning to have it listed (by far the more
common route). Once an animal or plant is on the list of endangered
species, no public action can be taken that imperils any member of that
species or its critical habitat, and private actions are seriously circumscribed. From a statutory perspective, then, the ESA is clear about its
purpose, clear about its procedures, and clear about what can and cannot be done in light of it.

Notably, the ESA is facially neutral as to the types of endangered species protected—whether mammals, plants, spiders, or worms. In light
of that, how should we expect the broad protections of the act to be
allocated in practice? One prediction might be that all types of species
would be more or less equally likely to be protected. If so, we would
expect to see the number of species of various types that are protected
be roughly proportional to the total number of that type of species in
the world. An alternative prediction might be that types of species that
are more endangered, for example by changing climates, would be more
likely to be protected. In that case, for example, cold-blooded animals
should tend to be more protected than warm-blooded animals, the latter
of whom have more options for adapting to changing climactic conditions. Still another prediction might be that types of species that are
particularly important to larger ecosystems, and that might therefore
cause more wide-ranging damage through extinction, will tend to be
more protected. In that case, we should expect to see species that are at
the bottom of food chains, such as insects, being more protected than
those at the top of food chains, such as reptiles or mammals.

All of these predictions, however, appear to be wrong. In fact, warm-
blooded mammals are protected at far greater rates than any other type
of species: 7 times the rate of reptiles, 23 times the rate of plants, 70 times
the rate of insects, and 87,500 times the rate of spiders. Why?

At least part of the answer is human psychology. For an animal to be
protected by the ESA, someone—whether an individual, organization,
or agency—must both *notice* and *care* enough about the species in question to go through the effort of getting it on the list. And the processes

that lead to attention and care are cognitive and emotional—they are psychological processes. Which species garner enough attention to trigger listing? Larger, more photogenic, and more vivid species. This advantages mammals and reptiles over plants and insects. Which are most likely to trigger caring sufficient to justify the effort of listing? Those that provide the greatest basis for emotional connection, such as animals that share features with human babies—again, think fuzzy mammals—and *not* those that trigger deep-seated phobias, such as arachnids. Which animals, then, are *least* likely to find their way onto the list of protected species, regardless of their potential value to ecosystems and degree of endangerment? Those that are easy to ignore and that trigger little to no emotional connection—like insects and plants. Note that, again, there is no reason to think that such species are more resilient against extinction risks. If anything, the opposite may be true. Some scientists warn, for instance, of a coming "insect apocalypse" and estimate that as much as 40% of insect species are in measurable decline (Sanchez-Bayo & Wyckhuys, 2019). Yet only 0.1% of insect species are protected by the ESA—versus 7% of mammal species.

This serves as an example of how human cognitive and emotional processes can affect how the law operates, and indeed, whether it is effective at serving the ends for which it was created. Note again that there is no evidence that legislators intended the Endangered Species Act to be a Cute, Noticeable Animal Protection Act—that is just how the act has come to function in practice. Importantly, this result is not inevitable, even if it is predictable: Once they are aware of how the ESA functions in light of human biases and other mental processes, legal decision makers have the option of responding. If some species are not being noticed but should be, the law can intervene to make them more noticeable, can specifically direct action targeting neglected and disliked species, and/ or otherwise incentivize their inclusion on the endangered species list. Yet the direction such corrections might take, and the need for them in the first place, becomes apparent only once a psychological analysis of the ESA has been done.

With this example in mind, then, we can see that psychological analysis of environmental law offers descriptive, predictive, and prescriptive payoffs. Descriptively, psychology enriches environmental law's understanding of why, when, and how people engage in behaviors that affect the environment, by illuminating human cognition, motivation, and emotion. Predictively, psychology can help environmental law more accurately anticipate the impact of laws on human choices and human behaviors. And prescriptively, psychology can help environmental law identify opportunities for more effectively achieving its policy goals, whatever they may be.

Now that we have (hopefully) mounted a compelling case that psychology has something valuable to offer environmental law, the remainder of this book presents the building blocks for creating a psychology of environmental law. Chapter 1 articulates what we see as distinctively *environmental*, distinctively *psychological*, and distinctively *legal* about such a field. Subsequent chapters expand and develop our claims that the particular characteristics of environmental injury generate identifiable psychological implications, and that laws, legal institutions, and legal decision makers can be more effective in achieving environmental goals when they apply psychological analysis to environmental law. We pursue these claims through two means. First, in chapters 2, 3, 4, and 5, we outline what we see as the key psychological building blocks for performing psychological analysis of environmental laws. Three of these chapters are dedicated to highlighting psychological research that is particularly relevant to environmental law, in that it informs people's perceptions, processing, and responses to the diffuse (Chapter 2), complex (Chapter 3), and nonhuman (Chapter 4) character of environmental injury. These explorations, in combination with a more generalized overview of key research findings in law and psychology (Chapter 5), present readers with the tools they need to perform psychological analysis of environmental laws in specific applied areas.

The remainder of the book applies the research canvassed in these earlier chapters, presenting concrete examples and displaying some of the intellectual payoffs of applying a psychological approach to the environmental law of pollution control (Chapter 6), ecosystem management (Chapter 7), and climate change (Chapter 8). The book concludes with a final chapter containing suggestions for how the psychology of environmental law might develop from here, and ideas about future research that would further capture the benefits of psychological analysis for policy makers and other legal actors in environmental law.

Why Read a Book About the Psychology of Environmental Law?

Psychology has several features that can contribute to environmental law and policy.

- Focuses on mental processes. Psychology describes, explains, and predicts the mental processes of humans, which in turn affect their behavior.
- Uses mental processes to understand/predict behavior. Knowing how cognitive, emotional, and motivational processes (and consequent behaviors) work can help legal actors design environmental policies that have the effects they intend.
- Experimental methodology. Methodologically, psychology supplies tools for a rich understanding of causes and effects in environmental law, and for predicting human behavior in light of social and environmental change.
- Nonnormative. Psychology does not commit the user to any particular normative framework or set of environmental goals.

These features offer descriptive, predictive, and prescriptive payoffs, which can be used to make environmental laws more effective at achieving their goals.

1

Key Features of Environmental Law and Psychology

Environmental law scholars have long argued that environmental law is distinctive, and that failing to appreciate that distinctiveness can lead legal decision makers into error, by obscuring the ways in which environmental injury operates differently than other types of legally cognizable injury. We build on those claims here to argue that environmental law is also *psychologically* distinctive and that failing to appreciate the psychological distinctiveness of environmental injury can also undermine legal decision making. A psychology of environmental law should account for these distinctive characteristics, while respecting the normative goals and institutional constraints through which environmental law and policy is created and enforced.

What makes environmental law environmental? We begin the chapter by summarizing legal scholarship that explores what makes environmental law distinctive. In doing so, we draw particularly on the well-known work of Richard Lazarus in articulating the important characteristics of environmental harms. This line of scholarship will be familiar to environmental scholars, though it may be new to readers coming from law and psychology. In sum, that work suggests that harms to the environment tend to involve a set of characteristics that are otherwise unusual within law, and that legal institutions and legal decision makers need to recognize what makes environmental injury distinctive in order to effectuate their ends. In some cases, Lazarus and other scholars even call for structural, institutional, or doctrinal changes in environmental law to allow for more effective management of environmental injury. By the end of this part of the chapter, it should be clear (if it is not already) that the characteristics of environmental injury matter, and that understanding and addressing those characteristics helps determine whether environmental laws can achieve their ends.

The chapter then highlights where recognized characteristics of environmental injury match with influential bodies of research in psychology—that is, we describe what is distinctively psychological about environmental law. Many of the characteristics that make environmental injury distinctive also implicate distinctive psychological phenomena, and understanding those phenomena can help in crafting, enforcing, and understanding the impact of laws that seek to manage environmental injury. In particular, as we will develop further throughout the remainder of the book, the distinctively diffuse, complex, and nonhuman character of environmental injury has psychological as well as legal implications, and trying to tease out the legal implications without considering the psychology creates a needless handicap in developing effective legal regimes.

Finally, we discuss the law part of the psychology of environmental law. This begins with an overview of the origins and history of environmental law. We then discuss two key features of environmental law that are important for lawyers to recognize and psychologists to understand. First, we explain that, unlike psychology, environmental law is normative. That is, it does take a position on what is good versus bad, worth preserving versus safe to dispose of, and so on. This normative dimension motivates action and activism in the field, and determines the goals that environmental laws seek to achieve. Second, we note that environmental law is institutional. That is, environmental law has purchase via the multiple legal institutions responsible for creating, enforcing, and interpreting it, as well as via individual decision making. Psychologists, who are more prone to thinking about how people operate individually, or in dyads or small groups, must remember that the law operates through institutional actors of various stripes (including individuals!) who are constrained and enabled by their roles.

What Is Environmental About Environmental Law?

Environmental law is law, of course, but it is also environmental. Indeed, a key attribute of environmental law is that it concerns the environment: the surroundings in which humans, plants, and animals live. This is not merely a tautology; it is a defining feature of the field that differentiates it from most other areas of law, which seek to regulate human behavior directly.

Richard Lazarus has argued that what is "environmental" about environmental law is its focus on environmental or ecological injury; that is, on harm that accrues to the environment, rather than (directly) to people (Lazarus, 2000). Lazarus's analysis, first presented in his article "Restoring What's Environmental About Environmental Law in the Supreme Court" (2000) and further articulated in his book *The Making of Environmental Law* (2004), seeks to articulate what it is that makes environmental harm distinctively challenging to address and resolve through typical legal approaches. Explaining that "[e]nvironmental law is concerned, in the first instance, with impacts on the natural environment," Lazarus identifies ecological injury as the common denominator among environmental laws—and as the common source of the special challenges that environmental law presents for lawmaking. Importantly, Lazarus highlights that ecological injury is often irreversible, catastrophic, and persistent; is both physically and temporally distant; implicates uncertainty and risk; has multiple causes; and has a "noneconomic, nonhuman character" (Lazarus, 2000, p. 748).

Lazarus's analysis has been widely excerpted in environmental law textbooks and is frequently used as a jumping-off point for environmental scholarship. In part because of Lazarus, then, a now familiar claim within environmental scholarship is the notion that environmental law is distinctive because it addresses environmental harm. A number of legal scholars—including Lazarus (2000)—have gone one step further, however, to argue that legal institutions (such as the Supreme Court) and legal decision making cannot effectively manage environmental injury without understanding and addressing the qualities that make environmental injury distinctive. Lazarus goes on to identify a series of doctrines—in property law, Article III standing, Dormant Commerce Clause jurisprudence, regulatory takings, and even corporate law jurisprudence—that relate to environmental injury and that are prone to mistake and mismanagement without a full understanding of the ecological nature of environmental injury.

Other scholars have built on Lazarus's argument that the law needs to address distinctive qualities of environmental injury in order to be effective. Such arguments range from doctrinal claims that elaborate on the idea that doctrines of standing need to adjust to allow for claims of environmental injury (Nash, 2008), to claims that forms of environmental legal decision making cannot effectively address environmental injury because of challenges to expressing environmental goods meaningfully in economic terms (Ackerman & Heinzerling, 2002). Other scholars have emphasized the mismatch between the complexity of nature and the simplified account of nature upon which environmental laws often seem to rely (Doremus, 2006; Fischman, 2007). Still other scholars, addressing similar concerns (though not following Lazarus in particular) have made related legal and institutional critiques, for example, by arguing that environmental injustice is meaningfully distinct from other forms of injustice and deserves its own recognition and management (Bullard, 1993). Finally, scholars, most notably Elinor Ostrom, have also argued that different types of environmental injury (or types of environmental resources) should be understood to call for different kinds of management, depending upon their characteristics and qualities (Ostrom, 1990).

What Is Psychological About Environmental Law?

Throughout this book, we will build upon the common view within environmental legal scholarship that environmental law and legal institutions must address the distinctive characteristics of environmental injury. What we add to this discussion is an argument that the distinctive characteristics of environmental injury also have distinctive psychological implications—and that recognizing and understanding these implications can help environmental law by informing how people perceive, respond to, value, and make decisions about the environment. Furthermore, and as we will see, where environmental law fails to incorporate insights from psychology, it risks misunderstanding and mispredicting human behaviors that affect the environment, and therefore misprescribing legal tools to shape those behaviors.

Though we follow Lazarus's lead in focusing on the distinctiveness of environmental injury, our approach to exploring environmental harm differs somewhat from his. This should not be surprising; Lazarus was particularly focused on judicial decision making and in helping courts to see what and where they might want to think about environmental injury as a logically separate category. Our focus is different—broader in some ways and narrower in others. We aim to address what makes environmental law not just generally distinctive but *psychologically* distinctive. To our knowledge, we are the first to explore this question. And so we think it is reasonable to channel our focus toward those aspects of environmental law about which psychological processes have something helpful to impart.

To this end, we believe it is helpful to boil down the key psychological aspects of environmental injury into three general concerns. These are that environmental impacts tend to be (1) diffuse through time and space; (2) complex, insofar as they are interactive with other human behaviors, nonlinear in their impacts, and multicausal; and (3) nonhuman in character, insofar as they implicate and interact with nonhuman "natural" processes and implicate nonhuman stakeholders. (Though this list differs from Lazarus's typology, readers familiar with his work will still note the substantial influence of it.) We have a great deal more to say about each of these characteristics, and we devote a chapter to each. As a very general thumbnail sketch, however, we will suggest that the diffuse quality of environmental impacts makes environmental injury difficult to perceive; the complex nature of environmental impacts makes them difficult to understand; and the nonhuman character of environmental impacts makes them difficult to care about. These three characteristics, we argue, can explain a wide range of environmental behaviors. At the same time, failing to account for these characteristics can undermine the ability of environmental laws to effectively implement preferred environmental policies.

We hope that readers will find this structure to be helpful in addressing the distinctive character of environmental law, as it relates to environmental injury and the natural world. That said, psychology also has other and more general lessons to offer law, including environmental law, and many general law and psychology resources will also be valuable to environmental scholars and practitioners, just as they are to scholars and practitioners in other areas of law. While general law and psychology resources are available elsewhere, we devote a chapter to more general psychological phenomena, and highlight where they specifically interact with environmental impacts.

What Is Legal About Environmental Law and Psychology?

Although environmental law can be deeply informed and helped by psychology, the field should, of course, be about the *law*. This section begins by describing the origins and history of the field; environmental law scholars will be familiar with this history, but psychologists and nonenvironmental scholars may find this context to be helpful. We then discuss two important features of environmental law that any psychological approach must contend with: That the law is *normative,* and the law is *institutional.* By "normative" we mean that law is written, implemented, interpreted, and complied with (or not) by legal actors who have goals. These goals are selected because those actors think that it would be better if those goals were achieved, all things considered, than if those goals were not achieved. They believe that the law therefore *should* pursue them. Second, and importantly, legal actors have particular and circumscribed roles in the legal system. They are entitled, or even required, to act in particular ways because of those roles. In other words, the law is "institutional." Recognizing these features of the law is important to understanding what use the law can make of psychology, because to be valuable, psychology must work within these limitations and structures.

A Brief History of Environmental Law

The environment—or the surroundings in which people and organisms live—exists separate from law: It predates humans, and it persists (even if in an altered state) regardless of legal institutions and human behavior. Yet humans have always affected their environments. Indeed, environmental archaeological evidence suggests that even very small-scale societies routinely and measurably impact the environments in which they live, often through deforestation and hunting, and that semisedentary and agricultural societies have been measurably changing the surface of the planet for over 8,000 years (Reyes-Garcia et al., 2017). More recently, the emissions associated with industrialization have changed not only local environments but the composition and function of the global climate—impacts so profound that the current planetary epoch is now commonly called the Anthropocene, or the "Age of Humans" (Crutzen & Stoermer, 2000; Purdy, 2015).

In many cases, both in the past and today, the environmental impacts of human behavior are inadvertent or incidental. Often, the environmental impacts of behaviors like acquiring and burning fuel, planting crops, killing animals, or gathering resources—impacts that may be latent, distant, and hard to perceive and understand—are invisible to individuals bent only on living their lives. Still, where environmental impacts become acute or otherwise apparent, states have sometimes responded by developing environmental laws: purposeful codes of behavior intended to shape human actions to desired environmental ends. Records from early imperial China, for example, reveal laws undertaken for purposes of conservation and environmental stewardship, including ordinances attempting to protect young animals and birds from being overhunted (Sanft, 2010). The ancient Romans, in addition to building enormous public infrastructure projects for the provision of clean water and the management of municipal sewage and solid waste, also issued laws addressing pollution. They banned lime kilns in highly populated areas because of their impact on air quality and prohibited wagons and chariots being used at night to limit the impact of noise pollution (Havlíček & Morcinek, 2016). In the late Middle Ages, King Edward I of England famously outlawed coal burning in an attempt to clean up London's highly polluted air. "[W]hosoever shall be found guilty of burning coal," the law warned, "shall suffer the loss of his head" (Newton, 2007, p. 3; Vesilind et al., 2013). Subsequent English monarchs attempted to enforce similar bans over several centuries, even prior to the Industrial Revolution—though these seem largely to have been ineffective in achieving improved environmental quality (Vesilind et al., 2013).

Indeed, many early environmental laws struggled to achieve their intended ends, whether because of limitations on scientific knowledge (Sanft, 2010; Newton, 2007) or because they failed to effectively understand the motivations underlying regulated behaviors. Still, these laws were distinct from early nonenvironmental laws in their focus on environmental or ecological harm, whether that harm was overhunting, sewage, noise, or smog. These laws sought to change behavior not for its own sake but instead because of the harm that behavior might do to the environment—and which the environment might then impose upon the people who lived within it. Environmental law thus developed only as people began to be purposeful in how their behaviors affected their environments, and as they saw opportunities to address behaviors with undesirable environmental impacts.

In the United States, efforts and laws addressing conservation date at least to the establishment of the National Park Service in 1891. That said, modern environmental law—and particularly pollution control— are conventionally traced to the 1960s and 1970s. That era saw increased awareness of environmental issues, sparked in part by the lyrical scientific writing of Rachel Carson in her book *Silent Spring*, which introduced many Americans to the notion of ecological injury for the first time. This awareness combined with the movements of the Civil Rights Era and with a string of high-profile, well-publicized disasters, including the Great Smog Disaster of London, which killed 12,000 people in a few days, the Santa Barbara oil spill of 1968, which at that time was the largest in American history, and the well-publicized Cuyahoga River fire, also in 1969.

This social attention and activism culminated in what is sometimes called the "Environmental Decade," a time of extraordinary social and legislative activity on environmental issues. The decade was kicked off on January 1, 1970, with then-President Richard Nixon signing the National Environmental Policy Act into law. The same year saw the establishment of the Environmental Protection Agency (EPA), the celebration of the first Earth Day, and passage of the Clean Air Act and the Occupational Safety and Health Act. These were followed by an avalanche of environmental legislation at the federal level, including most of the statutes that remain the backbone of environmental law today. These also include the National Environmental Policy Act (1970), the Clean Water Act (1972), the Endangered Species Act (1973), the Safe Drinking Water Act (1974), the Resource Conservation and Recovery Act (1976), the Toxic Substances Control Act (1976), significant amendments to the Clean Air Act and Clean Water Act (1977), and the Comprehensive Environmental Response, Compensation, and Liability Act ("Superfund"/CERCLA) (1980). Although in recent years environmental law and environmental issues have become increasingly partisan (Karol, 2018)—about which we shall say more in subsequent chapters—at the time of passage, the burgeoning environmental movement had such broad support that many foundational environmental statutes generated little to no political controversy, even when they established legal approaches that are now viewed with partisan suspicion. The National Environmental Policy Act, the Clean Air Act, and the Endangered Species Act, for instance, all passed unanimously in the Senate.

The pace of new legislation slowed during the 1980s under the overtly deregulatory presidency of Ronald Reagan, but other important environmental mechanisms developed during that time (Rowell & van Zeben, 2020). In particular, the 1980s saw the creation and entrenchment of new forms of regulatory analysis, including executive orders requiring quantitative cost-benefit analysis for most regulatory (including environmental) decisions. It also saw the participation of the United States in the influential 1987 Montreal Protocol on Substances that Deplete the Ozone Layer. The 1990s saw the substantive amendment of the Clean Air Act and substantial debate regarding U.S. participation in international climate change agreements, particularly the Kyoto Protocol—which the United States ultimately chose not to ratify. During the 2000s and 2010s, the relative scarcity of federal legislation on environmental matters—including climate change—left many substantive environmental policy decisions in the hands of environmental agencies, and the President. At times—as between the presidencies of Barack Obama and Donald Trump—this has led to substantial shifts in federal environmental policy between presidential administrations and has thus heightened the stakes of presidential decision making. Climate change policy, which in the absence of directed legislation on climate change is left largely to the executive to address (Rowell, 2015), has been particularly unstable.

The reasons for the extraordinary period of activity in the 1970s are complex, and commentators have highlighted a number of social, scientific, institutional, and political factors that came together in that period (Tarlock, 2010; Lazarus, 2004; Lewis, 1985). These factors may well have helped legislators of the Environmental Decade note, learn, and care about environmental impacts despite the types of psychological barriers we will discuss throughout the rest of the book that make environmental impacts generally difficult to notice, understand, and engage with emotionally. Yet even when politicians of the 1970s noticed and cared enough about environmental impacts to legislate, they were drafting legislation (which courts and agencies were interpreting) without the support of any substantial social science research to help them accurately understand, predict, or shape human behaviors. Indeed, commentators have rightfully noted that these core environmental statutes were in many cases built on inaccurate and incomplete assumptions—and particularly on an oversimplified account of nature and human impacts upon the environment (Doremus, 2006; Fischman, 2007; Tarlock, 2010). Perhaps unsurprisingly, then, in many cases they have failed to achieve their goals (Lazarus, 2004; Tarlock, 2010). As we will see, some of these inaccuracies and opportunities can be illuminated by research psychology, which can help both in describing and predicting how people engage with their environments, and potentially aid policy makers in more effectively shaping environmental behaviors in light of their preferred environmental ends.

Normativity: Psychology and the Ends and Means of Environmental Law

Environmental law seeks to achieve its ends by shaping human behavior—but what those ends are, or should be, remains controversial. Different value judgments about what the environment should be and how humans should relate to it result in varying—sometimes competing, sometimes overlapping—goals. Should environmental law seek to maximize social welfare, and if so, whose welfare counts, and how should that welfare be measured? Should humans seek to craft environments that serve humans, or should we adopt a nonanthropocentric goal, for example by trying to preserve, restore, and build healthy, self-renewing ecosystems for their own sakes, separate from their usefulness to humans? Does it matter if environmental risks and harms are spread unequally across the human population and the planet? How should the goals of environmental quality—however that is defined—be balanced against goals of economic growth or financial prosperity? How important is it for environmental quality to be sustainable over time?

These are hard questions, and often environmental laws reflect a series of compromises and attempts to build consensus that only partially respond to the puzzle of how humans should live on the earth. Psychology has nothing to say about which end or ends are the "best" for a society to choose. Psychology can, however, illuminate how, when, and why people behave in the ways they do; pay attention to the things they do; and, to some extent, respond to the environment in the ways they do. All of these functions are helpful regardless of which normative commitment(s) are held as the appropriate end(s) of environmental law. Psychological analysis can thus increase the effectiveness of any of the common normative ends of environmental law and policy.

In addition to furthering a variety of potential normative goals, environmental law also employs multiple means for shaping people's behavior toward preferred policy ends. Common tools in environmental law include command-and-control regulatory regimes, ex post liability regimes, economic incentives, and disclosure regimes (Richards & van Zeben, 2020). The choice between these tools—often called "instrument choice"—is a robust subfield within environmental law.

Psychological research has contributed to this domain directly by suggesting new forms of behavioral regulation, such as "nudges," choice architecture, and other forms of libertarian paternalism (Rowell, 2020a). As readers may know, choice architecture relies upon the purposeful structuring of decision-making contexts to shape people's behavior toward selected ends. Developed by Nobel Prize–winning economist Richard Thaler and law professor Cass Sunstein (Thaler & Sunstein, 2003) and popularized in their book *Nudge* (Thaler & Sunstein, 2008), choice architecture relies explicitly upon behavioral research to identify the ways in which context may affect decisions. Default rules and framing are particularly common techniques used to encourage people's behavior toward selected policy ends (Rowell, 2020a). Where the appropriate ends of environmental law are understood to be maximizing social welfare, the so-called "behavioral market failures" that nudges seek to address (Thaler & Sunstein, 2008; Sunstein, 2014) look like particularly important targets for regulation.

Behavioral mechanisms like nudges can be effective tools for achieving particular policy ends, and it is important to recognize the contributions that psychology has made to developing those tools (Rachlinski, 2011). That said, it would be a mistake to think that psychology is only or even primarily helpful to environmental law through the vehicle of choice architecture or nudges. Accurately understanding and predicting how people perceive, process, and engage with the environment is critical to crafting legal schemes that accomplish their desired ends— regardless of the tools and instruments used to further those ends.

Whose Psychology Matters? People and Institutions in Environmental Law

Many people and institutions behave in ways that impact the environment. In fact, environmental law is notable for implicating many different legal and institutional decision makers, each of whom acts in different circumstances and in light of different contextual cues. One of the key insights of modern cognitive psychology is that context matters to the substance of decision making. This means that the institutional and personal contexts in which people make decisions about environmental law and policy can affect the substance of those decisions.

This section provides an overview and orientation into some key institutional actors in environmental law, and how their roles affect them. To that end, the section begins by refreshing the reader on key aspects of how institutional context can matter to decision making. It then highlights legal decision makers who play important roles in environmental law, including international actors, the executive, legislatures, judges, and agencies. The chapter provides an overview of the role(s) these actors play in environmental law, and the kind of environmental decisions in which they are most influential, before identifying the contextual aspect(s) of decision making that make that actor's decisions psychologically distinctive.

WHOSE PSYCHOLOGY MATTERS TO ENVIRONMENTAL LAW?
Individuals acting within a range of roles.
- actions as subjects of the law to whom laws are directed
- economic actions via market or business decisions
- political actions as through voting or lobbying
- legal actions as through citizen suits or petitions

Legal institutions in which individuals work.
- international legal institutions
- legislatures
- executive
- judiciary
- administrative agencies
- states and local governments

THE ROLE OF ROLES IN DECISION MAKING

Broadly speaking, psychology organizes its research by looking at the individual alone (in the subfields of personality, cognitive psychology, and the psychology of the self), the individual embedded in particular circumstances (classic social psychology), the dynamics of groups (as in research on social identity, group decision making, and interpersonal conflict), and finally, to a lesser extent, the psychology of social movements (research that more traditionally has been left to sociologists). Each of these contexts can affect the psychology of decision making.

In many, perhaps most, contexts, the impact of this context is the same in environmental law as in other areas of law. But sometimes the particular contexts in which environmental law arises are distinct and psychologically interesting. For instance, zoning and land use decisions tend to be made by local decision makers such as zoning boards, whereas climate change policies are often impacted by the decisions of international bodies like the United Nations. Generally, for a legal decision to be perceived as procedurally just, at a minimum people think they need a voice in the process (Lind & Tyler, 1988). But what counts as "voice" may vary dramatically in different settings. In a zoning decision, for example, citizens may expect to act in their individual capacity and to actually speak and tell their individual story to decision makers. Having a "voice" at the United Nations, however, may be satisfied by having one's country's ambassador, appointed by the executive, present and voting.

Motivation and decision making can interact with institutional roles in interesting ways as well. In particular, the goals of public institutions, who are charged with protecting public welfare, may motivate public actors differently than private actors, who often have profit motives (as with industry). These different motivations may impact the way that profit-oriented private and welfare-oriented public actors see the same environmental problem, even when both are operating with identical information. That said, not all private institutions are profit oriented; nonprofit institutions like the Sierra Club, the Center for Biological Diversity, and the Defenders of Wildlife play a formative role in many environmental legal contexts, and often their motivations may be more similar to agency actors than to industry actors. Understanding the way that motivations can affect perception of information may help to explain not only conflicts as they arise between public and private institutions in environmental law, but also the complex relationships that environmental nonprofits have traditionally had with other environmental legal actors.

In addition, insofar as many of the important actors within environmental law are comprised of largely like-minded individuals working to promote environmental quality, environmental law frequently implicates the psychology of group decision making. In particular, research suggests that groups tend to exhibit "polarization," where "group members become even more aligned in the direction they were already tending" (Turner et al., 1987, p. 142). That is, a secret straw poll of the individual members of a group might have indicated that they were leaning somewhat toward a fairly modest environmental regulation. But for various psychological reasons, after open discussion, the group's final decision is likely to lean strongly toward a more aggressive environmental regulation than their initial, individual inclinations would have been. Polarization can be a valuable lens for understanding the evolving decision making of environmental agencies, who are generally peopled by public-oriented civil servants, and even for contrasting this decision making with that of industry and of environmental nonprofits.

SPECIFIC ACTORS AND INSTITUTIONS

This portion of the chapter highlights ways that psychology interacts with specific and important actors and institutions in environmental law. These actors and institutions will be highly familiar to legal and environmental law scholars, though they may be less so to psychologists. For psychologists in particular, then, it is important to note the key actors and institutions that create, interpret, implement, and respond to environmental law. Legal and social limits may affect the psychology of decision making within these institutions.

First, consider the multiple roles private individuals play within environmental law. Often, private individuals are the intended subject of environmental laws. Consumer recycling policies, for example, are directed toward everyone who might recycle. Yet they also impact law and policy via economic decisions, as through individual consumption choices or business decisions; through political decisions, as by voting or direct contact with representatives and policy makers; and when taking direct legal action, as by bringing citizen suits, filing petitions, and/or commenting on pending regulatory rules. In all of these instances, individuals are prone to identifiable cognitive phenomena when addressing environmental impacts.

Now consider the range of institutional actors, working in different contexts, who also play an important role in environmental law and policy. These include international as well as domestic actors.

As readers may know, international law—including international environmental law—is made through several different processes. Two important processes for international environmental law are the making of international agreements and treaties, such as the Declaration of the United Nations Conference on the Human Environment (the 1972 "Stockholm Declaration"), the Rio Declaration on Environment and Development (the 1992 "Stockholm Declaration"), and international tribunals. There is no international court dedicated to environmental issues, though disputes between states concerning international environmental law are sometimes heard at the International Court of Justice, and other international institutions hear cases about specific environmental issues such as those arising out of trade by the World Trade Organization (WTO).

In both treaty-making and judicial functions, the key institutional feature of international environmental law is that it is made by states rather than by individual persons. Perhaps because of this focus, relatively little has yet been written on the psychology of international law, much less on the psychology of international environmental law (Broude, 2015; van Aaken & Broude, 2019; Rowell & van Zeben 2016). This is unfortunate, as around the world—though admittedly less so in the United States (Rowell & van Zeben, 2020)—international law has a greater impact on environmental law than on many other areas of law. Because of the impact international bodies have on environmental decisions, the psychology of these international bodies—and of various actors within them—has heightened importance in environmental contexts.

Though the psychology of state actors remains relatively understudied, individual psychology also plays an important role in international environmental law because international legal bodies are still made up of people. States are legally responsible for and obligated by international law, but individual persons are still necessarily involved in negotiating, implementing, and complying with international legal requirements. This at least makes it possible to speculate about how typical individual decision-making processes apply when people act as international institutional actors.

For instance, and as we discuss in more detail in the chapter on general law and psychology, psychological research suggests that, across a wide range of decision contexts, people tend to experience loss aversion. This makes them highly sensitive to behaviors just as with they identify as failing to meet a baseline. International agreements, like domestic law, can create psychological focal points against which an individual's future judgments can be formed (Rowell & van Zeben, 2016). When international law is effective at creating a perceived norm, it may trigger the power of the endowment effect and loss aversion against diversions from it (Rowell & van Zeben, 2016). This effect may operate independently of traditional enforcement mechanisms, meaning that high-salience agreements such as the Paris Agreement may impact the perceptions—and thus the behavior—even of individuals and institutions who are not a party to the relevant agreement. The psychological impact of international agreements may be heightened through additional contextual factors, including unanimity and the selection of quantifiable measures of success or failure (Rowell & van Zeben, 2016). In this light, the Paris Agreement's decision to adopt a quantified and ambitious goal—keeping global warming "well below" 2° C and aiming to keep it at less than 1.5° C above preindustrial levels—may generate significant psychological stickiness on that perceived baseline, even without an international police, court, or other entity to enforce it.

Individual judgment and decision making in the context of international law is not the only psychological feature of international law that may matter. Other aspects of international law may be responsive to the same sorts of cues to which domestic legal institutions respond. The psychology of international tribunals, for instance, may be informed by research on (domestic) judicial decision making. International agreements are drafted communally. Thus, they may be influenced by many of the same things that domestic legislatures are influenced by. For instance, both international legal actors and domestic legal actors like legislatures must often come together to represent divergent voices and interests.

As such, international treaty making may be informed by research on (domestic) political psychology.

Speaking of domestic legal institutions, perhaps it is helpful also to highlight important ways in which environmental law interacts with the legislative, executive, and judicial branches, as well as in administrative agencies, and the areas of psychology that may be most relevant to understanding decision making in those realms. In some cases, recognizing the role psychology plays in various institutions may be helpful in crafting effective laws or even government designs (Rachlinski & Farina, 2002). Or it may simply help in providing a richer understanding of how and why environmental laws operate as they do.

First, consider the psychology of legislatures. Legislatures, of course, are empowered to make law and do so as a group. As we have noted, the period that saw the greatest federal legislative activity in U.S. environmental law was the so-called "Environmental Decade" of the 1970s. To legislate, legislatures must pay attention to an issue—in some cases, a tall order, given it is impossible for modern legislatures to address all possible issues that might deserve their attention. The selection of particular issues to legislate upon, or to vote to support, is thus likely to be particularly subject to psychological phenomena that affect their cognitive availability. One aspect of this may be socially constructed, as with the growing attention to ecological impacts after *Silent Spring*. But disasters—such as the Santa Barbara oil spill, Love Canal, or Bhopal—present another method to grab the attention of constituents as well as of legislators themselves. Once attention is grabbed, group psychology may matter: Legislatures are composed of many people and are thus subject to group polarization, availability cascades, and other dynamics that particularly affect groups making decisions. Such dynamics may merely be exacerbated by the impact of partisanship, including in triggering in-group/out-group dynamics and motivated cognition in support of the political party with whom they identify.

Second, consider the role of the executive in environmental law and policy. In the United States., the President, as the head of the executive branch, has a number of legal powers and responsibilities that can significantly impact environmental law and policy. These include issuing executive policy through executive orders and other means; appointing (and firing, if necessary) most heads of administrative agencies, including the EPA, the Secretary of the Interior, the Secretary of Agriculture, and the Secretary of Energy; enforcing the law; and, in the continued absence of significant legislative action on climate change, setting substantial portions of U.S. climate policy.

In areas of law where the President has significant power, personal psychology may play an outsized role in executive actions (as we argue it does in climate change policy). This extends our consideration of the psychology of the executive even to the level of personality (Rubenzer & Faschingbauer, 2004), psychopathy (Lilienfeld et al., 2012), or mental health (Davidson et al., 2006).

For obvious reasons this can be problematic, as is well illustrated and well documented by the example of U.S. President Richard Nixon, whose personality flaws and increasingly erratic behavior affected the behavior of his staff as they sought to manage him (Reeves, 2001). Infamously, in the waning days of the Nixon White House as impeachment loomed, Nixon's Secretary of State and Secretary of Defense secretly told military commanders to ignore any military orders from Nixon that were not signed by the Secretaries. Apparently, they were worried that Nixon's mental health had deteriorated to a state where he might precipitously launch a nuclear attack.

Because U.S. presidents have historically been members of political parties, the role of partisanship and political psychology can play a role as well. Consider what happens when new presidents take office and have to consider what to do with policies set by their predecessors. Where both presidents share a party affiliation, the new President might see the prior President as a fellow in-group member and thus give prior policies some deference (even subconsciously), simply because of that shared affiliation. On the other hand, if the new President is a member of a different party, prior policies may be perceived as unwise or even dangerous merely because of their out-group source. In an extreme version of this, the President may even construct his or her identity in deliberate contrast to that of the prior executive.

Third, consider the judicial role in environmental law. There is a growing literature on the psychology of judicial decision making that we cannot do full justice to here (Klein & Mitchell, 2010). A number of studies in political science look at the effect of the political affiliation of elected judges, or of their appointing executive, on the outcomes of judicial decisions. Most of it shows—perhaps as one would expect—that politics matter, even though federal judges, at least, are politically independent (Epstein et al., 2013). There has also been a smaller spate of studies, mostly conducted by the research team of Jeffrey Rachlinski, Chris Guthrie, and federal judge Andrew Wistrich, that test for various cognitive heuristics and biases in sitting judges (see Guthrie et al., 2000, 2007; Rachlinski et al., 2006; Wistrich et al., 2005 for just a small sample). That line of research shows that, for the most part, judges are subject to the same cognitive failings as most other people, with certain notable differences, such as their ability to ignore certain irrelevant evidence for purposes of Fourth Amendment exclusionary rule decisions. Generally speaking, however, we would note that the diffuse, complex, and nonhuman character of environmental impacts present a number of practical and psychological challenges to judicial decision making just as they do for everyone else. More sharply, we would simply flag that judges, like other people, can experience substantial cognitive challenges in processing environmental impacts and that those cognitive challenges can then turn into important and substantive distortions in the substance of judicial decisions in environmental law.

Finally, agencies—units of government created by statute or by direction of the President—play a distinctive and important set of roles within environmental law and policy (Rowell & van Zeben, 2020). Many of these functions mirror those of the executive, legislature, and judiciary: Environmental agencies are routinely responsible for enforcing environmental laws, for issuing environmental regulations, and for adjudicating environmental disputes. In performing each of these functions, however, agencies are empowered to act by other branches of government—Congress, the President—rather than acting on their own behalf.

Agencies are particularly important in environmental law in large part because of the complex nature of many environmental problems, which has led legislatures over the years to delegate significant authority to environmental agencies, who theoretically have the expertise and capacity to research and monitor complicated environmental problems. In the United States, much of this authority (though by no means all) has been delegated to the EPA, which is responsible for administering most of the nation's key environmental statutes. The breadth and depth of the authority delegated to the EPA makes the agency a central legal actor in environmental law, and makes the psychology of the EPA—and of various actors within it—particularly relevant to environmental decision making.

The particular directions agencies are tasked with implementing can also play an important role. Congress generally uses statutes to issue directions to agencies regarding what goals they are supposed to achieve and how. Some of these goals are articulated quite broadly. In exercising their substantial discretion to interpret these general directions, actors within agencies may be subject to a whole slew of cognitive biases, including those generated by the availability heuristic and by motivated cognition (which we discuss at more length in Chapters 2 and 5). On the executive side, a particularly important institutional direction to agencies has come from executive orders on centralized planning and review. Since 1980, those executive orders have centralized executive review of agency actions, and required agencies to perform cost-benefit analyses for the majority of major federal regulations. The centralization of agency review gives particular weight to the psychological characteristics of individuals who hold key oversight roles, particularly the Administrator of the Office of Management and Budget and the Office of Information and Regulatory Affairs. More generally, the substantive requirement that agencies default to cost-benefit analysis—and regulate only where the quantified and monetized benefits of a proposed action justify its monetized costs, unless otherwise directed by statute—has influenced the focus of the analysis performed to justify many environmental regulations. This procedure is often justified as improving decision quality (Adler & Posner, 1999), though the psychological implications of monetization remain understudied. At the least, and as we discuss further in our chapter on ecosystem management, the fact that environmental agencies must generally monetize the impacts of proposed rules—including on nonhuman plants and animals—should be presumed to trigger a set of psychological phenomena related to monetization and quantification.

Conclusion

In developing a psychological approach to environmental law and policy, it may be helpful to consider what is distinctively environmental, distinctively psychological, and distinctively legal about the psychology of environmental law. In this chapter, we have suggested that much of what is distinctively environmental about environmental law—namely, its focus on diffuse, complex, and nonhuman environmental harms—also implicates a distinctive psychology, which should focus on those same characteristics. We have also suggested that the legal and institutional mechanisms used to implement environmental law and policy may interact with the environmental and psychological qualities of environmental injury in ways that legal decision makers would do well to note. We expand on all of these ideas in subsequent chapters.

Key Aspects of Psychology as Applied to Environmental Law

What Is Environmental About Environmental Law?

- Environmental or ecological injury. Environmental law addresses harms to the environment, which tend to be diffuse, complex, and involve nonhuman stakeholders and processes. This distinguishes environmental law from other areas of law.

What Is Psychological About the Psychology of Environmental Law?

- The psychology of diffusion. The psychology of diffusion makes environmental injuries hard for people to *see.*
- The psychology of complexity. The psychology of complexity makes environmental injuries hard for people to *understand.*
- The psychology of nonhuman things. The psychology of how we interact with others who are unlike us (such as animals and ecosystems) makes injuries to them hard for people to *care about.*

What Is Legal About the Psychology of Environmental Law?

- Through history, people have sought to purposefully shape their environments through environmental law. The effectiveness of those attempts is likely to relate to the law's ability to accurately understand and predict the impacts of law on people's decision making.

- Environmental law incorporates a variety of potential normative goals, as well as a variety of different means for shaping people's behavior to those ends. Although psychology is not helpful in determining which goals it is best to pursue, it can help in illuminating how, when, and why people may select the ends that they do and in identifying more effective means to accomplish selected ends.

- Large portions of U.S. environmental law were created in the "Environmental Decade" of the 1970s, and predate the vast majority of research on social science and the law.

- Environmental law is implemented by people acting within various roles and institutions, such as international bodies, national and subnational bodies, branches of government, administrative agencies, and even at the individual level. The role in which someone is operating will sometimes expand and sometimes limit why, when, and how they perceive, understand, and respond to environmental injury.

2

Diffusion

The environmental consequences of human behaviors are often both literally and psychologically distant from the human actions that caused them. In this chapter, we present research in psychology to explain how and why effects that are diffuse through space and/or time are so hard for people to perceive, respond to, and appreciate. The cognitive and emotional barriers people face in addressing diffuse environmental impacts have profound implications both for how environmental law operates and for how it might be made more effective.

Diffuse environmental injuries pose a particular problem for environmental law. Regulations that have little obvious or immediate beneficial effects on individual citizens might have large effects in distant places or on future generations. Consider an example of diffusion across time: Exposure to a carcinogenic pollutant such as arsenic, asbestos, or benzene is likely to cause cancer (if it causes cancer at all) years, if not decades, in the future (Revesz, 1999). Or an example of diffusion across space: Air pollution routinely drifts across state borders. On certain days, the EPA estimates that as much as a quarter of the particulate matter air pollution above Los Angeles was emitted in China (Lin et al., 2014). And as example of both kinds of diffusion simultaneously, consider that most of the harms of climate change are expected to accrue to future generations (Revesz & Shahabian, 2011) in foreign lands (Rowell, 2015; Rowell & Wexler, 2014). Indeed, as we discuss in our chapter on climate change, the failure of environmental law to effectively and comprehensively deal with climate change may in no small part be explained by the diffuse nature of climate injuries, and the psychological obstacles that diffusion presents.

In other words, there is often a physical distance, temporal distance, or both, between a behavior the law might seek to regulate and the apparent effects of that behavior. This can make it difficult for both policy makers and citizens to connect behavioral causes with environmental effects. Even when people take on the complex cognitive cost of tracking down the relationship between behavior and impact, they may find that the environmental benefits of behavioral change would accrue to future or distant others rather than to themselves. Particularly where diffuse environmental impacts must be traded off against more prominent cognitive considerations—such as immediate and proximate cost, convenience, security, or aesthetics—the cognitive distance of environmental impacts tends to make them fade into the background.

This chapter proceeds by first discussing the general phenomenon of diffuse impacts, focusing on the psychology of externalities. Next, the chapter explores the cognitive and emotional/motivational phenomena that are likely to affect the way that people perceive, process, and respond to diffuse environmental impacts.

The Psychology of Externalities

Behaviors that incur costs or benefits for a third party create what economists call *externalities*, or spillovers. The full costs (and benefits) of externalities are not experienced by those who generate them, often because the effects are distant from their cause in space and/or time. As economists have long noted, unless there are adequate incentives to internalize them, rational and self-interested people will produce negative externalities (Pigou, 1920; Coase, 1960; Ostrom, 1990). Indeed, creating adequate incentives to internalize the social cost of environmental injury provides the primary economic justification for environmental regulation (Baumol & Oates, 1988; Stavins, 2019).

As environmental economists have explained, a well-functioning environment is a public good: All can benefit from it, whether or not they individually contribute to it, because those who created it cannot effectively shut out those who did not (Olson, 1965). This creates the potential for public goods dilemmas, and particularly for "free riding," where people capture benefits for themselves while creating externalities for others (Baumol, 1952). The economic notion of free riding is straightforward: People like free things, so if someone can get the benefits of something without having to pay for it, then that person has the incentive not to contribute. They will just take without giving. When the same opportunity arises for multiple people, it can generate what is now famously called the "tragedy of the commons": degradation, even collapse, of common resources as a result of individual incentives to overuse (Hardin, 1968). Land may be overgrazed to the point of barrenness; fisheries may be fished to the point of extinction; the air may be clogged with smoke, soot, and heat-entrapping greenhouse gases.

Precisely because the environment is external to every individual, the environment provides countless and pervasive opportunities for generating externalities. In fact, by definition, a person who takes an action that affects the environment has created an externality. So it should be no surprise that much of the field of environmental economics is devoted to identifying and managing them (Stavins, 2019). What may be surprising—particularly with the behavioral turn that economics has taken in the last decade—is that although environmental economics often incorporates rich understandings of social norms (see, e.g., Ostrom, 1990), the *psychology* of externalities has been largely neglected.

This is a missed opportunity, as psychology has much to say about how externalities are perceived and how those perceptions may relate to the motives, biases, and social influences that lead people either to free ride by externalizing harm, or instead to engage in pro-environmental behaviors that externalize benefits. What mental states, for instance, allow people to engage in behavior that they know will harm others—to generate negative externalities? Psychological research suggests that people are reluctant to engage in behavior they recognize as harming others—behavior widely viewed as antisocial (Bandura, 2002; Gini, 2006; Bandura, 2015). As a result, people tend to use one (or many) of a series of psychological mechanisms to morally and cognitively disengage, minimize, and protect themselves from negative feelings—such as guilt or shame—that otherwise follow from harming others (Bandura 1991, 2002). These include the following techniques of what is sometimes called "moral disengagement":

- Moral justification. Portraying the act as serving moral ends ("We have to use this pesticide to keep people from getting sick!").
- Palliative comparisons. Making harmful acts look better by comparing them to even worse acts ("Sure, I emit greenhouse gases, but my emissions are tiny compared to the whole country.").
- Euphemistic labeling. Using language to minimize the emotional aspects

of the harm ("endangered species" rather than "dying species"; discussing the killing of aquatic organisms in water-cooling intake systems as "entrainment" or "entrapment" rather than "squashing" or "smashing"; referring to "debeaking" of chickens rather than "mutilation").

- Displacement. Obscuring or minimizing one's agentive role in the harm being caused ("Yes, airplane emissions are bad for the climate, but I have no choice—I have to travel for work.").
- Diffusion of responsibility. Obscuring or minimizing one's obligations or ability to mitigate the harm ("I can see that there is a problem that needs to be resolved, but other people are more capable or more responsible for fixing it than me.").
- Minimizing consequences. Disregarding, distorting, or downplaying the consequences ("It's not like me riding my bike to work is going to magically fix local air quality"; "One more plastic bag isn't going to do anything that isn't already done.").
- Depersonalization and dehumanization. Grouping victims with animals or as a group rather than as individuals ("It's just a bunch of animals/foreigners anyway.").
- Psychic numbing. The larger the size of the externality, the less important any subset of it is ("If hundreds of species go extinct every year, then what difference does it make if a few more go?").
- Attribution of blame. Blaming victims or portraying them as threats ("If people don't like living near trash dumps, it's their fault for not moving.").
- Pluralistic ignorance. Not recognizing there is a problem *because* no one else is doing anything about it ("If it were really a problem, the government would have outlawed it by now.").

For purposes of regulating environmental externalities, the important implication of this line of psychological research is that moral disengagement may lead nonsadistic individuals to systematically underperceive the extent of the externalities they cause. It is as if one's own externalities are perceived through a psychologically concave lens, making objects appear smaller than they actually are. Disturbingly, this effect will often be subconscious, and it may also be resistant to many attempts to debias, because convincing someone that they have harmed others more than they realized risks triggering the same protective emotional and cognitive mechanisms that led to the initial moral disengagement (Bandura,

2015). As we discuss in subsequent chapters, this may lead polluters to inadvertently (but perhaps stubbornly) minimize the likely effects of their pollution, and may lead individuals to psychologically discount the effects of their greenhouse gas emissions. Counterintuitively, this may also mean that public policy communications that emphasize the scope and scale of environmental harm in an attempt to generate urgency and pro-environmental responses risk triggering denial and other minimization strategies. The exact extent of such consequences, however, is ripe for additional empirical research.

Moral disengagement is peculiarly relevant to the psychology of externalities, because it informs what happens when a person externalizes harm on another. The tendency to minimize the harm that one does to others may be further exacerbated when those harms are distant in space and time.

Cognitive Limitations and Techniques for Dealing with Diffuse Environmental Effects

Diffusion interferes with humans' ability to appreciate the environmental effects of their actions. Humans are creatures with limited cognitive resources who must conserve those resources for when they count. It would be impossible to fully attend to every feature of the world when making decisions, computing all outcomes and possibilities before making decisions or changing attitudes. We have only so much processing capacity, let alone time in the day. As we discuss in more detail in this section, distant and diffuse effects simply struggle to compete for attention with more immediate and obvious concerns. As a result, the diffuse environmental impacts of people's actions are prone to systematic underperception and underresponse.

Cognitive Heuristics—Availability and Representativeness

One important set of phenomena related to diffusion has to do with people's tendency to use various shortcutting techniques to limit the effort spent solving problems and making decisions. These shortcuts can further worsen the ability to see remote effects. We are mainly "cognitive misers" (Fiske & Taylor, 1984/1991) who in most circumstances only attend to the features of a decision that are most obvious, pressing, and large—not those that are hard to detect, distant, and incremental. Many of these shortcuts or "heuristics" were first described by Amos Tversky and Daniel Kahneman in the 1970s and are by now likely to be familiar to many readers. We will discuss general heuristics in greater detail later; here we focus on two common ones with particular implications for people's perception, understanding, and response to diffuse environmental impacts. These are the "availability" heuristic, where a more easily recalled feature is assumed to occur more often than it actually does in fact, and the "representativeness" heuristic, where one or more shared features of a person or object leads an observer to assume there are many more such shared features (Kahneman & Tversky, 1979; Tversky & Kahneman, 1974). Each of them can significantly reduce the salience of diffused effects.

The availability heuristic is what it sounds like: Easily thought of instances of a phenomenon—that is, ones that are more "available" to a person thinking about them—are estimated to be more frequent than more obscure ones. Kahneman and Tversky (1973) famously demonstrated this heuristic with the "K" study: Participants were asked to report the number of English words that start with the letter K and the number of English words whose third letter is K. People can retrieve words that start with K with relative ease (kangaroo, kid, kayak), but coming up with words with K in the third position is devilish (acknowledge, lake, unkind). As a consequence, people estimate that there are twice as many of the former as the latter. In fact, there are about three times as many of the latter as the former, but the ease of retrieval of words that start with K made participants overestimate their frequency.

In many contexts, the availability heuristic operates according to the aphorism "out of sight, out of mind": The less visible, immediate, or vivid a risk or event, the more likely people are to underestimate its likelihood and severity (Kahneman et al., 1982; Kuran & Sunstein, 1999; Weber, 2006; Wiener, 2016). Vivid, highly newsworthy environmental disasters can thus trigger heightened awareness of environmental issues, and may help to explain the tradition of postdisaster environmental legislation, including the passage of CERCLA after Love Canal and the Clean Water Act after the Cuyahoga River fire and the Santa Barbara oil spill. Less-visible or imaginable harms, however—particularly those that are likely to affect foreign persons (Rowell & Wexler, 2014)—are far more likely to be neglected. This may create special challenges for environmental policies seeking to address problems, such as climate change, where the harms from emitting behaviors are likely to be felt far away and many years in the future (Weber, 2006; Rowell, 2015). These challenges are all the greater for unprecedented problems—such as extreme-scenario climate change, or nuclear war (Baum & Tonn, 2015)—for which humans have no mental template for comparison. Despite their catastrophic potential, the fact that such events have not occurred in living memory may make them unavailable, which in turn may lead to underinvestment and even mismanagement of attendant risks (Wiener, 2016).

Availability may also have profound effects on how people perceive the harms of more chronic, common environmental behaviors—particularly when the consequences of those behaviors are separated from their causes by space or time. Consider, for a homely example, that modern trash pickup programs, combined with dedicated landfills, are generally effective at making municipal waste management largely invisible to the average person (Nagle, 2013). As waste is managed through removal, it becomes less observable, and thus less cognitively available. Or consider that many people are at least theoretically aware that plastics can take over a thousand years to biodegrade, that enormous trash islands of plastic are floating and dispersing into the oceans, and that even on land, plastic presents ecological risks (Rochman et al., 2016; M. L. Taylor et al., 2016). A few may also be aware of recent research showing that human exposure to microplastics—in the air we breathe, the water we drink, even the table salt we sprinkle on our food—is utterly pervasive (Zhang et al., 2020). Yet plastics use—including single-use, "disposable" plastic products—remains widespread around the globe; 18 billion tons of plastic flows into the ocean each year, of which 40% are single-use products (Parker, 2018). The seeming intractability of casual plastics use may be at least partially ascribable to the fact that in general their harms, particularly to marine ecosystems, are invisible to the average person. Indeed, such harms are often brought to mind only by media campaigns highlighting sea life mutilated by six-pack rings, plastic bottles, and plastic straws. Such campaigns—which heighten the vividness, and thus the availability, of the harms caused by plastics—can be highly effective. One video of a sea turtle with a straw imbedded in its nose, for instance, has been credited with sparking an avalanche of local plastic straw bans (Rosenbaum, 2018). Such "availability cascades," where a previously invisible and neglected issue becomes suddenly salient, triggering an avalanche of behavioral and policy responses, have been chronicled in other contexts as well (Kuran & Sunstein, 1999).

Cognitive shortcuts can also systematically distort information that could be used to generate decisions and minimize externalities. Consider the representativeness heuristic, which might be thought of as the "if it looks like a duck and quacks like a duck, it must be a duck" shortcut. Things that share features of a class are estimated as more likely to be part of that class. In Kahneman and Tversky's (1983) classic demonstration of this phenomenon, they described a person named "Linda" to research participants like this: "Linda is 31 years old, single, outspoken and very bright. She majored in philosophy. As a student, she was deeply concerned with issues of discrimination and social justice, and also participated in antinuclear demonstrations." They were then asked to rank the probabilities of various facts about Linda, among them that 1) Linda is a bank teller and 2) Linda is both a bank teller and a feminist. Linda seems very representative of the second category. Nevertheless, it cannot be more likely that she is a member of the second category (both a bank teller and a feminist) than that she is a member of the first (only a bank teller)—the former is a subset of the latter. And yet, by large margins, people rank the second likelihood as higher. Because Linda "looks like" a feminist, they fail to account for the underlying probability of being just a bank teller.

The representativeness heuristic can lead to a number of cognitive errors. One of the more well known is "base rate neglect," which is a failure of the perceiver to account for the underlying distribution of something when estimating its current probability. The more remote the underlying baseline probability to be accounted for, the worse the distortion caused by the availability heuristic. A different (and perhaps more literal) sort of "diffusion" than being remote across time or space is actually very common in environmental harms: Often pollutants are literally microscopic or highly dilute but still consequential. Yet their diffuse, invisible nature makes it hard to take them seriously—we tend to forget their effects or their importance in favor of more immediate, visible phenomena.

To see how this can work (or fail to work!), imagine a toxicologist is trying to determine whether a particular chemical is present in a sample of water drawn from a large wastewater supply on a particular day. As a whole, there are usually 50,000 parts per million (ppm) of one common chemical and only 1 ppm of a very rare chemical. The toxicologist uses a test that is 99% accurate at discriminating between the two chemicals, and after applying the test, announces that the chemical she found in the sample is the very rare one. What is the probability that she is right? Most people's first-order, intuitive answer is "99%," because the test is 99% accurate. However, upon a little further reflection, more sophisticated answerers will realize that the probability is lower than 99% because it is necessary to compensate for the fact that on an absolute measure, there will be *many* times that the test will identify the chemical as "rare" when in fact it is "common," given that it will be wrong 1% of the time. So a second-order answer, without actually breaking out a calculator, might be something lower—98%? 75%? 50%?

In fact, the real probability that the toxicologist's result is accurate is more like 0.2%. How could intuition be so far off? The representativeness heuristic helps explain it. (To see an explanation for this number, complete with the math for the above example, check out this endnote.[1]) We know that the general underlying probability of finding the common versus the rare chemical are worlds apart. But once we get *new* diagnostic information (namely, a positive identification of the chemical), we tend to forget what came before and assume that the new odds represent the old odds too. So we learn that a test is 99% accurate, and we tend to neglect the fact that finding the "rare" chemical is still wildly unlikely. There are some circumstances where people will correct for the underlying probabilities at least somewhat, but it is a remarkably sticky cognitive bias.

This base rate neglect cuts both ways: Not only might it make us less willing to take steps to mitigate a diffuse but real harm, it can make us think that pro-environmental efforts we are taking now have *more* effect than they actually do because we fail to appreciate the magnitude of the underlying problem. Recycling plastic bottles is a pro-environmental behavior, for example, which the EPA recommends in part because of its impact on reducing climate emissions. Yet the impacts of each bottle recycled are truly tiny compared with the magnitude of the problem. As a comparative measure, you would have to recycle roughly 40,000 plastic bottles to equal the climate emissions of one round-trip coach flight between New York and London (Berners-Lee, 2011). This is not to suggest that recycling plastic is a bad choice—after all, the climate impacts of air travel are notoriously terrible. It might suggest, however, that base rate neglect can encourage people to overestimate the impacts of small actions like recycling, even as they underestimate the impacts of higher-impact actions such as shifting to plant-based diets or reducing air travel.

The availability and representativeness heuristics are at heart demonstrations that humans are bad at certain kinds of probabilistic cognitive processing, which can make appreciating diffuse environmental effects harder. But diffusion may not just affect the likelihood of seeing or understanding environmental phenomena in an abstract sense, it may also affect actual perception, particularly where the diffusion occurs across time. Psychological research demonstrates that people's ability to process information that is temporally distant from them is far more complex than conventional environmental law approaches assume—even those approaches that are economically sophisticated and take into account concepts like discounting. Temporal diffusion can affect the relationship between people's perceptions of value and the time value of money, subjective experience of time as continuously flowing, and even the felt experience of time as unidirectional. These distortions make meaningful interactions between present and future people—or even between present and future selves—impossible (Rowell 2014), and they trigger a number of powerful psychological phenomena, which we discuss further below.

Cognitive Limitations in Temporal Diffusion

It is simply not possible for people to know everything about what the future will look like. The world may change in unexpected ways, and people themselves may change and develop new values and new ways of thinking about it. These changes can matter to environmental policy. If we forgo economic gain today, for instance, by forbidding overfishing a particular species in the ocean, we have guaranteed a present loss, undertaken in the hopes it will mitigate overall loss when averaged with the future. But what if technology develops to allow us to farm that species in a way that makes its flourishing in the open ocean unimportant? We will have delayed consuming and enjoying that species today with no corresponding future benefits. As with public goods dilemmas, it is irrational for us to invest fully in a future event when we cannot guarantee we will fully internalize its benefits.

Such problems can be addressed at least partially by adjusting for future probabilities based on what we do know. That is, we can estimate the possible future scenarios, weight them by their likelihood, and calculate an expected value. This is a practical and highly rational approach to future impacts, and is particularly suitable where there is good information about probabilities. Indeed, it is the approach that regulators generally take in the United States to valuing future environmental impacts (Sunstein & Rowell, 2007). But as we discuss further in Chapter 7, this approach is imperfect. Most obviously, as a practical matter, even hyperrational decision makers cannot use expected value to generate prescriptions when there is insufficient information about probabilities. In such cases, decision makers must adopt other methods of choosing (Farber, 2010)—but, unfortunately, all those other methods (such as the precautionary principle) still depend upon decisions about how to value the future.

In addition to simple informational limitations, there are cognitive quirks associated with how we think about time that complicate our ability to fully internalize future effects. These include how we manage future uncertainty, our ability to accurately predict how we will feel in the future ("hedonic forecasting"), how much we value the present versus the future ("present bias"), and our perceptions of our ethical obligations to the future. We focus on each of these problems below.

MANAGING FUTURE LOSSES AND GAINS
Before we know how much effort to put into seeking or avoiding some future outcome, we have to figure out how much it is worth. To do this, we do not just estimate the absolute worth of the outcome, we also view it as either a "loss" or a "gain" relative to some comparison state of affairs—and the reference point we choose affects our calculations. Prospect theory, also developed by Daniel Kahneman and Amos Tversky (1979), describes how people value losses and gains and how they

treat uncertainty and risk regarding each of them. Their basic finding is that losses hurt more than gains feel good: The magnitude of negative emotion people feel when experiencing a loss is greater than the magnitude of positive emotion people feel when experiencing an equally sized gain. This heightened sensitivity to loss is what is typically called "loss aversion." In addition, people are risk-avoiding for losses and risk-seeking for gains. For instance, if I were to ask you which you prefer: $6 outright or $7 if you roll a 1 on a six-sided die, most people take the guaranteed gain over the gamble, even though the gamble has a higher expected value. In contrast, if you had to pay $6 with certainty or $7 if you rolled a 1, most people would take the gamble over the certain loss. This is prospect theory.

Prospect theory is the foundation for the "endowment effect," a phenomenon whose discovery began with research into how people value environmental goods. As we discuss further in Chapter 7, this research revealed contingent valuation puzzles—specifically, people in these studies would consistently offer to pay far less for things they didn't currently have, like a national park or clean air, than they would demand to sell that same thing. But prospect theory is even more interesting when we think about the subjective nature of framing something as a loss versus a gain.

It turns out that the temporally delayed nature of most environmental effects (relative to when we either invest or fail to invest in them) affects whether we see them as gains or losses. Prospect theory says that people evaluate outcomes as either losses or gains based on departures from a relevant reference point, and for most decisions, that reference point is the current status quo (Kahneman & Tversky, 1984). In the context of decisions that affect the environment, then, we are most likely to see how we live and consume today as our "endowment," which must be traded off to achieve some future possible set of circumstances—the loss or gain. Thus, people tend to give greater weight to entitlements they "own" (such as their time or their freedom to use as many paper towels as they want, or to not compost, or to produce smoke in their widget factory) versus speculative future potential environmental goods (which are probably not fully internalizable to the actor to boot). This phenomenon leads to a form of "status quo bias," which we discuss in more detail below.

A continuing puzzle for contingent valuation and prospect theory is why people in contingent valuation studies seem to code future environmental goods as gains for which they are relatively unwilling to pay. Why, for instance, aren't they seeing the *failure* to get some future environmental good as a painful loss? Since the respondent owns the money she is contemplating exchanging, she could code the transaction as either a loss of her money or a gain of the good (Novemsky & Kahneman, 2005). A barter example may make this framing effect more clear: I own one good (say, a bicycle) and am considering trading for another (say, a laptop). I could see this transaction as losing a bike (loss frame) or getting a computer (gain frame). More research on intuitive framing of environmental goods would be valuable in this realm.

In any case, for policy makers and norm entrepreneurs, the status quo may be sticky, but it is not immutable. Psychology research has shown a number of wrinkles in prospect theory that planners should be aware of, and which in some cases they may take advantage of.

First, although the default reference point for decisions is the status quo, it is *only* the default and can be overridden. The law can make efforts to reset it (Thaler & Sunstein, 2003; Thaler & Benartzi, 2004; Korobkin, 2014). It might, for example, set aspirational goals in international environmental agreements like the Paris Agreement—which set an aggressive (and perhaps impossible) goal of keeping global temperature change below 2° C and which might recast what is perceived to be the minimum acceptable baseline goal. The threat of missing this new goal may trigger loss aversion in individual actors, who may then work that much harder to achieve it (Rowell & van Zeben, 2016).

Second, if environmental quality changes, people might actually focus on the way things *were* as their reference point. When changes are for the worse, this may induce people to take otherwise unfavorable risks to regain what they see as the baseline. Think of gambling at a casino to get back to even (Thaler & Johnson, 1990). In environmental contexts, this effect may heighten people's attention to and concern for degrading environments, and may underlie the common environmental policy goal of antidegradation, which seeks to hold on to the status quo of environmental quality, and to prevent downward changes from that baseline. The Clean Water Act, for example, has as one of its principle objectives to "maintain the chemical, physical, and biological integrity of the Nation's waters" (Clean Water Act 101(a)). A number of other environmental regimes both in the United States and around the world embed some form of antidegradation, antibacksliding, or antiregression norm (Glicksman, 2012).

Notably, preoccupation with the perceived status quo will not always lead to pro-environmental behaviors. When environmental quality *improves* from the perceived status quo, the same effect could lead people to undervalue those improvements, especially when they are categorized as a gain rather than a loss. This could be particularly important in large-scale social and economic disruptions, such as may be generated by the COVID-19 pandemic (Rowell, 2020c). In some cases, the changed behaviors postpandemic may lead to increased environmental quality, for example by lowering pollution from decreased production and transportation. Yet if these changes are generally perceived as gains from the prepandemic status quo, people will tend to intuitively assign these improvements less value.

Policy makers may have options for shaping how people perceive the status quo. When we have expectations that the status quo will certainly change, for example, it can shift our reference point to the future context and make us willing to incur certain costs now to prevent it (Kőszegi & Rabin, 2007). Indeed, even reminding people in subtle ways that it is their own future self who will suffer can induce them to change their behaviors now. For instance, people's discount rates for future rewards drop significantly when the timing of the future reward is described in terms of their own age ("when you are 47") rather than in terms of years ("in 10 years")—an effect that is more pronounced the younger the person (Frederick et al., 2008). In short, to the extent people can be induced *not* to focus on the current status quo as the referent, their loss aversion to investing and changing present behaviors (and willingness to risk future harms) can be muted. Similarly, a focus on improved environmental quality as the "new" status quo may encourage people to hold fast to those improvements.

Finally, it is also worthwhile to consider that the usual pattern of risk seeking for losses and risk avoiding for gains flips for very low-probability future events. This phenomenon is compounded by people's overestimation of high-salience low-probability events and underestimation of low-salience, high-probability events, and it leads them to over- and underinvest and insure accordingly. People buy too little flood insurance in the United States, for instance, even though it is federally subsidized and sometimes even required (as for those with federally backed mortgages), because they underestimate the fairly common risks of their area being flooded (Atreya et al., 2015). Yet many of these same people are also willing to pay insurance premiums, often using unreasonably high deductibles, for very low-probability losses like their house burning down, and are willing to buy lottery tickets, which offer notoriously bad odds for vanishingly small chances of winning. Combining prospect theory with these over-/underestimation tendencies, we can see why people tend to underappreciate some high-probability environmental outcomes, underinsure for them, take suboptimal precautions to prevent them, and demand too little from lawmakers to mitigate them.

Still further factors come into play when considering mega-catastrophic outcomes, meaning that extremely bad risks are systematically neglected (Wiener, 2016). When risks are extraordinarily rare, there are unlikely to be any instances of recent occurrences that can be brought to mind, and they are therefore less cognitively available (Kahneman et al., 1982; Kuran & Sunstein, 1999; Wiener, 2016). Moreover, as we discuss further in Chapter 8 on climate change, the catastrophic nature of such risks also triggers "numbing," a cognitive phenomenon whereby extremely large, "mass" risks elicit less emotional affect than smaller, more manageable risks, presumably as a result of a cognitive strategy to tamp down excess trauma (Slovic et al., 2007; Slovic et al., 2013; Wiener, 2016). Consequently, extraordinarily large and unprecedented risks—such as mass extinction (Ceballos et al., 2017) or a nanotechnology accident (Phoenix & Treder, 2008)—are routinely underestimated and undervalued. At the same time, massive *gains* from the status quo—such as the development of highly effective geoengineering technologies or successful colonization of outer space environments—will also be underpredicted and undervalued, as they will also lack availability and be perceived as underappreciated "gains" rather than as "losses to be avoided" (Rowell, 2020b).

Again, social science research does offer hope for how to recalibrate people's risk- and benefit-taking behavior for these kinds of events. People do respond to government's attempts to educate them on the magnitude of risks. Thus, easily accessible, accurate flood maps do improve the likelihood of people buying appropriate levels of flood insurance (Shao et al., 2017). Moreover, a trust in government translates to a trust in government's estimation of risks. Working to increase trust in government may therefore pay dividends in people's willingness to plan/spend appropriately for environmental risks, in addition to all the other benefits of such trust (Shao et al., 2017).

HEDONIC FORECASTING

Perhaps surprisingly, people are not particularly good at anticipating how they will feel about things in the future: They cannot predict their own preferences well. As an objective matter, for instance, though we might think various life events will change our overall level of happiness permanently, in fact adaptation quickly sets in—something evocatively called the "hedonic treadmill." One of the earliest and most colorful demonstrations of this was a comparison of the happiness levels of three types of people: those who had in the past won the lottery, those who had suffered a paralyzing accident, and controls who had experienced neither. After a certain period of time, all three groups exhibited roughly equal levels of happiness (Brickman et al., 1978). The explanation is presumably fairly simple: On any given day, one gets used to what one has and focuses mainly on the task at hand. Paraplegics still have personal relationships and jobs that bring them gratification; lottery winners still must deal with difficult relatives and attend their children's umpteenth baseball practice of the season. This is related to the "present bias" issue discussed below (O'Donoghue & Rabin, 1999): People lose focus on the shock of the disrupting event of yesterday and concentrate more on living their lives today. In addition, they learn various coping mechanisms for dealing with the new reality, including simply readjusting their expectations and preferences to comport with their new circumstances—a sort of affective "immune system" response (Gilbert et al., 1998).

Subsequent experimental work begun by Daniel Gilbert and Timothy Wilson demonstrated that despite the robustness of a happiness set point, people are relatively oblivious to it, even for events that they experience repeatedly (Gilbert et al., 1998; Wilson & Gilbert, 2003). For whatever reason, when trying to predict how an event will affect them, people focus on the event itself and fail to appreciate the compensations, mitigating circumstances, and adaptations that attend it (Wilson et al., 2000). The phenomenon is somewhat similar to how intentions fail to accurately predict action—people simply forget the myriad ways that intervening events and competing priorities can distract and subvert us from accomplishing even the sincerest goals (Poon et al., 2014; Poon & Koehler, 2006). Hedonic adaptation has its value, not least in preventing emotional swings that could otherwise interfere with daily functioning. After all, whether you are a lottery winner or a paraplegic, you still need to deal with your irritating cousin at Thanksgiving. But this just explains why hedonic adaptation is adaptive—it does not explain why people would routinely fail to *anticipate* it. And yet people do. They are perennially surprised by the finding that lottery winners and people who have been paralyzed are roughly equally happy.

Possibly, overpredicting the joy of good events and the despair of bad ones maintains incentives to seek out the former and avoid the latter. Regardless of the cognitive reason for the hedonic treadmill, however, such failures of affective forecasting have clear implications for environmental policy. When people are deciding the appropriate way to act today, based on the effects that action will have in the future, it is obviously important that they accurately anticipate what those effects will be. In the next section, we discuss the ways in which people's predictions of future events might be incorrect based on distorted discount rates and loss aversion. Here we note that such errors can also arise because of their emotional impact. Even if we correctly predict the actuarial likelihood of a future outcome, if we misperceive its "goodness" or "badness" in an affective sense, then our incentives to seek it out or avoid it will be distorted.

How can we improve people's affective forecasting capabilities? Calling people's attention to the phenomenon of adaptation and encouraging them to consider intervening circumstances and events that would reduce the emotional impact of the future event have been shown to improve affective forecasting in at least some experimental circumstances (Ubel et al., 2005). Present emotional states also color our estimates of the effect of future outcomes (Loewenstein, 2005; Schwarz, 2000). Fear and anxiety, for instance, concentrates attention and so worsens the "focalism" problem of ignoring likely mitigating circumstances (Elster, 1998; LeDoux, 2002). Another promising ameliorative approach to the problem of affective forecasting is encouraging "mindfulness." A tendency to-ward mindfulness (which is a nonjudgmental, present-focused internal state) has been shown to be negatively correlated with overestimating the effect that a future event will have on someone (Emanuel et al., 2010).

Interestingly, Gilbert, Wilson, and colleagues showed that one of the most effective interventions for improving affective forecasting is simply getting people to ask another person who has experienced the event how they responded to it. This is even more effective than telling them facts and details about the event itself. Unfortunately, this is of limited utility for future environmental impacts that nobody on earth has experienced (like the melting of polar ice caps) or where decision makers do not have easy access to those who might have experienced them. Moreover, people don't tend to *believe* that others' affective responses are better predictors of their own reaction than a careful consideration of the facts and details of the future event would be. Thus, even when they have access to both methods of estimation, they are likely to reject the tech-nique that actually works better (Gilbert et al., 2009).

DISCOUNTING AND PRESENT BIAS

Valuing goods through time triggers the possibility of investment. This is particularly true for valuing monetary or monetized goods: Money has a time value because a dollar today can be invested and made to grow. The process of "discounting" quantifies this time value (Heal, 1999). Conven-tionally, for instance, a 5% discount rate indicates that decision makers believe that a dollar can be expected to grow 5% in value over the com-ing year. Because money has a time value, people may reasonably value an immediate dollar over a dollar they get next year.

The fact that the environmental impacts of many actions are latent, occurring long after the behavior that caused them, can significantly af-fect the value people place on them (Revesz, 1999; Rowell, 2010). In the United States, regulators generally address the timing of environmental and other policy impacts via the practice of discounting (Sunstein & Rowell, 2007; Rowell, 2010). This practice allows economists and regu-lators to account for the time value of money (Heal, 1999). Economists and regulators routinely discount future environmental impacts after monetizing them on the basis of people's willingness to pay money to protect them (Sunstein & Rowell, 2007).

Unfortunately, a number of cognitive distortions affect individuals' perceptions and understanding of future value, leading people to routinely exhibit a constellation of phenomena known as "hyperbolic discounting," "time inconsistency," and "present bias." These phenomena affect how people value future environmental goods and harms, especially when the possibilities of future environmental impacts are being weighed against immediate actions or immediate costs.

For instance, people's discount rates in most instances are "hyperbolic"—that is, they decline as the temporal period increases (Frederick et al., 2002; Laibson, 1997). They might prefer $1 today to $2 a week from now, yet prefer $2 in a year plus a week from now to $1 in a year. As we discuss further below, this creates problems of time inconsistency—preferences that shift depending upon when they are elicited. But it also means that individuals' valuation of money or monetized goods through time diverges substantially from the valuation by economists of the same goods over the same period. Time-inconsistent preferences mean that *when* you ask people to value an environmental good can affect *what* valuations you get.

Thus, it can generate troublesome inconsistencies—even mistakes—when policy makers build their environmental policies on valuations generated by members of the public without being careful to identify in what time frame, exactly, the environmental good or harm is being valued (Rowell, 2010). This is particularly important where, as is often the case in the United States, environmental policy is being informed by monetized cost-benefit analysis. Because money has a time value, time-indeterminacy (where there is no particular time signature attached to a cost or benefit) undermines the ability of the analysis to coherently quantify the value of the underlying good (Rowell 2010, 2014).

Relatedly, people's preferences often exhibit inconsistency when comparing immediate choices over delayed choices. One common way to understand hyperbolic discounting is to think of it as a form of "present bias," where people attach a special premium to instant gratification (O'Donoghue & Rabin, 1999; Frederick et al., 2002), and thus will work particularly hard to avoid immediate injury. For example, Liberman and Trope (1998) found that when students were offered a choice of doing an interesting but hard assignment or a boring but easy one, they chose the easy, boring task if they were asked to decide immediately but chose the hard, interesting one if deciding for the future. These inconsistencies are exacerbated with longer latency periods between the decision and its impact: The longer the wait, the more people devalue the impact, and the more inconsistent they get (Thaler, 1991). This hints that as environmental effects become more distant from the people and behaviors that generate them, those impacts might affect behavior less and less.

All of these distortions exist simultaneously not only with one another but also with the other effects we have discussed, including loss aversion and failures in affective forecasting. In principle, of course, such phenomena could at least partially offset each other. Imagine that we think global warming is relatively unconcerning because present bias leads us to hyperbolically discount future harms, and imagine that our loss aversion makes us less willing to inconvenience ourselves now on the chance of avoiding that future, since it's an uncertain loss that not only might not happen, but might not happen *to us*. If so, then perhaps a failure of affective forecasting could serve as a corrective measure, making us take more steps to avoid that bad future than we otherwise would because we wrongly overestimate the degree to which that future will make us miserable. In short, while the temporally induced biases cause us to underprepare for bad events, perhaps the temporally induced emotional exaggeration of hedonic forecasting might sometimes cause us to overprepare.

It is very tempting to dismiss these interactions among heuristics and biases, hoping that they will balance out on net, leaving people close enough in the end to the cognitively "right" place. But it seems a bit convenient to believe that they would cancel each other out in anything close to an optimal fashion, and there is certainly no evidence for it. Instead, determining the impacts of the combination of such effects should be a priority for psychological science, with further experimental and psychological research designed to tease apart the multiple and interactive impacts of these heuristics and biases. We, of course, would be especially happy to see such research as it specifically applies to the environmental context. In the absence of such research, though, basic research into figuring out ways to avoid suffering from biases in the first place, or designing debiasing techniques to mitigate their impact, would obviously also be useful.

Unidirectionality and Bargaining with the Future

A final distinctive aspect of temporally diffuse impacts is that time, unlike space, is unidirectional: It moves in one direction, from past to future. This observation triggers a set of phenomena that make it challenging to "bargain with the future" (Rowell, 2014). While the present can convey resources, information, harm, and risk *to* the future—say, by building a nuclear waste depository that will inevitably leak at some future point, or by preserving a valuable landscape or species from destruction—the future cannot reciprocate. This creates a consistent barrier to intertemporal bargaining, which works on top of the general challenges of seeing or imagining the future. These challenges have particular relevance to environmental impacts, where again many, if not most, of the impacts of policies may accrue to the future.

Notably, the barriers to bargaining with the future are psychological as well as practical. Imagine that decision makers today are considering a policy with likely impacts on future stakeholders. Unlike in a contemporaneous negotiation where, say, the policy would immediately impact stakeholders in a neighboring state, our decision makers would have to act without representatives from the future commenting on impacts they would experience. Neither could the future stakeholders deploy techniques of social influence and persuasion that contemporaneous stakeholders would have at their disposal. These barriers to intertemporal relationships are particularly worrisome given the latency of many environmental impacts. This has led a number of commentators to argue that ethical obligations to the future—and particularly to future generations—are substantively different than ethical obligations to present people (Farber & Hemmersbaugh, 1993; Revesz, 1999; Portney & Weyant, 2013), yet fulfilling those obligations is rendered more difficult by the very same barriers the currently living have in noticing, perceiving, and connecting with future stakeholders.

Some partial solutions to this problem have been proposed. One is the creation of so-called "ombudsmen for the future." The idea is that individuals might be appointed to act as voices for future stakeholders (Beckman & Uggla, 2016.) The country of Hungary, for instance, has famously established an Office of the Hungarian Ombudsman for Future Generations. Although such ombudsmen lack the power to sanction, compel, or incentivize via traditional means, their ability to take advantage of soft forms of influence and persuasion might still make a practical difference in decision making.

Another possibility is that decision makers could simply be induced to imagine the future and how their current decisions might affect future people, animals, and ecosystems. Presenting decision makers with members of an imaginary future generation, for example, has been shown in lab contexts to encourage pro-environmental choices that would benefit future generations (Kamijo et al., 2017). In one study, 60% of participants selected a policy option that promoted sustainability when future generations were made salient, versus just 28% when not so prompted (Kamijo et al., 2017). This suggests that merely increasing the salience of future generations in this way may make a substantial difference.

Although these approaches may help in increasing the salience and power of future stakeholders, we should note that cognitive barriers to imagining the future continue to operate; a major psychological battle in dealing with future impacts is to get decision makers to notice that they exist in the first place. This is a problem largely of low salience and is subject to all the phenomena potentially affecting subjective salience—but it is also amenable to solutions that increase salience.

The problem is not just cognitive, of course—even if salience or other problems we have discussed so far are addressed, people may not *care* about future impacts, in the same way that they may not care about other externalities that they generate. We take up this problem in the next section. The tendency to feel numb or uncaring may increase with diffusion through both time and space. And finally, even if people notice future impacts, and even if they care, recall that well-meaning people may simply get what is best for the future *wrong*. Even ombudsmen for future generations may suffer from problems with hedonic forecasting, for instance, as may well-meaning policy makers who have been primed to think about future generations.

Emotional and Motivational Limitations on Dealing with Diffuse Environmental Effects

Above we suggested that diffuse impacts will in many cases be difficult for people to "see" and process. But people may also be insufficiently motivated to mitigate harms (or pursue gains). This is a not a cognitive limitation—we might see exactly how we could achieve such goals but just not want to bother. This is especially so where the affected populations are different from us in ways that are easily categorized in social identity terms. Human psychology developed in the context of small, cohesive tribal groups—not large, abstract, global populations—and this developmental history introduces emotional and motivational obstacles to dealing with diffuse environmental effects. Temporal diffusion is part of the problem—we simply may not care about "future us" (or even "our descendants") to the same degree we care about "present us." But spatial diffusion is an even bigger concern here, because spatial diffusion triggers identifiable in-group/out-group dynamics and the problem of generating sympathy for others.

In-Group/Out-Group Dynamics

People are inherently prone to creating and maintaining groups, identifying with them, and even favoring them to the detriment of outsiders. Groups are social constructs, and they simply consist of agglomerations of individuals who perceive themselves as members of the same social category and who therefore share an identity with others in that category (Turner et al., 1987). Triggers to creating groups can be tiny and even arbitrary. In some of the earliest experimental research in this area, for instance, groups of research subjects were brought into a lab, shown slides of collections of dots, and asked to quickly guess their number. Then (irrespective of their answers) they were randomly told either that they were "underestimators" or "overestimators." Afterward, they engaged in a task where they could assign money to others who were either fellow estimators or the opposite. Despite the fact that they knew nothing about the others except that they were a "member" of one or the other entirely manufactured and artificial "groups," research subjects consistently allotted more resources to their fellow in-group members (Tajfel, 1970).

This early finding spawned much more research, supporting the idea that group creation and a preference for giving advantages to fellow in-group members is a deeply ingrained human tendency. By creating groups, we create social identities from which we derive intense pride and esteem (Tajfel & Turner, 1979), plus a sense of belonging in the world (Baumeister & Leary, 1995). To increase that esteem, we strive to increase the status of our group—which leads us to discriminate in favor of fellow members (Hewstone et al., 2002). This usually takes the form of increased cooperation with in-group members (Balliet et al., 2014; Cremer & Vugt, 1999), but it can also take ugly and even perverse forms, where people actually take pleasure in harms experienced by members of an out-group (Cikara, Botvinick & Fiske, 2011) or even become willing to actually harm their own group in order to inflict damage on the other (Balliet et al., 2014). These tendencies are further exacerbated when the out-group is perceived to be a competitor (Cikara, Bruneau & Saxe, 2011).

And unfortunately, in a world of scarce resources, people have lots of competitors (Kurzban & Neuberg, 2005; Schaller et al., 2003). Even worse, scarcity makes people more likely to classify another as a member of an out-group in the first place. For instance, making economic troubles more salient to white research subjects makes them more likely in a subsequent task to identify a biracial face as black (Rodeheffer et al., 2012). A perception of threat to their own status also makes people denigrate out-groups more—particularly members of lower-status out-groups, and even when the threat came not from the lower-status group but from a higher-status one (Cadinu & Reggiori, 2002).

This fundamental "groupiness" of human organization makes it easier to ignore the bad effects of environmental impacts that diffuse across space to harm members of out-groups—even, or perhaps especially, as it makes the benefits to in-groups loom that much larger. And, in particularly pernicious versions of in-group/out-group dynamics, it might even cause people to get value out of inflicting such harms! Where an environmental problem involves scarcity—as it often does—these in-group/out-group effects are exacerbated.

As we discuss further in subsequent chapters, in-group/out-group dynamics may complicate environmental regulation in multiple ways. Regulation (or lack thereof) in one place may affect environmental outcomes in another, with no (or little) overlap across populations. A farmer who fertilizes his field in Iowa gets the benefit of that fertilization in bigger, more lucrative crops—and incurs almost none of the harm caused by nitrogen runoff into the Mississippi watershed nor of the sprawling dead zone in the Gulf of Mexico. Others, separate and remote from that farmer, suffer effects such as destruction of fishing stocks, decreased recreation opportunities, and risks to health. The farmer and the farmer's representatives may underestimate and undervalue those harms, where they are perceived to accrue to out-groups. In some perverse contexts, polluters may even perceive a benefit to externalizing harm onto those they perceive as outside their group—people in other cities, states, or just marginalized communities. In this light, the likelihood that most climate impacts will accrue outside the borders of any single country (Rowell, 2015) may lead to systematic underestimation *and* undercaring about those climate impacts.

In other words, diffusion of the harm through space and in-group/out-group dynamics exacerbate the typical problem of externalities, and may create distributional problems as well. Again, part of the problem is cognitive: The farmer may not know how his fertilization practices lead to distant environmental problems, and the fact that the harms caused by his actions are so distant—and involve such diffuse stakeholders—makes it even less likely that he will ever learn of those impacts or be reminded of them if he does. Moreover, he has cognitive strategies to minimize the extent of the harms that he does know about: He may tell himself that his contribution is tiny compared to everyone else's, that he needs to feed his family, and that it's just a bunch of fish anyway. But another part of the problem is that the harms are experienced by out-group members—non-farmers, non-Midwesterners, perhaps even foreigners. And he has a motivational incentive not to care as much about harms to them.

Another and more extreme example is the Amazonian rain forest, half of which is in Brazil. That forest constitutes a significant carbon sink that, if released through deforestation, would significantly affect not just Brazil but the entire planet (Pan et al., 2011; Phillips et al., 2008). Yet citizens of Brazil can make great productive use of the rich forest land for cattle grazing, mining, and harvesting other products of the forest—all activities that destroy the forest and release carbon. Forest-consuming choices that Brazilian companies (or the Brazilian government) make within their borders will redound mainly to the benefit of their own economy—the in-group—but mainly harm non-Brazilians—members of the out-group. In other words, if Brazilians forewent the benefits of using the rain forest, the out-group would essentially be freeriding on their sacrifices. When free riding occurs in a small community under, say, a unified political or social system, the solutions are clearer and easier, in no small part because of the greater likelihood of social unity between cost payers and benefit receivers. Social pressures to fall into line are more effective when imposed by in-group members. But more formal solutions will work better too: The polity will have an easier time taxing or punishing free riders because there will be more political support to protect harms to the in-group by a few bad actors. For similar reasons, the polity might also have an easier time compensating harm sufferers. But conventional approaches to solving public goods dilemmas (which is what these are) are weaker when the dispersion is large, because in-group/out-group dynamics are also large.

The solutions become even more complicated when they must cross political jurisdictional lines. For example, while international bodies can urge Brazil to restrict economic activity that destroys the forest, there is no obligation for Brazil to do so and no way consistent with international law to unilaterally make them. Negotiation and bargaining is always an option in principle, of course. If there were agreements or treaties to which Brazil was a party that required restrictions on Brazil's destruction of their own forests, then of course there might be meaningful and legal enforcement mechanisms—but Brazil would have to have entered into such agreements willingly. Similarly, Brazil might be paid off by other countries—but it would have to agree to any such payoff and to an enforcement mechanism for living with the terms of the deal. Classic economic theory holds that rules are irrelevant in perfect markets where there are no transaction costs because stakeholders will bargain to the efficient solution (Coase, 1960). But one big transaction cost, and thus obstacle to a negotiated solution, is that Brazil—and Brazil's decision makers—are likely to fall prey to self-justification, minimizing the harm that they cause through deforestation and mentally bolstering the value of the deforestation to themselves. Such self-serving distortion is made that much easier because Brazil will not see most of the harm of climate change—though they will see much of the benefits of the activities that cause deforestation. The result may be an inflated value attached to continued deforestation and a refusal to bargain "rationally" with international actors.

Moreover, even if Brazil's domestic laws or international treaties, freely entered into by them, manage to protect the forest, these are, at heart, political solutions—and in democracies, at least, such solutions are driven (or resisted) by individual perceptions of what is important and what is tolerable. As a result, they are subject to individual psychology and to the full range of psychological effects we are discussing. They are furthermore subject to destabilizing social phenomena like availability cascades—self-reinforcing processes of collective belief formation, where an expressed perception triggers a chain reaction that leads to widespread adoption of an idea (Kuran, 1995; Kuran & Sunstein, 1999). Whether because of cascades or not, preferences have proved unstable recently in Brazil (Schiffman, 2017), and laws designed to preserve the rainforest have begun to be reversed after a regime change. As a consequence, while deforestation of the Amazon had slowed over the last decade, it has recently begun to increase in earnest again. And note that, while cascades can arise wherever a risk or issue gains prominence, they are systematically less likely to occur where the risk or issue has been cognitively shoved into the background, as distant environmental risks are prone to be. In short, regulation of agricultural runoff, the use of the Amazon, and countless other spatially diffused public goods dilemmas are at least in part in-group/out-group problems for environmental regulators to solve—ones for which the usually available solutions are likely to be weak or even nonexistent.

Although we believe the psychological challenges of in-group/out-group dynamics in environmental law and policy should be recognized as worrisome, there *are* less conventional potential solutions. One glimmer of hope is that the in-group/out-group dynamic is malleable: The tendency toward "groupification" is itself something that can be magnified or muted depending on the context. For the dynamic to trigger at all, intergroup identities must be salient, and their interaction must be thought of as relevant (Turner et al., 1987). Also, individuals will engage in group-based bias less to the extent they perceive the in-group as permeable, unstable, or illegitimate (Tajfel & Turner, 1979). Structural or procedural shifts can also minimize the dynamic: Lack of interdependence among in-group members decreases bias against out-group members (Balliet et al., 2014), and sequential interactions with out-groups decrease bias versus simultaneous-exchange interactions (Balliet et al., 2014). Furthermore, except where the groups are defined by moral positions, many people at least exhibit reluctance (though not complete unwillingness) to display out-group hate by actively harming out-group members (Wiesel & Boehm, 2015). These features may be, or perhaps can be made to be, more or less prevalent in different environmental regulatory contexts. More importantly, the *perception* of their existence might be something that can be shaped through careful choice architecture and regulatory action.

Another possible solution to the problem of in-group/out-group dynamics in the environmental arena is actually suggested by the phenomenon itself. Groups are a matter of social construct and therefore perception. Groups may be arbitrary, but they are more saliently and robustly consequences of gender, race, religion, political affiliation, and geographic location. This means that at every moment humans are members of multiple groups that nest and overlap. Preferential treatment of the in-group is generally driven more by self-love than other-hate (Brewer, 1979; Balliet et al., 2014), and the choice of "group" frame is driven by the relative salience of the relevant grouping (Turner et al., 1987). This means that regulators can try to create a sense of solidarity with a larger, superordinate group in order to inspire self-sacrificing but group-protecting impulses.

A surprising demonstration of this comes from studies that expose research subjects to their national flag. Rather than inspiring denigration of out-groups, such exposure can trigger a larger sense of community. Exposing American research subjects to a large American flag actually causes them to report *less* hostility to Arabs and Muslims, particularly among the most highly nationalistic participants (Butz et al., 2007). A similar phenomenon was demonstrated after exposing Israeli citizens to their flag—it moderated nationalistic impulses about the Israeli–Arab conflict (Hassin et al., 2007). Moreover, this effect has now been conceptually replicated in several settings (Butz, 2009). We can speculate about how this might work for the Amazon forest problem. Citizens of Brazil are also members of the superordinate class of "South Americans" or even "humans"; many are also "parents." Carefully describing the problems of deforestation in terms that reference the superordinate category can convert a seemingly intractable in-group/out-group inflected environmental problem into a *more* tractable, simple public goods problem—at least psychologically.

Identifiable Victim Effect

Another aspect of diffusion that tends to make environmental impacts harder to for people to care about relates to the so-called "identifiable victim" effect. Generally speaking, the willingness to forgo benefits or to incur costs in order to avoid harming another person or group of people is a form of prosocial, altruistic behavior. Many things, both personal (Penner et al., 1995) and situational (Dovidio et al., 2006), predict willingness to make such sacrifices for the benefit of others. One large predictor is a feeling of identity with the other as suggested by the previous section. Another, though, is the ability to indivdualize the other.

To the extent environmental effects are diffused onto remote individuals—especially those whose particular identities may be hard or even impossible to distinguish—people may empathize with them less than with more easily distinguishable, closer victims. his phenomenon has been experimentally demonstrated: identifiable victims are perceived as more sympathetic, and are more likely to receive our aid than "statistical" or unidentified and unindividuated victims (Loewenstein & Lerner, 2003). Nongovernmental aid organizations have intuited this phenomenon for a long time: Appeals for donations are often accompanied by names and pictures of individual victims of, say, poverty or famine, as a way to increase contributions. In an evocative experiment, merely including a single victim's name, age, and picture on a donation appeal increased actual donations by 60% (Kogut & Ritov, 2005).

While people's tendency to empathize with identifiable people may seem benign, even laudable, the phenomenon also has a darker side. Although people empathize with identifiable humans, that empathy can be undermined relatively easily, for instance, simply by telling them that a problem is large or dispersed. In another donation study, for instance, researchers found that people told about the extent of the hunger problem in Africa would donate *less* to feed a 7-year-old African girl named Rokia than similarly situated people who were told about Rokia but not about the larger problem (Small et al., 2007). Telling people about very large and distant problems is particularly likely to trigger a phenomenon called "psychic numbing" or "compassion fade," whereby people dim their emotional response to harm (Slovic et al., 2007; Rowell & Wexler, 2014).

The diffusion of many environmental impacts makes it extraordinarily difficult—and sometimes impossible—for individuals to connect the harm of their actions to any identifiable group, much less an identifiable person. Over the coming decades, climate change is expected to substantially increase the likelihood of severe, pervasive, and irreversible outcomes for people and ecosystems around the globe (Pachauri et al., 2015)—but which persons in particular will be affected by drought, heat-related deaths, hurricanes, increased infectious disease, flooding, and famine remains extraordinarily difficult to identify. Similarly, a factory that incinerates an extra 15 tons of hazardous air pollutants may well cause someone's painful and lingering death from cancer—but *whose* cancer is impossible to predict ahead of time, and even afterward may be extraordinarily difficult to trace.

This research suggests that increasing the identifiability of environmental "victims" may help in raising concern about environmental harms. Perhaps people would be more willing to refrain from flushing expired prescription medicines down the toilet when it might lead to an antibiotic resistant staph infection in a 6-year-old girl named Lucy who lives in Anaheim than when it might lead to .01% of the population of Anaheim falling ill from antibiotic resistant staph infections. Similarly, news stories that highlight particular families whose homes will be lost to rising sea levels may evoke significantly greater care than mere information about the widespread harms that sea level rise is likely to cause. Importantly and counterintuitively, such communications may even be *more* effective when *not* bundled with information about the scope of the problem; such communications, as with the study on famine in Africa, may risk triggering psychic numbing (Small et al., 2007).

Interestingly, while individual identifiability increases willingness to engage in prosocial behaviors, it also increases a willingness to engage in punitive behaviors—the identifiable perpetrator effect (Small & Loewenstein, 2005). This effect, too, has relevance to the psychology of environmental law. Legislators may be more willing to support strong penalties for polluting engaged in by specific, identifiable companies than they would be for polluting engaged in by American industry more generally. Presumably, identifiability is also a matter of degree. Support for penalties for polluting by "coal companies" would fall somewhere in between.

Conclusion

In many contexts, environmental impacts are "diffuse"—distant in space and time from the causes that preceded them. This has an effect on decision making about environmental harms and benefits because people tend to process distant and latent impacts differently than nearby and immediate ones. As a result of multiple psychological phenomena, this makes diffuse environmental impacts difficult for people to see and measure let alone, care about.

Key Aspects of the Psychology of Diffusion as Applied to Environmental Law

Environmental injuries may be immediate and proximate, but more likely they will be spread across time or place relative to their source. When people engage in behaviors that benefit themselves but that consequently inflict harm on someone or something else, we say they create *negative externalities.*

Externalities may trigger moral disengagement, and where harms caused are diffuse, those externalities will be harder to see and easier to discount. Cognitive, emotional, and motivational phenomena that affect the psychology of diffusion include:

- Heuristics. Harms that are remote are less *available* to our conscious awareness, making them harder to count. Harms that are remote may be easier to ignore because of *base rate neglect,* which arises because of the *representativeness* heuristic. That is, harms that are in the background are easy to discount relative to immediate, present ones.
- Prospect theory/loss aversion. People devalue losses relative to equal magnitude gains, and they prefer to gamble to avoid losses but take certain gains. What counts as a loss or a gain tends to be evaluated from the current state of affairs because of the *status quo bias.* Thus, effects that happen in the future tend to be coded as a loss or a gain relative to the current state of affairs. Putting these things together, when faced with keeping a certain, immediate gain at the risk of causing an uncertain, future, or distant loss, people are likely to take the present benefit (gain) and gamble that the future harm (loss) won't occur.

- Hedonic forecasting. People are not good at estimating how they will feel about either positive or negative events in the future. This causes them to overweight future events and fail to plan for them properly, meaning they may also inappropriately account for future environmental harms.
- Hyperbolic discounting and present bias. People experience temporal inconsistencies when thinking about future value. They overweight present value and overdiscount future value the further away it gets from them. This, again, can cause them to underappreciate the true future costs of environmental harms.
- Bargaining with the future. Because of the unidirectionality of time, it is not possible for stakeholders of the future to negotiate with those presently living to prevent future harms to themselves. This is another reason people undervalue future harms—there is literally no one at the table to make the case.
- In-group/out-group effects. To the extent environmental harms are spatially (and sometimes temporally) distant from those who cause them, it is easier for people to undercount them because they tend to undervalue the lives and needs of the "other."
- Empathy and the identifiable victim effect. People are more likely to connect with and help/avoid harming individuals they can directly identify. When environmental harms are diffuse, they become more abstract and less individually identifiable, which interferes with people's desire to help or avoid harming them.

3

Complexity

Recognizing, processing, and understanding environmental impacts is difficult and cognitively costly, because it requires understanding the relationships between human behavior and nature, which is made up of notoriously complicated and interactive natural systems. Furthermore, the human stimuli that affect the environment introduce additional complexity, as they, too, arise where many small individual actions combine in complicated ways to create a single outcome, or where a single action has multiple impacts. Actions that would have little to no effect on their own can become damaging when engaged in widely or when combined with other behaviors that might also have been harmless on their own. As a result, individuals, firms, and governments will often struggle to identify and respond to the environmental impacts of human activity.

This chapter proceeds in two major parts. First, we explain more specifically what we mean by complexity, and how perceiving, understanding, and responding to environmental impacts meets that definition. Many domains of the law have patches of complexity, but in few is it as pervasive and deep as in environmental law. Second, we describe psychological research about how people cope with complexity, including cognitive, emotional, and motivational responses to it that can complicate how environmental law operates. Understanding how people deal with complexity can help environmental lawyers and policy makers predict how people will respond to environmental phenomena, which in turn will make it easier not just to regulate but to know how people will respond to that regulation. Where possible, we flag potential approaches that environmental law and policy makers can use to effectively manage the challenges that complexity presents.

Defining and Identifying Complexity

While there are formal mathematical descriptions of complexity (e.g. Standish, 2008), and other models of complexity in other disciplines, we are concerned here with systems and cause-and-effect relationships that are complex from a psychological perspective. As we shall discuss, people process complex problems differently than they do simple ones. In particular, they tend to deploy simplifying heuristics designed to break difficult problems down into easier chunks. This common approach to simplification can be helpful in minimizing cognitive and emotional effort, but where it washes away important nuance, it also runs the risk of causing systemic errors. The more underlying complexity that attaches to a system or cause-and-effect relationship, the more risk simplifying heuristics create. Here, we suggest that the extraordinary complexity of the natural environment itself, combined with the intricacy of human/ nature interactions, make psychological heuristics particularly prone to misfire in environmental policy contexts.

Natural systems such as ecosystems nest and interact in hard-to-predict ways and tend to adapt to and impact neighboring (and sometimes distant) systems (Solé & Bascompte, 2006; Levin, 1998; Doremus, 2010a). The complexity of these interactions is only increased where, as is often the case with environmental impacts, there is more than one input. As Richard Lazarus has explained, ecological injuries are rarely the product of a single action at an isolated moment in time (Lazarus, 2000). Many people, processes, and actions may contribute to nutrient load in a watershed, to the health of a horned owl's habitat, or to the emission of greenhouse gases. The cognitive challenges are further increased where—as is constantly the case in environmental law and policy—complex human systems such as communities, economies, and societies, interact with other complex systems such as the environment. Indeed, the same behaviors can have different effects depending upon other behaviors and how the environment itself adapts (Nagle, 2013). Attempting to predict and map the interaction of social and natural systems thus presents environmental law and policy with a distinctively enormous task—and yet, a task that is necessary to be able to accurately shape the impacts of human actions on the natural environment.

In the subsequent sections, we map several features that make natural environmental systems particularly complex and that therefore trigger identifiable psychological phenomena related to thinking about and responding to complex things. In subsequent sections, we engage with the psychological factors that make managing human behavior in the environmental context so challenging.

Statistical Anomalies in the Environment

First, consider that complex systems are more likely to be marked by various statistical and nonlinear anomalies, which as we discuss below, tend to trigger a set of simplifying approaches that can lead people into error.

One important source of complexity relates to the role of thresholds and tipping points, past which change occurs suddenly rather than smoothly (Standish, 2008). Research suggests, for example, there may be nonlinear tipping points where even small changes may destroy entire ecosystems (Dakos et al., 2019). Moreover, in such complex systems, new states ("catastrophic shifts") tend to be sticky. Reversal may not be possible without a massive new change in the underlying parameters (Solé & Bascompte, 2006). It is exceptionally difficult to dig an economy out of a depression; arguably, harder still for an ecosystem to un-degrade. It is impossible for a bumblebee to un-die. As another example, consider that many dangerous substances exhibit a nonlinear relationship between quantity of exposure and harm caused. Drinking tiny amounts of disinfectants, in the quantities used to kill microorganisms in public water systems, may not harm and may even help; yet in higher quantities and concentrations, the same substances (such as chlorine) can kill. Failing to recognize the complexity of those relationships between dose and response may fundamentally undermine the law's ability to effectively regulate them (Sunstein, 2002a, 2002c; Rowell, 2012a).

Note that, with complex systems, extreme outlier events may be possible, unlike in most less-complex systems, where events are more likely to be described by a normal curve, and in which events several standard deviations from the mean are essentially impossible (Solé & Bascompte, 2006). As evocatively described by Dan Farber, the weight of house cats follows a normal distribution. In such a distribution, if 10 lb. tabbies are the median, you'll find that the vast majority of cats are a couple of pounds heavier or lighter than this, and you'll even find the barest handful of 25 lb. cats. But we can confidently dismiss the possibility of a one-ton cat. Not so in some complex systems; specifically, those whose distributions follow a "power law." In such systems, extreme events might be exceptionally rare, but they are at least still possible. Mathematically, such distributions have extremes that don't peter out into nothing as quickly as they do in a normal distribution; they have "fat tails." As Farber explains, "If feline weight were subject to a power law, we would find that the vast majority of cats were tiny or even microscopic but that one-thousand-pound house cats would cross our paths now and then" (Farber, 2003–2004, p. 147) and indeed, given enough time or enough such distributions, at least one such anomalous event happening (if not a one-ton cat, then a one-ton dog, or a microscopic horse) is even *likely* (Farber, 2003–2004). While many environmental phenomena follow a normal curve, it is nevertheless a domain where many others follow a power law. Examples are population densities, body size across different species (Farber, 2003–2004), the size of wildfires (Brown et al., 2002), and rainfall across seasons and places (Zinck & Grimm, 2009). Many climate change scientists worry that climate change is particularly fat-tailed, and warn that extreme-downside climate change is therefore very possible (Nordhaus, 2011; Pindyck, 2011; Weitzman, 2011).

Feedback Effects and Adaptation in the Environment

On every dimension, the environment as a whole is a classic complex system (Solé & Bascompte, 2006; Levin, 1998). "The environment" operates in a nesting hierarchy from individual units, to ecosystems, to the biosphere (Ruhl, 1997). Each of these pieces themselves can be described with more or less particularity, and even this "hierarchy" is not strict (Brown et al., 2002), being marked by constant feedback effects. While changes in the biosphere affect ecosystems, ecosystems (and the individuals within them) obviously also can affect the biosphere, as in the phenomenon of human-induced climate change.

The environment changes and adapts as its parts interact with one another, often in quite surprising and unpredictable ways (Levin, 1998). Evolution, of course, is well documented in various plant and animal

populations (Darwin, 1859), and is a perfect example of an adaptive response to environmental challenge. We all learned the story of the pep-
pered moth as high schoolers: As the coal industry expanded in England,
black moths became more common than their white counterparts since
it became increasingly easy for the black ones to blend into their newly
dirtied surroundings. Consequently, they flourished and increased in
number. The white ones, in literal contrast, stood out, making them easy
prey. But scientists have recently discovered equally fast adaptations by
humans to environmental contamination: A 6,000-member indigenous
group in the Andes mountains has quickly—as evolutionary time scales
go—developed the genetic ability to metabolize arsenic, a potentially
deadly pollutant to which they are highly exposed both through naturally occurring arsenic deposits in drinking water and through human
mining activities (Schlebusch et al., 2015).

Pieces of the environment can also go through periodic catastrophic
shifts that may fundamentally change or destroy whole ecosystems or
even climates (Levin, 1998; Dakos et al., 2019). Again, as school children
we all learned about the climactic shocks that killed off the dinosaurs,
but seismic shifts in the environment are far more frequent and localized than that example suggests. Most of the time, of course, nature re-
sponds slowly and smoothly to changes in inputs. Woods emerge out
of meadows over decades or even centuries as winds, temperature, and
bird migration patterns slowly shift; lakes slowly salinate over thousands
of years of rain and evaporation cycles; rivers change course as silt gets
deposited; mountain ranges rise, inch by inch, as tectonic plates crash
slowly together. But the environment also suddenly shifts to drastically
contrasting states when a sufficiently severe perturbation in the ecosystem occurs and crosses critical thresholds. Clear lakes suddenly turn
green and hypoxic when nutrient levels cross the threshold for supporting aquatic life; fisheries collapse from pollution and overharvest-
ing; lush land rapidly turns to desert in response to a critical shift in
temperature and precipitation; coral reefs bleach and die en masse in
response to threshold changes in ocean temperatures and acidification
(Scheffer et al., 2001). These tipping points may either be extremely difficult or impossible to reverse (Hughes et al., 2018; Dakos et al., 2019).
And once again, additional complexity arises from the fact that humans
interact with these natural processes: People might accelerate deserti-

fication by deliberately damming water supplies for human uses (Van Dijck et al., 2006); bathers might accelerate the dying of coral reefs near popular shorelines by using sunscreens to protect themselves from skin cancer (Raffa et al., 2019), and farmers might both cause hypoxic waters through their agricultural practices and reverse them for the same reason (Mee, 2006). As a result, it is both very difficult and remarkably high stakes for environmental law and policy to find ways to accurately predict the likely impact of human behavior on natural systems—and similarly critical for it to adopt methods for shaping those behaviors in a way that leads to desired outcomes.

The Psychology of Responding to Complexity

Psychological research has established a number of ways that people approach complex problems differently than they do simple ones. As a result, understanding how people respond to and cope with complex systems may be helpful in understanding how people deal with the natural environment, and with their impacts upon it.

In general, psychological research suggests that people struggle to manage complex systems, and that they typically find complex causes and effects difficult to parse accurately. As a result, they use cognitive, motivational, and emotional shortcuts for simplifying and comprehending complex situations and systems. People also have techniques—sometimes faulty—for detecting patterns to help them make sense of complicated information. We expand on these techniques and phenomena below.

Distortions in Perceiving Cause and Effect

When a system is complex, cause and effect are harder to tease out simply because there are more candidates for causality and the contribution of each one may be obscured by the others. How does a person decide which causes are real, and if real, how much they contribute to an effect? When systems are complex, how can a person determine whether any particular behavior is necessary and/or sufficient to cause an effect?

Obviously, as a gold standard for how to assess cause and effect, an observer would personally perform a deep and careful quantitative analysis (Jameson & Kostinski, 2002). But for the vast majority of circumstances, and for many reasons, this is a deeply impractical recommendation. Virtually no individual person can—or does—perform such analyses, especially for environmental effects like damage from pollution or climate change.

At least sometimes, the reason for not doing even a rough individual quantitative analysis is lack of skill. Many people are not particularly good at math. They are "innumerate" (which is the numerical analogue to "illiterate") (Peters et al., 2006; Dieckmann, 2008; Kahneman, 2011). Innumeracy leads to more errors in estimating probabilities and understanding risks, and it causes people to suffer more from framing effects (Gurmankin et al., 2004; Paulos, 1988). It can even lead to distortions in the perception of what the law requires about risk (Rowell & Bregant, 2014).

Similarly, while numbers that are infinitesimally small or colossally large do not make the concepts they describe more "complex," most people are just not good at comprehending scale at such extremes (Peters et al., 2006). This limitation seems to be hardwired, as with the early psychophysics phenomenon of the "just noticeable difference" threshold: While we might be able to detect a very small increase in the length of time a light is flashed from a previous short flash of light, for instance, the same small increase from a longer initial flash is undetectable (Butterworth, 1999).

Combining general innumeracy with problems comprehending extremes of scale makes understanding environmental threats doubly hard, because not only are many environmental threats probabilistic, but the probabilities themselves may be quite tiny (even while the consequences are perhaps unimaginably large) (Salkind, 2010; Rowell, 2020b). As a consequence, people's ability to process information about environmental threats into clear legal conclusions may be limited, again leading to errors in their estimation of cause and effect.

But innumeracy cannot fully explain people's common reluctance to accept scientific conclusions about environmental harms. Another explanation is that people rely on various shortcuts to assess causal relationships, and these shortcuts introduce systematic errors that lead them astray. For instance, where there are multiple possible causes for an effect, some are likely to be more salient than others. If a feature is salient, people are more likely to assume it is causal (Taylor & Fiske, 1978). And the more salient the stimulus, the more causal it seems—irrespective of the magnitude of its actual contribution to the outcome (Posner, 2004). These salience effects are very robust. Even when an actor is paying attention, interested in the issue, and trying to assess causality accurately, he can be misled into thinking salient "causes" explain an outcome (Taylor et al., 1979).

What makes a potential cause salient? Anything that makes it "stand out," such as its distinctiveness, rarity, emotional evocativeness, and recency/proximity (Higgins, 1996). None of these qualities, though, have any necessary, logical connection to actual causation. For example, when researchers in northeastern England wanted to assess whether the public perceived the link between air pollution and health, they found that the thing that made people most likely to link the two was whether or not there was heavy industry in their immediate neighborhood (Howel et al., 2003). Because people could literally see the pollution source, making it more salient, they were more likely to connect it to health outcomes. While such simple heuristics may sometimes result in accurate estimates of probabilities, estimates are less and less likely to be accurate where systems are increasingly multicausal, interactive, and nonlinear.

Another shortcut to assess causality comes not from cognition but motivation. The more desired the outcome, the more causal it seems as well. The phenomenon of motivated reasoning (Kunda, 1990) leads people to interpret obscure (and sometimes even clear!) data in a manner that accords with their existing political and cultural beliefs. For example, society is deeply polarized on the causes, or even the existence, of climate change. Science communication specialists often assume the problem is a lack of information or of the cognitive skills to process that information. This has been called the "science comprehension thesis" (Kahan, Peters, et al., 2012). The problem, though, is that lack of knowledge does not in fact seem to drive disbelief in climate change. Instead, it is a function of how credible the knowledge seems and how it is processed by people with fundamentally different value systems (Kahan, 2007; Kahan, Peters, et al., 2012).

It turns out that people are simply more likely to credit bad outcomes to causes they already believe are harmful or morally bad, and they are reluctant to believe that things they like or think are good could lead to bad outcomes. What they believe are good and bad are, unsurprisingly, linked to political identities and cultural views about how the world does and should operate. Consider people with a "hierarchical, individualist" worldview, who believe in the validity of social rankings and are skeptical about collective interference with the prerogatives and activities of those high on the social order (like believing that businessmen have earned their place and should not be told what to do by government regulators). Dan Kahan and colleagues showed that these hierarchs/individualists were quite skeptical of climate change science not because they didn't understand it but because they worried about the implications of crediting it. If climate change science were valid, it would give a legitimate reason to regulate industries—something that clearly conflicted with their values. Contrast this with the egalitarians and communitarians, who are less likely to give privilege to social position and who are happy to embrace collective interventions in individual and business behavior. They embrace climate change science not because they know more but because the usual top-down regulatory solutions to it are consistent with their prior philosophical commitments (Kahan, Peters, et al., 2012). Even scientifically and statistically sophisticated people suffer from motivated reasoning; they process and interpret data in a manner that conforms to their values. Ironically, Kahan and colleagues have found that the sophisticates might sometimes even be *worse* in this regard (Kahan et al., 2017; Kahan, Peters et al., 2012).

Sometimes, cognitive and motivational biases can interact in interesting and very surprising ways. For instance, people's beliefs about climate change follow recent weather patterns—an example of a cognitive "recency" bias. But people's perceptions about what the recent weather actually has been are influenced by their cultural worldview and political ideology—a motivational bias (Goebbert et al., 2012). This feedback effect obviously makes comprehension of the already complex science surrounding climate change even more difficult.

The situation is not hopeless, though. First of all, many environmental harms are *not* value laden, even in today's polarized world (Sunstein, 2006b; Kahan, 2007). The risks and effects of many environmental phenomena, like perhaps leaded gasoline, chlorofluorocarbons, earthquakes, and so on are not (yet?) extremely politically loaded determinations, either because they are obscure and people have not thought much about them or just by chance. In such cases, cultural meanings will not distort people's ability to understand complex risks. Of course, other things might—there will still be the pure cognitive biases to overcome in comprehending causes and effects, but at least they will not be compounded by the failings of desire. Second, it turns out that when communications (and solutions) are designed in a way that pays attention to motivational considerations, both comprehension and acceptance go up. Kahan and colleagues, for instance, conducted an experiment in which they exposed people to information about carbon dioxide (CO_2) risks but put them in one of two different treatment conditions (plus a third, control condition): They were exposed to an article describing traditional regulatory approaches to limiting carbon emissions or to one describing novel, commerce-friendly geoengineering solutions to the problem. (Geoengineering solutions involve technological innovations that control or remove greenhouse gases already in the atmosphere.) The researchers found that when climate change science information was followed by information about traditional, government-interventionist regulatory solutions, hierarchs and individualists tended to reject both evidence of the problem and the viability of the solution. But when presented with information about the geoengineering solutions, they *credited* both. In other words, the viability of a worldview-consistent solution made them more able to accept the science demonstrating the problem (Kahan et al., 2015).

Careful attention to cultural values can help people to comprehend complex environmental harms that they otherwise might dismiss. This is not as easy a solution as it appears, though. First, there need to be solutions that comport with people's desires and worldviews. And second, what satisfies one worldview may offend another: While presenting the geoengineering solution made individualists and hierarchs more likely to understand and accept climate change science, it made egalitarians and communitarians—who are skeptical of market solutions to social problems—*less* receptive (Kahan et al., 2015). So effectively designing communications and policies that successfully navigate the worldviews of *all* listeners is quite a challenge—but nevertheless not impossible.

Acts and Omissions

An additional distortion that looms particularly large in processing environmental harms is that, for whatever reason, people tend to judge errors of commission much more harshly than errors of omission (Baron & Ritov, 1994, 2004). While this is not an issue of complexity on its face, it bears a family resemblance. It is usually straightforward to see how affirmative actions cause a result in an almost physical sense. Omissions are more obscure. While it is true that many actions can contribute to an effect (the body of water is polluted by Actor X dumping a chemical directly into it, by Actor Y damming it so that it cannot drain properly, and so on), there are an almost infinite number of actors who could have cleaned it up but did not—that is, actors "guilty" of omissions rather than commissions. And actors who have *not* done something are usually harder to notice than those who have, unless there is some strong prior reason to expect them to have acted (like, perhaps, a particular water zoning board with jurisdiction to clean up a particular body of water). One has to use more conjecture and even imagination to think about omissions as causes, as compared to commissions. Since omissions are harder to see, they are easier to ignore, even when they actually might be, pragmatically speaking, a very large cause of an environmental outcome.

We are all by now familiar with Philippa Foot's (1967) "trolley problem" and its almost infinite variations. Imagine a trolley is racing down a track and will hit five people if you do not push an innocent bystander in front of it first. What should you do? The permutations of this problem have generated a cottage industry in the philosophy world (Moore, 1993; Kamm, 2015), but one consistent empirical finding across them all is that people generally think it is worse for someone to directly *act* in a way that causes harm (pushing someone in front of a runaway trolley car) than to simply let something bad that is already happening continue (letting the trolley hit five people) (Moore, 1993; Shallow et al., 2011).

In the context of the environment, this means that people will tend to attach less condemnation to passive or continuing harms (say, failing to discontinue a long-standing but harmful industrial practice that leaves hazardous waste) relative to more active ones (starting a *new* harmful practice that would kill members of a species). Consider the long tradition in environmental ethics that emphasizes noninterference in nature as a virtue. Aldo Leopold, for instance, famously argued that "[a] thing is right when it tends to preserve the integrity, stability, and beauty of the biotic community. It is wrong when it tends otherwise" (Leopold, 1949). This ethic is often connected to early ecological scholarship, which emphasized the equilibrium model of ecology, which assumed that nature would attain maximum diversity and stability if left undisturbed by human action (Clements, 1936). Though the equilibrium model in ecology has been challenged in subsequent years on multiple grounds (Lowenthal, 1998), the continuing underlying inclination many environmentalists feel toward noninterference may be best understood as having a psychological foundation.

The tendency to prioritize "acts" over "omissions" will, in some cases, put a thumb on the scale toward one policy choice over another. An example is the perennial question in wildfire policy: Is it better to implement active fire management through small, planned burns, which burn up the fuel of grass, underbrush, and other detritus in managed quantities under (relatively) controlled conditions, or instead to adopt passive management strategies—allowing fuel to build up until a wildfire is ignited at some point by lightning, a careless cigarette butt, or an unquenched campfire (Bradshaw & Lueck, 2012; Engel & Reeves, 2012)? Generally speaking, scholars have suggested that risks associated with unplanned fires are much greater because they can occur during dangerous weather and climatic conditions and without prior preparation on the part of firefighters, they can burn much hotter and longer as a result of increased fuel load, and as a consequence the heightened concentrations of woodsmoke in the air from unplanned fires are more harmful than lower concentrations of woodsmoke from planned ones (Engel & Reeves, 2012; Rowell, 2012a; Shultz et al., 2019).

Legal scholars have noted that environmental law creates perverse incentives in this realm by exempting wildfires—the result of passive fire management policy—from their calculations of whether a state is meeting its obligations under the National Ambient Air Quality Standards in the Clean Air Act, while *counting* emissions from active planned burns (Engel & Reeves, 2012; Engel, 2013; Shultz et al., 2019). A psychological analysis may help in solving the mystery of why this seemingly perverse policy continues: It preferences passive "omissions" of fire management over the active "actions" involved in planned burns. While such simplifying heuristics may operate effectively in some circumstances, the complexities of fire management and woodsmoke exposure may not be the optimal policy space for applying a simple psychological preference for omission over action.

That said, we do not mean to suggest that the mere existence of a psychological preference for omissions over acts makes all distinctions between acts and omissions in the law unreasonable. Legal scholars in other subdisciplines have strongly supported the use of the act/omission distinction in some contexts (Moore, 1993), and it is possible that some environmental contexts would also support such a distinction. The best candidate for such distinctions may be when action but *not* omission risks disrupting complex environmental systems and thus generating substantial additional harm. This may provide a justification, for example, for the predominant form of wilderness management, which seeks primarily to preserve wilderness areas from human intervention (Nagle, 2015), or for biodiversity schemes that emphasize preserving existing biodiversity over the restoration of damaged ecosystems (Jones et al., 2018). Regardless, whether environmental actions are coded as acts or omissions is likely to affect how people process them.

Pattern Detection and Simplifying Heuristics

Pattern detection is a critical skill for all animals with anything more than a rudimentary brain, and it helps them to cope with complexity in the world. Some neuroscientists have gone so far as to argue that superior pattern processing is the essence of the evolved human brain (Mattson, 2014). The ability to detect patterns is highly developed in higher-order animals, especially humans (Mattson, 2014). Perhaps as a result, the ability to detect patterns begins remarkably early in human development, and some patterns are hardwired into our brains rather than learned. Not only do babies easily identify faces, for instance, but high-resolution sonograms recently revealed that even fetuses preferentially track images of human faces while still inside the womb (Reid et al., 2017). But most patterns are gleaned from processing and categorizing the sensory information contained in the world around us. The development of pattern-detection capacities enabled animals to identify and find water and water sources, recognize kin and avoid enemies, and even communicate with others (Mattson, 2014). Humans, perhaps uniquely among animals, have the additional capacity to generate new patterns from whole cloth, an ability that enables humans to have imagination and generates robust problem-solving capacities (Mattson, 2014).

In short, pattern detection allows—even requires—animals to reduce complex patterns into simpler ones. When it works well, pattern detection allows us to directly "map" the essential features of a situation down to their most important parts. This capacity helps us to navigate and manage our world and to make sense of otherwise difficult-to-understand phenomena. It allows humans to create algorithms that themselves can detect patterns that are not observable directly. Some researchers, for instance, recently created a mind-bogglingly sophisticated set of tools for mining and analyzing big data sets of weather patterns in a way that would allow them to predict the very kinds of extreme and rare events that are more likely to occur under the weather's power law distribution (Ashraf Vaghefi et al., 2017).

Unfortunately, while our patterning faculties are very impressive, and our creative capacities more impressive still, human pattern detection can go awry. For example, we can detect the wrong patterns, or we can "detect" patterns that are not actually there. When pattern detection goes wrong, it can introduce errors—and the more complex a pattern, the more likely it is that pattern-detection abilities will misfire. When do our pattern-detection capacities go astray? Again, there can be glitches for cognitive, emotional, and motivational reasons.

Most of the time, the pattern-detection shortcuts our brain uses assist us well in accurately making sense of complex information quickly. We have already discussed one example of heuristic pattern detection: the availability heuristic. In estimating frequencies, things that come easily to mind are seen as more abundant (Tversky & Kahneman, 1973; Slovic, 1987). Since tornadoes get covered by the news and people post about them in dramatic detail on their social media feeds, and the deaths they cause tend to happen in clusters, people tend to assume that tornado deaths are more common than less-discussed weather-related deaths like heat stroke (Lichtenstein et al., 1978). (In fact, heat kills twice as many people per year as tornadoes; see www.nws.noaa.gov.) The representativeness heuristic, too, is a pattern-detection device: We take some features of a phenomenon and assume other features about it are true, sometimes even where such assumptions might violate formal logic. When we learn Linda is bookish and interested in social justice, she seems more like a "feminist bank teller" than just a "bank teller" (Tversky & Kahneman, 1983), because "feminist bank teller" better fits a social pattern we know.

But there are other cognitive heuristics that, while enhancing the accuracy of the patterns we detect under most circumstances, can lead us astray. People tend to assume that the most recent event they've encountered is representative of the whole field—a bias that also, obviously, affects prediction (Slovic, 1987; Slovic, 2000). Within limits, we tend to think how things have been recently tells us more about how they will continue to be than is actually warranted; that is, we suffer from a "recency" bias (Chen et al., 2019). Ironically, there is also a "primacy" effect, where we overweight the first piece of information we encounter in estimates of its frequency or importance (Asch, 1946; Deese & Kaufman, 1957). Yet another similar cognitive heuristic is "anchoring," where perceivers focus heavily on one salient piece of information in describing the whole (Bahník et al., 2017)—sometimes even when that piece of information is entirely irrelevant.

In detecting patterns, we must also contend with "contrast effects" and opposite "assimilation effects," where the magnitude or valence of a stimulus depends on what it is being compared to (Bless & Schwarz, 2010; Sherif & Hovland, 1961). A low-level example of a cognitive contrast effect happens when one plunges a hand in either a bowl of hot or cold water. The temperature of a lukewarm bowl of water will feel hotter or colder depending on the temperature of the water you felt immediately before (Wundt, 1904/1969). Similarly, and at a much higher level of cognition, how hostile a person seems depends on whether you are comparing his bad behavior to person who is a bit rude, or to Hitler (Moskowitz & Skurnik, 1999).

Humans also experience an interesting "peak-end" bias—experiences are evaluated not by an average evaluation of them but by their peaks (most intense moments) and end states, with the latter being particularly important (Do et al., 2008). As a famous example using a now-outdated and painful procedure, doctors gave patients colonoscopies after first putting them into one of two conditions: either the procedure ended

immediately after the "peak" pain (which in the usual procedure happens right at the end), or the procedure was deliberately extended after
this peak pain moment, a period during which the pain subsided but did
not disappear. The latter form of the procedure, of course, arithmetically
involves the highest quantum of pain over the course of the procedure,
since it lasts longer than necessary. Nevertheless, patients strongly preferred it and were more likely to come back for future colonoscopies in
that condition (Redelmeier et al., 2003).

Which among this panoply of biases dominates in any one perceptual, complexity-reducing task depends on many factors, like how complex the task actually is, the extremity of the values involved (Chapman
& Johnson, 1994), the relative availability of the different pieces of information (Tversky & Kahneman, 1974, 1981), and so on. All of these
biases make accurate pattern detection and subsequent prediction less
reliable. Apply them to environmental phenomena, and they may seriously interfere with impression formation about environmental harms
(Nicholls, 1999; Slovic, 1987).

Just as with cause-and-effect perceptions, pattern detection is also affected by motivational and identity processes in addition to lower-level
cognitive ones. For example, researchers found that impressions about
the level of pollution on local beaches in England was a function of perceivers' attachment to their local towns or to their nation—the more patriotic they were, the less likely they were to see their beaches as polluted
(Bonaito et al., 1996). Pattern detection is also affected by emotions. For
example, strong emotions (like fear and anger) will amplify relevant features in pattern perceptions and enhance memory of them (Phelps et al.,
2006). This in turn can interact with cause-and-effect perceptions—the
emotion increases perceptual salience, which makes features seem more
causal. The intuitive nature of this process is perhaps why policy makers
tend to appeal to emotion when trying to win approval for regulations
or motivate individual actions. Strong emotions like fear, anger, and
hope do seem to energize climate change activism, for instance (Kleres
& Wettergren, 2017).

A final interesting problem with human pattern-detection capacities
is an occasional tendency to see patterns that are not really there—a
phenomenon called apophenia. At a very low level of abstraction, humans tend to see faces everywhere, even though we are also good at

distinguishing actual faces from what is merely "face-like" (Grill-Spector et al., 2004; Meng et al., 2012). But we also tend to have more general overperceptions of patterns, either visual (like seeing shapes in clouds) or aural (like hearing words in music played backward), which we cannot blame on dedicated modules in our brain, as we can for our over-perception of faces (Uchiyama et al., 2015), and for which our ability to distinguish truth may also not be as intrinsic. Our overdeveloped pattern-recognition system can cause us, for instance, to see meaning in stock market prices, develop superstitions, and falsely believe in conspiracies (Liu et al., 2014; Whitson & Galinsky, 2008).

Both perceptual overdetection of patterns (like in random noise or in clouds) and high-level, substantive overdetection (like searching for meaning or seeing conspiracies everywhere) is driven by a desire to understand and control our environment (Douglas et al., 2017). Indeed, being made to feel out of control increases our likelihood of perceiving signals in noise of all kinds (Whitson & Galinsky, 2008). This association between feeling out of control and conspiracy theorizing can perhaps help explain some of the resistance to things like climate change science. The complexity of environmental phenomena, coupled with the diffused nature of its effects, may lead many people to feel helpless when contemplating environmental harms. One response to feeling helpless is demotivation and a failure to take actions to ameliorate a bad situation—a species of "ignoring the problem" that we discuss again at the end of this chapter. But another response to feeling overwhelmed by the chaotic immensity and complexity of environmental problems is to try to impose order—though illusorily—by generating conspiracy theories to explain them.

As we would predict, this phenomenon is indeed quite common in the environmental domain. A 2019 YouGov poll in the United States, for example, showed that 17% of the public believed climate change was a "hoax that was invented to deceive people" (Milman & Harvey, 2019). We should also not forget the ease with which many people accepted "Climategate," (wrongly) believing that a set of email messages among climate scientists suggested a massive cover-up (Lewandowsky, 2014). Climate change conspiracy theories, in fact, are ubiquitous, and relatively impervious to challenges based on their lack of support or internal consistency (Lewandowsky et al., 2018). One of the most troubling things about conspiracy theories is their "self-sealing" nature—evidence of their falsity is taken as evidence for their *truth* by the conspiracy minded, in the sense that exonerating evidence is interpreted as official whitewashing. As such, conspiracies tend to linger and even expand, at least in the subpopulations who are most inclined to indulge them in the first place (Douglas et al., 2017; Lewandowsky et al., 2018; Sunstein & Vermeule, 2009; Keeley, 1999). Worse still, the discourse of skepticism about climate change affects how scientists themselves speak and even think about their work, leading them to inadvertently reinforce public skepticism about climate change and understate its peril (Lewandowsky et al., 2015).

Managing Limited Information and Uncertainty

When they address strategies for managing limited information, economists conventionally distinguish between "risk" (where the likelihood of a bad thing occurring is quantifiable) and "uncertainty" (where the likelihood is nonquantifiable) (Knight, 1921; Farber, 2010). There is a long tradition of psychological research on risk perception (Slovic, 2000), to which we refer throughout this book, and much of which also applies to how people perceive and respond to uncertainty. That said, some research also suggests that when people know probabilities for sure—as in experimental gambling contexts—they may sometimes perceive and act differently than when probabilities are ambiguous (Weber & Johnson, 2009). For example, acute stress affects how people engage with probabilistic "risk" tasks but not "uncertain" ones (Buckert et al., 2014).

Given information constraints individuals face particularly when making decisions about deeply complex issues, such as their own effects on the environment, people often perceive, process, and respond to potential environmental threats in contexts of functional uncertainty. Even where the likelihood of bad events would be theoretically determinable, if they lack access to full information, they cannot use it to generate accurate probabilities. As a result, many of the strategies people use to cope with risk—like using mental heuristics to minimize it, seeking out experts who will help them to understand and maybe reduce it, and even simply living with it—are also strategies people use to manage uncertainty.

Generally speaking, people are motivated to reduce perceived uncertainty wherever possible (Hogg, 2000; Inglis, 2000). They deploy three common strategies for doing so: using heuristic shortcuts to save cognitive effort, deferring to trusted others such as experts, and finally simply ignoring or living with it. Each of these approaches is worth considering in some detail, as each can lead people to misperceive and/or misunderstand complex systems.

THE STRATEGY OF HEURISTIC SHORTCUTS

The dislike of perceived uncertainty is the reason humans seek information about cause and effect and why they try to detect patterns in confusing noise—they use that information to predict and perhaps then control their environment (Fiske & Taylor, 1984/1991). The gold standard of uncertainty reduction is, again, a mathematically rigorous, top-down analysis of the probability of events occurring (Fiske & Taylor, 1984/1991; Kahneman, 2011). In a perfect world with no limits on our resources, time, or abilities, we would all be perfect Bayesian analysts. But as cognitive misers (Fiske & Taylor, 1984/1991) who live in a world of physical and cognitive scarcity (Arthur, 1994), it is essentially impossible for humans to live up to that standard on any kind of consistent basis.

And indeed, in the context of risk assessment and uncertainty reduction, humans do frequently fail to deploy Bayesian analysis. In very simple English, if a Bayesian wants to know the likelihood that some proposition is true, then she would multiply the probability of each component of that proposition together, giving each piece its due weight, to come up with a final probability of truth. The order in which she processed the evidence would not matter. If, for instance, she were trying to decide if a particular pollutant had caused a cluster of townspeople to suffer a disease, she would find out the odds that those individuals would have suffered from the disease independent of the pollutant as well. What are the odds of the disease arising based on population genetics alone? What are the odds based on their diet? Their sun exposure? And so on. Then she would add to this the odds they were exposed to the pollutant. After putting it all together using simple algebra, she could come up with a final estimate of the probability that the pollutant caused the disease cluster. It would not matter whether she considered sun exposure first or instead considered the pollutant exposure probabilities first. The math would spit out a clear answer.

In the real world, people depart from organized, clean Bayesian analysis in several ways. First, and most distinctively, they fail to do the math properly. Instead of using *all* pieces of evidence that contribute to a probability, most people tend to let whatever the newest or perhaps most salient piece of evidence they are processing (like the odds that the population was actually exposed to the pollutant) dominate their estimates. If the odds that the population was exposed to the pollutant were 80%, for instance, they might say the probability that the pollutant caused the disease cluster was 80%. This is often referred to as the tendency to fail to "update their priors"—that is, forgetting to use the new information to simply modify the baseline probabilities of an event rather than using it to estimate the probability of the event by itself. (We have already described this kind of error in in our discussion of base rate neglect.)

Second, people have a tendency to actually distort the underlying probabilities of each piece of evidence so that they cohere and are maximally consistent with one another. In Bayesian analysis, not only does it not matter in what order you consider evidence, it also does not matter if independent pieces of evidence are contradictory. When estimating the odds that a pollutant caused a disease cluster, it would not matter if there is some evidence, for instance, that while most people exposed to the pollutant got the disease, some subset of people exposed to the pollutant not only did not get the disease but were actually *less likely* to get it. A Bayesian would simply add that probability into the equation, which would then reduce the odds that the pollutant caused this particular disease cluster. But many, perhaps most, people are uncomfortable with such seeming inconsistencies (Cialdini et al., 1995). And one psychological response to inconsistency is to simply cognitively distort all the evidence to fit a single, coherent theory. In this process, evidence does lead an evaluator to a conclusion—but the conclusion itself in turn leads the evaluator to read *subsequent* pieces of evidence in a way that makes them more consistent with that emerging conclusion. In other words, evidence and conclusions feed back on one another (Holyoak & Simon, 1999; Simon et al., 2004). With such "coherence shifts" in evaluation of evidence, the order in which evidence is presented obviously matters a great deal.

Third, people *seek out* information in a distorted way, either because of some of the cognitive biases we have already discussed or from motivated desires for particular outcomes (Stanovich et al., 2013)—a phenomenon usually referred to as the "confirmation bias." The confirmation bias actually works on many levels. People are more likely not only to seek out but also to notice (Nickerson, 1998; Simon et al., 2004; Stanovich et al., 2013), credit (Talluri et al., 2018), and remember (Sanitioso et al., 1990) evidence that is consistent with their prior beliefs; to interpret ambiguous evidence in a way that supports their prior beliefs (Kahan et al., 2009; O'Brien, 2009); and to avoid information that might contradict it (Kunda, 1990). In other words, people test their hypotheses in a biased way, inadvertently cooking the books so that their previously believed conclusion is more likely to be supported (Kunda, 1990).

One of the clearest and most robust demonstrations of the confirmation bias is the Wason task (Wason, 1968). Imagine an array of four index cards on a table in front of you. Each one has a number on one side and either a shape or a squiggle on the other. The cards you see show the following faces: 3, 6, triangle, and squiggle. Which cards should you turn over to test the following proposition: "If a card shows an even number, then the other side shows a shape"? The correct answer is the 6 card and the squiggle. If the other side of the 6 is a squiggle, or the other side of the squiggle is an even number, then the proposition is false. Turning over the 3 tells us nothing, as the proposition makes no claim about what should be on the other side of an odd number. Turning over the triangle likewise tells us nothing—turning it over can *confirm* the hypothesis if there is an even number on the other side, but it cannot *disprove* it, since again the proposition makes no claim about what is on the other side of a card with an odd number. When faced with this problem, fewer than 5% of people turn over the correct cards. The vast majority turn over either only the 6 or turn over the 6 and the triangle (Wason, 1968; Wason & Shapiro, 1971). In other words, they seek to confirm, and forget to try to disconfirm, the proposition, which is the opposite of what scientific hypothesis testing is designed to do (Popper, 1968). Turning over the triangle does not give us good information about the proposition's truth—but it might unhelpfully satisfy our expectations.

To be fair to the lay public, the confirmation bias is a scourge of scientists as well. The gold standard of double blinding in laboratory experiments (where both experimenter and research subject are unaware of which condition they are in) is a response to the risk that researchers will simply, though unconsciously, find what they expect to find (Rosenthal & Fode, 1963). And certain branches of environmental science may be particularly prone to confirmation bias. Some fields (for instance, conservation studies) are founded on a bed of normative commitments (such as that invasive species are bad or biodiversity is good), which may make research in their domains particularly at risk of motivated confirmation biases and their attendant errors (Kareiva et al., 2017).

THE STRATEGY OF TRUSTING AUTHORITIES

Rather than testing a hypothesis themselves, another technique people use to cope with complexity and to reduce associated uncertainty is simple deference to trusted others (Cooper et al., 1996). Deference to subject-matter experts is especially likely with environmental phenomena, which because of their complexity can be especially technical or scientific and far beyond the ability of laypeople to evaluate directly themselves. Indeed, in environmental science, even the experts defer to experts. Single-authored research papers are increasingly rare, since analysis of complicated environmental problems typically takes expertise in multiple specialties (Sonnenwald, 2007). Gaining traction on environmental phenomena thus requires teams of scientists working together (Eigenbrode et al., 2007; Wuchty et al., 2007).

Deference to qualified experts is, naturally, a rational and pragmatic way to cope with uncertainty engendered by complexity. The problem, though, is that it requires a person first to figure out that he needs such an expert and then to decide who qualifies as one. People can make errors at both stages.

Recognizing Expertise

Unsurprisingly, recognizing one's own ignorance can be a tricky business. One part of the problem is that some of the strategies described above can actually lead people to be overconfident that they have understood or solved a problem when they have not. More specifically, people tend to suffer from an "overprecision bias," thinking that their judgments are more accurate than they actually are (Harvey, 1997; Moore et al., 2015). There are two sources of imprecision. First, people may draw overly narrow "confidence intervals." For instance, they might estimate a value and think that, at most, they are off 5% in either direction, when in fact, the true value is something like 10% higher or lower than their estimate (Jain et al., 2013). In other words, people are too confident about their risk of error. Second, people may make reasonable parameters of error based on the beliefs they have come to, but because of biased evidence-gathering techniques (see the confirmation bias, above), their belief itself is simply off (Juslin et al., 2007). Either way, people might be wrong but more confident than they should be in their rightness—a state of mind unlikely to lead them to seek out help from an expert.

Another phenomenon that can interfere with awareness of one's own limitations is the Dunning–Kruger effect—an ignorance about one's own ignorance (Dunning, 2011; Kruger & Dunning, 1999). Dunning and Kruger experimentally demonstrated that people of low ability seem to lack the metacognition necessary to recognize their incompetence. This happens because, many times, the very skills one needs to *be* competent are the skills needed to *evaluate* one's competence (Dunning, 2011). Moreover, the crucial feedback one needs to estimate one's accuracy is often itself biased, obscure, or ambiguous (Carter & Dunning, 2008). Figuring out what we don't know, in other words, is an intrinsically difficult task. There are gender, class, and cultural differences in the tendency to suffer from the Dunning–Kruger effect: Men suffer it more than women do (Reuben et al., 2012), people in higher social classes more than lower (Belmi et al., 2019), and in some contexts Westerners more than East Asians (Muthukrishna et al., 2018). And perhaps ironically, increasing a person's skill in a domain will actually reduce their confidence in their competence—highly competent people if anything tend to *under*estimate their abilities (Kruger & Dunning, 1999). But the ignorance-about-ignorance effect is widespread, and it is obviously likely to impair people's recognition that deference to a qualified expert in a field as complex as environmental science is a good idea.

Though there is not yet much direct analysis of the Dunning–Kruger effect in the environmental domain, at least one recent study does show an example of the effect in action. On population samples in three different countries (the United States, France, and Germany), a group of researchers recently found that those who were most opposed to genetically modified foods knew the least—yet thought they knew the most—

about the technology (Fernbach et al., 2019). Such mistaken confidence can affect environmental law and policy through multiple vectors, including through individuals participating in legal and political action, and more directly where regulators and other legal decision makers suffer from it. The Dunning–Kruger effect may also provide psychological support for the continued viability of the *Chevron* doctrine in administrative law, whereby generalist courts—who might otherwise be tempted to overestimate their abilities—are doctrinally encouraged to defer to specialist administrative agencies (*Chevron U.S.A, Inc. v. NRDC*, 1984). Such a doctrine may look particularly wise when it is used to discipline overconfidence in highly complex realms such as environmental law.

Identifying Experts

Even if someone realizes she should defer to an expert, she still faces the obstacle of identifying a reliable one. There is not even an obvious gold-standard for how a person should perform this task, because as the Dunning–Kruger phenomenon would predict, it involves a catch-22—an expert is one who understands things and knows the right answers, but unless one understands things and knows the right answers, it is impossible to use that knowledge to identify a true expert. Because of this, people are relegated to other criteria for deciding who is an expert. An obvious one is an appeal to credentials. This is a reasonable approach but nevertheless can lead people astray—particularly if they are unable (or perhaps unwilling?) to evaluate the relevance or legitimacy of particular credentials.

This infamously happened with the "Global Warming Petition Project," which purports to be a declaration by over 31,000 scientists that "[t]here is no convincing scientific evidence that human release of carbon dioxide, methane, or other greenhouse gases is causing or will, in the foreseeable future, cause catastrophic heating of the Earth's atmosphere and disruption of the Earth's climate. Moreover, there is substantial scientific evidence that increases in atmospheric carbon dioxide produce many beneficial effects upon the natural plant and animal environments of the Earth" (www.petitionproject.org, n.d.) While the petition received a fair bit of media attention and has continued to live on in internet searches and the blogosphere, only 39 of the signatories were actually climatologists, and most of the rest were nonclimate scientists (including most with just a bachelor's degree) in fields as varied as veterinary medicine, astrophysics, and metallurgy. Nevertheless, the imprimatur of scientific expertise was credible enough that the National Academy of Science felt the need to issue a press release rejecting the authority of the petition (Brown, 2006).

Even worse than deferring to (what may be faulty) credentials, people have a tendency, especially when not motivated to pay particularly close attention, to defer based on irrelevant characteristics such as likability (Chaiken, 1980), attractiveness (Horai et al., 1974), the sheer number rather than quality of arguments offered (Petty & Cacioppo, 1984), or even the perceiver's mood at the time (Biggers & Pryor, 1982). Naturally, these cognitive processes can interact with motivational ones, such that whether or not someone qualifies as an expert is at least in part a function of whether the expert's conclusions comport with the perceiver's own worldviews (Kahan et al., 2011).

On the other hand, research shows people do use at least some reasonable guidelines for deciding who is an expert worth deferring to. For instance, they are more likely to accept the conclusions of a source who seems honest (Priester & Petty, 1995), consistent (Ziegler et al., 2004), and un-self-interested or otherwise biased (Walster et al., 1966). Also, when the issue is important or relevant to her, the listener is more likely to attend to the quality of the argument and less to the heuristic but irrelevant features of the expert (Petty et al., 1981). In short, once a person decides that deference to an expert on a complex issue is a good idea, the task of deciding *which* expert to trust may be daunting but is not hopeless.

Fortunately, as a class, most Americans still seem to trust scientists on the whole, and when it comes to environmental issues in particular, they still seem inclined to believe them. About 78% of Americans, for instance, believe that scientists can be trusted to give "full and accurate information" on issues of genetically modified organisms (GMOs) and on climate change—levels of deference that have been steady in recent years (National Science Board, 2018; Biggers & Pryor, 1982). (Not every country fares so well. Around half or fewer of Germans trust scientists on issues concerning renewable energy, climate change, and GMOs [National Science Board, 2018].) At the same time they are trusted, however, scientists are not especially *liked* (Priester & Petty, 1995; Fiske & Dupree, 2014). Given that deference to an expert involves cognitive, motivational, and emotional considerations, environmental scientists, policy makers, and activists should take great care in how they communicate with the public and who they pick to front their cause, because congeniality does matter (Nisbet & Markowitz, 2016).

THE STRATEGY OF IGNORANCE AND DENIAL

After assessing problems for themselves and deferring to experts, there is a final tactic people may deploy in the face of uncertainty: ignoring it or denying that there is a problem at all. Disregarding or discounting problems we don't fully comprehend can be easier than trying to understand and act on them. One form of ignoring a problem is outright rejection. This is at least in part because people are motivated to eliminate unpleasant clashes between their own beliefs and actions, a phenomenon known as cognitive dissonance reduction. When we engage in behaviors that are convenient and hard to change (say, flying in airplanes) but learn unsettling facts about flying (like that it is among the very worst sources of greenhouse gas emissions), we might simply choose to dismiss the validity of the belief (deciding that flying in airplanes isn't really that bad after all) rather than change our actions.

Even if we accept the validity of troubling environmental science conclusions, if we feel we cannot do anything about them, we might experience a state of "learned helplessness." In this state, people are essentially demoralized to the extent that they do not take actions that would ameliorate bad situations, even when doing so would be relatively easy (Maier & Seligman, 1976). And in fact, there is evidence that even for those with high levels of environmental awareness and concern, a sense of helplessness leads people to fail to take pro-environmental actions (Landry et al., 2018).

Finally, we might just choose not to think about these issues at all. When information might make us miserable, we often have a desire to avoid it—like not looking at our retirement investment accounts when the stock markets are plunging (Karlsson et al., 2009), or not going to the doctor for medical tests when we are worried something is very wrong (Ganguly & Tasoff, 2017). As we saw earlier, we are also particularly likely to minimize or disengage from information that suggests that we may be harming other people (Bandura, 2002, 2015). Finally, we are a particularly likely to avoid unpleasant information if we think there is nothing we can do about it. Indeed, avoiding bad information in such circumstances can be rational, where such disappointment can do nothing but lower our overall utility curve (Golman & Loewenstein, 2016).

In the case of environmental harms, we often can take some measures to address the underlying problem, and sticking our head in the sand in those cases is not rational. However, a large number of the behaviors we could engage in to protect or mitigate damage to the environment may indeed be *individually* pointless. As we discussed earlier, because of the diffusion of environmental impacts, no individual can fully capture ("internalize") the gains from individual environmental actions. It is similar to the decision to vote—no individual's vote will win any modern election of any appreciable size (Stubbings & Carmines, 1991), and no individual's decision to recycle used food cans and carry reusable grocery sacks is going to measurably stall climate change. To the extent our individual pro-environmental actions are not pointless, therefore, they are often largely altruistic or identity-related (Schultz et al., 1995; Whitmarsh, 2009). It is exactly in such circumstances that we might expect people to choose to ignore the unpleasant information about environmental harms, since learning about them does little more than make us feel bad.

Yet while information acquisition can be costly and upsetting, people do sometimes seek out information, perhaps out of mere curiosity (Loewenstein, 1994), or perhaps because they are not aware that their individual behaviors are small and that a prisoner's dilemma analysis would reveal that the only rational action to take is none at all. The science in this area is still emerging (Golman et al., 2017), and there is much to learn, but it seems like people's desire to know about (and act on) the state of the environment is driven at least in part by moral considerations rather than instrumental ones (Bilz & Nadler, 2009). Perhaps they feel they have an ethical obligation to know, even if they don't think they can do anything about it. In any event, for regulators who must try to get whole populations to behave in certain ways, it is important to know that tendencies toward denial, while powerful, are by no means absolute.

Conclusion

In sum, environmental impacts are distinctively complex, particularly insofar as they implicate multiply-causal and interactive nonlinear systems in mathematically atypical ways. This complexity leads to difficulties in perceiving, predicting, and understanding the environmental impacts of human behavior. People engage in various techniques to manage and even reduce that complexity, sometimes rationally and sometimes in ways that merely supply confidence without actually increasing their ability to comprehend and control their world. These techniques include heuristic strategies to tease out the causes of effects, underweighting omissions in favor of focusing on commissions, and detecting patterns from what looks like noise. When this fails to resolve complexity, people might defer to experts. Finally, when all else fails, people may cope with complexity by simply ignoring or denying it. All of these strategies complicate the tasks of environmental law.

Key Aspects of the Psychology of Complexity in Environmental Law

Environmental effects are complex. That is, they are often unpredictable, interactive, and nonlinear. Psychological research suggests that people try to simplify complex problems in order to process them—but doing so washes away nuance and can obscure important aspects of an issue. This can be particularly problematic where the underlying problem is legitimately complicated.

Cognitive, emotional, and motivational challenges arise in dealing with complex environmental impacts. These include:

- Causes and effects. Teasing out causes and effects is particularly hard in the environmental domain, especially where doing so requires technical expertise. In the main, people are *innumerate*—essentially meaning they are bad with math. This causes them to use techniques other than precise calculation to estimate causes. In general, they are likely to focus on salience to determine causality; that is, focus on what "stands out" and assume it is causal. Things "stand out" when they are distinctive, rare, evocative, vivid, recent, or proximate. People also assume that bad effects are from causes they think are independently bad. None of these things has any necessary, logical connection to actual causation.

- Acts versus omissions. When assessing causes, people tend to favor acts over omissions. This can distort their assessments in various ways. For instance, they may fail to condemn failures to act. It also leads them to prefer *noninterference* as a solution.

- Pattern detection. People try to make sense of complex stimuli by detecting patterns. Humans have well-developed pattern-detection capabilities—but sometimes they are too developed. We have a tendency to see patterns that are not there. *Various cognitive heuristics* can be thought of as pattern-detection devices (like the availability heuristic, which assumes that things that are easy to recall are therefore more frequent)—and heuristic thinking is prone to errors. Our tendency to seek patterns in complex situations can also lead to a tendency toward conspiracy theorizing.

- Distortions in information seeking and uncertainty reduction. To reduce complexity, people may interpret and seek out information in biased ways. People tend to forget their base rates when calculating probabilities (a product of the *representativeness heuristic*). They also suffer from the *confirmation bias,* where they fail to seek out information that might disconfirm their beliefs. Their preference for consistency also leads them to suffer from *coherence shifts,* where they interpret ambiguous information in ways that make it consistent with their prior beliefs.

- Ignorance/denial. In the face of unsurmountable problems with complexity, people may simply ignore problems altogether. This can obviously have pernicious effects when it comes to interacting with and regulating the environment.

In the highly complicated and technical domain of environmental effects, people may also seek out experts to help them resolve complexity. Doing so, though, requires overcoming two problems.

- They must know they need an expert. The same processes that make it hard for people to understand complex things like the environment may make it hard for them to know they do not understand it. This is the *Dunning–Kruger effect.*

- <u>They must be able to accurately identify expertise.</u> The Dunning–Kruger effect also makes it hard for people to know who is a qualified expert. Consequently, people will often rely on other social and contextual cues to determine who is an expert. Some of these are helpful, such as credentials, consistency, and the like. But some are unrelated to expertise, such as attractiveness, likeability, and whether they share the person's values.

4

Nonhuman Impacts

The environmental consequences that law seeks to manage operate through and affect the nonhuman animals, plants, geography, and processes that make up much of human surroundings. The centrality of these nonhuman concerns is possibly the greatest distinction between environmental law and other areas of the law (Lazarus, 2000). In this chapter, we argue that psychology can help inform our understanding of people's perceptions of and response to the nonhuman aspects of environmental harm. We believe that the nonhuman character of many environmental impacts triggers a distinctive set of psychological phenomena. More particularly, people experience systematic psychological barriers in recognizing, comprehending, and caring about harms to the nonhuman environment. These barriers have particular import in environmental law, particularly through their influence on the process of valuation, on which many environmental law and policy decisions depend.

This chapter proceeds in three parts. First, it identifies the institutional contexts in which questions regarding nonhuman impacts often arise, and flags an example of the type of nonhuman impacts that environmental law and policy is often asked to address. Second, it outlines cognitive limitations that people face in evaluating and addressing nonhuman impacts. Third, it develops the emotional and motivational complications that come into play with nonhuman impacts. Throughout, the chapter pays special attention to the psychology of nonhuman impacts as it relates to the legally important task of valuation.

Nonhuman Impacts in Institutional and Practical Contexts

Legal institutions frequently assign value to nonhuman environmental impacts, in order to know how to trade them off either for money or against each other. The task of valuation arises in a number of legal contexts. Courts (in the form of judges or juries), for instance, have to assign a value to environmental goods when calculating damages, as for oil spills like the Exxon-Valdez spill in Prince William Sound or the BP Deepwater Horizon spill in the Gulf of Mexico, and as they must do when computing cleanup costs for contaminated lands under CER-CLA. Valuation may also determine legal status itself. When courts evaluate purported negligence for environmental injuries, for example, liability depends on whether the cost of precaution outweighed the value and probability of harm at the time the decision was made. Furthermore, whether an environmental law is invoked to protect a species, an area of land, or a community will often be a function of whether anyone values those goods enough to seek that protection. Courts are also routinely asked to review agency decisions about nonhuman impacts, such as agencies' management of public lands, or EPA rulemaking.

Agencies themselves routinely assign value to nonhuman environmental entities and processes. Indeed, quantified regulatory valuations play a particularly important role in U.S. environmental law because of its general dependence on monetized cost-benefit analysis (Rowell, 2015). Typically, to attach monetary values to nonmonetary goods, agencies try to determine what people would be "willing to pay" to secure those goods, or in some cases, "willing to accept" to forgo them (Sunstein, 2002c; Sunstein & Rowell, 2007). Agencies then consider whether the quantified, monetized benefits of a proposed rule—such as human lives saved, or ecosystems protected—justify its quantified, monetized costs, such as to industry (Sunstein, 2004; Executive Order 12,866). While the normative desirability of cost-benefit analysis remains a matter for scholarly debate (Ackerman & Heinzerling, 2002; Sunstein, 2004; Revesz & Livermore, 2008), the importance of the approach within U.S. environmental law is widely recognized.

Even advocates for cost-benefit analysis concede that monetization grows more challenging when the goods being valued are not traded on open markets, as is the case with almost all environmental goods. As we discuss further in Chapter 7, economists have developed a number of methods for addressing this issue, mostly centered on so-called "contingent valuation" methods, which ask people directly about their willingness to pay, though also through the careful valuation of so-called "ecosystem services," which are benefits that ecosystems present to humans. Through these methods, U.S. environmental law is directly informed and affected by the way that individuals quantify and monetize the value of environmental goods.

In this chapter, we argue that these conventional approaches to valuing the nonhuman environment can be enriched and improved by a better understanding of psychology. Conventional approaches to valuation do not adequately account for predictable human cognitive quirks and failures in the valuation of nonhuman animals, processes, and things, nor do they fully address the motivational and emotional phenomena that can affect, and even create, value. This, in turn, can make environmental regulations that depend on accurate (or even just consistent!) valuations problematic. Such regulations can fail to anticipate or change behaviors in predicted ways, and can be politically unacceptable.

An example of the sort of nonhuman impact that legal institutions may be asked to address and balance against human concerns is the question of how aquatic biota should be valued—a question that arose before the EPA, and subsequently the Supreme Court, in *Entergy Corp. v. Riverkeeper, Inc.*, 556 U.S. 208 (2009). The court was reviewing a rule by the EPA that set standards for how power plants may use cooling water intake structures. Power plants rely on some method of cooling to reduce the massive heat created by power generation. A common solution is cooling water intake structures. These generally work by sucking up huge quantities of water from a nearby water source. The water intake systems kill aquatic organisms by squashing them against screens (impingement) or entangling them in the system itself (entrainment). The number of animals killed is enormous. One plant can kill 3–4 billion fish and shellfish in a year—enough to destabilize local ecosystems. Across the country, trillions of aquatic organisms (including plankton, fish, crustaceans, shellfish, sea turtles, marine mammals, etc.) are killed each year in this way.

Under the Clean Water Act, the EPA faced the question of determining what constituted the "best technology available for minimizing adverse environmental impacts" of cooling water intake structures at existing plants. One available technology would have essentially eliminated impingement and entrainment (so-called "closed-cycle" cooling systems) at a cost of $3.5 billion per year. Other cheaper technology cost only $389 million per year but allowed the continued deaths of trillions of aquatic animals.

To determine which technology to require, the EPA followed the now-standard regulatory practice of cost-benefit analysis, requiring them to express the expected impacts of a regulation in monetary terms (Executive Order 12,866; *OMB Circular A-4*; Pearce et al., 2006).

In this case, that meant the EPA was faced with the question not only of how much the different potential technologies would cost but also the much thornier question of how to value the impingement or entrainment of billions of aquatic organisms a year. In this case, the EPA chose to monetize only that portion of animals that had easily measurable recreational and commercial value. This was only 1.8% of the total kills: 1.4 billion fish, primarily. It valued those fish according to their human uses forgone—$83 million a year. The remaining trillions of aquatic organisms were thus valued at $0 (Rowell, 2012b). Valued this way, the $3.5 billion price tag of the closed-cycle cooling systems looked unjustifiable, and the EPA chose to require the less effective (but much cheaper) technology instead. The Supreme Court upheld this analysis, affirming the agency's authority to perform valuations of this type and in this way. In doing so, neither the court nor the agency noted or addressed any psychological aspect of these valuations.

Throughout the remainder of this chapter, we aim to describe what this conventional analysis is missing as a way to hopefully improve and enrich it. We catalog the cognitive and emotional/motivational phenomena that affect how people attach value to nonhuman goods such as these and how these phenomena can systematically disrupt the way people value the nonhuman environment. We then discuss a broader psychology that informs how people attach value to the environment—namely, religious/spiritual and cultural sources of value. Finally, we talk about the psychology of valuation itself and how the very act of attaching value can alter the perceived value of a good.

Cognitive Limitations in Valuing the Nonhuman Environment

As we have seen, environmental impacts can be challenging to cognitively process because of their diffusion and complexity. An additional set of challenges arises as a consequence of their nonhuman character.

These include the triggering of the social brain and anthropomorphism, selective attention and availability of some nonhuman aspects and species over others, and the instability of preferences about nonhuman effects.

The Specialized Social Brain and Anthropomorphism

As social psychologists have long emphasized, the human mind is extraordinarily well adapted to understanding and predicting human behavior. The brain includes many specialized systems that mediate social interaction, ranging from a "fast path" for recognizing faces; to special circuits for perceiving tiny emotional cues from faces, intonation, and body language; to systems that identify and ascribe intent to others (Baars & Gage, 2010). Infants are born with a number of tendencies that facilitate social interaction, such as making eye contact and recognizing faces. Other skills develop over childhood and adolescence. The theory of mind develops to help people understand other people's intentions, thoughts, and feelings. Indeed, the need for complex brain systems to support social interactions is widely viewed as the evolutionary explanation for humans' enlarged brain size (Brothers, 2002; Dunbar, 2016).

These social parts of the brain are optimized for understanding human interactions. Yet cognitive structures that developed to understand other humans can struggle or even misfire when asked instead to manage nonhuman behavior and processes. Consider anthropomorphism, which arises when humans ascribe human characteristics to animals, inanimate objects, or natural phenomena. Although people can consciously differentiate between humans and nonhumans, neuroscience research suggest that humans use similar brain regions—those related to theory of mind—when thinking about the behavior of both humans and nonhuman entities. These perceptions can influence whether the agent is perceived as accountable for its actions or worthy of moral care and consideration (Waytz et al., 2010). Anthropomorphized entities are generally perceived as more deserving of punishment and reward. Ironically, then, anthropomorphism can negatively affect the treatment of wildlife, as where wolves in ranchland are perceived as wily and sneaky, or where an orca attacking a handler is seen as mean or worthy of punishment.

People do not anthropomorphize everything—or at least not everything equally. The more similar the target is to humans, the more people anthropomorphize it (Waytz et al., 2010). This is likely due to a set of emotional responses sometimes called "biophilia" (Ulrich, 1993; Wilson, 1986). For instance, we seem to have a genetically based attraction to and preference for "cute" nonhuman animals, like small mammals, that share features with human babies (*Kindchenschema*) (Bradshaw & Paul, 2010; Lorenz, 1943). Some researchers believe such preferences may have served an evolutionary function, particularly among hunter-gatherer societies (Bradshaw & Paul, 2010). Such preferences could lead people to attach higher value to animals that are phylogenetically similar to humans—but it may also lead them to anthropomorphize and thus misunderstand those animals' behaviors. As we discuss further in Chapter 7, such distortions in attention and caring may have significant implications for the selective operation of environmental schemes that seek to protect particular species, such as the Endangered Species Act.

Heuristics and Salience

Other, more quotidian cognitive biases can also contribute to or detract from our understanding of nonhuman entities. Availability, for instance, has a role to play here as well. Understanding the needs of nonhuman animals or places requires noticing them in the first place. Insects, for example, may be easily neglected not just because they are phylogenetically quite different from us but simply because they are so small. Moreover, their very commonness may make them nonsalient—they are so much a part of our background noise we may fail to think about them at all. Similar availability issues may attach to remote, difficult-to-observe ecosystems versus vast or scenic ones. It is easy to think about the Colorado Rockies as they loom above us, or stare down at us from picturesque landscapes hung on our walls. It is much harder to detect and imagine, and thus to care about, the microbial and fungal ecosystems buried deep beneath the ground, or even the aquatic and marine ecosystems teeming below the surface of our rivers, lakes, and oceans. Imaginability here may matter. The abstractness of some nonhuman environmental goods may also cause them to be relatively ignored—as in the problems people have thinking about things as vast as "the atmosphere" or "the nation's waterways."

Notably, although the social brain can be misled when it comes to understanding nonhuman animals and surroundings, it is quite helpful for predicting other *people's* behavior to those same nonhuman entities. Thus, while the nonhuman character of environmental impacts is a barrier to understanding the environment, the social brain—and social psychology—can still generate meaningful predictions of human behavior.

Instability of Preferences About Nonhuman Effects

Other cognitive problems in valuing the nonhuman environment concern not errors in estimating value but the worth of making such estimates altogether. Conventional views of valuation do not categorically reject the idea that valuations can change—people can learn new things, or what they value can change over some period of time. Nor do they fail to recognize that valuations may vary with who is doing the valuing—courts assign value differently than agencies do, for instance, and both may differ from valuations by private individuals or institutions. But there should ideally still be some fundamental stability in valuation in order for those valuations to be usable by policy makers.

To see the problem, consider a seminal 1997 paper published in *Nature*, in which researchers calculated the value of "ecosystem services and natural capital" at $33 trillion per year (Costanza et al., 1997). This number is especially notable because not only was it double the entire global gross national product at the time, it was a conservative estimate. As such, it may in fact have underestimated (perhaps substantially) the economic use value of nature—and indeed, the authors updated their research several years later, revising their calculations upward by over fourfold, to $145 trillion per year (Costanza et al., 2014).

The fact that these two estimates could vary so much when computed by the same research team at two different times indicates part of the problem of valuation in the environmental domain. Not only can these valuations be deeply subjective—with some people valuing, say, a forest for its logging and others for its hiking potential—but they can also be unstable. This is because valuation by its very nature involves compressing diverse ways of valuing things onto a single metric (typically, though not necessarily, a monetary one) so that they can be compared and traded off. Yet for humans, value is often subjectively experienced as pluralistic, contextual, and sometimes conflicting (Anderson, 1995). This means—among other things—that *how* you ask about value matters significantly to the values elicited. In one setting, or framed one way, the very same person might value the forest primarily for its logging; in another setting or framed another way, primarily for its hiking potential. Which framing reflects their "true" value? Even limiting the value of environmental goods to their economic uses to humans can generate numbers that vary wildly, depending on who is asked, when, and how.

The subjectivity and instability of value affects all areas of law, of course, not just environmental law. But because environmental law involves the regulation of such incredibly diverse things and processes—especially including ones that involve hard-to-value nonhuman entities like animals, landscapes, and particular weather patterns, all of which must generally be valued outside traditional markets—the problem of valuation is especially difficult there (Mullainathan & Shafir, 2013), and may be particularly prone to the sorts of distortions and biases that we discuss further below.

Emotional and Motivational Factors in Perceiving and Valuing the Nonhuman Environment

Economists commonly rely upon subjective valuations without interrogating their source. Yet it may be helpful to understand the sources of people's subjective valuations, in part because that analysis may help reveal where psychological influences can affect them. In cases where policy makers seek to build legal policy on the basis of people's subjective valuations, such knowledge should be seen as fundamental to developing meaningful and predictable estimates. It may also help—eventually—in understanding and managing the instabilities and even inaccuracies (Kahneman et al., 1999) that so frequently occur within environmental valuations.

Though many psychological techniques used to make quick valuations apply across legal domains, in environmental law we are particularly concerned with nonhuman entities, which are even more prone to the gyrations we discussed above. Thus, we focus here on those psychological characteristics that apply particularly to valuing animals, natural landscapes and features, and the like. We discuss motivational and emotional processes and signifiers of value that enable people to reduce the vast array of use values to a more manageable set they care (most) about.

Emotional Benefits of Interaction with the Environment

Humans interact with their nonhuman environments in varied and rich ways. The study of environmental psychology, which focuses on the relationship between an environment and its inhabitants (Gifford, 2007), is particularly focused on informing and recognizing those interactions. Although a significant portion of environmental psychology focuses on the psychology of built spaces (Devlin, 2018), it also includes research on humans' interactions with natural and outdoor environments.

Exposure to the natural world affects humans in a number of ways (Maple & Morris, 2018). In particular, time spent "in nature" has measurable emotional and psychological benefits. One study, for instance, found that just looking at trees can measurably reduce stress levels, even when the trees are located in the middle of a city (Jiang et al., 2016). Another found that just looking at still *images* of nature generates emotional and stress-reduction benefits (van den Berg et al., 2015). Recreational settings that simulate nature—such as zoos, aquariums, and botanical gardens—improve brain function and overall mental and physical well-being (Maple & Morris, 2018). By contrast, degraded environments generate psychological and emotional stress (Pretty et al., 2005; Wyles et al., 2016).

Although there is not (yet) a tradition of incorporating the psychological and emotional benefits of environmental goods in legal and regulatory valuations, at least in theory, these benefits should be perfectly amenable to being counted. Why, then, have they been neglected? One part of the explanation may be psychological: While emotional and psychological benefits can be measured once noticed, these effects often happen outside the perceiver's awareness (Bratman et al., 2012). So while interaction with the environment can have fairly profound consequences on the human psyche, the fact that people may not even be aware they are happening means that people may not fully appreciate the value of urban green spaces or the preservation of wild areas. And this in turn may mean they can be easily neglected, both by individuals and as a matter of policy.

The Effect of Uniqueness and Identity on Value

Environmental goods and processes are frequently, though of course not always, unique. Ecosystems themselves are unique. The Redwood Forests of the west coast of the United States are not interchangeable with the rainforests of Brazil, which are not interchangeable with the rainforests of Alaska. Even if one were to regard individual members of a species within a given ecosystem as commodities (a contestable notion), the particular *array* of species in that ecosystem is unique. Uniqueness contributes to saliency; that is, to what "stands out" to observers. To the extent something is unique, it is therefore more likely to be noticed and assigned a value, either positive or negative.

Beyond its effect on whether a target gets assigned a value at all, people simply treat unique goods differently, generally preferring them to commodities. This preference, moreover, is linked to concepts of self. People associate with objects and places in the world around them as a way of expressing their identity (Csikszentmihalyi, 1993). Connection with unique or at least distinctive goods and places helps us to construct an "optimally distinctive" social identity—one that is a part of groups or affiliations with which we wish to be identified, but which also allows us to express our own individuality (Leonardelli et al., 2010). Presumably, then, people value those goods and places that help them to express their identity more than those to which they have no particular connection.

The preference for uniqueness/distinctiveness starts early, and is revealed in a behavior very common in small children: an attachment to a favorite toy or other object. In a creative study on 3- to 6-year-olds, researchers used a "copying machine" to "create" a perfect duplicate of the child's attachment object, and then invited the child to take either the "original" or the "copy" (Hood & Bloom, 2008). Almost all selected the "original"—though four refused to allow their attachment object to be copied at all! This could not be explained merely by an aversion to copies—the children were more than happy to take a duplicate of the experimenter's own toy. A follow-up study showed that "identity" was indeed connected to the unique: 6-year-olds preferred an object that they believed had been owned by the queen of England to its "copy." Additional permutations of the study also demonstrated that the effect could not be explained by some perceived objective value of the unique good—the children had no preference for an object they knew was expensive versus its identical "copy." Another study demonstrated that children as young as 3 years old understood that the value they had for their own attachment objects was idiosyncratic; children did not assume the researchers valued the children's used toy as they themselves did (Gelman & Davidson, 2016). In other words, by a very young age, we understand that objects can be meaningfully affiliated with people, and we prefer those objects that are meaningfully affiliated with ourselves or with those we like, admire, or even see as an extension of ourselves (like a parent who finds it hard to throw out the child's object of affection, perhaps even after the child has long since grown into adulthood and abandoned it herself) (Phillips & Sego, 2011).

What might be seen as "magical thinking" of this sort does not end in childhood. The value adults place on uniqueness explains the high value for original art (and the low value for counterfeits) (Bloom, 1996) and why they pay lots of money for things that have been owned (and especially touched) by celebrities (Newman & Bloom, 2014) but feel disgust at objects that were owned by murderers (Nemeroff & Rozin, 1994). But the preference for uniqueness and socially identified goods may also help to inform why people value particular unique environmental spaces, such as the Grand Canyon or Yosemite. It may also help explain some urges to eliminate invasive species. Consider New Zealand's ambitious and controversial plans to eradicate (through killing) all nonnative animals from their land by 2050. Their conservation minister justified the plan by explaining, "New Zealand's unique native creatures and plants are central to our national identity" (Greshko, 2016, n.p.) Conversely, note that the value of uniqueness and distinctive identity in the environment can also explain the desire to *keep* invasive species. Consider the monk parakeets of the Hyde Park neighborhood in Chicago, Illinois. The birds began populating the area in the 1970s, probably as a result of pets escaping or being released deliberately. They quickly became iconic, and residents rebelled against and blocked a plan by the USDA to remove them (Garcia, 2014). In both cases—for New Zealand, in eradicating invasive species, and Hyde Park, in retaining them—a portion of the subjective value attached to nonhuman animals flows from perceptions of their perceived distinctiveness and impact on identity.

The Effect of Scarcity on Value

By definition, unique goods are scarce; there is only one of them. But other features of the nonhuman environment contribute to the sense of scarcity. For one thing, the environment is constantly changing, and in many ways, constantly degrading or diminishing. For example, in the updated estimate of the "ecosystem services and natural capital" *Nature* article cited above, the recent (as of 2011) estimated use value is $125 trillion per year, down from the revised estimate of $145 trillion per year from a decade before. That is because, the authors argue, land uses have reduced the value of the ecosystem overall (including, for instance, destruction of coral reefs, tropical forests, and wetlands) (Costanza et al., 2014). Each year, they estimate, we have lost between $4 trillion and $20 trillion in value from the environment, largely, if not entirely, as a result of human behaviors.

Humans respond to scarce things by valuing them more (Mittone & Savadori, 2009). In this sense, of course, the psychology of scarcity is the same as the conventional economics of scarcity: Limited supply in the face of constant demand increases prices. From an environmentalist's perspective, this may sometimes generate positive outcomes. The psychological value attached to scarcity may help to explain why endangered species are protected (in preference to common species) and why rare landscapes are preserved as National Parks (Nagle, 2019). People are simply willing to invest more to preserve and protect nonhuman animals, features, and resources that they perceive as scarce.

Scarcity has other psychological consequences as well, though. Of particular interest are those elaborated by Shafir and Mullainathan in their compelling book *Scarcity: Why Having Too Little Means So Much* (Mullainathan & Shafir, 2013). Perceived scarcity can become a "mindset," triggering a whole set of cognitive effects. In particular, a scarcity mindset uses up cognitive resources, making it hard to focus on other things. Scarcity draws mental attention to itself and uses up space in working memory. This has an upside: Scarcity increases concentration on a problem, which can actually enhance the ability to deal with it. But this concentration can easily turn into "tunnel vision," leading to a prioritization of short-term solutions at the expense of long-term ones. It also leads to a sort of myopia, where intense focus on the problem causes one to fail to notice relevant information outside the "tunnel" that could alleviate the problem. Ironically, these poor reactions to scarcity can actually lead to the kind of mismanagement that causes yet more scarcity. On this front, consider an example from Morocco, which sits on the edge of the Sahara Desert. The government of Morocco decided—in the face of water scarcity—to dam and divert limited groundwater sources so that they would be more abundant for urban and agricultural uses. The result was immediate increase in supply—but at a cost of increased desertification, which exacerbates the scarcity that prompted the intervention in the first place (Chelleri, 2014).

The psychology of scarcity generates still other concerns. For one thing, and in contrast to classical economic theory, which traditionally treats preferences as fixed, scarcity shifts *demand itself*. People are not just willing to pay more for scarce things than abundant things, they *want* scarce things more than abundant things. This is due to several factors, one of which is a perceived loss of freedom or control in the face of scarcity. Parents of teenagers will recognize this in the phenomenon of "reactance"—when you try to limit a someone's access to something, she reacts against the restriction by desiring it more (Brehm, 1966). It is also a function of social proof: If something is scarce, it is reasonable to assume that others desire it, and it is therefore desirable (Cialdini, 2001). The consequence may be a perverse attitude that causes a run on the scarce resource for no other reason than that it is scarce.

This can have obvious bad effects when it comes to environmental goods. People may seek to travel to Yosemite precisely because it is both unique and scarce; the resulting overtourism damages the very thing that people so value (Simmonds et al., 2018). Trophy hunters often particularly value killing rare animals that their trophy hunting pals have not (yet) killed. A permit to hunt an endangered black rhino in Namibia, for instance, recently sold for $350,000 at auction (Herskovitz, 2014). Birders and wildlife enthusiasts seek to capture the moment of seeing rare wildlife, but their presence and behaviors (such as use of camera equipment) may disturb animals' typical behaviors or the habitats on which those animals depend (Knight & Cole, 1995). The extraordinary sums paid in Japan's Tsukiji fish market for the first bluefin of the year—as much as $2 million!—are often understood to follow from the endangered fish's increasing rarity (Narula, 2014).

The Psychology of Intrinsic Value

Many people have a sense that some things are valuable in and of themselves, perhaps partly *because* they exist apart from the interests and design of humans. The sentiment is captured somewhat by Alfred Joyce Kilmer's classic and oft-quoted 1913 poem: "I think that I shall never see a poem so lovely as a tree . . . Poems are made by fools like me but only God can make a tree." The value of Kilmer's tree seems based not so much on its loveliness as on the awe it inspires, on its sacredness. Animals, plants, mountains, landscapes, waterways—for many people, these things seem to have value worth protecting for their own sake, even beyond how humans value them.

This is perhaps the hardest psychological feature of valuation for environmental law to grapple with. What does it mean for something to have value outside the human use for it? Trying to assess the biocentric or "intrinsic" value of a thing, beyond its value to humans, comes up against psychological barriers to imagination that are arguably insuperable. The human mind inevitably can only see and assess intrinsic value as a human would. And humans put value on things to the extent they, as humans, *perceive* their value (Justus et al., 2009). In other words, even when we try to ascertain the intrinsic value of environmental goods separate from human interests, it's turtles (or at any rate, humans) all the way down.

Nevertheless, many people experience a sense of value that *feels* distinctly different from the instrumental values most commonly ascribed to use value (Sagoff, 2009). And while there may be conceptual problems with distinguishing the two, psychologically, many people report seeing a difference between the use to which they put something, and its intrinsic value, such as may be grounded in religious, moral, or cultural commitments and obligations (P. W. Taylor, 1983). Furthermore, people often exhibit reluctance to trade off items they see as having intrinsic value, especially with explicitly monetary use values (or even with other items of intrinsic value) (Tetlock et al., 2000; Ackerman & Heinzerling, 2002). Below, we discuss the psychology of these kinds of valuations and how they play out in the environmental context.

EMPATHY AND IDENTIFICATION

Psychologists have long understood that people's sense of self encompasses not just their physical bodies, but also the things and places that surround them (James, 1890). If we perceive ourselves as intrinsically valuable—as many people do—then we will also be more likely to intrinsically value those things and places that are connected deeply to, and seen as extensions of, ourselves (Bloom, 2004).

As a result, we discriminate in favor of people we identify with, both in terms of our attitudes toward them (Perdue et al., 1990) and resources allocated to them (Brewer, 1979; Tajfel et al., 1971). This seems to be a function of "the other" merging with "the self": The more we identify with someone, the more we empathize with them, and the more likely we are to help them (Batson et al., 1997). Psychologically, we are more likely to identify (and therefore merge) with an "other" to the extent they are easily identifiable as opposed to abstract. For instance, as we saw earlier, people are more likely to donate to help a particular, named person in need over "statistical" persons who are merely described in terms of their group (Small & Loewenstein, 2003). Sheer numbers matter too: When the number of victims in need increases (presumably in a way that makes it harder to differentiate them), people are less willing to help (Västfjäll et al., 2014). This well-documented phenomenon has been called "compassion fade" or "compassion fatigue" (Butts et al., 2019).

These studies, though, focus on identification with and valuing other *human* lives (Butts et al., 2019; Pratto & Glasford, 2008). Yet as we have emphasized, environmental law distinctively also deals with valuing *nonhuman* organisms, processes, and even places. Research demonstrates that people do incorporate both places (Belk, 1988; Proshansky et al., 1983; Williams et al., 1992) and nonhuman animals (S.-E. Brown, 2004, 2007) into their sense of self—we discussed that very phenomenon in the discussion of unique objects, above. This opens the possibility that they could therefore also experience compassion fatigue in the same ways as they do for human lives. And indeed, some research suggests they do.

One study (Markowitz et al., 2013) showed that people were less willing to help a relatively large and undifferentiated mass of wood storks than a smaller, more identifiable grouping. Similarly, they were less willing to help when shown a photo of a large group of polar bears versus a single adult polar bear. (On what might be an optimistic note, the effect disappeared for those who considered themselves environmentalists.) Still, it is early days for research in this area, and the evidence is a bit mixed: Another, earlier study showed that when the question was not one of direct helping/giving but was instead about broad support for protective environmental policies, participants were *more* willing to help large numbers of polar bears than individual ones (Hart, 2011). The bottom line is that empathy and identification may matter to both the extrinsic and the intrinsic value people attach to the environment.

SIMILARITY

A sense of intrinsic value can also come from perceived similarity to ourselves. Some evidence suggests that the more similar we perceive ourselves to be to a person, the more empathetic we feel toward him, and the more likely we are to help him. Support for this hypothesis has been strong (Brown et al., 2006; Krebs, 1975; Stotland, 1969), though not perfectly uniform (Batson et al., 2005) when it comes to human strangers. But for humans versus nonhumans, the differences vary from moderate (humans versus apes) to extreme (humans versus fruit flies). Perhaps as a consequence, the evidence for a similarity-empathy effect for nonhuman animals is much clearer. For instance, one study (Westbury & Neumann, 2008) demonstrated that when human participants were shown film clips with humans, primates, quadruped mammals, and birds in distress, human participants showed greater physiological empathetic responses the more phylogenetically similar the animals displayed were to them, with far greater empathy demonstrated for primates than birds. Similarly, recall the tendency people have to empathize with animals that share features with human babies (Bradshaw & Paul, 2010; Lorenz, 1943). In this sense, the likelihood that people will perceive intrinsic value in an environmental good—such as the preservation of an animal species—may be importantly tied to the level of similarity that the individual perceives between that good and themselves.

RELIGIOUS OR SPIRITUAL CONCERNS

Like Joyce Kilmer and his awe of God's tree, many people derive a sense of the intrinsic value of nature from religious or spiritual commitments. Sometimes, nature's intrinsic value is even explicit holy doctrine. Many American indigenous traditions, for example, are deeply place oriented, and nonhuman animals are sometimes seen as connected with both humans and landscapes in the community, all the members of which are entitled to respect and honor (Pierotti & Wildcat, 2000). Many Eastern religious traditions incorporate a respect for nature, and some sense of its intrinsic value, as part of their core beliefs. Buddhist traditions treat all things in nature (animals, objects, and even things like sunlight) as "dharmas," which have religious and moral significance (Batchelor & Brown, 1994). The Japanese Shinto religion is animist—landscapes, rivers, rocks, animals, plants, and so on can all embody a spiritual essence called "kami"—a belief that has made it a prime target for increasingly global adoption by some environmentalists (Rots, 2015).

But it is not just people in indigenous and Eastern cultures that derive a sense of commitment to nature from a spiritual practice. A burgeoning environmental movement has arisen among some Judeo-Christian believers based on concepts of "dominion" and "stewardship" in the Bible (Gould & Kearns, 2018). Even outside this explicitly religious group, one survey of Westerners involved in the environmental movement revealed that over 90% of them reported a sense of "awe," "wonder," "transcendence," and similar spiritual experiences when in nature, which motivated their environmental commitments (Palmer, 1998). Another study interviewed Texan environmentalists who reported that the local land was a religious symbol for them (Bartkowski & Swearingen, 1997). In fact, well over half of Americans, both religious and not, report feeling a profound spiritual connection to nature (Deal & Magyar-Russell, 2018), and some researchers suggest these "dark green religious" sensibilities are growing, along with a commitment to the spiritual underpinnings of environmentalism (Taylor, 2010). In short, an important explanation for some environmentalist beliefs and protective practices is a sense that nonhuman nature is sacred, a conception that may be grounded in explicit religious belief or just in a nontheistic sense of the divine.

The psychological consequences of sanctifying something leads both to a greater willingness to expend resources to protect it, such as by engaging in pro-environmental behaviors (Tarakeshwar et al., 2001; Taylor, 2010), and a revulsion toward threats to it, which may be seen as defiling (Rozin et al., 1999). In other words, and as we discuss in more detail in Chapter 6 on pollution control, people value those things they regard as sacred more (Pargament & Mahoney, 2005)—and recoil from those things they perceive as profane (Douglas, 1966; Douglas & Wildavsky, 1982; Khare, 1996). However, what features of a target cause people to sanctify it in the first place remain unclear (Douglas & Wildavsky, 1982). Obviously, religious doctrine or culture is one source, as the examples above suggest—but religiosity does not by any means automatically increase sacred respect for nature. Indeed, there are strains within some religions, or within some members of some religions, that actually denigrate environmental respect. Consider the Christian biblical concept of dominion by man over Earth. While some do find grounding for environmental protection in it, many other Christians take this to mean Earth and its contents are there entirely for humans to use and exploit (B. Taylor et al., 2016; White, 1967). And empirically, this latter view is unsurprisingly correlated with disdain for environmentalism (Tarakeshwar et al., 2001). Undoubtedly cognitive processes, particularly availability, explain some part of sanctification, as do culture, history, and even just happenstance. Yet as little as we know about why some people think of "nature" as sacred, we know even less about which *pieces* of the environment they see that way. Anecdotally, people often become connected to particular features of a landscape or to specific places, or perhaps to particular animals or even kinds of animals, for reasons we discussed earlier in this chapter. And those things to which people feel connected are presumably more likely candidates for sanctification. But again, the psychology in this domain is still developing (Pargament & Mahoney, 2005).

CROSS-CULTURAL CONSIDERATIONS
All of the considerations we have described above can interact with culture in surprising ways. Some of these differences we have already mentioned—certain religions may be animistic or otherwise support (or deny) a sacred view of nature that will affect the environmental valuations of their adherents. But cultural differences are far broader than just religious ones, and multiple aspects of culture may have important effects on individual psychology (Bruner, 1990; de Oliveira & Nisbett, 2017).

Indeed, an influential hypothesis within cultural psychology—the social orientation hypothesis (Varnum et al., 2010)—suggests that social patterns prevalent in a culture reinforce particular ways of thinking. One well-studied cultural distinction with psychological implications is the difference between collectivist and individualist cultures. Prototypical collectivist cultures are East Asian (like China, Japan, and Korea), and individualist cultures are countries in Western Europe (like England, Germany, France) and the United States. But the terms are also relative. The South in the United States is more historically collectivist than the Mountain West, blacks more collectivist than whites, and women more collectivist than men, for instance (Vandello & Cohen, 1999). The terms also can be used to define an orientation across individuals within the same cultural background, and even a single person can be more or less individualist or collectivist depending on the context (Trafimow et al., 1991).

People with collectivist attitudes tend to be less interested in uniqueness and in defining a distinctive, individual self-conception. Self-esteem, for instance, is not a particularly important motivator for collectivists, who are more interested in identification with their group (Fiske et al., 1998). Individualists, by contrast, tend to exhibit greater motivation to protect their personal self-esteem, as well as to protect objects and possessions they associate with themselves and their identity (Morrison & Johnson, 2011). Such differences may affect which features of the nonhuman world a person values, or indicate whether different kinds of incentives will motivate their environmental behaviors. More specifically, how people respond to various incentives and messages might vary with their cultural orientation (or, *which* cultural orientation is triggered within them). Research suggests that individualists, for instance, recycle more or less depending on how convenient it is perceived as being; collectivists do so depending on how important they think it is (McCarty & Shrum, 2001).

Finally, it is worth noting that the generalizability of the research we canvass throughout this book may be cabined by cultural concerns. As we discuss in much more detail in Chapter 5, research in cultural psychology has shown that even some things that psychologists initially thought of as hardwired—such as the fundamental attribution error—show variance across cultures (Bruner, 1990; Markus & Kitayama, 1991; Choi et al., 1999).

The Psychological Effects of Valuation

Assigning monetary values to human-centric environmental goods and processes is difficult and prone to numerous psychological tics and errors. Yet people do it all the time, including in environmental contexts (Sunstein, 2005a). Moreover, people can and do evaluate non-human environmental goods and processes, and they can even trade them off against one another. Such trade-offs may be perceived as both cognitively and emotionally unpleasant (Tetlock, 2003), however, and may sometimes leave valuers with a feeling that something important has been lost (Ackerman & Heinzerling, 2002), or that there is some "remainder" that has not been successfully monetized or traded (Rowell, 2012b). So while it is possible to attach monetary value to nonhuman items that are not traded in markets, it is important to recognize the psychological consequences to doing so.

In classical economics, preferences are presumed to be fixed, and simply assessing their value cannot change them. But psychology allows the possibility that, like the observer effect in physics, the very act of measuring can distort the object being weighed. Furthermore, the distortion of the valuation process may be particularly large where the valuation is expressed in monetary terms. Studies on the priming effect of money show that merely being encouraged to think about money, or having a picture of a dollar bill in the background, can measurably change people's thoughts, feelings, motivations, and behaviors (Caruso et al., 2013; Vohs, 2015). The effect is significant enough that it can even measurably effect people's expressed normative values. One set of studies, for instance, found that even incidental exposures to money led subjects to indicate greater support for inequality, socioeconomic differences, free-market economies, and group-based discrimination (Caruso et al., 2013; Rohrer et al., 2015).

Or consider the large body of literature showing that intrinsic motivation can be undermined by extrinsic incentives and trade-offs (Deci et al., 1999). An easy example to demonstrate this is to imagine paying someone enough to engage in altruistic behavior; say, donating blood (Titmuss, 2018). The act of giving and receiving payment literally converts the act from altruism into a market exchange. Those whose motivation to give blood was to engage in altruistic behavior may now not give blood at all. An experiment has demonstrated exactly this. Women were half as likely to donate blood when they were paid $7 as when they were paid $0. Yet when the $7 was given not to them but to a charity of their choice—preserving the act as altruism—blood donations went back up to baseline (Mellström & Johannesson, 2008). (The effect did not hold true for men, possibly because they were not as altruistically motivated in the first place.) Another example is if a couple in a marriage begin to keep exacting and careful records of who does what household chores. Tracking turns behavior that might once have been done in solidarity, or as a contribution to a joint enterprise, into something more transactional (Fiske & Tetlock, 1997)—and can actually change the partners' perception of the marriage itself. This kind of score keeping can erode the affection and harmony of an affectionate partnership (Grote & Clark, 2001).

In the context of valuing nonhuman environmental entities, this research raises the disturbing possibility that the process of quantifying and monetizing people's preferences regarding environmental goods may change the underlying values that policy makers are trying to measure. That is, the very act of monetizing a previously unmonetized thing could actually change people's willingness to engage in proenvironmental behaviors to protect it. There is some research suggesting this can indeed happen. Bruno Frey and his colleagues conducted an experiment where they asked Swiss residents if they were willing to allow a low-level radioactive waste site to be built in their community. Over half of the respondents did not object. However, when they asked another set of residents the same thing, but included the fact that the Swiss government was offering to pay each resident some compensation (a few thousand dollars) if the site were to be built in their community, the number who agreed to the site plummeted to less than a quarter (Frey & Oberholzer-Gee, 1997).

Of course, the downsides of valuation (and especially explicit monetization) may be worth the benefits it brings, at least under some circumstances. For instance, in the Frey study, one response might be to say that the Swiss government simply didn't pay *enough*. That is, maybe paying between $2,000 and $4,000 would get 25% of the population to agree, and paying $0 would get 51% of the population to agree, but paying $20,000 might get 90% of the population to agree—even though they'd only be doing it for the money. Does that mean the Swiss government should pay $0? Obviously, it depends—on how many resources it has to pay, on how much consensus it feels it needs, and on whether it worries about undermining pro-environmental attitudes on other projects by paying more for this one. Regardless, there will be challenges for the Swiss government if it seeks to use studies like this one to determine participants' underlying values, or to determine whether the site should be built at all. To be fair, the use of monetization in its most familiar form by U.S. agencies—where agencies use market and other data to attach estimates of what people would be willing to pay to secure environmental goods—may be relatively less subject to distorting valuations. Or perhaps more research in this area will further support economists' general preference for market-based studies that look at people's actual behaviors in markets rather than survey-based or stated-preference studies, in which the salience of the monetization may be heightened by the questions posed to participants. Regardless, environmental valuation should be undertaken with the recognition that asking people to attach quantified or monetized values to nonhuman environmental goods may actually influence how those goods are perceived.

Conclusion

In this chapter, we have argued that environmental law is marked by its distinctive focus on nonhuman impacts (including on animals, plants, landscapes, weather patterns, and the like), and that a core challenge of environmental law involves finding a way to attach value to those goods. The process of attaching value to such things is influenced by psychological phenomena. Cognitively, people's brains are well designed to evaluate human behaviors—but this very responsiveness to human cues makes people more likely to anthropomorphize nonhuman entities, which can distort their value. The usual panoply of cognitive heuristics can also distort valuation, causing people to attend to particular environmental goods not because they are important but also because they are salient or available. Emotionally and motivationally, valuations of nonhuman environmental goods and processes are governed by considerations that do not always work well with the conventional methods that legal actors use to elicit them, and which are not necessarily functions of use value alone. Often people value environmental goods according to how unique or scarce they are perceived as being, or how well they connect with them as expressions of their identities. People also tend to attribute intrinsic value to environmental goods in ways that are difficult to measure. Moreover, all of these emotional and motivational processes interact with religious/spiritual and cultural values in sometimes surprising ways. Finally, the very act of valuation itself can change the underlying value of the good. All of these psychological phenomena and processes further complicate the already daunting task of valuing the nonhuman environment in regulatory settings.

Key Aspects of the Psychology of Nonhuman Effects in Environmental Law

The target of environmental law is the natural environment, which distinctly includes the *nonhuman*: plants, nonhuman animals, landscapes, ecosystems, and natural processes such as weather patterns. Much of environmental law concerns valuations and trade-offs among these goods. Psychological research suggests that the value people attach to environmental goods departs from the assumptions conventional environmental law makes. In some cases, the nonhuman character of environmental goods may create barriers to empathy; in other circumstances, it may trigger hypersalience of some (but not all) environmental goods. Moreover, the very act of valuing such goods can change how they are perceived.

Cognitive, emotional, and motivational factors in valuing the nonhuman environment include:

- Anthropomorphism. People have a strong tendency to anthropomorphize nonhumans. This can increase how much people value the anthropomorphized good, but it can also cause misperceptions and false expectations about what the nonhuman thing is capable of, which can lead to its mismanagement.
- Availability/salience. People's tendency to rely on heuristics to make judgments can cause distortions in valuations of nonhuman goods. Nonhuman goods can be cognitively unavailable, for instance, because of their size, location, abstractness, etc.

- Instability of preferences. The nature of the environment is that it constantly changes and adapts. This contributes to instability in our valuation of it. And the fact that environmental goods are so often prized for multiple subjective reasons contributes to subjectivity and instability in valuing them.

- Uniqueness/identity. Nonhuman environmental goods are often literally unique. People have a general preference for unique goods over commodities. This preference is linked to concepts of *self*. People feel connected to unique goods around them as expressions of their *identity*.

- Scarcity. Even where nonhuman environmental goods are not perceived as unique, they are often perceived as rare. People prefer rare things to common ones and seek to acquire them before they disappear. This can lead to cognitive consequences such as increasing *salience/focus* or even *tunnel vision* about the good. These cognitive consequences can also lead to mismanagement of environmental goods.

- Perceiving intrinsic value. Some people attach intrinsic value to nature, and may even resist attempts to monetize or quantify it. People are more likely to see intrinsic value in things with which they identify and things that are similar to themselves.

- Religious/spiritual concerns. People also connect with the environment on a spiritual or religious level, again making it difficult to "measure" its value in any traditional (or tractable) way. We know that many people sanctify nature, but we do not yet understand what features of the environment (or of themselves) are likely to make them do so.

- Cultural values. How people process value differs across culture, which adds complication to the task of valuing nonhuman environmental goods.

- Distortions. The process of valuation can affect and distort the thing being valued. Problems may arise in particular from the process of quantification and monetization.

5

General Law and Psychology in Environmental Law

In the prior chapters, we have emphasized and discussed the aspects
of environmental law and environmental injury that we think can be
distinctively informed by psychological science: namely, those aspects
relating to the diffuse, complex, and nonhuman character of environmental injury. Yet psychological research has also revealed a whole host
of phenomena that affect how and whether laws can effectively regulate
in *any* area—environmental or not. Although readers may be familiar
with many of these findings, we believe we would be offering an incomplete account of the psychology of environmental law if we were to omit
fundamental findings in law and psychology from the book. With that
in mind, this chapter addresses what psychology has to say that may be
helpful to environmental law, as it is to other areas of law.

Very generally speaking, all law is concerned with shaping both attitudes and behaviors. This is not the only thing that law does or cares
about, of course. Law also allocates goods and bads; resolves disputes;
serves as a coordinating focal point for individuals, institutions, and
markets; supplies security and safety to its members (and even to outsiders); puts moral parameters on activities via rights and duties; and so
on. But while the law is not *only* about changing attitudes and behaviors,
it is *importantly* about doing so.

Attitudes are made up of, and shaped by, cognitions and emotions.
Behaviors are influenced by many things, including attitudes, but also
incentives, motives, and social norms. Interestingly, just as people's attitudes can affect their behaviors, people's behavior can feed back into
and affect their own attitudes. The whole process is socially contingent,
sensitive to how things are framed, and ironically often more influenced
by subtle mechanisms than by strong or obvious ones. Nevertheless, the
effects are often predictable.

In this chapter, we focus on what law and psychology can tell us about
getting people to change their attitudes and their behaviors—when at-

tempts to change might work, when they might fail, and why. Again, much of law is interested in doing this; this function does not distinguish environmental law from other domains. But it is a critical component of environmental law, and so we address it here.

Even limiting ourselves to this feature of the law, there are a number of ways to divide up the landscape, and any parceling will be imperfect. We also recognize that any attempt to summarize all of the relevant general empirical research and theoretical insight from psychology into a single chapter will necessarily be incomplete. So in this introductory chapter we have chosen to focus on the "biggest" phenomena—meaning those most commonly discussed in the literature in law and psychology more generally. We have grouped these into four broadly influential categories: persuasion, motivation (with emphasis on motivated cognition), cognition, and social influence. This organization reflects similarly broad categories often used within psychology—that said, these subtopics are clearly linked, and in many cases, readers may note that the phenomena we discuss could fit under more than one category. In each category, we first describe the broad strokes of the psychological research, and then give examples of how it might be used to understand the law generally, with particular emphasis on examples from environmental law. Note that some of these topics we have already discussed in the prior three chapters; we focus here on their applications as they apply specifically to attitude formation and change as well as behavior.

The field of psychology is only helpful to the law to the extent it is reliable, reproducible, and representative. With that in mind, we end the chapter by taking up two issues that have been the subject of a great deal of recent consideration in the field of psychology: the "replication crisis" and the move away from an overreliance on research subjects from Western student populations toward a more inclusive, and therefore representative, set of demographics.

Persuasion

Much of the earliest work in the field of experimental social psychology focused on how and why people change their minds—including how to get them to do so. Robert Cialdini (1984) summarized most of the classic research in the area in his straightforwardly named, best-selling book *Influence*, now in its 5th edition. In addition to compiling empirical research data, Cialdini spent three years embedded with what he calls "compliance professionals"—that is, salesmen, advertisers, PR executives, fundraisers, and the like—often even training to become one of them. From these experiences, Cialdini boiled the world of professional persuasion down to six bullet points: reciprocity, scarcity, authority, consistency, liking, and consensus. We discuss two of these themes (consistency and consensus) in greater detail under more directly relevant subtopics of this chapter, but we expand on the other four now.

Cialdini notes that people are fundamentally *reciprocators*—when they are given something, they feel a deep obligation to somehow return the favor. They are also predisposed to worry about *scarcity*—when a resource is (perceived as) low or fleeting, people are inclined to snap it up or even hoard it. People also tend to defer to the *authority* of experts—even if they are not always very sophisticated about discerning them. And finally, people are more likely to be influenced by those they like—who turn out to be, among other things, those who are *similar* to them. By intuiting these principles, compliance professionals can induce people to believe things they might not otherwise believe—and of course do things they might not otherwise do. And by exploiting these mechanisms of persuasion, people can be persuaded to believe and do a wide variety of things.

You have probably noticed that when you receive solicitations from charitable organizations in the mail, you are often given—with no obligation!—a "gift" such as a calendar, blank greeting cards, or address labels. Since people find it aversive to receive a gift and give nothing in return, the norm of reciprocity makes them far more likely to send money to the organization, even though they never wanted the gift in the first place, and even if it immediately ends up in the trash can. Another familiar example from daily life is the use of perceived scarcity by industries. These days, when you purchase airline tickets, you are often faced with a notice in red declaring "only three seats left at this price!" Through this technique, airlines expect that you will commit quickly to purchasing the ticket, cutting short a longer search that might reveal a lower price elsewhere or later. Airlines themselves, of course, are in control of how many seats they "release" for purchase at any given time and at any given price—and most people even know this. Yet the threat of scarcity can feel irresistible, and as Cialdini repeatedly shows, these techniques do work to increase sales for compliance professionals.

Persuasion research has fairly obvious applications to the law, including environmental law. Legal regimes frequently wish to change prevailing beliefs and dispositions and to alter behaviors of their constituents. They can use reciprocity and scarcity to help in doing so. Notably, such approaches contrast with the conventional approaches in political science and economics of emphasizing incentives (or compulsion) as a way to encourage contribution to public goods. Indeed, Dan Kahan showed that in many domains—tax compliance, policing, and the placement of environmentally noxious sites—reciprocity norms do a better job of explaining citizens' behaviors than do simple rewards or punishments (Kahan, 2003). The power of norms of reciprocity has been further established through laboratory experiments, where people contribute more to a public good when they believe others are contributing to it (Frey & Meier, 2004; Gächter, 2006). Such impacts have been shown for indigenous and place-based communities in maintaining fish stocks and forest management (Diver et al., 2019), and have also been shown in urban populations. We have already discussed Frey and Oberholzer-Gee's (1997) finding that the placement of noxious sites is accepted better by communities when they think it's a matter of civic duty. Another example is a finding by Monin and Norton (2003) that water conservation behaviors during a crisis were best explained by whether or not people believed their neighbors were conserving. Other psychological phenomena also explain why people do not act in a purely self-interested manner in these contexts, including as a result of as norms of fairness (e.g., Marwell & Ames, 1981), altruism (Batson, 2011), or other things (Dawes, 1980, for a review). But reciprocity norms do play a role (Frey & Stutzer, 2008).

In addition to exploiting (and even manipulating) scarcity and reciprocity, lawmakers often use authority pressures to change minds. For instance, they will try to garner support for bills and initiatives by deploying experts to argue the case in media outlets. Better still if these appeals to authority are coupled with the mechanism of liking. The most convincing experts, for example, are attractive (Hovland et al., 1953) and share the listener's worldview (Cooper et al., 1996; Kahan et al., 2010).

As evidence for the interest that the legal system as a whole takes in understanding how to persuade, consider that much of the earliest research in the field of persuasion in social psychology was funded by the United States government. As one of the earliest examples, in response to the need to ration meat and other agricultural products during World War II, the Department of Defense hired Kurt Lewin (later known as the father of social psychology) and other social psychologists to try to persuade housewives in Kansas to accept "variety" meat cuts (that is, animal organs as opposed to the more conventional muscle tissue) as edible food (Wansink, 2002). When these studies were eventually declassified and revealed via a Freedom of Information Act (FOIA) request in the mid-1990s, it became clear that many of the basic principles of persuasion in social psychology were elucidated and advanced by this early applied work.

Lewin—and the U.S. government—learned that extolling the patriotic and other virtues of a policy are not enough to change attitudes and behaviors. Successful persuasion also requires incentives and the reduction of barriers to change. People reject the unfamiliar and the surprising, and they do not tend to select goods that are hard to access. They also take cues from their surroundings—if their neighbors buy into something, they are more likely to do so themselves. In the context of organ meats, this means that if they are introduced slowly, made easily available, and come with instructions to prepare them in ways that are familiar, and if people see their neighbors eating and enjoying them, then other people will go ahead and try them too (Wansink, 2002). These lessons from the history of "variety" meat acceptance generalize for any preferences or behaviors the government wishes people would take on.

As it relates to the environment in particular, these sorts of techniques of persuasion have been shown to affect behaviors as diverse as encouraging resource conservation (Dickerson et al., 1992) and recycling (Schultz, 1999), and discouraging littering (Cialdini et al., 1990). Interventions to encourage pro-environmental behaviors need to be crafted carefully. If they are insufficiently attentive to psychological phenomena, not only might they not work; they can backfire (Cialdini, 2003).

Motivation

Motivated Cognition

The classic findings of persuasion continue to be relevant to the law today, but the field of attitude research has undergone a sea change in the last couple of decades or so with recognition of the phenomenon of *motivated cognition*. Learning and believing, it turns out, are guided by motives. A crude way to put this is that people tend to believe what they want to believe. Yet how this basic phenomenon plays out in practice can be extraordinarily complicated.

Consider the motive to be accurate. In most circumstances, such a desire leads to careful, unbiased decision making (Chaiken et al., 1996; Kunda, 1990). But human desires encompass much broader goals than accuracy—and these desires can lead to *less* careful, and indeed systematically biased decision making. Modern social psychological research has described how attitudes are not merely a function of objective information or reference points but very fundamentally are also a product of values, self, and identity. You do not merely know certain things, but you are the *kind of person* who knows certain things—and this affects how you learn them, and it can bias your beliefs.

The desire for specific outcomes affects memory, processing, and inferences. That is, people literally perceive the world differently depending on what they wish to perceive. People remember information that is consistent with their preferred positions better than that which is inconsistent (Croston & Pedersen, 2013; Eitam et al., 2013; Hennes et al., 2016). They even perceive things differently in the first place depending on their desires (Hastorf & Cantril, 1954). In one of the earliest and most evocative demonstrations of this point, poor children overestimated the physical size of coins relative to their richer peers (Bruner & Goodman, 1947). Motives cause people to process information differently as well. For instance, they tend to internally counterargue against positions they don't like while letting preferred positions alone, and they seek out consistent but not inconsistent information (Taber & Lodge, 2006), which biases them toward their preferred conclusions. People also tend to accept as correct conclusions that are consistent with their prior convictions more readily than those that conflict with them (Kuhn, 1989). Ironically, their prior convictions often actually *strengthen* when faced with opposition evidence (Lord et al., 1979; Redlawsk, 2002). Some of the most interesting work of recent years has demonstrated the cognitive effects not just of motivation but of emotion. While classically emotion has been described as contrary to reason, more modern scholarship sees emotional commitments as *central* to reasoning (Damasio, 2006; Zajonc, 1984; Abelson, 1963).

For a legal regime governing a diverse population that—often vehemently—disagrees with one another, these findings have important implications. It is one thing to convince people of something they had not previously thought about, which had little or nothing to do with their personal identity, or that they just did not care much about one way or the other, like eating organ meats or ceasing littering. It is a different thing altogether to regulate in areas where beliefs signal membership in particular communities or express commitments to fundamental values. Yale Law School has an entire center dedicated to research on how motivated cognition affects a wide variety of laws and policies that touch on highly contested areas of gender, race, class, power, and sexuality, including: the willingness to vaccinate one's child against the sexually transmitted HPV virus (Kahan et al., 2010), how juries (and even, critically, judges) evaluate the reasonableness of police seizures (Kahan et al., 2009), the speech/conduct distinction in constitutional law (Kahan, Hoffman et al., 2012), perceptions of consent in rape (Kahan, 2010), and more. Changing attitudes and behaviors in domains of strongly motivated cognition is one of the biggest problems the law faces.

Whether it should be so or not, environmental law is rife with areas of regulation where citizens have strongly motivated beliefs. Climate change, in particular, is an example of this phenomenon underscored, bolded, and italicized—at least in the United States. We live in a world where many citizens refuse to acknowledge the importance, or even existence, of climate change—yet for the most part, evidence suggests that people who resist it do not know less about it, nor are they scientifically illiterate or innumerate (Kahan, Peters et al., 2012), as we discussed earlier. The refusal to believe in human-made climate change is instead strongly correlated with political affiliation and worldview. Democrats are more likely to believe in it than Republicans (O'Connor et al., 2002), for instance—a dichotomy that has increased over time (Dunlap, 2008). As such, people are not as motivated by scientific communications that attempt only to appeal to their cognitions as they are to ones that appeal to their emotions and cultural commitments. This obviously complicates efforts to regulate in this domain.

The Desire for Consistency

People have a desire to be, and to appear to be, consistent. They prefer to mean what they do and do what they mean. This desire is so powerful that when people are induced to act in ways that are inconsistent with their attitudes, either their behavior or their beliefs will eventually give, a phenomenon known as *cognitive dissonance reduction.*

In the foundational experiment demonstrating the phenomenon, students were paid to engage in a mind-numbing task of rearranging pegs on a board (Festinger & Carlsmith, 1959). At the end, all students were told that the next research participant was waiting outside, and they were asked to tell him that the task was fun. Half of the students were told they would be paid $1, and half $20, if they told the white lie—and all did. Immediately afterward, they were asked to rate how fun the experiment *actually* was. Those who were paid only $1 rated it as significantly more entertaining than those who were paid $20. Why? Both sets of students had acted inconsistently with their actual (initial) feelings: The task was objectively dull, but they had said it was not. But was their behavior really inconsistent with their true beliefs? The students paid $20 weren't really acting inconsistently at all—what college student in 1959 *wouldn't* tell a harmless lie for the then-whopping sum of $20? But the students paid only $1 had no such covering explanation. They had told the lie with little incentive at all. Once uttered, they could not undo the behavior of having told a white lie in order to make their actions consistent with their true beliefs. But they *could* change their beliefs! To make their actions and beliefs consistent, they simply had to decide that the peg-rearranging task wasn't so bad after all.

The basic finding that people seek to reduce the unpleasant sensation of cognitive dissonance through either changes in their behavior or (more usually) changes in their attitudes has since been replicated in literally hundreds of studies, using various paradigms (Harmon-Jones & Mills, 1999). It has even been found to be true of nonhuman primates (Egan et al., 2010; Egan et al., 2007). It is not a limitless phenomenon, however, and the different paradigms for demonstrating the effect shed some light on those limits.

To induce dissonance, the behavior must be engaged in willingly. This is another reason for the Festinger and Carlsmith findings. The Festinger and Carlsmith study used what is now known as a "forced compliance" paradigm—the students paid $20 were "forced," in the sense that they were made an offer they couldn't refuse. When people feel they were *forced* to engage in a behavior inconsistent with their attitudes, no dissonance occurs, because the behavior is easily explained by the coercive influence. If, on the other hand, they are more subtly manipulated into engaging in an inconsistent behavior (like being paid $1, with the *real* coercion—social pressure—being relatively invisible to them), dissonance ensues. Dissonance can occur when one chooses among similarly valuable options (Brehm, 1956) and then rates their value after the fact. Compared to those who were simply assigned an option, the choosers rate the selected options more highly than the unchosen options. Why? People would like to think they act for a reason—to the point where they will impute a preference for a choice that in fact they made essentially randomly. Again, in short, we only feel dissonance between our behaviors and our actions when we think we have actually *chosen* to act.

In another experimental technique to test cognitive dissonance (the "effort justification" paradigm), researchers get participants to either expend effort of some kind on some task or not, and then they measure how valuable the task (or outcome) is to them. Participants typically rate the task as more valuable when they have expended more effort (broadly defined) on it. Why? When we choose to work for things, we would like to think it was worthwhile to do so. To think otherwise introduces unpleasant dissonance. Indeed, the more effort we expend, the more value we attach to the object of the effort. In other words, experiments have shown not only that you spend more effort on things you find valuable but that spending effort *causes* you to think it is valuable. This effect is so fundamental that the effect has been shown in monkeys and young children (Egan et al., 2007) and even in rats (Lydall et al., 2010).

The applications to law are clear. The law mandates unpleasant or difficult experiences all the time: paying taxes, going to school as a child, getting licenses for a profession, deploying soldiers, and on and on. But to the degree these experiences are seen as at least partly voluntary and also effortful, citizens are likely to value the underlying goals or results *more* for having done them. After willingly paying a tax or voting up a bond offering, public works projects are seen as necessary. After attending school past the age one could legally drop out, education is seen as important. After going through the burdensome process of registering for a profession or activity, licensing is seen as ensuring quality control. After willingly enlisting in an all-volunteer army, wars appear increasingly just.

In environmental law, cognitive dissonance reduction can help explain some otherwise surprising findings about public perceptions. For example, studies have shown weak or even negative relationships between closeness to a refinery and self-reported health symptoms (Luginaah et al., 2002; Luginaah et al., 2000). Similarly, students chronically exposed to smog are more likely to deny or ignore its existence compared to newcomers to the pollution (Evans et al., 1988). These findings can be explained by attitude change spurred by dissonance reduction: If citizens have chosen to live near a polluting site, then it is probably easier to conclude that the pollution is not so bad after all than to move away. Of course, other explanations are plausible as well. People who simply mind pollution less might be more likely to choose to live closer to it. Or, after living with pollution, perhaps they objectively learn it really is not as bad as they would have guessed. The point is not that cognitive dissonance is *all* that explains the differences in perceptions about environmental stressors—but it may explain some of it.

Not only does cognitive dissonance help explain why people might mind (some) pollution less than may be good for them, it also suggests that there are effects from *how* governments decide to site sources of pollution. We should expect people to mind pollution less to the degree they perceive (either accurately or not) that they *chose* the exposure (Slovic, 2000). True enough, providing large and obvious incentives to locate polluting conditions within a community might well lead a community to (grudgingly) acquiesce to the siting. But if the dissonance theory works here, then ironically, providing *lower* and *less* obvious incentives might cause the community not just to acquiesce but possibly to embrace it (Frey & Oberholzer-Gee, 1997). And both as cognitive dissonance research would predict and as researchers actually found, providing *no* monetary incentive at all is likely to lead to the highest levels of attidunal acceptance, since that condition demonstrates the highest level of voluntarism (Frey & Oberholzer-Gee, 1997).

Cognitive dissonance reduction can also help explain support—or lack thereof—for things like recycling. Although a person might think recycling is a good idea, if they do not have easy access to it, they are of course less likely to do it (Purdon et al., 2010). But a psychologist would predict that as people find themselves *not* recycling because of its inaccessibility, over time, their *support* for recycling will diminish, and they are likely to lower their estimates of the value of the activity. This is because, ironically, people look at their own behavior to assess how they feel about something. This can cut both ways: As engagement in an environmentally responsible behavior is induced (preferably through subtle means), support for the value of that activity would be expected to increase. Moreover, the more cognitive dissonance a target can be induced to feel, the stronger (and more lasting) should be the effect on behavior. Inducing a feeling of hypocrisy is a particularly effective and long-lasting way to induce environmentally responsible behaviors. This dynamic has been demonstrated in the realm of water conservation efforts. Research subjects who were induced not only to advocate for water conservation to peers but who were then reminded of ways they themselves had failed to live up to their stated beliefs in water conservation subsequently used less water than controls in whom a sense of hypocrisy had not been induced (Dickerson et al., 1992).

Finally, cognitive dissonance reduction may help to explain some otherwise counterintuitive findings about how people engage with and understand the law itself. One study found, for instance, that when people's beliefs about the law are inaccurate, they tend to get the law wrong in ways that comport with their own normative preferences and desires (Rowell, 2019). For example, whether participants *believed* they lived in a state with a constitutional right to a clean environment was better predicted by reference to their views about whether such a right was normatively desirable than by whether they *actually* lived in such a state. One way of understanding such findings is that people may feel incentivized to reduce dissonance by aligning their beliefs about what the law is with what they believe the law should be—even though doing so will sometimes lead them into factually inaccurate beliefs about the law. Whether or not this explanation is right, however, the finding itself has practical and theoretical implications, and it suggests that environmental law (like other areas of law) may need ways to overcome barriers to tasks as simple as putting people on notice about what the law is.

Cognitive Heuristics and Biases

Perhaps the most familiar set of psychological phenomena for most legal readers falls into the category of cognitive heuristics and biases such as those we have already touched upon in the prior three chapters. Psychologists and their behavioral economist friends have now accumulated robust evidence that human cognition operates along two coexisting systems. In terms popularized by psychologist Daniel Kahneman's best-selling book *Thinking, Fast and Slow*, these dual systems are now often called "System I"—a fast, emotional processing system that allows people to process information intuitively and quickly—and "System II"—a slower, deliberate system that allows people to process information coolly and reflectively (Kahneman, 2011). System I generally relies on heuristics: quick, easy-to-apply "rules of thumb" that help people speed up their analysis but that also run the risk of misfire.

In part because of heuristics, people's expressed preferences will often shift measurably in response to nonsubstantive changes in how information is presented—a phenomenon sometimes called "context dependence" or "framing" (Kahneman & Tversky, 2000). Small changes in contextual cues can therefore be used strategically to shape, or nudge, people's behaviors in a process called choice architecture (Thaler & Sunstein, 2003, 2008). In many cases, choice architecture builds directly on dual-process cognition by channeling behaviors via appeals to the affective, heuristic-based "System I."

In the subsections that follow, we provide a deeper treatment of the heuristics we have already described in prior chapters, and catalogue more of the most familiar or common heuristics. As we go, we highlight how such heuristics might particularly inform environmental law.

Loss Aversion, the Endowment Effect, and Status Quo Bias

As we saw earlier, research on the important phenomenon of loss aversion first grew out of research on prospect theory from psychologists Daniel Kahneman and Amos Tversky (1979). The basic insight underlying prospect theory is that losses hurt more than gains feel good: The magnitude of negative emotion people feel when experiencing a loss is greater than the magnitude of positive emotion people feel when experiencing an equally sized gain. The heightened sensitivity to loss is what is typically called loss aversion.

Researchers have built on the basic findings underlying prospect theory to identify a constellation of related phenomena, including the endowment effect and status quo bias (Kahneman et al., 1991; Korobkin, 2000; Korobkin, 2014). We discussed these in Chapter 2, but it is worth drawing attention to them further here, given how relevant they are to law generally and environmental law in particular.

Consider the basic findings of research on the endowment effect, which show that people value things they own more than things they do not own (yet). Most people are intuitively familiar with this phenomenon. How many of us have at least initially demanded a high price to sell, for instance, a well-loved used car, even though we would not have purchased the same model and year at that price? In daily life, such discrepancies can be explained by sentimental value or asymmetric information about the value of goods. But the phenomenon has also been demonstrated with newly acquired, interchangeable goods in controlled experimental settings (Kahneman et al., 2008). The original experiments on students, for instance, involved giving a group of them either a chocolate bar or a mug that they could easily have bought for themselves at the gift shop on campus (Knetsch, 1989). When the students were given the choice of either the mug or the chocolate, preferences for one or the other were about evenly divided. When instead researchers *assigned* them to get a mug or a chocolate bar, and then opened a market where the participants were invited to trade, things changed. Based on the free-choice condition, one might have expected about 50% of the goods to swap owners, since only half would have randomly been assigned what they would have chosen for themselves. Instead, hardly anyone traded. The mere fact of having been given one of the goods made the students value it more than they otherwise would have.

As with cognitive dissonance studies, endowment effect studies now easily number in the hundreds. And as with cognitive dissonance studies, the effect has even been found in nonhuman primates (Brosnan et al., 2007; Flemming et al., 2012; Lakshminaryanan et al., 2008). But as fundamental as the phenomenon is, there are both limits to it and situations that exacerbate it. The more commodity-like the good is, or the more commercial the market, the weaker the effect. For instance, the effect disappears altogether among professional sports memorabilia traders (List, 2003). And the more blood, sweat, and tears the individual puts into creating the good, the stronger the effect is, a phenomenon researchers dubbed the "creativity effect" (Buccafusco & Sprigman, 2011). Recent research also suggests that different populations might experience the endowment effect in different ways. Specifically, when a person is in a condition of perceived scarcity, she will be hyperaware of the "true" value of resources, making her less likely to suffer from the endowment effect at all (Mullainathan & Shafir, 2013; Shah et al., 2012).

The endowment effect is not monolithic. Trades do happen, and most markets do, after all, clear—at least eventually, even if not optimally. Indeed, when given extensive instructions, lots of practice, and generally making it as clear as possible that valuing interchangeable goods more just because you happen to own them is irrational, experimental research subjects will stop exhibiting the effect altogether (Plott & Zeiler, 2005, 2007). But the effect as experienced in real-life circumstances seems both common and powerful.

Research on the endowment effect has been particularly influential within law (Jolls et al., 1998; Korobkin, 2000; Plott & Zeiler, 2013), and there are a number of applications of the endowment effect within environmental law. The endowment effect has been used, for instance, to explain why people are willing to pay relatively little for clean air but demand many times that amount to give it up (Knetsch, 1990, 2007). Indeed, gaps between the willingness to pay (WTP) and the willingness to accept (WTA) for environmental goods provided the inspiration for the original experimental research on the endowment effect. Furthermore, a review of the research suggests that the impact of the endowment effect is particularly large for goods—like environmental goods—which are not routinely traded in markets (Horowitz & McConnell, 2000); for these goods, willingness to pay (WTP) to secure an environmental amenity is often only one-tenth what participants identify as their willingness to accept (WTA) the loss of the same environmental amenity. As a result, which measure is used to inform environmental policies can have an enormous impact on which policies look to be desirable (Knetsch, 2007).

Another aspect of research on loss and endowment concerns people's perception of the status quo, or what they perceive to be the background or default rule. This research suggests that a perceived status quo works as a baseline of entitlement, against which subsequent losses and gains are measured (Kahneman et al., 1991). As a result, people work both consciously and subconsciously to justify and promote what they perceive as the status quo (Jost et al., 2004). These findings have special import in law. Once people identify a rule or an allocation as the status quo, they tend to stick with it (Thaler & Benartzi, 2004; Korobkin, 2014). This phenomenon has been used to explain why legal grants of entitlements, as in property disputes, tend to stick, even when—contrary to the Coase Theorem—you might otherwise expect at least a few of the parties to successfully negotiate around the final legal decision (Korobkin, 2014; Farnsworth, 1999).

Because the framing of something as a loss or a gain can change how people understand (and whether they will accept) various legal regulations, knowledge of this discontinuity can be used to effectively promote regulations to lawmakers and the public. Framing effects are also foundational to literature on choice architecture. The famous behavioral intervention of the nudge, which seeks to alter people's behavior in a predictable way by shifting the context in which the decision is made (Thaler & Sunstein, 2008), relies on the stickiness of default rules to encourage people to act in ways that serve their own ends. Although the use of behavioral instruments in environmental law offers significant opportunity (Byerly et al., 2018), thus far it continues to lag behind uses of more traditional instruments, such as command-and-control and economic instruments (Rowell, 2020a).

Other Cognitive Heuristics and Biases

There is a large number of other cognitive biases and heuristics, ranging from the well known to the as yet uncatalogued, all of which have a tendency to affect behavior in predictable and frequently (but not always) irrational ways. We have already described availability and representativeness biases and their close cousins at length in other chapters. Below, we add two more cognitive biases that we believe are most relevant to the law generally, while again also explaining ways we think they apply to environmental law in particular. We conclude this section by discussing how seriously regulators should take the panoply of cognitive biases from which humans have been demonstrated to suffer.

HINDSIGHT BIAS

Hindsight bias (Fischhoff & Beyth, 1975) is the "knew it all along" phenomenon, and it can sharply affect the estimation of the likelihood of risks. The first scholars to describe its application to law noted that the fundamental task of jurors in negligent torts is to determine the ex ante odds that an event would happen. Kim Kamin and Jeff Rachlinski (1995) demonstrated that research participants gave higher probabilities that a potentially tortious accident *would* happen after they learned it actually *did* happen, relative to a condition where they did not know it happened. Such a bias, of course, would systematically inflate findings of negligence by jurors. The hindsight bias in practice could thus effectively convert a negligence regime into something closer to a strict liability system, possibly causing industry to take excessive precautions to avoid injuries. Jeff Rachlinski used this notion to argue for the value of a regulatory compliance defense for environmental tortfeasors, to safeguard against the excessive liability that the hindsight bias might otherwise inflict on industry (Rachlinski, 2000a).

It may be worth noting that there is a troubling lacuna left by research on hindsight bias. While Kamin and Rachlinski showed that research subjects rate the probability of risks as higher when assessed after the fact, it is unclear whether the inflated likelihoods that people perceive after the fact are necessarily less accurate. Indeed, it could be that people *under*estimate risks when assessed in advance—that a hindsight evaluation can actually be *more* accurate. As Richard Posner put it, "[H]indsight bias is often rational (for example, when the occurrence of an accident shows that a hypothetical possibility was a real one) and thus not an illusion at all" (Posner, 1999, p. 1528). Moreover, people are quite bad at assessing many kinds of risk" particularly many forms of environmental risk. This may be especially true for risks that are legitimately rare or hard to imagine, such as those attached to catastrophes or to very-uncommon events (Wiener, 2016). Depending on which kind of environmental risk is being evaluated and potentially regulated, a cognitive estimation "bias" (either in foresight or hindsight) could either correct for or *exaggerate* the true probability of the event. Thus, environmental regulators should not only be aware of the differences between evaluating risks in hindsight versus foresight—but also mindful that they do not jump to conclusions about which one is an error when the estimates differ.

Other cognitive phenomena that can distort people's estimations of risks are the availability and representativeness heuristics, first described by Kahneman and Tversky and since identified in thousands of settings, and the affect heuristic, which operates at the boundary of cognitive bias and emotion. Since we have already addressed the availability and representativeness heuristics at some length in Chapter 2, we turn now to the affect heuristic.

THE AFFECT HEURISTIC

Another cognitive phenomenon with important implications for environmental law is the affect heuristic, a phenomenon that operates at the boundaries of cognitive biases and emotion (Rowell 2019). The affect heuristic is the tendency to make decisions based on immediate, intuitive emotional reactions (Slovic et al., 2002). In such cases, "hot," emotional, System I feelings overtake "cool," reflective, System II opinions. Within environmental law, fear and disgust may play particularly important roles, as may the triggering of empathy. When the affect heuristic is triggered, it forges an insidious mental connection between costs and benefits: When people perceive something to be high risk, they perceive it to be low benefit, and vice versa (Slovic et al., 2002; Sunstein, 2002a, 2002c). This means that people often struggle to process policies that provide both risks and benefits, particularly if the policy's impact generates strong emotional reactions. When an activity or policy is perceived as frightening, disgusting, or risky, its benefits may be discounted. This can impact people's views about high-emotion environmental policies that generate both risks and rewards, such as nuclear power generation or the propagation of genetically modified foods. Emotional responses can also contribute to an "all or nothing" response to chemical substances, where people act as intuitive toxicologists, believing that a substance is either healthy in all quantities or dangerous in all quantities (Neil et al., 1994; Sunstein, 2002a). We discuss this effect in more detail in

Chapter 6, as we have much to say about the relationship between emotional responses like disgust, and people's management of pollution risks in particular.

REFLECTING ON COGNITIVE HEURISTICS AND BIASES

In environmental law, as in other areas of law, heuristic shortcuts can bias decision makers in unfortunate ways. The availability heuristic, for instance, is why people overestimate some remote but vivid environmental risks, such as a meltdown at a nuclear power plant—their visualizable and exotic (and consequently well-publicized) nature makes them easier to recall. It may also lead people to think easily of the importance of saving large and charismatic mammals, like polar bears, from extinction, while neglecting small and ugly animals—like worms or insects—even if the impact of extinction is as great or greater for the less salient animals. Since environmental law is fundamentally concerned with estimating and regulating risks, practitioners, scholars, and decision makers are well served to be aware of these potential cognitive biases as they do their work.

That said, one might fairly make the point that the sheer number and variety of heuristics makes it difficult, if not impossible, to be certain which one will apply in any given circumstance and in what direction. Consider again the finding that people overestimate remote, vivid risks and underestimate common or hard-to-imagine ones. The availability heuristic might explain this phenomenon because remote but vivid risks are exotic and memorable, and therefore easily recalled—but then again, why aren't *common* risks more "available" because they are more frequently encountered and comprehensible? Or consider loss aversion. As we discussed, almost any given exchange can be coded as either a loss *or* a gain. When I purchase a coffee mug, I can either see it as a gain of a coffee mug or a loss of the cost of the mug (say, $5). Which is it? Or consider the hindsight/foresight pairing—if people sometimes make errors from estimating risks before the fact, as Posner contends, and sometimes make errors from estimating them afterward, as Rachlinski points out, how can we know in advance which will be the error? The study of heuristics and biases can start to feel like Karl Llewellyn's famous article on dueling canons of statutory construction, in which he described, for every canon, an equal and opposite one (Llewellyn, 1949).

As with canons of construction, one can be left with the sense that the study of heuristics and biases will inevitably lead to just-so explanations for attitudes and behaviors with no real predictive power.

But this argument against the utility of learning heuristics and biases is weaker, ultimately, than even the argument against canons of construction. First, as with canons of construction, one heuristic often just seems to apply in a given situation in a given way for most people (such as, for instance, how most people, most of the time, code the sale of an object as a loss of that object rather than the gain of money). But second, psychology researchers have also considerably refined their understanding of these cognitive shortcuts so that we increasingly do have a good sense for when and how they apply even in more ambiguous cases, and we are at least starting to understand more about how they interact with one another (Fiedler & von Sydow, 2015).

For example, the classic work on environmental endowment effects considered fairly simple trades of money for environmental goods. But it turns out how a good was acquired in the first place might affect whether the subsequent exchange of that good is considered a loss or a gain. When a good was acquired for money in the first place, rather than endowed (essentially, gifted) to the owner, the sale of that good is more likely to be coded as a gain of money to the seller (Novemsky & Kahneman, 2005). To the extent environmental goods are seen as affirmatively acquired commodities, their exchange for something else (money, another environmental good, or perhaps another intangible good like social justice) similarly is less likely to be coded as a loss. In contrast, to the extent that an environmental good can be described as an entitlement (like a political right of a citizen), its exchange would be coded as a loss and thus more resistant to exchange. Of course, people working in environmental law cannot be expected to stay at the cutting edge of all this research, but being familiar with the most common heuristics will at least point them in the right direction for further investigation and help them to avoid obvious pitfalls.

There are other heuristic phenomena that are relevant to understanding environmental law and regulation, ones that lead us to fail in various ways to understand why others do what they do, or whether they even believe what we think they believe. We tend, for example, to think that others agree with us when they do not (Ross et al., 1977), or that others agree with each other when they do not ("pluralistic ignorance") (Katz & Allport, 1931), or that if they do disagree with us, it must be because they are craven or ignorant rather than because we are wrong (Ross & Ward, 1996). These cognitive and emotional quirks can also affect how policy makers and citizens perceive the distribution of environmental goods and bads across and within communities. The interpersonal nature of this last set of heuristics leads now to our discussion of another critical class of psychological theories relevant to the law—those that deal with the social environment.

Social Influence

People are social animals (Aronson, 2011) with a fundamental need to belong. When this need is not satisfied, it has wide-ranging consequences, from the emotional, to the cognitive, and even to the physical (Baumeister, 2012; Baumeister et al., 2007; Baumeister & Leary, 1995). As we discussed in Chapter 2, people are also fundamentally "groupy"— they form group identifications based on thin and even arbitrary criteria, like, for instance, whether they tend to "overestimate" or "underestimate" the number of dots printed on a card (Tajfel & Turner, 1988). They then immediately begin to preferentially treat their fellow in-group members relative to the out-group—sometimes even at material cost to themselves (Brewer, 1979).

As a consequence, people are motivated to maintain good relationships with others who share their social identity—and this leads to a tendency to conform to the observed behaviors of others, a tendency that grows the more people share a group identification. The reasons for this phenomenon are many: At a visceral level, groups provide safety, and exile in the earliest days of humankind could be deadly. Even more potently today, when an individual departs from group consensus, the individual might conclude that the group simply knows something he does not know ("informational conformity"). Or, a nonconforming individual might worry that a failure to go along with the group would result in embarrassment or ostracization ("normative conformity") (Deutsch & Gerard, 1955).

The informational conformity phenomenon was first demonstrated in 1935 by Muzafer Sherif. He exploited a low-level cognitive phenomenon called the autokinetic effect: When people are shown a spot of light in a dark room, it appears to move, even though it is perfectly still. Sherif asked participants to estimate how far the light "moved"—though of course, in reality, the light had not moved at all. When tested individually, the estimates ranged widely between people. But when tested in groups of three, the groups quickly converged on a consensus opinion (Sherif, 1935). Moreover, these estimates persisted over subsequent generations as new participants were gradually swapped in (MacNeil & Sherif, 1976). In the absence of any objective information about an ambiguous situation, people turn to each other, and the socially constructed judgments that result are prone to stick.

Even when the situation is *not* ambiguous, people are still influenced by those around them. Normative conformity was most famously demonstrated by Solomon Asch (Asch & Guetzkow, 1951), in what are now collectively referred to as the Asch experiments. Asch brought students into the laboratory and asked them to engage in a simple, repeated test. Participants were shown a line, and then directly below it, three other lines. One of the lines was identical to the line to which they were comparing it; the other two very obviously were not. Their job was to identify the correct match. The testing occurred in groups, and individuals gave their answers out loud and in turn. Asch's ingenious wrinkle was that there was actually only one research subject in each group. The rest were planted confederates who were instructed to occasionally answer wrongly but uniformly. In other words, if the correct answer was "A," the confederates would occasionally all answer "C." When the real research subjects were the first to answer, they essentially never made a mistake—unsurprisingly, as the task was purposefully a simple one. When research subjects went last, however, after all the confederates had answered incorrectly, the real subject frequently also answered incorrectly, either agreeing with the confederates or at least taking a middle ground (though still wrong) position. (Intriguing, though less well known, is the fact that Asch conducted an additional, inverted version of the study, in which the tested group was made up of all real research subjects, with only one confederate in the room. In an interesting demonstration of the social risk people take when they defy the group, the research subjects in this version of the study were visibly incredulous—and openly contemptuous—when the stone-faced confederate repeatedly defied the group and got the simple task wrong.)

These core social influence studies have begotten decades of subsequent demonstrations and extensions of the power of social influence. For instance, people generally assess the quality of their situation not in objective terms but relative to others ("relative deprivation") (Bernstein & Crosby, 1980; Crosby, 1976). Thus, receiving a raise of $1,000 is no longer gratifying once you learn all your colleagues received a raise of $2,000. People even assess their own emotions relative to how others are behaving. Schachter & Singer (1962) showed that when taking a survey while in a nonspecific physiological state of arousal (induced by a dose of epinephrine), people coded their own feelings as either angry or happy based on whether a confederate in the room, who was supposedly taking the same survey, was expressing irritation or delight at the questions.

One of the most famous demonstrations of the power of the social situation is the question of when a bystander will intervene in an emergency (Latané & Darley, 1970). Darley and Latané showed that, ironically, the more people who are nearby in an emergency, the *less* likely anyone is to help. And the reason is not apathy (as is often assumed by pundits in the wake of crimes where no Good Samaritans step forward), or even entirely because of a diffusion of responsibility (that is, the sense that you do not need to help out in an emergency because someone else is likely to do it). Instead, it is the fact that people decide whether there is an emergency *at all* by carefully looking to others to see how they are responding to it. Is the man lying on a stoop in the street a drunk sleeping off a bender, or has he just had a heart attack? We dread overreacting and being seen as a meddler, so we wait to see how others respond before we intervene. Since everyone is doing this simultaneously, in groups of bystanders often no one will act at all. But since there is no fear of such social embarrassment when we are alone, single actors respond quickly and decisively in the face of identical possible emergencies. The power of this phenomenon is so strong that it occurs even when *we* are the one who might be in danger. In one study, Darley and Latané slowly filled a room with smoke through the vents while a research participant was filling out a survey. When the participants were alone in the room, 75% immediately notified an experimenter. But when taking the survey in a room filled with seemingly unconcerned confederates, fewer than 40% of participants did so. Indeed, several stayed in the room, silently working, even to the point where they could no longer see their papers.

The relevance of the power of social influence to the law cannot be overstated. People are motivated at least as much by what their fellow citizens think, and what they *think* their fellow citizens think, as they are by direct sanctions and incentives or by objective outcomes. Consider the Minnesota tax experiments. Researchers convinced the state's department of revenue to send different versions of letters to taxpayers, one of which (truthfully) emphasized that their fellow citizens were fully paying their taxes. Recipients of that version of the letter reported more income in the subsequent year relative to those who instead received a letter that simply told them how often taxpayers were audited (Vihanto, 2003). Social influence has been shown to induce legal compliance for many criminal and regulatory rules as well (Kahan, 1997; Lessig, 1996; Meares & Kahan, 1998) and to affect whether people are willing to report offenses (Goudriaan et al., 2005; Ruback et al., 1984).

Moreover, compliance is tied to whether or not a citizen believes he has been treated well by law enforcers. Why? Because respectful treatment makes the citizen infer that he is a valued member of the group (Tyler, 1990; Tyler & Lind, 1992), which makes him in turn more likely to support its rules and norms. Tom Tyler, for instance, describes how police find it frustrating that they can reduce crime in an area through aggressive enforcement, yet nevertheless still face the specter of a hostile and resistant community who fails to appreciate their efforts or work with them to investigate crimes. But by understanding that people care not just about outcomes (safe streets) but also about social respect, police officers can perform their jobs better (Trinkner & Tyler, 2016; Trinkner et al., 2016).

In environmental law, too, social influence plays a large role. Obviously, it is relevant to whether people will support, or comply with, various mandates to engage in environmentally responsible behaviors. But it is also relevant to, for instance, selecting sites for pollution emitters. Support or opposition to such sitings or other burdensome regulations is likely to be based at least in part on whether affected people perceive support or opposition by their neighbors (Sokoloski et al., 2018), whether they think they are being treated fairly in the procedures used to make the decisions (Baxter, 2017), and how attached they feel to the social identity most affected by a regulation (Devine-Wright & Batel, 2017). And, of course, even whether they believe in things like climate change at all will be at least in part a function of whether those around them (or those like them) believe in it (Fielding & Hornsey, 2016). Even their willingness to discuss environmental issues can be a function of what they think their neighbors think—and ignorance about their neighbors' actual beliefs may well entrench false understandings (Geiger & Swim, 2016).

Other General Issues in Psychology Relevant to Law

We have already discussed those lines of psychological research we believe to be distinctively and pervasively relevant to environmental law. Furthermore, when a psychological effect seems particularly and perhaps uniquely applicable to one substantive area of environmental law—as for instance the discussion of disgust to pollution control—we reserve our discussion for where it is most relevant. Yet there are, of course, many other psychological theories and findings relevant to the law generally, and this chapter has aimed to curate an overview of the most important of these, rather than create a comprehensive catalogue of all of them.

While we have done our best to draw attention where we believe attention is most due, there are necessarily some areas of psychology that, while potentially relevant to environmental law, we have nevertheless left out. Partly, this omission is for the sake of brevity. But it also reflects a sense on our part that, while these areas may be relevant to environmental law in some circumstances, they are perhaps no more relevant there than elsewhere (and sometimes less so).

So, for instance, we have not discussed at length theories of stereotyping, prejudice, and discrimination (Fiske, 2000; Nelson, 2009). Stereotyping is when individuals make false generalizations or predictions about another based on their membership in a group, prejudice describes animosity toward targeted groups, and discrimination is the behavioral treatment of members of targeted groups. They can operate independently—a concept with which lawyers are very familiar in the distinction between laws that are intentionally discriminatory versus those which "merely" have disparate impact. The psychological literature here is voluminous and helps to explain when and whether these phenomena will occur, and is relevant to, for instance, understanding where stereotypes apply specifically to environmental behaviors—as is arguably the case with the so-called "ecological Indian" stereotype (which we discuss further below). It is also relevant to the immensely important field of environmental justice (Bullard, 1993; Bullard, 2005; Schlosberg, 2009; Taylor, 2000), which has shown quite convincingly how marginalized groups tend to suffer the most from environmental harms. Still, while we think research in this area is highly relevant to the law generally (particularly employment law, criminal law, and the study of housing, education, poverty, and the like), and we do discuss it somewhat glancingly in several places in this book, we believe this area of psychology is not uniquely relevant to environmental law, and so would point the reader to more general treatments of the psychology of prejudice (e.g., Sibley & Barlow, 2016). In the remainder of this section, we address two general sources of controversy in general psychological science that have arisen in recent years: the question of generalizability from so-called "WEIRD" (Western, educated, industrialized, rich, and democratic) experimental subjects and concerns about replicability. There is no reason to think that these concerns loom larger over the psychology of environmental law than over any other area of law and psychology, but we believe it may be helpful here to flag them as concerns and describe the current state of the field in responding to them.

The Generalizability of Psychological Research

Recent years have seen a positive trend in general psychological research: a deliberate move away from a primary focus on so-called "WEIRD" research participants. Historically, psychologists have tended to draw from Western, educated, industrialized, rich, and democratic subject pools to do their work (Henrich et al., 2010). Perhaps more troubling still, they have often used the most convenient subject pool of all—undergraduates at their own educational institutions who are participating in research experiments for course credit.

The problems with reliance on such a limited section of the human population dawned on psychologists several decades ago. First came anxiety about reliance on college student populations, a worry that began in the 1940s and has not abated since—though reliance on those populations continued, largely unabated, for decades afterward (Peterson,

2001). This reliance was particularly concerning because, while much of the mental architecture of the human brain is developed by the teenage years, important differences remain between late adolescents and fully grown populations. For instance, younger populations are more sensitive to incentives (Cohen et al., 2010) and less deterred by novel risks (Tymula et al., 2012). The even more circumscribed test population comprised of *American* undergraduates "tend[s], among other things, to have incompletely formulated senses of self, rather uncrystallized sociopolitical attitudes, unusually strong cognitive skills, strong needs for peer approval, tendencies to be compliant to authority, quite unstable group relationships, little material self-interest in public affairs, and unusual egocentricity" (Sears, 1986, p. 527).

It was even later that psychologists began systematically thinking about broader social and demographic influences, and how they would affect the generalizability of their results given the test populations they typically relied upon. Specifically, researchers first began to study what came to be known as "cultural psychology" in the late 1980s. As it turned out, even some things that psychologists thought were hardwired, fundamental features of human mental life and perception did, in fact, differ systematically across populations (Bruner, 1990; Markus & Kitayama, 1991; Triandis, 1989; de Oliveira & Nisbett, 2017). It's hard to overstate how surprising some of these findings have been within psychology. Even things regarded as so central to human psychology that they were given names like the "fundamental attribution error" (often affectionately referred to as the "FAE") have not turned out to be so fundamental after all. The FAE holds that people attribute others' behavior to character and disposition, while attributing their own behavior to situational pressures and circumstance (Ross, 1977). Yet people from East Asian cultures, who tend to be more collectivist (in focusing on groups over individuals) than the individualist Western subjects on whom this original research was based, are much more likely to pay attention to the situational pressures that might explain others' behavior (Choi et al., 1999; de Oliveira & Nisbett, 2017). A number of other phenomena have been found to similarly vary as participants become less "WEIRD" and less American (Arnett, 2008).

Notably, the psychological differences between various subpopulations sometimes extend even to low-level perceptual phenomena—some of which may be particularly interesting for a reader interested in environmental law.

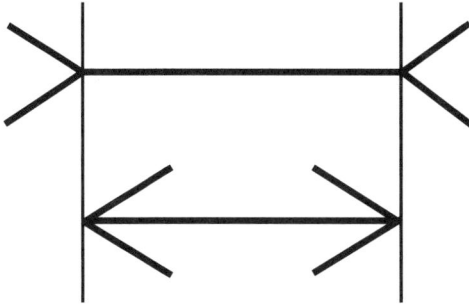

Figure 5.1. The Müller-Lyer illusion.

For instance, it turns out that people raised in urban environments suffer more from certain optical illusions, like the Müller-Lyer illusion shown in Figure 5.1, than do their rural counterparts (Segall et al., 1966).

Indeed, urban participants are worse at several other straight-line-based optical illusions too. Why? The researchers' working theory is that modern urbanites are raised in a world of "carpentered corners"; tall, upright buildings; and an absence of broad, uninterrupted horizons. During critical periods of early optical development, urbanites therefore developed "perceptual habits" that allow them to quickly comprehend and predict built spaces. As we know from discussions elsewhere in this book, cognitive shortcuts introduce risk of error—and that seems to be true here. What is novel is the notion that cognitive shortcuts can develop for cultural reasons.

The interaction of cultural psychology with environmental law can get quite complicated (Harris et al., 2017). Consider, for instance, the role that Indian tribes (who hold a complex quasi-sovereign status under U.S. law), and individual Native Americans, play in U.S. environmental law. They do so via their relationship with federal "Indian law" (U.S. law regarding indigenous peoples) and tribal law, and also as individuals. Since 1984, the EPA's policy for the administration of environmental programs on Indian reservations recognizes tribal governments as the primary parties for setting standards, making environmental policy decisions, and managing programs for reservations—though all such decisions are still required to comply with federal statutes and regulations.

Many tribes have traditional understandings of the appropriate relationship between humans and the environment that are different from, or even in tension with, U.S. federal policy. In some cases, behaviors that would be banned by federal or international law were guaranteed by treaty, as with the right of the Makah tribe to hunt whales (Treaty of Neah Bay, 1855). In other cases, specific federal laws make exceptions for some tribal beliefs and policies. For example, the so-called "eagle feather law" excepts individuals of certifiable American Indian ancestry from wildlife laws applicable to eagles and other migratory birds, allowing individual Indians and tribes to continue some traditional spiritual and cultural practices in which feathers play an important role (50 CFR § 22.2).

For some Indian tribes and individuals, the environment is related to cultural, social, and personal identity (Schure et al., 2013). As a result, cultural values may, in some cases, raise the salience of environmental impacts for Indian individuals or tribes. In addition, the role of identity-protective cognition has the potential to create distinctive challenges for Indians who identify with a cultural value of protecting the environment but who also may be faced with difficult economic and practical trade-offs in exchange for investing in environmental quality. In-group/out-group dynamics may play a role in decisions affecting indigenous populations too: Policy makers outside the indigenous group may underweight risks and harms to indigenous groups who are seen as out-groups, and similarly, indigenous people themselves may underweight environmental risks and harms to those who are seen as falling outside the tribe.

Finally, in the United States in particular, indigenous people may face a powerful psychological barrier in the form of the "ecological Indian" stereotype, which depicts them as the original environmentalists, living in harmony with their environment (Sturgeon, 2009). Imagery of Native Americans was particularly popular during the birth of the environmentalist movement in the United States in the 1960s and 1970s (the famous "crying Indian" anti-littering campaign being one example) (Deloria, 1998). In many cases, Indian actions continue to be interpreted against the backdrop of this stereotype, arguably increasing the salience of—and attention to—Native American actions that deviate from it. This has been used to explain, for example, ongoing controversy regarding Makah whale hunting, and also traditional tribal land use practices that alter local ecology (Sturgeon, 2009).

While it is true that psychologists have been thinking about cultural differences for some time now, it is also true that the field continues to struggle with how far to generalize their findings. Caution, at a minimum, demands that we assume psychological phenomena do not necessarily extend to populations meaningfully different from those on which the phenomenon has been tested—populations that have been predominately "WEIRD" in character. But researchers are not always clear about these limitations—and the problems get worse in a book like this, which reports hundreds of empirical articles describing research on various populations that can be described in a variety of ways. (And, of course, the problem for us is worse still: In many cases, we are reporting basic psychological research and then merely speculating about how it would apply to the phenomena of interest to environmental law.) The bottom line, we suppose, is that the research is evolving, and we hope that a book like this is taken as an invitation to do still more research that is more specific to environmental law, and on diverse populations, rather than as a statement of absolute confidence about what that research would actually find.

The Replication Crisis in Psychology

While we are in the business of striking cautionary notes, we also want to discuss developments that have roiled not just the field of psychology but both social and hard sciences more generally.

Though the crisis is not limited to social psychology, it started there. After a series of individualized failures to replicate findings (some of which involved outright research fraud), concerned psychologists created the Open Science Collaboration, inviting scientists from across the globe to systematically attempt to replicate 100 classic psychology findings reported in a single year in the three top social psychology journals. The results were sobering: The majority of findings failed to replicate at all, and of those that did, the mean effect size was considerably smaller than in the originals (Open Science Collaboration, 2015). Why? There are many explanations, including some mitigating ones (such as that even by statistical probability alone, many of the studies would have not been likely to replicate) (Gilbert et al., 2016). Nevertheless, the crisis has produced valuable introspection by scientists and a commitment by the field of psychology to at least try to minimize—or in some cases, abandon altogether—research practices that might result in false or misleading findings, like unacceptably low power, *p*-hacking, failure to report dependent measures that were not significant, and so on. Indeed, the crisis has spurred a number of creative research practices and suggestions that have filtered both from and out to other areas of science that are subject to replication crises of their own. These include a norm of publishing research hypotheses and even materials online *before* the data gathering even begins, and encouraging triple blinding of studies, in which not only are both the experimenter and research subject blind to condition, but the researcher is blind to condition while conducting her statistical analyses (MacCoun & Perlmutter, 2015). The methods and practices psychologists have developed in response to the replication crisis are voluminous, and by now well catalogued (Fidler & Wilcox, 2018).

In the end, the replication "crisis" has been a boon for rigor in the field. Future generations of psychologists (and, hopefully, other scientists too) are being trained in these better techniques and so producing research that is both more transparent and more reliable. While it is fair to say that the field was overdue for an overhaul with regard to questionable research practices, it is also fair to say that the field has taken the challenge very seriously, and there is reason to believe that the sciences will be vastly improved going forward because of it. Nevertheless, being aware of past challenges in replication—as with limitations from "WEIRD" research participants—can help readers in being educated consumers of the psychological science we report in this book.

Conclusion

While we have focused throughout this book on psychological findings that have special relevance to environmental law, the general field of law and psychology has pointed to a number of findings that may be as helpful to environmental law as they are to other areas. As research on the psychology of environmental law continues to develop, it will prove important to account for general phenomena as well as those that have a more targeted impact on diffuse, complex, and nonhuman environmental harms. It is also important to keep in mind both limitations about the generality of research findings that draw their participants from circumscribed populations, and methodological limitations of the field, particularly with older studies written before some of the best practices in the science had been developed.

Key Aspects of General Psychology and Law

While environmental law is psychologically distinctive in important ways (being diverse, complex, and nonhuman in character), it also shares a number of features with other areas of law. Generally speaking, all law is concerned with shaping both attitudes and behaviors, and psychology has much to say about that task.

Findings from general law and psychology that may also apply within environmental law include:

THE PSYCHOLOGY OF PERSUASION AND MOTIVATION

- Reciprocity/authority/scarcity/similarity. People have desires to reciprocate what others in society are doing, to defer to authority, to acquire/hoard scarce goods, and to associate with people who are similar to themselves. The law can exploit these preferences when designing laws or policies to encourage people to do or believe various things.
- Motivated cognition. Learning and believing are guided by motives. The desire for specific outcomes affects memory, processing, and inferences. This poses severe challenges in a legal regime where people value sharply different things—it means people may simply not credit information that goes against their values.
- Consistency/cognitive dissonance. People prefer consistency across their beliefs, attitudes, and actions. When these things are inconsistent, they will often change whatever is easiest to change to bring them back to a state of consistency—and the easiest things to change are often mental processes like attitudes or beliefs. This tendency to change attitudes or beliefs can pose challenges to the law where it tries to get people to act in ways that they may believe in in the abstract but that are inconvenient or otherwise costly—but it also provides opportunities.

COGNITIVE HEURISTICS AND BIASES, AND SOCIAL INFLUENCES

- Loss aversion/endowment effect/status quo bias. All of these are aspects of *prospect theory,* which shows that people dislike losses more than they like equally sized gains, and treat losses and gains differently in terms of risk preference.

- Hindsight bias. The hindsight bias can sharply distort measurement of risks that are estimated ex post (as in common law negligence cases) rather than ex ante (as in regulatory prescriptions).
- Affect heuristic. The affect heuristic is the tendency to make decisions based on immediate, intuitive emotional reactions. The affect heuristic can also distort perceptions of risk: People tend to assume things with high benefit have low risk, and vice versa.
- Social identity and social influence. People have a deep need to belong to groups with which they identify. They are motivated to maintain good relationships with others who share their social identity. They take cues, both perceptual and social, from people around them—and the more they identify with them, the more they rely on them for these functions. Social identity pressures can influence not only whether people obey the law but what they think the law is.

Psychologists in recent years have started to pay more attention to the generalizability of their findings and to methodological concerns in their field. These cautions apply to applications of psychological science to environmental law, as they do in other areas of law.

- Student research participants, WEIRD populations, and cross-cultural psychology. Historically, psychologists overrelied on convenience samples (often, college students) for testing their hypotheses. As concern about student samples grew, so, too, did concern about overreliance on Western, educated, industrialized, rich, and democratic populations. Research reveals that other populations often have their own distinctive psychological responses that depart from what were assumed to be fundamental human mental processes. Psychologists now make a point not only to draw from a wider range of subjects where possible but also to note the limits to the generalizability of their conclusions in their reports.
- The replication crisis. Even more recently, psychology (and all science) has undergone the revelation that poor but common research practices have undermined the reliability of some of their findings. This has caused a seismic shift away from these practices and toward newer, more scientifically sound techniques. Still, a note of caution is advised when relying on older empirical studies.

6

The Psychology of Pollution Control

This chapter argues that exploring the psychology of pollution perception and response can help in crafting more effective regimes for pollution control. The impacts of pollution—like other environmental problems—are often diffuse, complex, and nonhuman in character. Furthermore, pollution itself often generates an affective, disgusted response, and perceptions of pollution risk are mediated by who is polluting. Each of these characteristics has implications for managing human behaviors that create, promote, or reduce pollution. As a result, understanding the psychology of pollution control can help in understanding, predicting, and evaluating how existing environmental policies shape human behavior, and in developing policies that are better at controlling pollution.

The chapter begins by briefly defining the problem of pollution. It then outlines key psychological phenomena that can help in understanding the cognitive context in which pollution control decisions operate. After that, the chapter moves on to explore a series of concrete contexts in which doing a psychological analysis can generate meaningful payoffs in understanding, explaining, and sometimes even solving important puzzles in pollution control. In particular, it suggests that psychology can be helpful in informing which substances are treated as pollutants, when pollution is tolerated, and how pollutants are—and can be more effectively—controlled.

The Problem of Pollution

One of the greatest puzzles in environmental law is the question of how to manage pollution: the greater-than-desired concentration of dangerous or impure substances. Pollution is often classified and controlled by the medium through which humans become exposed to dangerous substances; thus, air pollution, water pollution, and soil pollution are commonly distinguished from one another and managed through distinct pollution-control regimes. Pollution is also sometimes classified by the reason for its generation: Potentially dangerous substances may be regulated differently depending upon whether they have been purposefully generated because they offer benefits as well as dangers, as with toxic substances like pesticides or pharmaceuticals, or whether they are waste byproducts of other substances or processes that are useful in industry or in daily life.

The stakes of pollution control vary from minimal to enormous, depending upon the type and extent of the pollution being controlled. One form of pollution—anthropogenic emissions of greenhouse gases, leading to global climate change—is now often viewed as the greatest problem of our time. The stakes and complexity of climate change are indeed so great that we devote an entire chapter to it. Even the stakes of conventional pollutants can be enormous, however; as an example, some estimates suggest that 200,000 Americans die each year from air pollution (Calazzo et al., 2013)—even as the legal protections of the Clean Air Act prevent another 200,000 premature deaths (Environmental Protection Agency, 2011).

In part because of the many types of pollution, and in part because pollution can have such an extraordinary impact on human health and environmental quality, pollution control is a massive field of law. In the United States, pollution control incorporates a number of sprawling statutes and regulatory regimes, including the Clean Air Act, the Clean Water Act, the Toxic Substances Control Act, the Resource Conservation and Recovery Act, the "Superfund," and the Safe Drinking Water Act. The length of the Clean Air Act alone is sometimes compared to that of the U.S. tax code (Revesz, 2015). Yet pollution and pollution exposure is affected not only by national or federal law, but also by laws and policies at the international, state, and local level. Furthermore, because of the breadth and complexity of the legal strategies applied to pollution control, it is common for many legal institutions to be involved in controlling pollution. In the United States, for example, many decisions are coordinated through federal regulatory processes in cooperation with state entities, Indian tribes, and local and municipal governments, as well as with private stakeholders, including industry and nonprofit environmental groups.

The Psychological Challenges of Pollution

Like other environmental problems, pollution presents risks that are diffuse, complex, and nonhuman in character. Pollution also poses some of its own distinctive psychological features, perhaps most notably the trigger of intuitive and affective responses to what is perceived as unclean (Douglas, 1966; Rozin et al., 2008). These characteristics interact and—as we discuss further in the next part of the chapter—generate important challenges and opportunities for environmental law and policy.

The Psychology of Pollution as Environmental Injury

Pollution presents the classic qualities of environmental injury (Lazarus, 2000). As we have argued throughout the first half of this book, those qualities have psychological implications that will tend to drive legal policy in some directions over others. Below, we flag some of the most notable of those implications for pollution-control law and policy. These include the likelihood that the diffusion of pollution effects through space and time facilitate minimization and dismissal of pollution externalities by both individuals and institutions; that the complexity of many causes and aspects of pollution leads to simplifying heuristics and approaches to controlling it, contributing to a gap between expert and lay perceptions of pollution; and that barriers to attention and empathy toward nonhuman impacts may contribute to neglecting or minimizing the impacts of pollution on nonhuman animals, plants, and ecosystems.

Diffusion

Pollution can exhibit temporal and spatial diffusion both in its generation and its impacts. The psychology of each is worth consideration.

First, consider that dangerous accumulations of pollutants often develop from the individual actions of many people. Nonpoint source water pollution presents one example: While the emission of fertilizer and municipal waste into the Mississippi River might present no significant problem if it were engaged in by one farm or one town, when thousands of actors introduce nitrogen and other nutrients into the river, the cumulative result is the massive dead zone in the Gulf of Mexico. Yet no single actor may see the polluting behavior of any other, making coordinated solutions particularly challenging. In fact, because the impacts of pollution tend to be far away from the polluting activity, polluters themselves rarely see the harms of their actions with their own eyes. Farmers in Minnesota applying nitrogen-rich fertilizer to their fields may never visit the Gulf of Mexico; the air pollution from a coal plant in Illinois may waft many miles into Indiana and beyond; and the harm of an improperly disposed-of battery, thrown casually into a municipal waste stream, may accrue hundreds of miles away, buried deep beneath a pile of other refuse.

Of course, the harm from pollution is often temporally distant as well. It is common, even expected, that for many pollutants there is some latency between exposure and harm (Revesz, 1999). This, too, implicates the diffusion phenomena discussed earlier, including time inconsistency, hyperbolic discounting, and present bias. In addition, it presents special challenges to eliciting people's preferences about pollution control in meaningful ways, and to distinguishing between present and future environmental risks (Rowell, 2012a).

Although many pollution problems involve some level of diffusion, it is worth noting that there are also pollution problems that are acute and immediate. As an example, consider emergency chemical releases, such as the one that tragically occurred at the Union Carbide plant in Bhopal, India. In that case, a series of terrible errors led to a pesticide plant releasing 30 tons of methyl isocyanate—an invisible, extremely toxic gas—into a highly populated area, exposing more than 600,000 (mostly sleeping) people, killing at least 20,000, and blinding and permanently disabling many tens of thousands more. The disaster was so shocking that countries around the world, including the United States, adopted emergency response plans—in our case, the Emergency Planning and Community Right-to-Know Act (EPCRA)—to manage emergency risks of this type.

Notably, the psychology of response to acute emergency is significantly different than that of responding to diffuse risk. In many cases, acute risks lead to extreme anxiety and may even trigger "fight or flight" responses. Many disaster policies attempt to ameliorate such concerns by encouraging significant up-front planning, such as is required under EPCRA for facilities that store dangerous substances, and such as is recommended by the Federal Emergency Management Agency (FEMA) and other disaster agencies for individuals in preparing for disasters.

But even these acute and immediate problems may generate diffuse impacts as well. In the case of the Bhopal disaster, some estimates suggest that hundreds of thousands of people continue to suffer lingering aftereffects (Broughton, 2005). Other environmental disasters also present both acute and diffuse aspects. The enormous BP oil spill, for example, which dumped about 4.3 million barrels of crude oil into the Gulf of Mexico, had terrible immediate impacts: Fish populations collapsed while fishermen watched, turtles and dolphins were pulled from the ocean coated in brown oil, coral colonies suffocated, and corpses of sea birds washed up on oily beaches. Yet research on the ongoing impact of the spill on the ecosystem continues, and scientists are chronicling a number of significant long-term consequences (Ainsworth et al., 2018; D'Andrea & Reddy, 2018; Lichtveld et al., 2016). Importantly, because of the attention-sapping psychology of diffusion, these lingering effects tend not to get nearly as much attention as the risks posed by the acute phase of the disaster.

Complexity

The effects of pollution exposure and the implications of various pollution-control regimes are complex in a number of ways. We have already mentioned the fact that pollution can accumulate when many individual actors contribute to it, making it harder to perceive or isolate the contributions of any one source. Other important complexities include the fact that there can be local adaptations to pollutants, making them either better or worse for humans and other living things, and that pollution is subject to nonlinear relationships between quantity and harm.

As we have discussed, a robust literature finds systematic differences in how experts and laypeople perceive the tolerability of risk (Kraus et al., 2001). Many of these phenomena relate to how risky people perceive pollution to be and relate to specific important qualities of pollution. We discuss these considerations further in the following section.

More generally speaking, the tolerability of a risk requires a weighting—whether probabilistic and magnitude-sensitive or not—of both the benefits and the harms of polluting activity. When the sources of pollution and their effects are complex, this makes these determinations of risk both harder and less predictable. Furthermore, a key challenge presented by managing pollution is that it often presents trade-offs between the usefulness of the activities that produce pollution (such as most industrial processes) and the harm the pollution can cause. Just how useful the polluting activities are can be a matter of significant disagreement, as can the likelihood and the seriousness of the harm that is caused. In addition, the countervailing benefits and drawbacks of the polluting activity can generate cognitive dissonance, making the question of what to tolerate—and how much—mentally costly to process. In many circumstances, as we discuss further below, people end up tolerating pollution of some kinds and in some amounts; in others, they take action to reduce the pollution to tolerable levels, or even to eliminate it entirely. Which substances and quantities are tolerated is likely to be in part a function of the psychology of complexity.

Nonhuman Character

Finally, pollution control often implicates both nonhuman processes and the possibility of harm to nonhuman plants, animals, and ecosystems. Furthermore, perceptions of harm may vary to the extent people identify with the entities that are being harmed. In some cases, such identification can vary cross-culturally. Some Native American tribes and people who practice the animist Japanese Shinto religion, for instance, might particularly care about damage to specific rock formations or landscapes or waterways, even where such damage could have no appreciable effect on humans. Generally speaking, however, the more people identify with the exposed entities, the more they are likely to support regimes designed to restrict or clean up the pollutants. And in many cases, people exhibit both sensitivities and barriers to attention and empathy toward nonhuman entities that they do not exhibit regarding human impacts. In pollution-control contexts, this will often contribute to neglecting or minimizing the impacts of pollution on nonhuman animals, plants, and ecosystems.

The psychology of nonhuman impacts also has a particularly interesting implication that affects how risky people perceive nonhuman sources of pollution to be. As we emphasize below, there is a common intuition that "natural" substances are less dangerous than manmade or artificial ones (Rozin et al., 2004). That is, people distinguish between human and nonhuman *sources* of pollutants, as well as between human and nonhuman *recipients*. Notably, this phenomenon holds true despite the fact that many potentially dangerous pollutants have both natural and manmade sources.

The Distinctive Psychology of Pollution

In addition to the general qualities of environmental injury that we have discussed throughout the book, some aspects of which we have highlighted above, pollution also triggers a set of pollution-specific psychological phenomena. Recognizing these phenomena may help in understanding the particular challenges presented by pollution-control law and policy, and it may even—in some cases—offer opportunities for improving the effectiveness of control strategies. To that end, here we flag three lines of psychological research that we believe may be particularly helpful in explaining how perceptions of and responses to pollution risks develop. These are (1) the psychology of disgust and impurity, (2) source effects, and (3) role-relative risk perception.

THE PSYCHOLOGY OF DISGUST AND IMPURITY

The world is full of substances and phenomena, all of which pose some risks of some kinds in some situations (Graham & Wiener, 1997). To choose among the substances, phenomena, and risks pervasive in the world requires some form of selection, which ranks some sources of danger or impurity as worse than others (Nagle, 2009). One man's cologne is another man's stench; one woman's pristine, sanitized swimming pool is another woman's chlorinated hellhole. In this sense, the choice to categorize any substance as "pollution" is fundamentally cognitive: Consciously or not, it involves a choice to identify the substance as undesirable or risky. And the processes that lead to prioritizing some risks over others are inherently subject to subjective psychological processes (Slovic, 2000).

What gets perceived as dangerous or impure enough to constitute "pollution"? One way of answering this question stems from a sister social science, anthropology. Anthropologists have characterized responses to pollution as a recoiling from the unclean (Douglas, 1966; Douglas & Wildavsky, 1982; Khare, 1996). What counts as "unclean" is informed by underlying normative values and is thus socially constructed (Douglas, 1966; Douglas & Wildavsky, 1982; Khare, 1996; Nagle, 2009). A related account is offered by Evernden (1992), who notes that "the ubiquitous term *pollution* did not acquire its current connotation . . . until quite recently" and that "[w]e must bear in mind that the current understanding of pollution is just that: the current understanding," as such conceptions are socially constructed (p. 4). Indeed, in their influential work *Risk and Culture: An Essay on the Selection of Technical and Environmental Dangers*, anthropologist Mary Douglas and political scientist Aaron Wildavsky argued that pollution is perceived as "risky" because it is embedded with highly tailored individual conceptions of what counts as dangerous, unclean, or impure (Douglas & Wildavsky, 1982; Kahan & Braman, 2006). Supporting their theory, and as we have discussed extensively elsewhere, substantial empirical work has now established that individuals who hold different social values actually perceive different phenomena as differently risky (Kahan & Braman, 2006; Kahan et al., 2007a). For example, individuals with more egalitarian and solidaristic values perceive global warming, nuclear power, and environmental pollution as riskier than do individuals with individualistic or hierarchical values (Kahan & Braman, 2006; Kahan et al., 2007a, 2007b).

Perhaps unsurprisingly, the specific substances and phenomena that people think of as "polluting" vary significantly across culture and worldviews, as well as through history (Douglas, 1966; Khare, 1996; Nagle, 2009). Early Americans, for example, worried much more about spiritual and cultural pollution than environmental pollution (Rome, 1996; Nagle, 2009), whereas modern Americans think about pollution as "the introduction of harmful substances or products into the environment" (*Random House Unabridged Dictionary*, 2001). But while what counts as unclean or polluted can vary (Nagle, 2009), the psychology of the response to whatever is perceived as unclean appears to generalize.

In psychological terms, once something is identified as unclean, the response to it becomes affective: sudden, instantaneous, and emotionally laden (Slovic et al., 2002; Rowell, 2012a). Affective responses are automatic and can be quite powerful. They can even cause measurable physical responses. Feelings of disgust are an obvious example. In one famous experiment by Rozin et al. (2008), experimenters offered participants a free glass of orange juice. The catch was that participants first watched the experimenters dip a carefully sterilized cockroach into the juice just prior to being handed the glass. Not only did participants not want to drink the juice; many reported feelings of nausea. We might also speculate that many of them felt little desire for a glass of orange juice for some time afterward, as a feeling of disgust is easily transferred to items associated with the object of disgust (Morales & Fitzsimons, 2007).

The participants' disgust response was characteristic: a recoiling from the unclean that creates a distinctive "all or nothing" affective response. Something is either repulsive or it is not, and a glass of juice might well strike most people as just as disgusting if one-quarter of a sterilized cockroach were dipped into it as if the whole bug were submerged. In the context of toxic substances, this same "all or nothing" response means that most people care far more about whether they have been exposed to pollution *at all* than the amount of exposure (Kraus et al., 2001; Sunstein, 2002c; Rowell, 2012a).

Research suggests that, in part because of these psychological phenomena, laypeople and experts think very differently about pollution risks (Kraus et al., 2001; Sunstein, 2002a, 2006). Laypeople tend to act like "intuitive toxicologists" when presented with dangerous substances. In comparison with professional toxicologists, laypeople are more likely to think that "[t]he fact of exposure to a pesticide is the critical concern, rather than the amount of exposure" (Kraus et al., 2001, pp. 290–291; Sunstein, 2002a, 2006). In toxicology, "the dose makes the poison," and toxicologists have developed sophisticated techniques to explore the complex relationships between amount of a substance and the harm that exposure to it might cause (Klaassen, 2008; Klaassen & Watkins, 2010). The same dose-response-based reasoning suggests that sometimes it might cause less harm overall to spread pollution over more people or time—that is, exposing *more* people to pollution—just at lower quantities (Rowell, 2012a). Yet the intuitive response of recoil from pollution makes this approach politically challenging. Similarly, the "all or nothing" disgust engendered by pollution may help to explain why people often struggle to accept that some pollutants may generate benefits and harms simultaneously (Nagle, 2013). In this sense, and as we discuss in more detail at the end of this chapter, the psychology of pollution can work against effective environmental policy.

The divide between laypeople and experts in this realm can also create other significant challenges for regulators, who must decide how much of a dangerous substance to tolerate, and who often rely both on quantitative risk analysis (which looks very carefully at the relationship between exposure level and harm) and on cost-benefit analysis (Sunstein, 2002c). The regulation of arsenic in drinking water is a good example of how this can play out. When the EPA considered relaxing regulations on arsenic in drinking water, the decision was met with significant public controversy, perhaps largely due to the difference in how the EPA and laypeople approach the problem of pollution (Sunstein, 2002a). Alternatively, consider a more colorful example, where the city of Portland, Oregon, decided to drain 38 million gallons of clean drinking water from its reservoir after a teenager was caught on video urinating into it. In defending their actions, the Water Bureau spokesman stated, "Our customers don't anticipate drinking water that's been contaminated by some yahoo who decided to pee into a reservoir" (Rayman, 2014, n.p.).

SOURCE EFFECTS

Another important aspect of the psychology of pollution relates to how the perceived risks of pollution vary according to the source of that pollution. Robust research suggests that whether or not a substance triggers disgust and recoil can depend upon the source of the substance, a phenomenon known as the "source effect" (Curtis et al., 2004). Generally, people are less disgusted by sources they view as familiar (Peng et al., 2013); mothers, for example, regard their own baby's fecal smell as less disgusting than someone else's baby's (Case et al., 2006), and people are less disgusted by odors and emanations from their parents, partners, friends, and acquaintances than those of strangers (Bužeková & Išová, 2010; Peng et al., 2013). People also find their own pollution less disgusting. In one smelly illustration of this effect, researchers found increased levels of disgust and negative affect when body malodors emanated from strangers than from themselves (Stevenson & Repacholi, 2005). Some researchers have suggested these adaptations are evolutionarily valuable as a behavioral response to potential disease, which is more likely to be dangerous when carried by strangers who may carry diseases to which the immune system has not yet had a chance to develop resistance (Navarrete & Fessler, 2006; Peng et al., 2013).

Another instantiation of the source effect is the perceived distinction between risks perceived as "natural" and those perceived as manmade or artificial (Nagle, 2009; Thorsheim, 2006). Modern Americans typically perceive manmade risks as more dangerous (Douglas & Wildavsky, 1982). This effect is so robust that people have even been shown to perceive "natural" disasters as less damaging than *identical* "manmade" disasters (Siegrist & Sutterlin, 2014). As a result of the perceived danger of manmade risks, people are more likely to categorize a substance as "pollution" when it has some connection to human behavior or when humans are perceived to be the source (Collman, 2001). Consider again the example of the Portland reservoir. The city of Portland chose to drain its reservoir after a single person was caught urinating in it—but no similar actions are considered or undertaken in response to bird and animal urine, though both substances are likely similarly biologically sterile, and the quantities of animal urine are presumably much larger. Or consider that the same Water Bureau that drained the reservoir because of human urine does not drain it when (as often happens) dead animals—rodents, birds, fish, etc.—are found floating in it; as one official explained, "We look at that as part of the business of open reservoirs" (Schmidt, 2011, n.p.).

POSITIONAL JUDGMENTS OF POLLUTION RISK

Individuals contribute to the harm of pollution in two important ways: as polluters (who themselves create or spread pollution) and as pollutees (who are affected by their own or others' pollution). In each of these roles, individuals may experience many of the psychological phenomena identified and discussed above—many of which may combine to lead to psychological minimization of the externalities of pollution.

The Psychology of Polluters

Polluters may exhibit particular psychological responses related to both their role in generating harm and to the particularly diffuse kind of harm that most pollution creates. Such responses may apply both to individuals engaging in industrial-level pollution as well as to the casual picnicker who opts to leave her trash in the park rather than carry it with her for disposal. We earlier noted the psychological responses people have to creating externalities, and they apply here as well. In particular, polluters may experience cognitive dissonance at the thought that they are harming other people, and they may therefore diminish that unpleasant sensation by mentally underestimating the total harm that they do—a tendency related both to egocentric bias (Shu et al., 2011) and to moral disengagement (Bandura, 2015). Sometimes, even when they know they are doing harm, people engage in self-serving justifications that minimize and excuse their behavior (Shalvi et al., 2015; Bandura, 2002, 2015). Although not well studied in pollution contexts, such a phenomenon falls comfortably within a more general phenomenon called cognitive distortion, in which people avoid conscious confrontation with the negative impacts of their own behavior on others by reducing the perception of such impacts (Burns, 1989; Bandura, 2002, 2015; Helmond et al., 2015). Worse still, individual cognitive distortions have been associated with a higher likelihood of actively engaging in behavior that harms others (Burns, 1989; Helmond et al., 2015; Bandura, 2015). One study, for instance, demonstrated that in a simulated overfishing context, people *do* engage in self-serving biases—and indeed, the more egocentric they were, the more they overfished (Wade-Benzoni et al., 1996). Since we can only speculate whether these findings would apply to polluters choosing to pollute, further research on the extent to which this effect operates in applied contexts—and how it might be interrupted—would be valuable.

Another potentially disturbing possibility is that individuals who pollute might seek out justifications for the harm that they do by targeting individuals or groups whom they perceive as "other" and offloading pollution harms onto them. Law offers a number of potential methods for allocating the harms from pollution (Rowell, 2012a). While these methods can be used to reduce the harm from pollution where there are nonlinearities in pollution's impacts—for example by "bunching" pollutants that cause high damage in low doses to minimize the total amount of harm done, or by concentrating waste disposal at one facility rather than having waste dispersed across multiple locations—they can also be used to cause *extra* harm or to distribute harm in ways that are targeted or unequitable (Rowell, 2012a). Where polluters (or legal decision makers) are motivated to reduce the dissonance caused by harming others, such allocation decisions could be affected by stereotyping and prejudice, (Fiske, 2000; Nelson, 2009). And indeed, environmental justice research shows that environmental risks, such as those created by locally undesirable land uses such as landfills and incinerators, tend to be disproportionately allocated in a way that harms minorities and communities of color (Bullard, 2005; Schlosberg, 2009; Taylor, 2000).

The Psychology of Pollutees

Individuals who are impacted by the polluting behaviors of themselves or others—pollutees—may exhibit some distinctive psychological responses of their own. First, people who are potentially impacted by pollution may experience cognitive load and anxiety at the thought of having been exposed to pollution. This anxiety can be significant enough that it may generate harm in its own right. Indeed, one Estonian study of 1,000 adults found that, for at least some pollutants, the *belief* that they had been exposed to pollution was more predictive of measurable physical symptoms than the exposure itself (Orru et al., 2018).

Another aspect of pollutee psychology may arise out of the cognitive link between familiarity and risk perception (Slovic et al., 2002). Studies have repeatedly shown that people tend to perceive familiar risks as less dangerous or risky than unfamiliar ones. This may help to explain how individuals sometimes tolerate living in highly polluted areas even when alternatives are available to them. As evidence at least consistent with this possibility, note that studies show a weak or even negative relationship between living close to a refinery and self-reported health symptoms over time (Luginaah et al., 2002), and that students chronically exposed to smog are more likely to deny or ignore its existence compared to newcomers to the pollution (Evans et al., 1988).

Finally, individuals' responses to polluted conditions may sometimes be informed by the phenomenon of learned helplessness, where repeated exposure to a negative circumstance that a person feels like they cannot control makes them feel increasingly powerless and therefore immobilized. Tragically, their immobility does not always reverse even when control is restored to them (Maier & Seligman, 1976). Such feelings of helplessness in the face of pollution may interfere with individuals' ability to act to address it. This possibility is particularly disturbing in environmental justice contexts: Poor communities and communities of color who accurately perceive that they have been subjected to additional pollution risks relative to their whiter or richer fellow citizens may be particularly at risk for developing feelings of helplessness and lack of control. And again, over time such feelings could persist even where opportunities arise that would otherwise allow them to actively address unacceptable pollution levels.

Payoffs in the Psychology of Pollution Control

In this section, we move to the psychology of regulators. There are three general stages of pollution control in which regulators must engage. First, they must recognize or categorize a substance as dangerous or impure enough to constitute a pollutant. Second, they must determine how much, if any, of the pollutant can be tolerated. And third, they must select some mechanism or tool (whether social, legal, or personal) to resolve the part of the pollution that they have decided is intolerable. Because each of these regulatory stages requires cognitive selection and processing, we believe psychology has the power to play a critical, even determinative, role throughout.

What Counts as a "Pollutant"?

Earlier parts of this chapter worked to outline a thick and interconnected set of psychological phenomena that affect the identification of some substances as dangerous and impure "pollutants," even as other substances are largely neglected. In sum, the categorization of a substance as a pollutant is subject to psychological phenomena that inform what people think of as polluting. In many cases, this is a function of social or personal norms, such as a belief that "manmade" pollutants are dangerous or impure, whereas "natural" pollutants are not; or because one pollutant is salient, while other (even similar!) pollutants are not.

In legal contexts, the categorization of a substance as a pollutant is typically the legal trigger for action. Prior to that categorization, however, the substance may not be controlled—and may even be promoted through legal and policy means. Consider that when the powerful insecticide DDT was first developed, it was hailed as a miracle rather than a pollutant. Proponents—including many governments—celebrated it as an extraordinary protection against deadly insect-borne diseases like malaria and typhus, as well as a convenient boost to food production by efficiently killing crop pests. As a result, early deployment of DDT was broad and largely indiscriminate. It was used liberally in crop and livestock production; in vast aerial sprays over American towns, forests, and farmlands; in institutions, gardens, homes—in other words, as if it were not a pollutant at all (Landon, 2003).

Notably, it was not until Rachel Carson's influential account of the environmental impacts—in her poetic and evocative *Silent Spring* (1962)—that most people developed the conception of environmentally persistent toxic substances like DDT as pollutants at all. Once recognized as such, countries around the world took legal action to control DDT and similar substances. The United States, partly in response to Carson's book, banned DDT in 1972, followed gradually by many other countries around the world. In 2001, more than 100 countries signed the Stockholm Convention on Persistent Organic Pollutants (POPs), committing to eliminate the use of 12 of the POPs of greatest concern to the global community, including DDT.

Perhaps unsurprisingly, our modern toxics statutes—including the Toxic Substances Control Act of 1976; Federal Insecticide, Fungicide, and Rodenticide Act of 1972; and Emergency Planning and Community Right-to-Know Act of 1986—postdate the realization that insecticides and related substances pollute. Until such substances were perceived as dangerous, however, there was no need to seek control of them as pollutants (though early regulations did regulate other risks, such as from misbranding).

Clearly, whether a substance is perceived as a pollutant or a miracle worker will affect how it is regulated, and the categorization of a substance as a pollutant is a critical trigger for legal action to control it. But as we emphasize and discuss further below, how regulators decide what counts as a pollutant will often be subject to psychological phenomena. As a result, psychology has an important role to play in determining when, why, and how pollution control addresses substances as pollutants.

"NATURAL" AND "UNNATURAL" POLLUTION

First, consider the psychological tendency—which we have mentioned above—to consider "natural" substances and sources to be safer and less polluting than artificial or "unnatural" ones. This tendency generates challenges for regulators, not least because many substances perceived as pollution when emitted by humans are in fact naturally occurring in some quantity. Indeed a brief browse through the periodic table will reveal a number of "natural" but toxic substances, including lead, arsenic, and mercury (U.S. Geological Survey, n.d.). Soil, for example, commonly contains detectable quantities of both lead and arsenic, which are released into the air in a number of natural occurrences, including forest fires (Environmental Protection Agency, *Learn about Lead*; U.S. Geological Survey, 2016; U.S. Geological Survey, n.d.).

Or consider that amounts of radiation occur naturally in soil, water, air, and vegetation, and humans are routinely exposed to measurable levels of cosmic radiation from space. As the United Nations has explained, "The exposure of human beings to ionizing radiation from natural sources is a continuing and inescapable feature of life on the earth" (United Nations Scientific Committee on the Effects of Atomic Radiation, 2008, p. 223). The worldwide average natural dose of radiation is about 2.4 mSv per year, about four times the average artificial dose (0.6 mSv/year). That said, average natural background exposure varies across the globe. The city of Ramsar in Iran, for example, has unusually high levels of naturally occurring radiation—as high as 260 mSv/year, or enough to increase chromosomal abnormalities of inhabitants by more than 50% (Ghiassi-nejad et al., 2002).

Yet conceptions persist that pollution necessarily results (only) from artificial or manmade sources. This presumption is reflected in a number of the most influential environmental statutes. The Clean Water Act, for instance, defines pollution as the "manmade or man-induced alteration of the chemical, physical, biological, and radiological integrity of the water" (33 U.S.C. § 1362(19))—a definition entirely dependent upon comparing the impacts of human activity with some presumptive prehuman baseline (Nagle, 2009). This focus on pollution as "manmade" triggers many of the psychological phenomena discussed earlier regarding nonhuman impacts.

The perception that "natural," versus artificial, substances are less polluting, or less unclean, has the potential to be quite dangerous. As an example, consider again the now-perennial problem of widespread wildfires in the American West. In many cases, these wildfires leave huge swaths of the West Coast's population centers blanketed in highly polluted air—in recent years, with higher levels of air pollution even than notoriously polluted cities like Beijing. The high level of fine particulate matter exposure from wildfires is extraordinarily dangerous, particularly (though not exclusively) for people with preexisting breathing issues and for the elderly. In fact, recent estimates suggest that about 17,000 people in the United States die each year from air pollution from wildfires. If current climate changes continue, further exacerbating wildfire seasons, that number could more than double by the end of the century (Ford et al., 2018). Yet individual and policy response to wildfire risks may be muted insofar as wildfires seem "wild" or "natural" and therefore less risky. This tendency may only be exacerbated where still other psychological biases, such as the preference for perceived omissions over actions, come into play. And indeed, there is evidence of exactly this kind of perverting effect on policy, as we noted previously: The emissions from "natural" wildfires are exempt from whether a state is meeting its obligations under the National Ambient Air Quality Standards in the Clean Air Act (Engel & Reeves, 2012; Engel, 2013; Shultz et al., 2019), even while those from controlled ("unnatural") burns are counted toward pollution-control standards.

WOODSMOKE CANDLES AND "POLLUTANTS OF THE MONTH"

Psychological processes may obscure some types of pollution, even as other pollutants gain hypersalience.

Many pollutants lack cognitive salience in part because of the diffuse character of their distribution and harm, and in part because their relationship to causing injury can be complex—multicausal, interactive, and nonlinear. Consider again the example of wood fire. Burning wood indoors or out generates fine particulate matter, or PM2.5, which the EPA regulates as a criteria pollutant under the Clean Air Act because of its danger to human health, and which the World Health Organization estimates kills—in conjunction with a variety of other toxic pollutants—7 million people a year (World Health Organization, 2018). The harm from fine particle exposures is likely cumulative over time. Moreover, the dose-response rate to each of the substances emitted may be nonlinear, or even interactive, and thus complicated to understand, and harms from exposure are likely to be latent for people without acute respiratory diseases. These factors tend to make the dangers of woodsmoke less likely to garner attention or response.

In some cases, positive emotional associations may further obscure the dangers of some pollutants. Many people, for instance, associate woodsmoke with happy memories of campfires and being in the outdoors, or the cozy feeling of snuggling up next to a warm fireplace. Indeed, the emotional associations are so positive that "woodsmoke" is a popular candle scent (Kelly, 2015). As a result, people may be less likely to take any self-protective actions against it that they might readily take in response to more recognizable or negatively valenced pollutants. Still less are they likely to demand regulatory action to diminish the risks.

In contrast, other pollutants may trigger hyperresponse, as where a pollutant is made salient by extended media coverage. Such occurrences can cause what Timur Kuran and Cass Sunstein have called "availability cascades": self-reinforcing processes of collective belief formation, in which an expressed perception triggers a chain reaction that gives the public the perception of increasing plausibility through rising availability in public discourse (Kuran & Sunstein, 1999). This can result in, among other things, what Kuran and Sunstein have called the "pollutant of the month" syndrome, where "expressed concerns about a particular substance fuel growing anxieties, which then generate an irresistible demand for regulation. These anxieties remain in the headlines until they are bumped off by a new perceived hazard" (Kuran & Sunstein, 1999, p. 698; Wildavsky, 1995).

An example of this type of oversalience is the extraordinary public concern regarding Alar, a pesticide long used on apples, after an alarmist 60 Minutes episode and a dubious report about carcinogenicity by the Natural Resources Defense Council (Koshland, 1991; Kuran & Sunstein, 1999). Another example is the extreme public concern about hazardous waste sites after the broad coverage of the discovery of toxic waste underneath the Love Canal community, despite experts suggesting that "hazardous waste sites pose an almost negligible risk to human health when compared with the many more fundamental risks we face" (Viscusi, 1998, p. 23; Kuran & Sunstein, 1999).

Even when there are legitimate environmental and health concerns attached to a pollutant, availability cascades may help to explain why "all of a sudden" there is attention to long-neglected pollutants—often even as similar pollutants continue to slide under the public's radar. Consider the quick social shift following Rachel Carson's *Silent Spring*, from categorizing DDT as a cure-all to categorizing it as a dangerous pollutant. Or alternatively, consider the explosion of attention paid to the inclusion of bisphenol A (BPA) in plastics. BPA, invented over 120 years ago, has a number of useful manufacturing qualities, and it has been used in very large quantities around the world for many decades. In the mid-2000s, however, concern over BPA's health impacts exploded as evidence arose suggesting that the National Institute of Health (NIH), who had long treated it as safe except in very large quantities, had conflicts of interest with industry. The House Oversight and Government Reform Committee launched an investigation, and in the ensuing media coverage, many Americans learned about BPA for the first time. The National Toxicology Program, part of the NIH, issued a report concluding that there *was* "some concern for effects on the brain, behavior, and prostate gland in fetuses, infants, and children at current human exposures" (National Toxicology Program, 2008, p. 38), and countries, states, and eventually the federal government responded with a series of laws meant to curtail BPA exposure. These actions, and the simultaneous media coverage, have been credited with a social shift toward the use of reusable water bottles, and they have also led to the now highly familiar—and availability-reinforcing—labels that we commonly see on plastics indicating they are "BPA free." They have also been credited with the ban on BPA in baby bottles in the United States, Canada, and the EU.

While the increasing cognitive availability of BPA risk as a result of availability cascades arguably led to better environmental regulation in this instance, it is worth noting that the selective attention generated by availability cascades may crowd out interest in assessing substitutes— substitutes that may be as dangerous (if not more) than the original item, yet which lack any availability cascade of their own. The attention and concern about the potential toxicity of BPA to humans, for example, led many manufacturers to switch from bisphenol A to other bisphenols— bisphenol F (BPF) and bisphenol S (BPS) in particular—in manufacturing plastics. Little to no public attention has attached to these potential pollutants, though exposure to these substitutes is ubiquitous, very little is known about their health and environmental impacts, and they share many physical and chemical properties with BPA (Lehmler et al., 2018). BPA thus remains highly salient and mentally categorized as a pollutant, while substitutes for BPA, despite extraordinary chemical similarities to it, remain in the mental background, their possible dangers languishing in cognitive obscurity.

DEFINITIONS OF "POLLUTION" AND REGULATORY DISCRETION

Perhaps because of the conceptual difficulty in developing consensus-based accounts of what should count as a pollutant, environmental statutes are sometimes characterized by extraordinarily broad definitions of "pollution," leaving most of the practical work of line drawing within the discretionary hands of environmental agencies. The Clean Air Act (1970), for example, defines an air pollutant merely as "any air pollution agent . . . including any physical, chemical, biological, [or] radioactive . . . substance or matter which is emitted into or otherwise enters the ambient air" (42 U.S.C. §7602(g)). While this type of comprehensive legislative delegation gets the trouble of defining pollution out of the hands of legislators, it passes a hot potato to agencies.

In exercising their broad discretion to determine the complex question of which substances do and do not qualify as "pollution," regulators—like anyone else—are inevitably subject to the constraints of their own psychology. For example, where issues are factually complex, political appointees at the top of agency food chains may suffer from motivated cognition, and may therefore be particularly subject to interpreting facts in ways that align with their political preferences. Furthermore, whatever regulators do decide is likely to stick. The judicial role in second guessing agency categorizations of what counts as a "pollutant," and under what circumstance, is limited because of the broad discretion generally granted to agencies who are interpreting statutes in their area of expertise (*Chevron U.S.A., Inc. v. NRDC*, 1984; *Massachusetts v. EPA*, 2007). Even where meaningful judicial review does occur, judges, too, may be influenced by motivated cognition (Sunstein et al., 2006).

As an example of how motivated cognition could interact with both agency and judicial decision making about what counts as a pollutant, consider the landmark case of *Massachusetts v. EPA*, in which the Supreme Court considered whether the EPA had appropriately refused to categorize carbon dioxide as a "pollutant" or an "air pollution agent" under the Clean Air Act. With little additional guidance from the act about what constitutes pollution, the two institutions came to different conclusions about the same pollutant. The EPA, with its head appointed by a President reluctant to act on climate change, concluded that carbon dioxide was not a pollutant, while the Supreme Court concluded that carbon dioxide "fit well within the CAA's capacious definition of air pollutant" (p. 532). Notably, it is rare for courts to second-guess agency categorizations of pollutants. One way to understand the opinion in *Massachusetts v. EPA* is that the court was correcting for a decision that had been overly influenced—consciously or not—by the EPA's politics at the time. An optimistic account of this might be that courts create structural safeguards not just for traditional political overreach by the other branches but also for "too much" psychological bias. A more cynical interpretation might be that the Supreme Court was merely substituting its own motivated reasoning for that of the agency.

When Is Pollution Tolerated?

In addition to illuminating when, why, and how substances and conditions are targeted as dangerous pollutants and deemed worthy of control, psychology can also help in explaining pollution-control "gaps," where potential pollutants, harms from pollution, and pollutant sources are minimized or tolerated by individuals and/or by the legal structures that individuals implement. It may also be helpful in illustrating the extent of that tolerance, which may inform the quantity of pollution that the law allows.

HOMETOWN POLLUTION:
GRANDFATHERING, ENVIRONMENTAL FEDERALISM, AND
THE POLLUTER PAYS PRINCIPLE

Pollution levels that people are accustomed to may fade into the cognitive (if not the environmental) background, becoming a familiar part of the accepted status quo. This may, in part, help to explain the common phenomenon of environmental "grandfathering," where existing pollution types and sources are regulated less stringently than new types and sources.

The grandfathering of old sources remains a common though controversial approach to regulating pollution (Damon et al., 2019). In the United States, the Clean Air Act is particularly (in)famous for its decision to exempt pre-1970 sources of air pollution from the vast majority of the statute's controls, and particularly from New Source Performance Standards (Nash & Revesz, 2007). That said, modified grandfathering regimes are also common throughout a number of other pollution-control regimes around the world and even throughout many land-use schemes (Cole & Ostrom, 2012). Although grandfathering has been addressed by environmental scholars through a number of interdisciplinary lenses, including through political science and economics (Damon et al., 2019), it has not, to our knowledge, been addressed from a psychological perspective. Yet the psychological explanation for grandfathering—for why policy makers would give existing sources preferential treatment, and for why stakeholders might tolerate such policies—is a relatively straightforward application of research on risk perception, familiarity, the act/omission bias, and the source effect. That research suggests that policy makers and stakeholders may actually perceive old, familiar pollution as less risky than new pollution. As a result, policy makers may draft preferential treatment of what they perceive as less risky behavior, and stakeholders (like voters) may tolerate that structure because it fits their own perception of relative risks.

Similar effects may occur where people are asked to judge the relative riskiness of pollution generated by sources they view as familiar or as falling within their in-group—what we might think of as a "hometown pollution" effect. First, as we have discussed, familiar risks are likely to be perceived as less risky (Slovic et al., 1981) and the pollution thus generated as less disgusting (Peng et al., 2013). Second, as we have also discussed, people view pollution itself as less risky and as less disgusting when it emanates from a source with which they identify (Bužeková & Išová, 2010; Peng et al., 2013). And third, people may adopt minimization strategies to avoid the stress and anxiety of believing themselves, or people they care about, to be exposed to pollution (Evans et al., 1988). All of these factors may obscure the real risks people face from local pollution from familiar sources. Notably, this minimization may actually apply particularly strongly for people who have a strong attachment to their hometown or place of residence. We already cited the research finding that impressions of the level of pollution on local beaches in England were inversely correlated with perceivers' attachment to their local towns or to their nation, with those who were more attached being less likely to see their beachfronts as polluted (Bonaito et al., 1996). In short, a panoply of psychological phenomena contributes to this "hometown pollution effect," perhaps causing people to mistake or downplay—even to themselves—the likely impacts of existing pollution sources within their town, county, or state. The same effect could even attach to polluters, who may be all the more likely to exhibit cognitive distortion and moral disengagement to avoid conscious confrontation with the negative impacts of their pollution (Burns, 1989; Bandura, 2002, 2015; Helmond et al., 2015).

Exploring the parameters of such a hometown pollution effect would be a valuable line for future research, not least because it could have important implications for environmental federalism, which seeks to identify the optimal level of governance to address environmental problems. Generally speaking, environmental federalism literature attempts to navigate between two countervailing risks: that central governments will impose a one-size-fits-all policy that ignores local heterogeneity, and that local jurisdictions will ignore interjurisdictional spillovers that they inflict (Oates, 2002). The typical presumption throughout the literature is that local jurisdictions will actually understand their own risks and conditions better than the central government will, and that although localities may simply attempt to externalize pollution (and other) harms out of self-interest, the attempts will be conscious and strategic. A psychological approach to pollution, however, suggests that this account may miss an important aspect of local decision making. Local governments may actually sincerely believe that the likely externalities of their polluting behaviors, or the polluting behaviors of their residents, are less than they actually are, both because of the externality-minimizing psychological strategies we discussed earlier and also because of psychological strategies that lead them to discount the familiar-seeming risks of their hometown pollution. In this sense, local governments' understanding of their own impacts may be *worse* than those of central governments, who can assess pollution impacts without the barrier of overfamiliarity, egocentric bias, or the temptation to psychologically minimize harm to avoid cognitive dissonance.

Alternatively, consider the implications of a hometown polluter effect on the "polluter pays" principle, which is the notion that environmental laws should make the party responsible for producing pollution pay for the damage done by that pollution. The principle is incorporated into many U.S. laws, and also plays a central role in many environmental laws around the world. It is particularly foundational in the European Union (EU), where it has been incorporated into the Treaty on the Functioning of the EU (van Zeben & Rowell, 2020).

Although exact formulations of the principle vary by context, a common and generally uncontroversial economic formulation emphasizes that the principle forces the internalization of pollution externalities (Baumol & Oates, 1988; Nash, 2000; Woerdman, 2008). Yet one implication of the psychology of pollution is that—as we have noted—polluters may often legitimately and sincerely struggle to recognize the full harms of their actions because they tend to perceive their own pollution as familiar and inoffensive. This may prove problematic for several reasons. Consider that a core goal of forcing polluters to internalize the externalities of their pollution is to encourage them to engage in socially optimal behaviors, such that they only pollute when the likely harms of the pollution are greater than the marginal harm of pollution abatement (Coase, 1960). If the hometown pollution effect interferes with the ability of polluters to accurately identify harms, their tendency to systematically underestimate the damage of their pollution may lead them to overpollute—in comparison to socially optimal levels—despite effective liability regimes based on the polluter pays principle. Furthermore, the polluter pays principle may face legitimacy concerns even where it does not attach to liability structures. That is because estimates—even accurate estimates—of the harm polluters cause may strike polluters as unfair, even ludicrous, in comparison to their own deflated estimates of the same harm. Attempts to convey the true extent of the harm caused by pollution may even face substantial cognitive resistance as polluters egocentrically engage in cognitive distortion to avoid confronting the negative impacts of their behaviors on others (Bandura, 2002, 2015).

INDOOR VERSUS OUTDOOR ENVIRONMENTS
Another aspect of the psychology of pollution control may go to the definition of which spaces or places deserve protection and which do not. Indeed, some spaces may trigger exceptional, even foolhardy, tolerance for pollution. On this front, consider the fact that environmental laws are often widely understood to apply only outside, while indoor pollution risks are widely neglected—or when addressed, managed through regulatory schemes like the Occupational Safety and Health Act, rather than through environmental laws. The EPA, for instance—though clearly tasked through the Clean Air Act with regulating air pollutants—does not regulate indoor air quality. This is despite the fact that most people spend over 90% of their time indoors (Klepeis, 2001), that millions of people are routinely exposed to air pollutants at levels that are not allowed outdoors (Seltenrich, 2014), and that there are well-established, serious health impacts resulting from poor indoor air quality about which the EPA is fully aware.[1] This includes lung cancer from radon exposure, Legionnaires' disease and other airborne infections, carbon monoxide poisoning, secondhand smoke, and exacerbation of existing respiratory issues such as asthma and chronic obstructive pulmonary disorder, particularly from mold and excessive moisture.

The result is that the expansive environmental protections of the Clean Air Act apply in backyards, front porches, and outside open windows—but no federal environmental regime regulates air quality on the inside of the open window, or once a person steps through the front door into her home. Such a sharp regulatory distinction should be particularly disturbing given risk perception research suggesting, again, that people tend to discount risks that are familiar (Slovic et al., 1981), such as presumably those that arise in their own homes. Notably, such underplaying of self-created indoor pollutants—such as from one's own cooking (Seltenrich, 2014)—might also be expected to combine with the egocentric tendency to find one's own pollution less risky (Shu et al., 2011), and even less disgusting (Stevenson & Repacholi, 2005).

Notably, this psychological account of indoor pollution risk perception would suggest both that there may be little "supply side" pull for regulation of indoor environments, given people's perception of those environments as safe, and also that people may do a particularly poor job, in the absence of regulation, of managing indoor pollution risks on their own, given multiple psychological phenomena encouraging them to discount them. Of course, decisions about what and where to regulate in environmental law are necessarily normative decisions. That said, a psychological analysis of indoor and outdoor pollution-control policies might suggest that the choice to have pollution-control laws apply only outdoors may be a psychological artifact rather than an all-things-considered determination, and that such an artifact may be particularly dangerous in combination with the cognitive tendency of individuals to discount familiar, domestic risks.

HUMAN HEALTH VERSUS ENVIRONMENTAL IMPACTS OF POLLUTION

Another aspect of how psychology may affect which pollution risks are tolerated, and to what extent, is the question of whether the pollution has primarily human or nonhuman impacts. One common characteristic of pollution-control schemes in the United States is their focus on the human health impacts of pollution (Bach, 2014; Rowell & van Zeben, 2020). The Clean Air Act, for example, sets National Ambient Air Quality standards—the centerpiece of the Act—at a level "requisite to protect the public health" (42 U.S.C. § 7409 (b)). This focus on the human impacts of public health has sometimes been criticized as minimizing or de-emphasizing the nonhuman effects of pollution (Uhlmann, 2014). This choice of focus was not inevitable; after all, scientists have chronicled an extraordinary number, magnitude, and scope of pollution impacts on nonhuman animals, plants, and ecosystems (Freedman, 1989). Rather, it reflects a set of normative choices about what environmental law should seek to do (Bach, 2014). Again, psychology has little to say about the selection of appropriate normative goals of environmental law, and that includes the question of the appropriate weight to attach to human and nonhuman interests in pollution-control contexts.

That said, people do not value what they do not notice; and as we have emphasized, common psychological phenomena present barriers to empathy and attention toward nonhuman animals and ecosystems. At the same time, egocentrism bias and moral disengagement may lead humans—polluters—to cognitively minimize the harms they inflict on them. The combination of these impacts may contribute to normative choices to focus on human impacts, both by backgrounding possibilities for pollution-control regimes that are directed toward nonhuman impacts and by making it easier to dismiss nonhuman impacts where they are impossible to ignore.

How Are Pollutants Controlled?

A final consideration in pollution-control law and policy is the question of how—with which tools, instruments, and principles—pollution will be controlled. We have noted several such examples throughout this chapter; here we give three further examples of the dividends a psychological analysis of law can pay in addressing pollution control.

First, consider the broad range of contributions psychology may make in the realm of instrument choice. Although legal regimes around the world have developed robust schemes for managing many types of pollution, no pollution-control regime attempts to eliminate all pollution of all types under all circumstances. Instead, decisions about pollution control are characterized by attempts to balance the externalities created by pollution against the benefits that flow from whatever behaviors are generating the pollution to begin with (Revesz, 2015). Any strategy for pollution control can be furthered using a variety of legal tools. As we discussed earlier, particularly common legal instruments in environmental law include command-and-control regimes, ex post liability regimes, economic incentives, and information regimes (Richards & van Zeben, 2020).

More recently, psychological research has also been the basis for the development of new regulatory instruments—particularly choice architecture and "nudges" (Thaler & Sunstein, 2008)—and these instruments are increasingly being incorporated into the general tools used to address pollution control (Rowell, 2020a). There are also now increasing treatments of how psychology can best inform the structuring and implementation of particular tools. Loewenstein, Sunstein, and Golman (2014), for instance, have carefully documented ways in which psychological research can be used to increase the effectiveness of information disclosure regimes (including—though not focused on—pollution risks). For example, they suggest that while limited and motivated attention can undermine the ability of disclosure regimes to operate effectively, it is possible to address these defects using techniques such as standardizing disclosure formats, simplifying the information presented, and using vivid, high-salience imagery.

Psychology may also be helpful in informing debates within the instrument choice literature. Consider, for instance, that pollution-control regimes in the United States have long been criticized for an overreliance on command-and-control instruments such as bans and mandates (Ackerman & Stewart, 1985; Keohane et al., 1998). Admittedly, some scholars have also provided a qualified defense of command-and-control, or "traditional" regulation (Driesen, 2003), and others have provided nonpsychological accounts for why command-and-control has been so durable, despite a number of theoretical and economic challenges to its efficacy (Keohane et al., 1998). Here, we note a low-hanging psychological account of the continued popularity of command-and-control in pollution-control contexts: namely, that command-and-control tools often straightforwardly satisfy an intuitive psychological responses to pollution: disgust and recoil. This may be particularly true for bans, which seek to eliminate substances or pollutants entirely, regardless of expected exposure levels, and regardless of the potential costs of the ban (Slovic, 2000; Sunstein, 2002a).

It is similarly possible to tell a psychological story about the general preference for pollution prevention, sometimes called source reduction, in U.S. environmental law, versus recycling, treatment, disposal, or release. Many U.S. pollution-control statutes mandate pollution prevention of various kinds (Environmental Protection Agency, *Pollution prevention law and policies*), and the strategy remains particularly central to approaches to solid and hazardous waste under the Resource Conservation and Recovery Act. More generally, the Pollution Prevention Act formalizes pollution prevention as the most preferred policy option throughout federal environmental law, saying that "pollution should be prevented or reduced at the source whenever feasible"—and only then turns to alternative forms of management (Pollution Prevention Act, 1990, §13101(b)). Of course, there may be a number of policy benefits to pollution prevention, and it may be that pollution prevention is the normatively best approach to controlling pollution. One additional benefit the approach has, however, is a psychological one: It prevents the production of something that may trigger an affective response to perceived uncleanliness. In contrast, the relative appeal of recycling, treatment, and disposal may be diminished by the fact that all such strategies permit the psychologically repellant pollution to be generated in the first place.

A similar set of issues may arise in pollution-control decisions that affect the distribution of pollution harms. Because it is not possible to reduce all pollution to zero, pollution control also necessarily embeds normative choices about where pollution will be tolerated and who will be forced to bear its burden. Site selection for locally undesirable land uses or "LULUs" is particularly fraught with conflict, and frequently implicates the "NIMBY" ("not in my backyard") phenomenon, which we discuss further in the next chapter, where individuals and communities compete to keep out new land uses they find repellent (Brion, 1987). The resulting phenomenon triggers a number of environmental justice concerns, with LULUs disproportionately sited within poor communities and communities of color (Bullard, 1983; Been, 1992, 1994). The analysis above suggests that a portion of NIMBYism may flow from the emotional, affective response that many people feel to uses and substances they find disgusting, such as (new) waste dumps or incinerators. Insisting that disgusting polluting uses be kept as far away as possible may tap into an intuitive recoil from the unclean—a phenomenon that may help to explain the relative intractability of many NIMBY issues, perhaps most famously in the case of the functional elimination of the United States' centralized nuclear waste storage facility at Yucca Mountain, on the basis of local objections.

Alternatively, consider that the psychology of pollution control may affect the operation of a number of general principles and decision-making approaches in pollution-control law and policy. The precautionary principle, for example—which we discuss in much greater detail in the next chapter—is particularly subject to distortion by psychological and cognitive phenomena (Sunstein, 2005b), since it exhorts precautionary action while leaving substantial cognitive discretion on which risks to be precautionary about. More salient and dreaded risks are therefore more likely to be addressed—perhaps via cognitively straightforward instruments, such as bans—leaving less salient, seemingly inane risks unaddressed. In pollution-control contexts, this can lead to the aforementioned "pollution of the month" issues, while simultaneously failing to address the risks of "hometown," or familiar pollution. Although often defended for its rigor (Adler & Posner, 1999; Sunstein, 2002c; Revesz & Livermore, 2008), cost-benefit analysis can fall prey to similar selective psychological mechanisms because of its dependence upon accurate and comprehensive identification of the costs and benefits to be considered. In some cases, this may lead to a skew in perceptions of costs and benefits, for example, by prioritizing concerns for the human impacts of pollution control above the nonhuman impacts or by distorting valuations of future harms from pollution. These concerns are also fleshed out in greater detail in the next chapter.

Conclusion

Psychological research can be helpful in understanding and addressing both the problems generated by pollution and the solutions selected to control it. Generally speaking, psychological research suggests that pollution may trigger a constellation of psychological phenomena that drive pollution policy in some directions over others. Understanding the psychology of pollution perception and response can be helpful in improving pollution control by illuminating which substances get identified as pollutants, when pollutants may be tolerated, and how mechanisms for pollution control can and do operate.

Key Psychological Challenges Presented by Pollution

Environmental Nature of Pollution Injuries

The environmental nature of pollution injuries drives pollution policy in some directions over others.

- Diffusion. Diffusion of pollution effects through space and time facilitates minimization and dismissal of pollution externalities.
- Complexity. The complexity of nonlinear dose-response relationships,

particularly as combined with the emotional and cognitive load of disgust, incentivizes use of simplifying heuristics and approaches to pollution problems, intuitive toxicology, and expert-lay perception gaps.

- Nonhuman character. Barriers to attention and empathy toward nonhuman impacts may contribute to neglecting or minimizing nonhuman impacts of pollution.

Pollution-Specific Phenomena

Pollution-specific phenomena help explain distinctive perceptions of and responses to pollution risks.

- Disgust and impurity. The psychology of pollution and purity triggers emotional and cognitive load as well as intuitive toxicology and "all or nothing" responses.
- Source effects. Perceived pollution risks vary according to the source of the pollution; familiar, "natural," and "hometown" pollutants may fade into the background while novel and manmade pollutants may be hypersalient.
- Role-relative risk perception. Polluters may tend to underperceive the harms of their actions as a result of interaction between general environmental heuristics and egocentric bias, while victims of pollution may manage the cognitive and emotional load of expected harm via anxiety responses and/or strategies of denial and minimization.

All these phenomena may affect which substances get identified as pollutants, when pollutants are tolerated (and how much), and the effectiveness of pollution controls.

7

The Psychology of Ecosystem Management

Ecosystems have many potential uses and values, and law and policy can affect ecological systems in extraordinarily diverse ways. This chapter argues that psychology can be helpful in generating legal strategies for more effectively managing ecosystems and natural resources. To that end, the chapter specifically addresses the operation—and psychological vulnerabilities—of influential decision-making frameworks within environmental law, including the sustainability framework, the precautionary principle, and cost-benefit analysis.

The prior chapter on pollution control addressed the heart of what many environmental lawyers and scholars think of as environmental law. That said, controlling pollution is by no means the only way that environmental law attempts to regulate the environment. Environmental law also encompasses a broad set of choices and behaviors related to natural resource management and extraction, the preservation and conservation of special places and ecosystems, the management of public lands, and biodiversity and wildlife. While these areas can be affected by pollution, and thus by pollution control, pollution is not the only source of ecosystem degradation and thus not the only target of schemes attempting to manage ecosystems to their best ends.

This chapter begins by further highlighting the core challenges in ecosystem management, and exploring what a psychological understanding of people's perceptions, motivations, and cognitions regarding ecosystems might offer for enriching ecosystem management. It suggests psychology may be particularly helpful in explaining which aspects of ecosystems are noticed, understood, cared about—and thus addressed—in environmental law and policy. The chapter then highlights a set of concrete intellectual "payoffs" that help to illustrate how psychological analysis can explain and even improve the operation of ecosystem management. It identifies examples of how existing law can be better understood through a psychological lens, and how psychological research might be used to counteract some of the biases and psychological phenomena identified. Finally, it explores the psychology of influential decision-making frameworks that environmental law and policy relies upon for balancing and prioritizing among the many possible uses and qualities in the environment: the sustainability framework, often combined with the precautionary principle; and cost-benefit analysis, which is particularly influential within U.S. environmental law. While these approaches are influential throughout domestic and international environmental law, they have a particular relevance in ecosystem management, which requires trade-offs among so many potential environmental values. We discuss how the operation of each approach can be affected by psychological phenomena, leading to selective attention and in some cases the possibility that unconscious bias may shape environmental law. We also identify opportunities for potentially strengthening each approach to provide some immunity against psychological vulnerability.

The Challenges of Managing Ecosystems

Modern ecosystem management seeks to manage ecosystems purposefully, to achieve some goal or set of goals by preserving or restoring aspects of ecosystems that are deemed valuable. In considering the core challenges presented by ecosystem management, and in how and where psychology may be most helpful, it is worth considering where the field of ecosystem management started and the key challenges with which it continues to grapple.

The early days of ecosystem management in the United States are generally traced to the conservation movement, which was in turn deeply influenced by the Romantic movement, and by writers like Ralph Waldo Emerson and Henry David Thoreau, who promoted new attitudes toward nature. In the mid-19th century, scientists began piecing together some of the earliest ecological notions: George Perkins Marsh, in his *Man and Nature; or, Physical Geography as Modified by Human Action*, traced for the first time a variety of the long-term and diffuse consequences of deforestation—such as soil erosion, wildlife impacts, and watershed changes such as spring floods and summer droughts (Marsh, 1864). At the same time, increasingly easy transportation meant more and more people were able to travel to remote natural areas, and advances in printing and photography meant that more and more people were able to see (pictures of) some of the United States' most distinctive landscapes—increasingly imperiled by industrialization, resource extraction, and population growth—with their own eyes. Indeed, the work of landscape photographer Carleton Watkins has been called "the spark that started the national parks movement in the United States" (Rothman & Ronk, 2016, n.p.; Hobson, 2018).

The United States' first national park—Yellowstone—was designated in 1872. While it was followed by a number of additional parks in subsequent decades, the parks were at first haphazardly funded and managed, and were often purposefully left open to private commercial use, with the goal of using the lands for revenue generation. Subsequent decades saw the gradual establishment of multiple public lands schemes, including the National Forest Service in 1891, established with the stated purpose of designating and cultivating "forest reserves" for productive use and timber extraction, and, years later, in 1916 the National Park System, intended "to conserve the scenery, the natural and historic objects, and the wildlife in the United States' National Parks, and to provide for the public's enjoyment of these features in a manner that will leave them unimpaired for the enjoyment of future generations" (National Park Service Organic Act of 1916, 16 U.S.C. §1). Over time, the public lands system grew to encompass more than a quarter of the United States' land.

This sprawling public lands system is often viewed as an archetypal commons (Huber, 2018). As such, it presents a constellation of challenges related to managing externalities, access, and competing interests. Modern approaches to ecosystem management are informed by increasingly nuanced ecological understanding. The term "ecosystem" was first coined by Arthur Tansley, a pioneer in the science of ecology, in the 1930s. In explaining the importance of the concept of an ecological system, Tansley explained that "[t]hough the organisms may claim our prime interest, when we are trying to think fundamentally, we cannot separate them from their special environments, with which they form one physical system" (Tansley, 1935, p. 299). The interconnected nature of ecological systems was further explored and articulated in subsequent decades, including famously by Aldo Leopold, whose concept of a "land ethic"—which remains deeply influential in environmental ethics and policy today—was explicitly based upon the notion of what he called "biotic communities," which included "the land"—soil, waters, plants, animals—as well as humans (Leopold, 1949). "We can only be ethical," Leopold warned presciently, "in relation to something we can see, understand, feel, love, or otherwise have faith in" (Leopold, 1949, p. 214).

The science of ecology grew in leaps and bounds over the next half-century, supporting the modern notion of ecosystems as geographic areas where living entities (plants, animals, and other organisms) and nonliving substances (water, air, oil, rocks) interact in mutually inter-dependent ways (Robbins, 2013). As ecology and environmental science advanced over time, an understanding of the relationships between law and policy and ecosystem quality developed as well. By the 1990s, this understanding had formalized into a conception of "ecosystem management," a term coined by Forest Service Chief F. Dale Robertson in 1992 and meant to indicate purposeful management of ecosystems that seeks to achieve some particular set of goals, policies, protocols, and practices (Christensen, 1996; Robbins, 2013).

The goals, policies, protocols, and practices sought in modern eco-system management are diverse. Indeed, policy makers may choose to allow, prevent, or mitigate ecosystem degradation, which occurs when-ever valued aspects of an ecosystem are harmed. Policy makers may also attempt to repair past degradation through ecosystem restoration or to purposefully change existing ecosystems to secure more of whatever is valued (Rowell & van Zeben, 2020). This may include decisions about development, conservation, land use, natural resources, and even agri-culture (Robbins, 2013).

As John Nagle and J. B. Ruhl (2007, p. 335) have pointed out, how-ever, "[T]his only begs the question: What *are* the goals, policies, pro-tocols, and practices of ecosystem management?" The question is only made more difficult by the fact that any particular ecosystem presents countless opportunities to provide value—yet not all sources of value can be maximized simultaneously. A wetland that is filled with soil to support fruitful agriculture or to build a much-needed hospital cannot also provide a home for frogs and marsh birds; a rushing river that sup-ports leaping copper salmon and the animals that feed upon them can-not also be dammed for hydroelectric power; a primeval forest that is preserved as a wilderness cannot also be cleared for its timber resources to be made into the pages of a book. Activities that change (or preserve) an ecosystem for one function necessarily give up much, if not all, of the potential benefits of other uses. As a result, managing ecosystems inevitably requires trade-offs between different worthwhile things—and often those trade-offs involve competing social, cultural, and environmental values, as well as the claims of competing stakeholders. Laws and policies regarding ecosystem management thus reflect specific judgments about which ecosystems, or which qualities of ecosystems, are viewed as most deserving of protection or promotion (Rowell & van Zeben, 2020; van Zeben & Rowell, 2020).

Consider, for example, the special protection of wetlands implemented in the United States under § 404 of the Clean Water Act, or the protections granted to geographic areas of special value under the various public lands systems, including the National Forest System, the National Park System, the National Wildlife Refuge System, the National Wilderness Preservation System, and the National System of Public Lands—not to mention further expansive public lands and park schemes at state and local levels. Under such approaches, particular types or particular ecosystems are protected for particular purposes. Or consider the multiplicity of statutes that protect special animal species and their habitats, such as the Migratory Bird Treaty Act, the Bald Eagle Act, the African Elephant Conservation Act, or the Marine Mammals Protection Act. Policies promoting agriculture or particular agricultural policies (such as restricting planting of genetically modified crops or the use of pesticides impacting bee populations) or development (such as with zoning for residential use or subsidies for development) often preference certain ecosystems or uses (such as agriculture or development) over others (such as maintaining wild habitat), and can also have important and wide-ranging impacts on ecosystems (Rowell & van Zeben, 2020). Finally, and as we discuss further below, decisions about how to administer ecosystem-based statutes—whether via regulatory policy, land use practices, or state and local laws—may also end up preferencing some ecosystems over others.

The determination of which ecosystems, or ecosystem qualities, are "best"—or most worth protection, or deserving of care and/or ethical treatment—is ultimately a normative question. As we have said, psychology is not particularly helpful in guiding choice among normative frameworks for making such decisions. That said, and as we discuss in the next sections, psychological research may still be helpful in informing both when and why particular ecosystems or qualities get selected as deserving of special care and attention, as well as the expected impact of legal interventions. In some contexts, it may also offer aid in adopting— and debiasing—decision-making frameworks, to help more effectively achieve whichever ends are selected.

The Psychology of Managing Ecosystems

Although what exactly counts as a worrisome injury to an ecosystem may vary depending upon ecosystem managers' legal or normative commitments, ecosystem injury clearly triggers the constellation of psychological phenomena that we have already articulated as central to environmental injury. Below, we highlight several particularly important aspects of how the diffuse, complex, and nonhuman character of ecosystem injury can be expected to affect people's perception, understanding, and caring about those injuries. In addition, we argue in this section that certain aspects of ecosystem management may trigger distinctive psychological phenomena—particularly regarding the psychology of place, scarcity, and uniqueness—and suggest that understanding these phenomena may help in crafting more reflective and effective ecosystem management goals, policies, protocols, and practices.

Ecosystem Injury as Environmental Injury

As we discussed throughout the first half of this book, the impacts of human action on nonhuman environments are often diffuse, complex, and nonhuman in character. In the context of ecosystem management, it is worth flagging a few specific aspects of each of these characteristics that might be expected to impact how people notice and respond to ecosystem impacts.

DIFFUSION
Ecosystem impacts can be spread across space and time, though the psychology of diffusion is likely to operate differently for the two.

First, consider spatial diffusion. Some behaviors generate harms that diffuse across large swaths of the planet: Consider, on this front, the increasing pervasiveness of microplastics throughout every media and ecosystem (Rochman et al., 2016; M. L. Taylor et al., 2016; Zhang et al., 2020). Other behaviors may cause only distant impacts, though those impacts may be concentrated and severe. Agricultural practices across the American Midwest, for example, contribute to eutrophication of the Mississippi River and have added to the vast "dead zone" in the Gulf of Mexico, which now has oxygen levels too low to support life. In such cases the causes of ecosystem injury are diffuse—as where many individual Midwestern farmers make choices about their own fields—but the impacts are concentrated in an identifiable "place" or ecosystem where substantial injury accrues, such as the Gulf of Mexico. This pattern distinguishes many ecosystem injuries from, for example, the harms from climate change, which may or may not be concentrated enough to be observable in any particular location. In such cases, where ecosystem injuries are obvious and localized, it may partially immunize observers from some of the psychological distortions (such as the availability heuristic or undersalience effects) that can otherwise attach to environmental harms whose impacts are diffuse. Yet it would be easy to overstate the impact of this potential immunization: Because so many ecosystem impacts are hidden from view, by time if not by space, they still trigger concerns about unavailability and unobservability, which may in turn translate into emotional distancing and relatively low salience of ecosystems risks.

Furthermore, as environmental scholars know, when ecosystems are affected by human behavior, both the causes and the impacts of that behavior may be spread over long time periods (Revesz, 1999). A degraded ecosystem may be degraded forever; a lost species may be lost forever. Nonrenewable resource extraction—such as oil drilling, mining for minerals, or depleting an aquifer—generally presents a one-shot opportunity; once extracted, such resources by definition do not renew. Even the harvest of renewable resources, such as timber, requires balancing costs and benefits over time; a tree cut today cannot be cut tomorrow or even a year from now. As a result, ecosystem management decisions routinely affect future and far-future environmental quality. In processing temporally distant impacts, both individuals and policy makers are likely to fall prey to the psychological phenomena related to temporal diffusion that we detailed previously, including difficulties with managing future uncertainty, hedonic forecasting, hyperbolic discounting, and present bias. On the whole, such phenomena may tend to lead ecosystem managers to attach a heightened value to preservation (preventing losses from the status quo); to be impatient about gathering value from ecosystems; and to miss and mispredict the value of delaying actions that are likely to have significant ecosystem impacts. As we discuss further below, such predictions are at least consistent with the long tradition of preservationism in environmental policy, and with analysis showing that even sophisticated agencies tend to neglect the value of delaying resource extraction (Livermore, 2015).

Where ecosystem impacts are intergenerational in scope, they may also implicate distinct psychological phenomena related to group identification. The cost to future generations of destroying an ecosystem, for example, may be easy to ignore in part because the stakeholders are so distant in time, or even because the stakeholders would be coded as out-group members. Finally, permanent and very-long-term ecosystem impacts may also trigger concerns about permanence and irreversibility—concerns sometimes used to justify precautionary decision making (Sunstein, 2006a), and which courts have used as a justification for legal requirements that mandate consideration of environmental actions prior to government action (*Sierra Club v. Marsh*, 1989; Sunstein, 2006a).

COMPLEXITY

Second, consider the complexities involved in gathering and interpreting information about ecosystems. Nature is extraordinarily complex, which creates substantial and systematic challenges to creating effective legal mechanisms to manage it (Doremus, 2010a; Doremus & Tarlock, 2005). To accurately predict the impacts of their own choices, decision makers are dependent upon information about how living and nonliving entities relate to and depend on one another, through time as well as across space. These relationships are complicated. Furthermore, not every potentially damaging behavior necessarily leads to the same amount of harm. Many ecosystems exhibit some level of resilience to disruption (Folke et al., 2002), yet research suggests there may also be nonlinear "tipping points" where even small changes may destroy the whole ecosystem (Dakos et al., 2019). Many of these tipping points are themselves interactive; a sudden increase in one species (or even young members of that species) can have surprising and stochastic effects on other inhabitants of the ecosystem (Pine et al., 2009). As a result, the same human behaviors may cause different levels of harm depending upon other people's behaviors, or even on when or where they occur. A few people fishing may leave local fish populations largely unaffected, but a few more people engaging in the same behavior (or at the wrong time of year) may decimate the same population. Yet while tipping points may be common, they are difficult to predict, not least because ecosystems are dynamic, responding and adapting to human impacts as they occur (Angeler et al., 2019; Pine et al., 2009).

In the past, when ecosystem management approaches have ignored these complexities, treating ecosystems as if injury to them is linear, predictable, stable, and fully subject to human direction, they have struggled to effectively achieve their policy ends (Folke et al., 2002; Doremus, 2010a). Holly Doremus, for example, has famously critiqued the Endangered Species Act for its "unrealistically static vision of nature," arguing that it undermines the act's ability to address dynamic and—with climate change—increasingly changing ecosystems, and the species that live within them (Doremus, 2010a, p. 175). Her account of the law's unrealistic oversimplification is partly social and political, and partly psychological: She flags what she calls the "psychological pull of a stable vision of nature" (p. 231) as a key stumbling block in developing ecosystem management practices that meaningfully address the dynamic and complex qualities of the natural environment.

Certainly, the complex nature of ecosystem injury increases the difficulty of the task for ecosystem managers. Institutional decision makers can respond by turning to experts—but while this approach may increase the quality of information relied upon, it does not eliminate the operation of heuristics and biases, and it may even *increase* their incidence. One entertaining study, for instance, found that self-proclaimed experts are more vulnerable to the illusion of knowledge than are people who perceive themselves to be inexperienced. In the study, people who reported themselves to be knowledgeable about a subject—such as biology or geography—were more likely to claim to be familiar with made-up words and locations, such as "meta-toxins," "bio-sexual," and "retroplex," or the imaginary town of Cashmere, Oregon (Atir et al., 2015).

Even where ecosystem managers can call upon high-quality scientific information and recognize the limits of that information, they still face substantial policy challenges (Doremus & Tarlock, 2005). These include defining the geographic and temporal spaces that should be protected; coordinating ecosystem management across multiple decision makers and with other environmental policies; and, most controversially, determining which qualities of ecosystems are valuable enough to justify policy intervention (Rowell & van Zeben, 2020).

NONHUMAN CHARACTER

The nonhuman character of ecosystem harms is very apparent. Harms to ecosystems may, of course, harm people; but the direct impacts of ecosystem degradation are on nonhuman animals, plants, and entities— all of which, as we have discussed, may struggle to induce the kind of emotional connection and empathy that converts into caring. In other words, the nonhuman character of ecosystems may create a kind of generalized empathy barrier to people caring about damage to it. To be fair, such impacts may be muted or even flipped in some circumstances, where the specific characteristics of nonhuman stakeholders overcome these barriers. Very beautiful landscapes, for example, may trigger appreciation and thus attention; very cute animals may trigger caring and thus protection, particularly where their features trigger tendencies toward anthropomorphism. Yet in general, psychological research suggests that ecosystem injuries will be harder to perceive and less likely to invite empathy and caring than human injuries would be.

In addition, ecosystem management implicates research in environmental psychology on the impact of nonhuman spaces, and the experience of wildness. Recall, on this front, that environmental psychology chronicles a number of measurable emotional benefits to humans from interacting with the environment (Gifford, 2007; Maple & Morris, 2018). Looking at trees (Jiang et al., 2016), or even just pictures of nature (van den Berg et al., 2015) measurably reduces stress levels, for instance. These findings may be helpful for understanding the value that people place on parks and green spaces, and for understanding the social impacts of policies that protect and create such spaces. Psychological benefits of ecosystems should also be thought of, on their own, as a form of ecosystem service that can generate benefits for people, the value of which should be incorporated into decisions about ecosystem management. While recent scholarship has begun to explore this (Bratman et al., 2012), there is not yet a policy tradition of addressing the psychological and mental health benefits of ecosystems as a distinctive category of ecosystem services. Even the more sophisticated approaches, such as the EPA's EnviroAtlas, deal only indirectly with these benefits, as by attempting to wrap them into concern about aesthetics.

Finally, as we discussed earlier and address in more detail below, the perception of scarcity and uniqueness tends to change how people perceive and value risks and opportunities. The nonhuman character of many ecosystem injuries may feed into the perception of ecosystems and ecosystem services as both scarce and unique—and thus worthy of special demand and (potentially) special protection.

Distinctive Aspects of Ecosystem Injuries

In addition to triggering psychological phenomena related to the diffuse, complex, and nonhuman aspects of ecosystem injury, we believe that ecosystem management also implicates two additional lines of psychological research, which bear particularly on the qualities of ecosystems as unique and scarce places and resources.

PSYCHOLOGY OF PLACE AND PROPERTY

The boundaries of ecosystems can be difficult to define. The exact extent of what constitutes "waters of the United States," for instance, remains a troubling legal problem, which has fundamental implications for which areas can be categorized and protected as wetlands under the Clean Water Act (*Rapanos v. United States*, 2006). Yet generally speaking, ecosystems are tied to geographic space (Doremus, 2000; Robbins, 2012). This is particularly true within the subfield of natural resources law, which addresses aspects of ecosystems that are thought to be economically or socially valuable "resources," via resource extraction, management of public lands, wildlife law, forest management, mining, and water law (Fischman, 2007). Because of its relationship with property law, and its tendency to address specific places and ecosystems "*in situ*," natural resources law is particularly reliant on state law, and on local and subnational legal structures that affect land use choices (Doremus, 2000; Fischman, 2007). Other state and local property doctrines, and land use decisions in particular, also substantially impact local ecosystems. These decisions are generally managed by local and municipal zoning boards, which are administrative bodies that decide the location and type of development and use that will be permitted.

The relationship between property law and many aspects of ecosystem management may be important for more than doctrinal reasons. As Stephanie Stern and Daphna Lewinsohn-Zamir (2020) have chronicled, property law implicates a broad range of distinctive psychological phenomena related to the acquisition, use, and transfer of resources. Where ecosystems are thought of as property, and where ecosystem management decisions must be made in light of natural resources, the psychology of property becomes particularly relevant.

One important aspect of this relationship with place and property relates to the tendency of property to trigger the endowment effect, loss aversion, and status quo bias. As we discussed in Chapter 5, the endowment effect relates to people's tendency to value things that they own more than things they do not (Kahneman et al., 1991). The effect operates even for newly acquired, interchangeable goods—suggesting that merely mentally categorizing something as one's own property is enough to trigger a heightened sensitivity to loss, or loss aversion—but it operates even more for goods that are perceived as unique, distinctive, or with which the person identifies (List, 2003; Buccafusco & Sprigman, 2011). This makes allocations of property and qualities viewed as the status quo particularly prone to "stickiness."

Such effects have a number of implications across legal contexts, and indeed were among the earliest phenomena in psychology to find their way into legal scholarship (Jolls et al., 1998). In ecosystem management contexts, these phenomena may operate to support continued interest in preservation, conservation, and sustainability as management strategies. The tie is likely strongest to preservationism, an approach that seeks to preserve places or ecosystems at a particular status quo. In U.S. environmental law, preservationism is particularly embedded within wilderness protections. The National Wilderness Preservation System, often characterized as the most restrictive of the United States' public lands schemes (Long & Biber, 2014), seeks to preserve designated areas to "leave them unimpaired for future use and enjoyment as wilderness," and to achieve "preservation of their wilderness character" (National Wilderness Protection Act, 16 U.S.C. § 1133(c)). Yet even conservation-based approaches, such as the National Park Service Organic Act, conceive of some baseline or status quo that they will seek to conserve: That act, for instance, tells the National Park Service to regulate the Parks "to conserve the scenery and the natural and historic objects and the wild life therein" (16 U.S.C. §1). And sustainability approaches necessarily require some concept of what it is that needs to be "sustained" (Gale & Cordray, 1994), a baseline that is also often set by reference to the status quo. This is not to say that preservationism, conservation, and sustainability are not valuable normative goals on their own. As we discuss further in the last part of this chapter, however, it is worth considering the ways in which the endowment effect, loss aversion, and status quo bias may interact with perceptions of the value of conservation and the desirability of sustainability.

PSYCHOLOGY OF SCARCITY AND UNIQUENESS

Ecosystems and species are unique, and resources are scarce. As a result, the distinctive psychology of uniqueness and scarcity may play particularly important roles in affecting how people respond to ecosystems, and thus in how ecosystems end up being managed.

First, recall the research on uniqueness that we canvassed earlier, which shows that people exhibit preferences for goods and qualities they perceive as one of a kind. This preference for uniqueness starts early in childhood, with children as young as three (Hood & Bloom, 2008), and it is heightened where people associate particular objects or places in the world around them with aspects of their personal identity (Csikszentmihalyi, 1993) or social identity (Leonardelli et al., 2010). In some cases, the value attached to a sense of uniqueness can interact with the psychology of place and lead to extraordinary protection of the perceived status quo; consider here again New Zealand's choice to kill all nonnative animals by 2050 in order to protect "New Zealand's unique native creatures and plants" which "are central to our national identity" (Greshko, 2016, n.p.).

Notably, copies of unique goods are insufficient replacements (Hood & Bloom, 2008; Bloom, 1996). Early work on these phenomena looked specifically at people's high valuation of original art and distaste for counterfeits (Bloom, 1996). Consider in this light the long-term debate in environmental ethics about the appropriate value to attach to ecological restoration projects, which seek to return damaged or degraded ecosystems to their prior status, or in some cases to generate new and similar ecosystems—such as wetlands—elsewhere (Elliott, 1982; Katz, 2012). In one influential essay, *Faking Nature*, Robert Elliot explicitly invoked a comparison to counterfeit art, arguing that even a perfect re-creation of an original lacks the value of that original (Elliott, 1982). Such arguments and intuitions have real legal and practical weight, insofar as they are then translated into policies of ecosystem management that disfavor restoration over other techniques such as conservation.

In some cases, the fact that uniqueness raises the salience of ecosystems or ecosystem qualities may act as a partial tonic against the human tendency to otherwise neglect environmental harms. This may be particularly true for aspects of ecosystems for which there are other factors increasing salience and/or emotional connection, including picturesque spaces, identity-related places, and appealing animal species. That said, while uniqueness may raise the relative salience of some goods, qualities, species, or ecosystems, it is not a cure-all. Especially where ecosystem impacts are easy to neglect for other reasons, they may still become mentally swamped by other considerations (Slovic, 2015).

Unique goods are by definition scarce. Nonunique environmental goods may also be scarce, however, as is the case with natural resources, multiple members of an endangered species, and vanishing ecosystem types. Like uniqueness, scarcity increases the perceived value of goods (Mittone & Savadori, 2009). Recall that perceived scarcity triggers a constellation of psychological phenomena, sometimes called a "scarcity mindset" (Mullainathan & Shafir, 2013). This can lead to tunnel vision, cognitive overload, and a type of durable preoccupation that can actually lead to the type of mismanagement that causes even greater scarcity.

The effects of perceived scarcity on ecosystems can be particularly perverse, potentially leading ecosystem managers to adopt policies that push people in exactly the opposite direction of what is intended. Consider, for instance, a study done by Cialdini and colleagues on thefts of pieces of petrified wood from the Petrified Wood National Park (Cialdini et al., 2006). Researchers planted pieces of petrified wood along the visitor trails, preceded by one of two signs. Either visitors saw a sign that read, "Many past visitors have removed petrified wood from the Park, changing the natural state of the Petrified Forest," along with an image of three different visitors pocketing pieces of wood (the "scarcity/social proof" condition), or instead they saw a sign that said, "Please don't remove the petrified wood from the Park, in order to preserve the natural state of the Petrified Forest," along with a sign showing one visitor pocketing wood, with a large red circle and hash mark over it (the control condition). Over the duration of the study, about 8% of the wood was stolen in the scarcity condition versus less than 2% in the control.

This study, and related research, should be understood as conveying an important warning to policy makers managing scarce resources. As National Parks struggle to deal with overtourism, for example, they should be cautious of strategies that emphasize the scarcity of the National Parks as a resource or that suggest to the public that at current tourism levels, there is a limited time before parks are degraded. Such messages may inadvertently convey to potential visitors that they should "get while the getting is good." The current tourism crisis in Venice—a city widely known to be at extraordinary threat of destruction from climate change—may be the result of this type of scarcity-based thinking (Hardy, 2019).

Note that crafting just the right communication strategy for the relative abundance or scarcity of environmental resources is complicated by the fact that abundance may also affect valuation. Just as scarcity increases subjective value, perceived abundance may decrease it. Consider how the passenger pigeon was hunted to extinction, although—perhaps in part because—flocks once covered the entire sky. Or recall again the relative indifference of the EPA to the deaths of trillions of aquatic organisms. Where there is seeming abundance, people may be that much more willing to engage in waste. We know this is true of household consumer products (Wansink, 1996) and food portion sizes (Zlatevska et al., 2014); perhaps it is also true of environmental goods. In short, both too much of an environmental good and too little of it may lead to its underprotection. Communicating about the relative scarcity or abundance of environmental goods should thus be thought of as psychologically fraught and risky in the sense that current research fails to provide meaningful, evidence-backed strategies for ecosystem managers. Additional research in this realm would be very valuable in crafting effective guidance.

Individual and Institutional Decision Making Regarding Ecosystems

Ecosystem management presents challenging and fundamental questions about the relationship between humankind and nature. We believe that legal management of these challenges may be improved through understanding how the psychology of ecosystem management, and the psychology of ecosystem perception, affects people. We provide concrete examples of such applications in the following section. Before we do so, however, it is worth explaining how the psychological research we have canvassed may shed light on people's choices regarding ecosystems in both individual and institutional contexts.

Individuals contribute to ecosystem management in two important ways: through their individual behavior and through political action. Both of these types of behaviors present individuals with substantial cognitive hurdles in dealing with ecosystem risks because the salience of ecosystem impacts tends to be quite low, and individuals will face systematic cognitive barriers in understanding the complexity of ecosystems while facing emotional barriers to engaging with and caring about ecosystem harms.

Individuals sometimes affect the law and policy of ecosystem management through direct involvement in legal and political decision making. This includes bringing citizen suits or filing petitions—as through the Endangered Species Act, making comments to environmental regulators, voting and participating in political processes, and filing suit in common law against neighbors or others who might be causing ecosystem degradation. For all of these activities, the actions of individuals are potentially susceptible to the same set of psychological phenomena we have been discussing throughout the book—phenomena that tend, on the whole, to make environmental harms like ecosystem degradation less salient and therefore less likely to be noticed and acted upon. These same phenomena may even make it challenging for individuals who do value ecosystems, or particular qualities of ecosystems, to learn when law and policy is being made that will affect the ecosystems or ecosystem qualities they care about.

Even when they overcome problems of low salience, individual attitudes and beliefs may influence individuals' perception of risk to ecosystems as well as the behaviors that follow from those perceptions. Cultural cognition research suggests that people's political and cultural beliefs can be used to predict their environmental risk perceptions (Overdevest & Christiansen, 2013). Such perceptions inform the general public—who then presumably take political (in)action on the basis of those beliefs—but may also guide individual participants in stakeholder processes, such as those that frequently occur in local zoning decisions and other more localized ecosystem management processes. For instance, one study on risk perceptions in a controversial water-supply planning process in Florida found that stakeholders who valued hierarchy and individualism tended to perceive less ecological risk, and individuals who valued egalitarianism and communitarianism to perceive more ecological risk, when presented with the same facts about a proposed project (Overdevest & Christiansen, 2013).

In the United States, ecosystems are managed by a variety of federal, state, local, and private actors, all of whom make decisions that can shape ecosystems (Rowell & van Zeben, 2020). As with any other type of decision, decisions about ecosystems may be context dependent, and institutions can play an important role in defining contextual cues. One source of context is the mission of the particular institution in question, which may have an impact not only on how it explains its decision making but also on how that decision making actually occurs. In some cases, those institutions do not present themselves as having affirmative environmental responsibilities or goals; in others, the environmental "mission" is strong, even explicit.

In addition to goal setting, another piece of psychological context to consider is priming, a phenomenon where exposure to one stimulus influences the response to subsequent stimuli—even without conscious guidance or intention (Bargh et al., 2001). At a basic level, priming affects what is most salient to a decision maker by bringing a particular word or concept into the forefront of the mind, making it cognitively and emotionally available. We have already discussed how priming with money can change the substance of decisions. Such impacts may attach not only to agency actors engaging in cost-benefit analysis, but also to private actors acting within for-profit companies, particularly when they are thinking about justifications to shareholders and a profit motive. But what happens when other important institutional decision makers—such as nonprofits and agencies—are primed in other ways? Consider the potential impact of mission statements—statements about the explicit purpose of the organization. By definition, all nonprofits have some mission other than seeking profit, and all agencies have some purpose identified by Congress. Perhaps vivid, clear statements about those missions can act as meaningful primes, keeping the mission of the nonprofit or the agency at the forefront of workers' minds. Another possibility is that required decision-making tasks—such as the requirement to consider environmental impacts prior to undertaking significant federal actions—may act as a prime, again potentially shaping institutional behavior, even in the absence of formal enforcement mechanisms.

Finally, consider that organizations and institutions of any type are characterized by group decision making. Research on group decision making suggests that it tends to be subject to distinctive psychological phenomena, including bandwagon effects, cascades (Heath, 1996), and group polarization (Myers & Lamm, 1976). These effects are likely to be particularly large when—as may happen within environmental organizations—members of the group share similar beliefs and starting points. In such cases, people tend to "end up accepting a more extreme version of the views with which they began" (Sunstein, 2005b, p. 98). These phenomena may influence the substance of groups' decisions about ecosystem management, and they may also distort demand for and analysis of environmental regulations (Kuenzler & Kysar, 2014).

Applying the Psychology of Ecosystem Management

In this section, we highlight examples of three ways psychology can help with the law of ecosystem management. First, we suggest that psychology can enrich our understanding of how existing environmental laws operate on the ground. To illustrate, we discuss the example of the Endangered Species Act, the operation of which can be better understood by looking at how psychological phenomena pull people's attention and empathy in identifiable directions. Second, psychology can highlight opportunities to use law to anticipate and respond to psychological phenomena, and even to shape behavior in light of that knowledge. Here, we give the example of the potential debiasing impacts of the National Environmental Policy Act. Finally, we suggest that psychology can be helpful in understanding the operation of important decision-making frameworks in environmental law that play a particularly important role in ecosystem management, including the sustainability framework, the precautionary principle, and cost-benefit analysis.

Understanding the Operation and Effects of Environmental Laws

Psychological research on cognitive availability and salience may be informative in considering which species and ecosystems garner legal and policy attention. People do not act to protect things they do not notice. As an important example, consider the Endangered Species Act (ESA). Before an animal or plant species can receive the substantial protection provided by the ESA, it must first be added to the federal list of endangered and threatened wildlife and plants. Species are added to the list either through an internal agency process or through a petition process, through which any interested person can ask the Secretary of the Interior or the Secretary of Commerce (for most marine life) to add (or remove) a species. If the agency determines that the species qualifies as threatened or endangered, it is directed to add the species to the list. Notably, the ESA itself does not prioritize some types of species over others: Under §2, any species of fish, wildlife, or plants may be protected, so long as the species is listed as "in danger of or threatened with extinction" (Endangered Species Act of 1973; Mann & Plummer, 1995; Nagle, 1998).

Being added to the list substantially improves the chances that a plant or animal species will survive. One recent study suggests that the ESA has saved 99% of listed species from extinction (Greenwald et al., 2019). Notably, in addition to providing powerful protections to the species themselves, the ESA also protects the species' critical habitat. In this way it has a direct impact on ecosystem management. The act is powerful enough that it has been used to stop even very large public projects, as with the famous decision in *Tennessee Valley Authority v. Hill* (1978), in which the Supreme Court ordered a halt to all federal operations to finish the almost-complete multimillion-dollar Tellico Dam upon discovery of the endangered snail darter—an economically insignificant fish—in the waters of the Little Tennessee River.

To date, 2,349 species have been listed as threatened or endangered under the ESA (U.S. Fish and Wildlife Service, 2019). Of these, 947 (40%) are plants, whereas 1,402 (60%) are animals. Within these kingdoms, the protection offered different types of species varies widely, despite the fact that the statute itself does not distinguish between them. Mammals, for instance, constitute 377 (or about one-sixth) of the total protected species, while only 17 species of arachnids are protected. Other less-familiar animals, like annelid worms (segmented worms such as earthworms), have zero species protected. This, despite the fact that only about 5,450 species of mammals have been identified, while there are over 16,500 identified species of annelid worms and over 60,000 arachnids. Similarly, of the 298,000 species of plants currently known to science (Mora et al., 2011), the ESA protects only 947.

In some ways, the differences in protection are even more striking when the percentage of species protected are compared to the number of those species thought to exist. If you count by percentage of species protected, the ESA is 7 times more protective of mammals than it is of reptiles, 3 times more protective of reptiles than plants, 3 times more protective of plants than insects, and 3 times more protective of insects than arachnids. If arachnids were protected at the same rate as mammals, there would be 4,200 protected arachnid species—4,183 more than there are now. Even arachnids, however, garner more protection than lowly annelid worms, many of whom toil through their largely invisible lives underground or underwater.

Levels of Protection Under the EPA for Plant and Animal Species			
Type	# of Species Protected	# of Species Known to Exist	% of Known Species Protected by ESA
Mammals	377	5,450	7%
Reptiles	141	10,000	1%
Plants	947	298,000	0.3%
Insects	89	91,000	0.1%
Arachnids	17	60,000	0.03%
Annelids	0	16,500	0%

Notably, there is no evidence that the varying rates of protection for different types of species reflect the actual threats to those species. If anything, climate disruption is thought to threaten reptiles more than mammals, as cold-blooded animals have fewer adaptive capabilities when faced with changing temperatures (Harvey, 2018; Rolland et al., 2018)—yet mammals are protected at greater rates than reptiles. Scientists warn that about a fifth of plant species are expected to struggle to survive in coming decades (Willis, 2017) and that 40% of insect species are in measurable decline, in large part as a result of changes in land use (Sanchez-Bayo & Wyckhuys, 2019). Yet only a tiny proportion of these species have been listed as protected.

Nor are varying protection rates best understood as evidence of different levels of ecological importance. As the Senate Environmental and Public Works Committee recognized in hearings before enacting the ESA, "Biologically it makes sense to treat all taxonomic groups equally or even to place some special emphasis on protecting plants and invertebrates since they form the bases of ecosystems and food chains upon which all other life depends" (S. Rep. No. 97-418, 1982, p. 14). This observation served as the basis for the legislative choice to protect all species "in danger of or threatened with extinction."

If the statute is facially neutral as to species types to be protected, and if the differing rates at which species are listed is not a result of varying threats, why are the species protected by the ESA so relatively heavy on mammals and light on reptiles, plants, insects, arachnids, and worms? We believe that that the answer lies in the listing process itself—and in the psychology of those invoking that process.

The vast majority of the species listed as threatened or endangered under the ESA—by one count, 80% (Puckett et al., 2016)—were added to the list because of the petition process (and in many cases, subsequent litigation). As a result, the portfolio of protected species is a product not so much of any vision or plan on the part of any single person or agency, but rather the result of many different actors identifying and following up on potentially threatened species about which they knew and cared.

This suggests that the portfolio of protected species under the ESA is at least partly a product of whatever leads people to know, and care, about animal and plant species. And here, the psychology of availability and empathy may provide insight. Someone must notice a species—and have research supporting their description of the species' endangerment—before the species can be protected. Less salient species are less likely to be noticed and therefore less likely to be listed. Bigger species—like elephants or sharks—may simply be easier to spot than smaller, shyer species like annelid worms and insects, and photogenic species may be appealing to picture and to visualize. These so-called "charismatic megafauna" are key attractions at zoos and wildlife preserves, and in other contexts, research suggests that thinking about and seeing large, charismatic animals promotes pro-conservation behaviors (Skibins et al., 2013). Furthermore, the problem of differential attention to big, attractive species versus small, less-attractive species may be exacerbated if similar psychological phenomena lead to research path distortions: If fewer people choose to study annelid worms and insects, there will be less scientific information to support potential endangerment findings. Indeed, there seems to be a shortage of qualified biologists to file and review listing petitions for insect species (Lugo, 2006).

Of course, even if a species is noticed and suspected to be endangered, there must be additional action taken before it can be listed. Here it matters how much people care about the potential loss of the species. Psychological research can help shed some light on what leads people to care more about some species than others.

Some accounts in evolutionary psychology suggest that there may be evolutionary reasons that humans feel empathy for some animals and not others (Bradshaw & Paul, 2010). These empathies may be so adaptive they are hardwired. Consider that many primates, including humans, have biologically predisposed aversions—sometimes called "biophobias"—toward venomous animals, particularly spiders and snakes (Bradshaw & Paul, 2010). Even 6-month-old babies in countries with no dangerously venomous spiders have been shown to have automatic fear responses to such animals (Hoehl et al., 2017). The evolutionary account for such biophobias is obvious: Human ancestors who avoided venomous animals likely lived longer. Presumably such biophobias could now make people (even subconsciously) less likely to advocate for endangered spiders and snakes, or other arachnids and reptiles. Yet it is unclear that withholding legal protection from arachnids and reptiles—most of which are not dangerous to humans, and many of which perform vital ecosystem functions—is an appropriate response to genetically induced fear of envenomation.

Other research also suggests that people may experience predispositions *for* some other species, a phenomenon sometimes called "biophilia" (Ulrich, 1993; Mather, 2019). Just as with biophobias, biophilias may have served an evolutionary function, particularly among hunter-gatherer societies (Bradshaw & Paul, 2010). There is evidence, for instance, for a genetically based attraction toward, and preference for, "cute" nonhuman animals—generally, ones (like small mammals) that share features with human babies (Bradshaw & Paul, 2010; Lorenz, 1943). Both the cognitive availability and empathy-producing qualities of a species may similarly affect the likelihood that an individual, or even an organization made up of individuals, would petition to have a species listed. Insofar as a species lacks the emotional appeal of *Kindchenschema*—such as plants or insects—it will garner less empathy, and thus less caring and fewer parties interested in going to the effort of petitioning for ESA protection.

The result is a portfolio of species (and ecosystem) protections based at least partly on the interplay of psychological phenomena. Thus, even though the ESA itself does not distinguish between species that are charismatic or repellant, enormous or tiny, plant or animal, the impact of the facially neutral petition process may be to embed psychological distortions into ecosystem management.

The ESA example may also help in showing how legal decision makers can be aided by an awareness of the interplay between environmental law and psychology. Policy makers and regulators might respond to the psychological undersalience of some species, for instance, by purposefully increasing their own attention to, or even the legal requirements to protect, those species who might otherwise be neglected as a result of psychological processes. They might also respond by communicating with individual legal actors, for example, by shining a light on possibly neglected species. One might imagine agencies deliberately issuing a call for petitions on ugly animals. Nor are opportunities for response restricted to government actors; individual attorneys and environmental groups can also be informed by a psychological analysis of environmental statutes like the ESA. In this instance, such actors might find it helpful to recognize the psychology underlying public demand for protection (and support for litigation) on more salient and appealing species, while simultaneously recognizing the potential work to be done on less appealing species who still meet legal requirements for protection. Individuals might also attempt to use their increased knowledge of psychological phenomena persuasively. For example, environmental groups might seek to find or "market" appealing species by emphasizing *Kindchenschema* or other features that attach to otherwise neglected species, and attorneys working with a more limited scientific record on a less obvious or less appealing animal may be able to better explain the lack of existing research. Judges, in turn, may benefit from recognizing the potential gap between the language and expressed purpose of the ESA versus how the act is applied by them, by agencies, and by petitioners.

Debiasing Ecosystem Management

In some cases, then, the operation of environmental laws—such as those protecting species and their habitats—may be influenced by psychological processes. But in others, the law may serve a debiasing function (Jolls & Sunstein, 2006), counteracting psychological phenomena that might otherwise affect ecosystem management. For instance, the law might be used to deliberately raise the salience of a particular—and otherwise neglected—ecosystem or ecosystem feature. This may be the case, for example, with the specific protections for wetlands embedded in the Clean Water Act § 404 and Executive Order 11990 on Protection of Wetlands. Such strategies may help to counterbalance a common affective disgust for swamps, mucky areas, and bogs, which might otherwise lead to undervaluation of those areas.

Still more ambitiously, law might seek to respond to the general challenges presented by ecosystem management by purposefully highlighting injuries to ecosystems that might otherwise fade into the background for psychological reasons. On this front, consider the operation of the National Environmental Policy Act of 1969 (NEPA), one of the United States' first federal environmental statutes, and still a centerpiece of environmental law and policy. The law is simple: It requires government agencies to "consider" environmental outcomes that will significantly affect the quality of the human environment prior to engaging in the behavior that will cause those consequences. Famous cases on this front include *Robertson v. Methow Valley Citizens Council* (1989) and *Strycker's Bay Neighborhood Council v. Karlen* (1980). Although simple and "merely" procedural, so far as NEPA is concerned—government agencies are free to take whatever action they like after they have considered environmental consequences—NEPA has been copied around the world, and it is widely viewed as a critical part of U.S. environmental law and policy. In addition to providing other benefits, such as increasing the transparency of agency action and thus potentially democratic legitimacy, our account suggests that laws like NEPA might be understood as a vital "priming" tonic for the psychological tendency to otherwise neglect environmental impacts.

Finally, consider that psychological research may be helpful in generating additional prescriptions for environmental policy when current policy is likely to suffer from distorting biases. For instance, the institution responsible for implementing any changes made to NEPA would likely be the Council on Environmental Quality (CEQ), the governmental body tasked with issuing guidance explaining how and when NEPA applies. Our analysis suggests that CEQ's guidance ought to urge NEPA to focus specifically on those types of environmental outcomes that are most likely to be neglected: those that are particularly diffuse through time and/or space, that are complex as a result of interactions or multiple streams of causation, and/or those that primarily impact nonhuman processes and ecosystems, plants, and animals. That said, NEPA is not the only possible avenue for balancing out dysfunctional levels of attention to ecological outcomes. In a number of cases, environmental agencies and other actors may have discretion to allocate their resources to address psychological distortions. The Fish and Wildlife Service, for instance, already chooses to list some endangered and threatened species without waiting for a petition to be filed. Though the agency may lack resources to increase listing activity across the board, and it may generally depend upon petitions to supplement movements to protect, our analysis suggests they might do well to purposefully focus the resources they do have on actively identifying and protecting unattractive and small species—species that, though they may be biologically critical, are also likely to be systematically neglected by the general public.

Common Approaches to Ecosystem Management

Ecosystem management necessarily requires policy makers to manage competing social, cultural, and environmental values. Two approaches to ecosystem management are particularly common and attempt to help policy makers manage the competing goals and values that are at stake. The first is the sustainability framework, which attempts to simultaneously promote economic growth, social welfare, and environmental quality. The second is cost-benefit analysis, which attempts to guide trade-offs between items of social value. Although the two approaches can be used simultaneously (Barbier et al., 1990), and they may both be informed by similar policies—such as through informational regimes like NEPA—the two approaches are widely viewed as distinct.

Importantly, these approaches are also used in environmental decisions other than ecosystem management—such as in some pollution-control decisions—and parts of our analysis here will also apply to other environmental problems. We choose to discuss these frameworks here because we think that each approach—both of which seek to inform which uses and functions of ecosystems should be supported—can be importantly affected by psychological phenomena that affect which values are prioritized over others, and how.

THE PSYCHOLOGY OF SUSTAINABILITY AND THE PRECAUTIONARY PRINCIPLE

Between these two approaches, sustainability—and its offspring, sustainable development—has been particularly influential worldwide. Although the exact parameters of sustainability remain under debate (Kates et al., 2005), the general intuition underlying it is that it seeks to simultaneously promote and sustain the three Es—economy, equity, and ecology. The sustainability framework is explicitly focused on managing these impacts over significant amounts of time. In one influential formulation, policy should seek "development that meets the needs of the present without compromising the ability of future generations to meet their own needs" (The World Commission on Environment and Development, 1987, p. 43).

Many sustainability advocates trace the approach to the Rio Declaration on Environment and Development, a product of the United

Nations' influential 1992 Rio Conference, which is widely viewed as a turning point in international environmental law (Weiss, 2011). And indeed, the sustainability framework is particularly important to international environmental law (Weiss, 2011) and to jurisdictions like the EU, who base internal policy on international environmental norms (van Zeben & Rowell, 2020). The EU's Integration Principle, for instance, requires that all EU policies and activities take into account "environmental protection requirements," "in particular with a view to promoting sustainable development" (Consolidated Version of the Treaty on the Functioning of the European Union, 2012, p. 53).

It is worth considering the psychological context and impact of the sustainability approach, both as a theory and as it is commonly applied. From a theoretical perspective, two aspects bear particular attention: the focus on "sustaining" over time and the attempt to simultaneously pursue multiple goals. From an applied perspective, we think it may be helpful to dig into the psychology of the precautionary principle, as that is perhaps the most commonly used tool for implementing sustainability policies.

First, consider the straightforward observation that the sustainability framework is focused on "sustaining," meaning ensuring that some level of economic, equitable, and ecological quality is maintained over time. This focus is often tied explicitly to views about the normative importance of future generations (Beekman, 2004; The World Commission on Environment and Development, 1987). As we have discussed, one significant challenge in managing environmental impacts is their latency (Revesz, 1999). The sustainability approach distinctively focuses decision makers on the very long run; on impacts that may not accrue until they are long gone (Heal, 1999). Although we are not aware of research testing this application, at least in theory this emphasis on future impacts could have a debiasing function against present bias and other time-related cognitive phenomena by making temporally distant impacts more salient. In this sense, the sustainability framework's focus on the (distant) future may act as corrective lenses to myopic decision makers. Research based on construal level theory suggests that priming people to think about the distant future may also help trigger creative, "insightful" problem solving, in contrast to the more typical focus on near-future impacts that triggers more systematic, analytical problem solving (Truelove-Hill et al., 2018). By encouraging consideration of future generations and the distant future, the sustainability approach may actually trigger different types of, and increasingly creative, problem solving.

Sustainability's focus may also account for some of the approach's broad appeal—although not necessarily for the better. Since the approach tries to prevent economic, equitable, and environmental quality from falling below some baseline, it may trigger loss aversion and status quo bias, both of which tend to make perceived losses from the status quo appear particularly harmful (Kahneman & Tversky, 1979). In this sense, the sustainability framework's focus on "sustaining" could be understood as a manifestation of loss aversion—or perhaps even worse, as a method of reaffirming loss aversion by focusing analysts on preventing losses below some minimal baseline, and thus drawing their attention away from potential improvements above that baseline.

A second psychologically relevant aspect of the sustainability approach is that it distinctively attempts to pursue multiple values at once: economic, equitable, and ecological. Adherents of the sustainability approach tend to view its commitment to multiple goals as an appealing feature that makes the approach comprehensive. Yet the decision to pursue multiple goals at once has psychological downsides. More specifically, research on pursuing multiple goals, sometimes called "multifinality," suggests that it can constrain decision making and can make it subjectively more difficult to achieve acceptable outcomes (Fernandez & Kruglanski, 2019; Kruglanski et al., 2012). Research on goal setting more generally suggests that it works best when the goals are challenging to achieve and when they are specific—vague goals such as "do your best" are significantly less effective (Latham, 2016). In this context, sustainability's selection of relatively lofty goals may be inspirational, but the vagueness and multiplicity of those goals may also create countervailing cognitive weight. As they do when facing other complex circumstances, people may end up using a simplifying heuristic, just choosing their favorite or the most salient among sustainability's multiple goals. Here again, however, despite the influence of the sustainability framework, there is distressingly little direct empirical work.

Psychology can also helpfully inform one of the most widely used tools for making decisions in pursuit of sustainability goals: the precautionary principle. Generally speaking, the precautionary principle is a formalization of the maxim "better safe than sorry." In most formulations, it encourages policy makers to take steps against potential harms, even if causal chains are uncertain. One highly influential formulation, the "Wingspread Declaration," states that "[w]here there are threats of serious or irreversible damage, lack of full scientific certainty shall not be used as a reason for postponing cost-effective measures to prevent environmental degradation." The principle was incorporated into Principle 15 of the Rio Declaration, and it remains a staple of international environmental law and—like the larger sustainability framework—of legal systems, like Europe's, which draw heavily on international legal tools (de Sadeleer, 2010; Trouwborst, 2002; van Zeben & Rowell, 2020). The 1992 Maastricht Treaty on the EU, for instance, requires that EU policy on the environment "shall be based on the Precautionary Principle" (Treaty on European Union, 1992, p. 29).

Although the principle is in widespread use and continues to enjoy significant support in many quarters (Bourg & Schlegel, 2001; de Sadeleer, 2007; Raffensperger & Tickner, 1999; Whiteside, 2006), it has been sharply criticized on psychological grounds. The most potent critique was mounted by Cass Sunstein in *Laws of Fear: Beyond the Precautionary Principle*, which argues that the precautionary principle broadly construed is incoherent and potentially paralyzing because there are risks on all sides of all actions (Sunstein, 2005b). The principle only appears to give guidance, Sunstein argues, because cognitive phenomena make some risks more salient than others. When cognitive and social factors make some risks more cognitively available than others, decision makers focus selectively on those risks and seek to be precautionary about them. But in doing so, they risk increasing other, less salient risks. For example, regulating one process, like nuclear power generation, might cause people to substitute into another, more damaging process, like more traditional—and dirtier—fossil fuels. In support of this critique, applications of the precautionary principle tend to vary on which environmental, health, and safety risks they choose to focus (Sunstein, 2005b; Wiener et al., 2011). Notably, this selective application of precaution may be endemic not only to jurisdictions like Europe that have built their regulatory systems explicitly on the precautionary principle, but also to jurisdictions like the United States, who use the concept of precaution selectively against some risks without having adopted an overarching commitment to the strategy (Wiener et al., 2011).

Attempting to be precautionary about risks to sustainability—which is so broadly defined on the basis of multiple values—may give decision makers particularly wide cognitive discretion to select (consciously or not) which risks to focus upon. Wherever there is substantial cognitive discretion, there is room for heuristics to play. And the combination of the precautionary principle with the multiple broad goals of the sustainability approach may present a particularly large playground.

To the extent that the discretion to select freely among too many risks is the problem, though the precautionary principle can be relatively easily adjusted, as Sunstein himself has noted. The trick is to purposefully select particular hazards to prioritize, such as those that risk catastrophe and/or irreversible harm (Sunstein, 2005b; Sunstein, 2007). Shrinking the total world of risks upon which the principle focuses also shrinks the cognitive discretion within which the decision maker operates, and may make it easier for decision makers to focus on specific goals (Latham, 2016). While sound as a cognitive strategy, there can be normative objections to this move, as it may shrink the risks addressed to much less than the whole of what decision makers care about. This is particularly true in applications of the precautionary principle to sustainability, which after all is attempting to be comprehensive in its approach. Decision makers may be stuck, at least to some extent, between choosing wide-ranging, comprehensive goals such as those embedded in the sustainability framework and allowing psychological biases to have substantial room for influence.

THE PSYCHOLOGY OF COST-BENEFIT ANALYSIS

Another key approach to ecosystem management is cost-benefit analysis, which attempts to facilitate decision making about trade-offs by highlighting, and in many cases quantifying, the positive and negative impacts of a policy. Though it remains controversial among some environmental scholars (Ackerman & Heinzerling, 2002; Ackerman, 2004), cost-benefit analysis forms a core part of modern U.S. regulatory policy, and it is commonly used by federal agencies to set policy, whenever Congress has not explicitly prohibited its use (Sunstein, 2002b; Revesz & Livermore, 2008; *Entergy Corp. v. Riverkeeper*, 2009; *Michigan v. EPA*, 2016). Even where statutes explicitly require a decision-making framework other than cost-benefit analysis, a form of cost-benefit analysis often influences their implementation (Kysar, 2010). The Endangered Species Act is one good example. The protections of that statute attach to any listed species, regardless of that species' economic or monetized value. In a particularly famous case, which we have already mentioned, this led to the enjoinment of completion of a $100 million dam to save the snail darter, an economically negligible endangered fish species (*Tennessee Valley Authority v. Hill*, 1978). Yet even the Endangered Species Act incorporates some balancing of costs and benefits; under § 1536 of the act, an Endangered Species Committee may, under rare circumstances, exempt a species from protection under the act, but they may only do so if they find that the benefits of a proposed project "clearly outweigh" the alternatives.

Regulatory cost-benefit analysis generally relies on quantifying the costs and benefits of proposed policies and expressing each in a single "currency": money (Sunstein, 2005a; Sunstein & Rowell, 2007; Rowell, 2010). One of the key ways to quantify and monetize the value of ecosystems is to focus on which benefits they provide to humans. These so-called "ecosystem services" range from providing food and water, to regulating climate and flood risk, to providing cultural and recreational opportunities (Farnsworth et al., 1981; Salzman, 1997; Millennium Ecosystem Assessment, 2005).

While quantifying and monetizing this range of ecosystem services presents one method for comparing across complex and interactive ecosystem impacts, it is also possible that the focus on quantification—and on monetization more particularly—may have a psychological effect on decision making. What is the psychological impact of quantifying, and specifically monetizing, environmental impacts like ecosystem services?

Some proponents of cost-benefit analysis—most notably, Cass Sunstein—have argued that cost-benefit analysis may serve a debiasing function (Sunstein, 2000; Sunstein, 2005a), at least when using careful analytical practices (Revesz & Livermore, 2008). Insofar as cost-benefit analysis requires systematic accounting, it may help to "slow down" policy analyses, converting them from System I (fast, automatic) to System II (slower, deliberate) procedures, possibly serving as a corrective to cognitive heuristics like the availability heuristic, base rate neglect, loss aversion, status quo bias, and the affect heuristic (Kuenzler & Kysar, 2014).

A complementary possibility is that cost-benefit analysis may present a method of managing cognitive dissonance and tendencies toward coherence shifts—phenomena that are particularly likely to arise in ecosystem management, since it involves trading off both positive and negative outcomes. As we have discussed, individuals tend to try to reduce cognitive dissonance by altering one of the attitudes, beliefs, or behaviors that is in conflict—usually, the one that is the easiest to change. Thus, when faced with a decision to allow or ban a pesticide that could cause both great harm and great benefit, there may generally be a cognitive temptation to minimize either the harm or the benefit in order to limit dissonance, rather than to recognize the full extent of each. To the extent that cost-benefit analysis allows both institutional and cognitive compartmentalization of different outcomes—both good and bad—it may present at least a partial immunization against this tendency to adjust factual perceptions to preferred outcomes.

On the other hand, some critics of cost-benefit analysis have argued that quantification and monetization may undermine decision making (Ackerman & Heinzerling, 2002; Ackerman, 2004). While these critiques have been largely philosophical rather than psychological, psychological research does support a cautionary flag on some cost-benefit techniques. In particular, it is worth considering that cost-benefit analysis may be subject both to general heuristics and biases, and to more specific psychological phenomena related to monetization and quantification.

First, consider that cost-benefit analysis is dependent upon the identification of costs and benefits to compare. This raises concerns similar in structure to Sunstein's critique of the precautionary principle as based upon risk salience (Sunstein, 2003). Omitting impacts from a policy analysis can affect the substance of policy outcomes (Rowell & Wexler, 2014). Yet the initial identification of any set of inputs is likely subject to the same kinds of psychological processes that go into any other decision-making process. In particular, the more salient a particular impact is, the more cognitively available it is likely to be—and the more likely it is to make its way into a cost-benefit analysis.

The reverse is also true. Because temporally and geographically distant, complex, and nonhuman impacts are likely to be less psychologically salient, environmental impacts may end up systematically more likely to be omitted from cost-benefit analyses than more psychologically prominent impacts such as immediate risks to national security (Slovic, 2015; Tversky et al., 1988). While this tendency may be balanced out with debiasing strategies, such as by making less-salient environmental impacts more salient via mandates to consider them, the general skew may still remain—and may be especially problematic where debiasing strategies are incomplete or missing. For example, while NEPA triggers significant analytical requirements for proposed actions with "significant" environmental impacts, the determination of whether impacts are significant may be systematically undermined by the psychological phenomena that make environmental impacts so easy to neglect. The possibility of such distortions more than justifies additional research in this realm.

Of course, the availability heuristic may affect any decision-making approach, not just cost-benefit analysis. But insofar as cost-benefit analysis generally focuses on the comparison of identified costs and benefits, rather than on supporting the initial identification of all relevant inputs, it may be especially vulnerable to distortions in which inputs get considered at all. And these kinds of "front-door" psychological challenges—where the decision about which costs and benefits are allowed in the front door, and therefore enter the analysis—are particularly likely to be subconsciously influenced by psychological phenomena. As such, institutional safeguards—such as debiasing via NEPA, thoughtful internal agency procedures encouraging broad identification of inputs (National Center for Environmental Economics [NCEE], 2014), and meaningful judicial review of whether important costs or benefits have been omitted (*Center for Biological Diversity v. National Highway Traffic Safety Administration*, 2008)—become particularly important for cost-benefit analyses. In the ecosystem management context, the EPA's years-long effort to think broadly about classifying and formalizing identification of ecosystem services, and how to then quantify and monetize their impact, looks particularly wise (Environmental Protection Agency, 2015).

Another distinctive aspect of—and potential psychological challenge for—cost-benefit analysis, at least as it is applied in the United States, is its approach toward valuation, and specifically its dependence upon monetization as a method for promoting comparison of disparate impacts. This quantified and monetized approach to health, safety, and environmental impacts gained real purchase starting in 1981, when President Reagan issued Executive Order 12291, ordering that "[r]egulatory action shall not be undertaken unless the potential benefits to society for the regulation outweigh the potential costs to society," and centralizing the review of major regulations to ensure that the order (and others) were carried out (Sunstein, 2002b). The order directs each agency—including environmental agencies—to conclude a regulatory impact analysis (RIA) that includes a cost-benefit analysis before publishing any major rule. Agencies are required to send the RIA to the Office of Management and Budget (OMB), and the OMB director may require the agency to do further analysis if she or he finds the cost-benefit analysis to be unacceptable, insufficient, or poorly performed.

Although initially perceived as a deregulatory strategy, the executive requirement for cost-benefit analysis has survived six presidents and four shifts in partisan control of the White House, and it has become so familiar a tool for U.S. regulators that critics worry that it is applied even where underlying statutes could best be read to reject it (Kysar, 2010). The methodology of cost-benefit analysis has developed over that time, and the centralized body responsible for reviewing agency analyses—the Office of Information and Regulatory Affairs (OIRA), in the OMB—exerts significant power in directing how cost-benefit analyses occur.

The valuation process is the foundation of cost-benefit analysis as practiced by U.S. agencies (Rowell, 2010). Any threat to the integrity of the valuation process thus risks undermining the practice. Both OIRA and other agencies are generally aware of this vulnerability, and there has been a lot of work both by individual agencies such as the EPA and OIRA to make valuation processes systematic and careful (NCEE, 2014; U.S. Office of Management and Budget, 2003). And occasionally, when agencies go too far afield in their approaches to valuing and monetizing regulatory impacts, courts will step in. Courts have said, for instance, that agencies may not tip the scales in their valuation processes by discounting one side of the cost-benefit equation and not the other (*Corrosion Proof Fittings v. EPA*, 1991), and that agencies may not utterly fail to monetize important impacts, such as greenhouse gas emissions, even if monetizing is difficult (*Center for Biological Diversity v. National Highway Traffic Safety Administration*, 2008).

To be thorough about quantifying all the impacts of a proposed government action—and to survive both OIRA review and the possibility of subsequent judicial review—agencies must monetize a wide variety of goods, risks, and services. They routinely do so with items as diverse as human mortality risk, loss of nonhuman life, and loss of ecosystem services (NCEE, 2014). Once items are monetized, agencies then use the process of discounting to make the monetized amounts comparable through time (Sunstein & Rowell, 2007).

How do agencies go about attaching a monetary value to things like loss of life or the degradation of an ecosystem? Generally speaking, they do it by figuring out how much money people would pay to secure (or demand to forgo) the particular cost or benefit (Rowell, 2010). Ideally, agencies will observe how much people pay for similar goods (or to avoid similar risks) in actual markets, but some things (like many environmental goods and services) are not traded (or sometimes even tradeable) in markets. For these, economists rely either on "revealed preference" methods that try to back out people's monetary preferences (for example, by looking at how much they demand in wage premiums to work in a very dirty job), or on "stated preference" studies, which ask people to directly report how much they would be willing to pay (WTP) to obtain the good, or how much they would be willing to accept (WTA) to give the good up. Many of these studies are relied upon again and again, as with estimates of the monetized "value of a statistical life" (VSL)—the amount of money that, on average, agencies will dedicate to saving a single human life. Other studies focus on single ecosystems or uses—in fact, an academic cottage industry has sprung up running studies to value particular uses of specific ecosystems. One evaluation identifies over 5,000 studies attaching dollar values to ecosystems (Carson, 2011).

The vast majority of agency analysts who work on valuation are economists by training; psychologists remain vanishingly rare in agency policy offices. Still, significant psychological research has trickled into economics via behavioral economics, and there has been a lot of work in behavioral economics attempting to identify key psychological processes influencing valuation. Among these, framing is particularly worth flagging, as it potentially affects a broad swath of environmental valuations.

The general concern is that the framing of contingent valuation studies—or small contextual shifts in how questions are asked and presented—may affect the valuations that people appear to attach to different goods. Recall that while agencies generally rely on market data to value goods that are traded in markets, they use contingent valuation studies to figure out how much money people would exchange for things—like outcomes to nonhumans—that cannot be bought and sold on the open market. Any framing effects in such studies have the potential to distort people's expressions of value and thus lead either to undervaluation or overvaluation. This is worrisome, as distorted valuations can undermine the effectiveness of cost-benefit analysis as a procedure when they are used as the basis for government action.

We have discussed framing and the endowment effect already, but their particular application in cost-benefit analysis is striking. One serious—and relatively well studied—aspect concerns willingness to pay (WTP) versus willingness to accept (WTA) measures. Although a hyperrational individual might be willing to give something up—say, a mug—for just 1 cent more than she would buy it for, as we know from research on loss aversion, prospect theory, and the endowment effect, real people usually do not act that way. Instead, they value items they already hold significantly more than identical items that they would have to purchase (Kahneman et al., 1990; Kahneman & Tversky, 1979; Knetsch & Sinden, 1984), demanding more to give them up than they would be willing to pay to acquire them. In other words, WTA is routinely higher than WTP, and this gap is particularly exacerbated for public goods that are not traded on markets (Horowitz & McConnell, 2000).

The WTP/WTA gap is well known within agencies and remains a perennially popular topic of analysis for economists, who have developed numerous different accounts for why and when it might occur and what agencies might do about it (Horowitz & McConnell, 2000; Kim et al., 2015). Many have warned that using WTP—which tends to be so much lower than WTA—may lead to systematic undervaluation of environmental benefits (Brown & Gregory, 1999). Yet for most regulatory impacts, including environmental impacts, agencies still generally default to WTP estimates. Thus far, their decision to do so has not been challenged in court. Such a challenge may come in the future, given the robust data showing that WTA routinely exceeds WTP.

While it is the best known, the WTA/WTP gap is by no means the only potential framing concern triggered by the use of valuation studies (Diamond & Hausman, 1994; Hausman, 1993; McFadden & Train, 2017). Another set of challenges has to do with the numerical scope or context in which questions are posed. For instance, one study found that respondents had roughly the same WTP to save the lives of 2,000 birds, 20,000 birds, and 200,000 birds, depending upon how the number of birds was presented (as "much less than 1% of a population" versus "2% of a population") (Desvousges et al., 1993). Such framing concerns interact, of course, with numeracy limitations as well (Peters et al., 2006; Rowell & Bregant, 2014). Unfortunately, if participants in these kinds of studies are innumerate, it can be difficult to know what their reported valuations actually reflect.

A similar issue arises with the framing of temporal impacts, which affects measurements of people's preferences about the future and their views about obligations to future generations (Frederick, 2003; Sunstein & Rowell, 2007). Merely being aware of challenges in framing can help decision makers who seek meaningful valuations and who strive to avoid mistakes such as inadvertently double discounting the benefits of environmental regulation (Rowell, 2010). Yet not every problem can be fixed through awareness alone. Note that even when carefully framed, valuation studies at their core are still asking people to value the underlying good. When that good is diffuse, complex, and nonhuman in character—as environmental goods so typically are—building policy on the basis of people's preferences also risks building policy on the basis of people's psychological quirks and limitations. Moreover, although economists within agencies are often well aware of concerns about valuation techniques, that does not necessarily mean that they have either the resources to counteract them or the alternative data sources they would need to adopt alternative valuations.

Finally, recall that psychological research suggests reasons to be concerned about the impacts of making decisions while primed to consider money (Caruso et al., 2013; Vohs, 2015). As we discussed in Chapter 4, the very act of valuing something may itself distort valuations. Merely being encouraged to think about money, or having a picture of a dollar bill in the background, may measurably change people's thoughts, feelings, motivations, and behaviors (Vohs, 2015). Recall here that one set of studies found that even incidental exposures to money led subjects to indicate greater support for inequality, socioeconomic differences, free-market economies, and group-based discrimination (Caruso et al., 2013; cf. Rohrer et al., 2015). Given research on group polarization and norm reinforcement, the impact of such effects might be even greater where relevant institutional decision makers' initial priming is reinforced through money-focused decisions—as occurs at agencies addressing monetized environmental impacts. Here, again, institutional safeguards, such as internal agency policies encouraging re-priming and/or meaningful judicial review where agency choices "drift" too much from legislative goals, may be particularly important in creating a counterweight to the psychological impacts of priming with money.

Conclusion

Psychological research can be helpful in understanding and addressing the problems presented by ecosystem management. It can be useful in illuminating how, when, and why people perceive and respond to ecosystem impacts as they do. By acting as an aid to understanding and even predicting human behavior in this realm, psychology also offers the possibility of improving the effectiveness of ecosystem management.

Key Psychological Challenges Presented by Ecosystem Injury

Environmental Nature

Their environmental nature makes many ecosystem injuries hard to perceive, difficult to understand, and hard to care about.

- Diffusion. Diminished salience for spatially diffuse behaviors, and heightened concern for permanent and irreversible impacts, may contribute to general neglect of ecosystem injuries. Pushing in the opposite direction, place-specific harms may sometimes be especially salient, and therefore garner more attention than other kinds of environmental injuries.
- Complexity. The extraordinary complexity of ecosystems triggers simplifying heuristics, motivated cognition, and phenomena related to the psychology of expertise.
- Nonhuman character. General barriers to empathy for nonhuman stakeholders may interfere with people's ability to care about some injuries to plants, nonhuman animals, and ecosystems, while anthropomorphism

and biophilia may draw selective attention to others. Environmental psychology and the emotional benefits of interacting with nature also engender psychological benefits from ecosystem protection.

Distinctive Ecosystem-Based Challenges

Distinctive ecosystem-based challenges may push toward entrenchment and maintenance of the status quo in ecosystem policy.

- The psychology of place and property. Attachment to property and to specific places may trigger the general psychology of property law and heighten the impact of loss aversion, the endowment effect, and status quo bias.
- The psychology of scarcity and uniqueness. Where ecosystems and resources are perceived as scarce and/or unique, it may trigger hypervaluation and a scarcity mindset.

These can affect how ecosystem management operates in practice; further research on potential debiasing strategies would be valuable. The multiple-goal nature of ecosystem management also triggers special concern in applying popular decision-making frameworks, including sustainability, the precautionary principle, and cost-benefit analysis.

8

The Psychology of Climate Change Law and Policy

This chapter argues that a psychological approach to climate change law and policy may be helpful in increasing our ability to effectively understand, predict, and shape human behavior regarding climate change. This approach requires developing an understanding of people's perceptions, motivations, and cognition regarding climate change. It then uses this understanding to help law and legal institutions more effectively regulate climate behavior. To that end, the chapter begins with a basic introduction into the extraordinary problem of climate change, which scientists expect to affect every ecosystem on earth. In addition to scientific, political, economic, and ethical puzzles—the difficulty of which trigger their own psychological phenomena—climate change also presents a series of psychological challenges to people's ability to understand and respond to climate injury. Some of these challenges relate to the diffuse, complex, and nonhuman character of climate harms; others are attached to distinctive aspects of climate change, including its extreme magnitude, its unprecedented nature, and the moral quagmire to which all of these characteristics contribute.

After laying out the groundwork of important psychological challenges presented by climate change, the chapter moves on to profile key legal and policy responses to it. It gives a brief introduction to climate policy, as well as an overview of basic legal strategies for addressing climate change, focusing particularly on the law of the United States. It then identifies opportunities for adopting a psychological approach to climate law and policy that may help policy makers more accurately understand and predict human responses to interventions—and hopefully develop more effective legal strategies to tailor human behavior in this area. Finally, the chapter flags strategies that policy makers and individuals can use for communicating effectively about climate change in light of its distinctive psychological features.

The chapter concludes that, because common psychological phenomena present barriers to accurately perceiving, understanding, and meaningfully responding to the risks and harms of climate change, a psychological approach to climate law may help in identifying and recognizing those barriers—and thus eventually in finding ways around them.

We have done our best in this chapter to meaningfully abstract key insights from a wide range of complex fields, including those in climate science, psychology, and climate law and policy. More so even than the rest of this volume, the breadth of this task has necessarily led to decreased depth, and to a number of hard calls about what to include and what to highlight. We hope that we have done enough to convey to readers from multiple disciplines that climate law and policy can in fact benefit from increased attention to psychological research, even as it continues to build on scientific and technical insights from other fields. Where readers note important lacunae, we hope they will be inspired to conduct further research and analysis in the psychology of climate change law and policy.

The Problem of Climate Change

Anthropogenic climate change is now widely recognized as the most important environmental issue of our time—and simultaneously the most difficult. This section provides an introduction into what makes climate change such a wicked problem. After defining climate change and flagging some of its expected (enormous) impacts, this section provides a thumbnail summary of a large set of literature addressing the scientific, political, economic, and ethical challenges climate change presents. It then discusses the common psychological challenges presented by climate change, which apply to climate-related decisions by both individuals and institutions. Failing to account for these challenges may undermine the law's ability to predict, understand, and shape human behavior in this area.

Effective legal policy must find a way to address all of the challenges presented by climate change while still cutting to the core of what makes climate change such a transformatively important problem. In subsequent sections, we describe key legal and policy responses to climate change, and suggest ways in which a psychological approach may help improve the effectiveness of climate change law.

Defining Climate Change

Climate change is any significant change in climate conditions— temperature, precipitation, wind, or other effects—that lasts for a significant period of time. These may result from natural variability and/or as a result of human behavior (Metz et al., 2007). In policy contexts, such as in the United Nations Framework Convention on Climate Change (United Nations Framework Convention, 1992), the term "climate change" is frequently used to refer specifically to changes in climate that are attributable directly or indirectly to human activity that alters the composition of the global atmosphere and that are in addition to natural climate variability observed over comparable time periods.

So-called "greenhouse gases"—including carbon dioxide, methane, chlorofluorocarbons (CFCs), and nitrous oxide—are gases that contribute to a "greenhouse effect," resulting in an average warming of the Earth's surface (Intergovernmental Panel on Climate Change [IPCC], 1992; Metz et al., 2007). The quantity of greenhouse gases in the atmosphere is an important determinant of climate. Prior to the Industrial Revolution, greenhouse gases such as carbon dioxide were emitted through natural, nonhuman processes, such as volcanic eruption and plant matter decay, and were absorbed through other natural, nonhuman processes, for instance, through absorption into the oceans and growth of carbon-fixing flora (Metz et al., 2007). Plants, animals, and ecosystems adapted to incremental changes, and over millennia, they developed into the rich, biodiverse mosaic of life that now populates the planet. During the Industrial Revolution, however, humans began emitting increasing quantities of greenhouse gases—significantly more than can be absorbed by natural processes—largely through extracting and then burning fossil fuels like coal and oil.

When more greenhouse gases are emitted than absorbed, the remainder end up in the atmosphere (Intergovernmental Panel on Climate Change, 1992; Metz et al., 2007). The current level of greenhouse gases in the atmosphere is causing changes in weather patterns that are so severe and rapid that they will likely have devastating and irreversible consequences for human, animal, and plant life (Masson-Delmotte et al., 2018).

Expected Impacts of Climate Change

The most authoritative analyses of climate change science and impacts are those created by the International Panel on Climate Change (IPCC), whose First Assessment Report in 1990 served as the basis for the United Nations Framework Convention on Climate Change (UNFCCC). The UNFCCC remains the foundational procedural structure for negotiating international treaties on climate change, which are commonly called "agreements" or "protocols." We have summarized the key factual findings of the IPCC in the table below. In brief, the IPCC is clear that humans influence climate change, that climate change has already had widespread impacts on human and natural systems, and that substantial additional changes can be expected worldwide that will affect both humans and ecosystems.

KEY CONCLUSIONS OF THE IPCC (PACHAURI ET AL., 2015)

Observed changes and their causes. Human influence on the climate system is clear, and recent anthropogenic emissions of greenhouse gases are the highest in history. Recent climate changes have had widespread impacts on human and natural systems (p. 2).

Observed changes in the climate system. Warming of the climate system is unequivocal, and since the 1950s, many of the observed changes are unprecedented over decades to millennia. The atmosphere and oceans have warmed, the amounts of snow and ice have diminished, and sea level has risen (p. 2).

Causes of climate change. Anthropogenic greenhouse gas emissions have increased since the preindustrial era, driven largely by economic and population growth, and are now higher than ever. This has led to atmospheric concentrations of carbon dioxide, methane, and nitrous oxide that are unprecedented in at least the last 800,000 years. Their effects, together with those of other anthropogenic drivers, have been detected throughout the climate system and are extremely likely to have been the dominant cause of the observed warming since the mid-20th century (p. 4).

Extreme events. Changes in many extreme weather and climate events have been observed since about 1950. Some of these changes have been linked to human influences, including a decrease in cold temperature extremes, an increase in warm temperature extremes, an increase in extreme high sea levels, and an increase in the number of heavy precipitation events in a number of regions (p. 7).

Future climate changes, risks, and impacts. Continued emission of greenhouse gases will cause further warming and long-lasting changes in all components of the climate system, increasing the likelihood of severe, pervasive, and irreversible consequences for people and ecosystems. Risks are unevenly distributed and are generally greater for disadvantaged people and communities in countries at all levels of development (p. 13).

Climate change beyond 2100, irreversibility, and abrupt changes. Many aspects of climate change and associated impacts will continue for centuries, even if anthropogenic emissions of greenhouse gases are stopped. The risks of abrupt or irreversible changes increase as the magnitude of the warming increases (p. 16).

The most important recent agreement under the UNFCCC was the 2015 Paris Agreement, which was adopted by virtually every county in the world. (The United States initially adopted the Paris Agreement under President Obama, but then announced its intent to withdraw under President Trump in 2017.) The Paris Agreement states a clear commitment to limit global temperature rises to 2° C and to attempt to hold warming to 1.5° C above preindustrial levels (Paris Agreement, 2015). It also puts in place legally binding procedural commitments for the parties to create "nationally determined contributions" for mitigation, and to report on them regularly.

A few years after the Paris Agreement, IPCC issued a special report on *Global Warming of 1.5° C* to explain why the quantity of warming matters and to assess the possibility that warming might be kept to 1.5° C above preindustrial levels—the Paris Agreement's aspirational goal (Masson-Delmotte et al., 2018). According to the IPCC, human activities are estimated to have already caused approximately 1° C of global warming above preindustrial levels. Given past and ongoing emissions, 1.5° C of warming is a plausible best-case scenario, though limiting warming to that level would require deep emissions reductions (of about 45% from 2010 levels by 2030) and rapid, far-reaching and unprecedented changes in all aspects of society. (Masson-Delmotte et al., 2018). Climate-related risks for natural and human systems are higher for global warming of 1.5° C—the IPCC warns us to expect increased risks to global health, livelihoods, food security, water supply, human security, and economic growth—but significantly lower than for 2° C. In fact, IPCC suggests that limiting warming to 1.5° C instead of 2° C could reduce the number of people exposed to climate risks and susceptible to poverty by up to several hundred million by 2050—although millions of people will still die, and hundreds of millions will suffer (Masson-Delmotte et al., 2018). By contrast, worst-case scenarios could result in as much as 5–6° C of warming, which models suggest would be sufficient to wipe out most life on Earth (Masson-Delmotte et al., 2018).

Understanding the Difficulty of Climate Change as a Policy Problem: Science, Politics, Economics, and Ethics

Climate change is characterized by a number of features that make it both exceedingly important and extraordinarily difficult to address. There is substantial and growing scholarship chronicling scientific, political, economic, and ethical challenges posed by global climate change. As this chapter emphasizes, climate change also presents distinctive psychological challenges.

Before getting to that point, however, it is helpful to understand some of what makes climate change so extraordinarily challenging from a *non*psychological perspective, as the very difficulty of managing climate change creates a psychological challenge of its own.

First, although the science connecting human emissions of greenhouse gases to climate change is now uncontroversial within the scientific community, it remains challenging to tie individual actions that cause climate change to specific impacts. There is widespread scientific consensus that the global climate is changing as a result of human activities, but there remains significant uncertainty regarding both short- and long-term consequences of those changes, complicated by the interactive qualities of many nonhuman processes and ecosystems. Although information about likely impacts continues to improve, there are also some types of impacts—such as ocean acidification—that scientists still struggle to explain and predict (Orr et al., 2005; Jiang et al., 2019). These uncertainties are further exacerbated by questions of how humans will change their mitigation and adaptation behaviors in the coming years (Masson-Delmotte et al., 2018; Pachauri et al., 2015), and of how changing pandemic behaviors will affect—and be affected by—climate change (Rowell, 2020c; Salas et al., 2020).

Second from a political and economic perspective, climate change has a multitude of diffuse causes, and thus seems unlikely to have a single "silver bullet" solution (Rayner, 2006). Every human action (including breathing!) results in the emission of some greenhouse gases, and it would not be possible, or desirable, to regulate each of these activities. While every person contributes to climate change in many small ways, the typical presumption is that no single person, state, or even country can meaningfully mitigate it alone. This generates substantial challenges in coordinating behavior, including collective action problems, where effective climate change mitigation necessitates action by a multitude of individual countries, and free rider problems where individuals and countries each prefer to have mitigation and adaptation paid for and performed by someone else. And even brilliant economists struggle with—and continue to disagree about—how to manage the extraordinary timescales across which climate change is expected to unfold (Stern, 2007; Nordhaus, 2008, 2015; Piketty, 2014).

Finally, climate change has also been called a "perfect moral storm" because it presents multiple mutually reinforcing major ethical challenges (Gardiner, 2011). Those who benefit from greenhouse-gas-emitting activities—primarily presently-living people and those in developed countries—do not necessarily shoulder the harms of climate change, which will accrue mainly to future and foreign vulnerable people, countries, and nonhuman plants, animals, and ecosystems. This means that most climate change impacts are externalities—the harms imposed are almost all experienced by someone other than the individual(s) responsible for acting—and most of the victims of climate change are peculiarly powerless to negotiate about those behaviors (Gardiner 2011; Posner & Weisbach 2010). As a result, climate change presents a series of acutely difficult moral and ethical puzzles, not the least of which is how much the current generation is—or should be—willing to sacrifice for the sake of future generation's well-being (Broome, 2012).

The Psychological Challenges of Climate Change

In addition to the scientific, political, economic, and ethical challenges outlined above, climate change also presents substantial psychological challenges to effective regulation—challenges that in many cases interact with the nonpsychological difficulties canvassed above.

In some ways, climate change is an archetypal environmental problem, which causes an archetypal kind of environmental injury: The harms are latent, likely to spread across decades if not centuries; will often be generated far from the location of the underlying behavior that causes them and are spread across political borders; are exceptionally complex—so much so that even individual specialists cannot hope to identify, let alone understand, all its interactive and nonlinear causes and effects; and are intrinsically tied to nonhuman stakeholders and natural processes. Notably, however, climate change also presents other distinctive psychological challenges that go beyond those experienced in addressing many other environmental issues. These include the extreme magnitude of potential climate change impacts, its unprecedented nature, and the moral quagmire to which all these characteristics contribute. While these characteristics trigger and interact with other psychological phenomena we have discussed throughout the book, they may also present special challenges of their own, and thus they are worth identifying before digging more deeply into the psychology of diffusion, complexity, and the nonhuman character of climate impacts.

Climate-Specific Challenges

First, consider the extraordinary magnitude of expected climate change impacts. As we have discussed, these are almost unimaginably large, and they may fundamentally change every ecosystem on earth. The magnitude and scope of these changes carry special cognitive, emotional, and motivational weight, both because they are difficult to imagine and because they are traumatic to consider. From a cognitive perspective, simply processing very large harms is costly and difficult. One cognitive response to managing the prospect of very large harms is "psychic numbing" (Slovic, 2007; Slovic & Zionts, 2012; Slovic et al., 2013). This phenomenon, which is actually a symptom in posttraumatic stress disorder, allows people to detach, and therefore protect themselves from traumatic information (Slovic et al., 2013; van der Kolk, 1994). This detachment can even be detected physically, as the psychically numbed decision maker emits fewer neurotransmitters related to emotion (Decety et al., 2010).

While this phenomenon can be psychologically protective, allowing people to cope with horrific events, it has a dark side as well. As psychologist Paul Slovic has explained, when harms or risks are overwhelmingly large, it can lead to a "collapse of compassion" (Slovic et al., 2013). In the face of overwhelming risk, psychic numbing can lead people to attach less affect to individual lives lost or risks incurred, and thus to become less interested in investing resources to prevent that loss. As we discussed earlier, in a foundational illustration of the phenomenon, Slovic et al. have shown that as more people's lives are threatened, people become less and less concerned about any one of them (Slovic et al., 2013). "[T]he importance of saving one life is great when it is the first, or only, life saved but diminishes marginally as the total number of lives saved increases" (Slovic et al., 2013, p. 129). A related finding is that people will invest more money to address a bigger part of a smaller problem than to address a smaller part of a very large problem. Fetherstonhaugh et al. (1997), for instance, found that people's willingness to allocate a $10 million grant required 100,000 lives to be saved where 290,000 were at risk, but only 9,000 lives to be saved when 15,000 were at risk. These phenomena are so powerful that they have been used to explain the continued recurrence of genocides (Slovic & Zionts, 2012; Slovic et al., 2013). Insofar as the likely impacts of climate change exceed the magnitude of any genocide, its overwhelming magnitude may—counterintuitively—drive *down* the total number of resources (cognitive and otherwise) that people are willing to spend to address it.

The unprecedented nature of climate change also generates distinctive psychological challenges as individuals and institutions do their best to address a problem of a type that has never before arisen in human history. This novelty is likely to further limit the ability of private citizens and policy makers to imagine what the world will look like in the future, and may therefore generate underresponsiveness to or undervaluation of the total dangers of climate change. More subtly, the unprecedented nature of climate change also undermines a number of potential tools for debiasing and learning. Consider, for example, the problem of affective forecasting. As we have discussed, one of the most effective interventions for improving affective forecasting, and being able to more accurately imagine how one is likely to feel after future events, is to gather information about how other people have responded to the same type of event (Gilbert et al., 2009). Where events are truly unprecedented in human memory, however—as with the melting of the polar ice caps, the bleaching of coral reefs, mass global extinctions, and so on—such strategies are unhelpful. Furthermore, research on salience and the availability heuristic has shown that uncommon, hard-to-imagine outcomes can trigger a kind of "tragedy of the uncommons," leading people to neglect or discount possible outcomes that they find difficult to visualize (Wiener, 2016) even as they overweight or overestimate the impact of high-salience large events, such as terrorism (Sunstein, 2007). One responsive policy prescription is to try to increase the cognitive salience of hard-to-imagine events (Sunstein, 2007). But where—as with climate change—it is legitimately difficult to predict and summarize the full extent of likely impacts, such interventions face special challenges.

Finally, as discussed above, climate change generates a series of deep moral and ethical questions, which can trigger a host of cognitive processes related to moral reasoning. Recall here the work of Bandura and others showing people's reluctance to engage in behavior they recognize as harming others—behavior that is widely viewed as antisocial (Bandura, 2002, 2015; Gini, 2006). Normal people experience discomfort at the possibility of harming others, and they engage in a number of strategies—minimization, displacement of responsibility, depersonalization and dehumanization, palliative comparisons, moral justification, and so on—to morally disengage and minimize their discomfort at causing pain (Bandura, 2015; Shalvi et al., 2015; Shu et al., 2011). Perhaps counterintuitively, this may suggest that denial of climate change may come, in part, from discomfort at the thought of harming others. Such tendencies interact with motivated reasoning, and with the general diffusion and complexity of the climate change problem, further enabling the ability to minimize and deflect.

All of these qualities together—the enormous size, the unprecedented nature of climate impacts, and the deeply held moral values that may be triggered by thinking about climate harms—can be emotionally overwhelming in ways that may affect people's ability to process and respond. As a result, the cognitive and emotional load of climate change may be a concern in and of itself. Just thinking about climate change has been found to lead to bad psychological consequences, separate and apart from the bad consequences that result from actually experiencing it (Doherty & Clayton 2011; Reser & Swim 2011). Emotional responses vary; for some, the huge, novel, and morally charged nature of climate change may simply overwhelm emotional capacity, leading to numbing and thus to apparent apathy (Moser 2007, Norgaard, 2011). For others, concern about climate change may also generate depression and/or anxiety (Doherty & Clayton 2011).

In addition to the bad feelings climate change (and thinking about climate change) generates, the cognitive and emotional load it induces can have behavioral consequences. Namely, it can demotivate action by inducing a sense of loss of control and helplessness. Many people enthusiastically engage in individual-level behaviors designed to slow climate change: driving less, moderating their thermostats, eating more plants, and so on. These are the sorts of individual actions we address in more detail in the subsequent section. Yet relentless media accounts of climate change continue, despite anyone's individual efforts. Feelings of acute lack of control and learned helplessness may follow, demotivating people from even simple individual actions and making them less likely to engage in pro-environmental behaviors, despite their level of concern (Landry et al., 2018).

These features of climate change psychology may also contribute to reluctance to support collective environmental protection efforts, as well. Much work has been done chronicling the pervasiveness of "climate change denial," where people deny or minimize the existence of anthropogenic climate change and/or the likelihood that climate change will have substantial impacts. Climate change denial as a phenomenon is particularly associated with the United States. In one recent study, for instance, 13% of Americans agreed with the statement that the climate is changing "but human activity is not responsible at all," while a further 5% simply rejected the possibility that the climate is even .changing (Milman & Harvey, 2019, n.p.). That said, some see the global response to climate change as underresponsive, as well (Thunberg, 2019), suggesting that general denial may underlie global as well as American lack of adequate response to climate change (Norgaard, 2011).

Within legal scholarship, climate change denial is most often treated through a political and cultural lens, and indeed there is robust empirical scholarship suggesting that the likelihood of climate change denial is at least partially mediated by ideological beliefs, partisanship, and endorsement of the status quo (Kahan et al., 2007a; Dunlap et al., 2016; Jylhä et al., 2016). In some cases, rejection or denial of information about the extent of climate change or its anthropogenic nature has been tied to "solution aversion," where people reject information that would have implications that are inconsistent with their values (Campbell & Kay, 2014). Individuals who hold antiregulatory values, for instance, may perceive information suggesting that tackling climate change requires federal and/or state regulation as threatening to their identity (Campbell & Kay, 2014; Kahan et al., 2015).

Understanding the political and partisan qualities of climate change denial is potentially helpful in a number of ways, including that it provides at least a partial explanation for legislative inaction in the United States. As climate change becomes increasingly associated with partisan identity, it may also become increasingly difficult for legislators to work outside their political parties. Understanding the politics of climate change can also help in generating prescriptions for effective communication about climate change. Dan Kahan and others, for instance, have suggested that policy makers will be most effective in conveying climate change messages when information is passed through ideologically approved messengers, who match the ideological identity of the person(s) hearing the information (Kahan et al., 2007a; Kahan, 2015).

That said, a purely partisan or ideological account of climate change denial is likely incomplete, not least because it cannot fully explain the reasons underlying the denial. Furthermore, it may obscure the relationship between "classic" American climate change denial and other, subtler forms of identity- and trauma-protective responses. "Classic" denial sometimes takes the form of extreme skepticism; for example, the insistence that there is a large conspiracy of scientists fabricating climate science, or as 17% of Americans said in a 2019 poll, that "the idea of manmade global warming is a hoax that was invented to deceive people" (Milman & Harvey, 2019, n.p.).

Contrast this with the "soft" denial associated with apathy and minimization, such as Kari Norgaard carefully documented in her book *Living in Denial: Climate Change, Emotions, and Everyday Life* (2011). Norgaard lived for a year in a small Norwegian city, interviewing people about their beliefs and attitudes about climate change. Though the population Norgaard studied was almost entirely egalitarian and progressive in their ideology, and many had personal experience with changing climate (for example, through seeing decreasing snow cover over the years), many still denied that climate change is a serious problem. Norgaard suggests that for the Norwegians she interviewed, it was emotionally and cognitively difficult for them to acknowledge that their country's large production of oil and gas contributes to the overwhelmingly bad consequences created by climate change. As a result, they actively avoided acknowledging disturbing information regarding climate change, often by simply steering clear of thinking or talking about climate change entirely. These individual responses were amplified through social processes, leading to political inaction and underresponse.

In sum, the distinctive qualities of climate change harms—their extraordinary size, unprecedented nature, and moral complexity—all combine to create special psychological challenges to perceiving, understanding, and responding to the risks. Perhaps counterintuitively, these characteristics may mean that some strategies commonly used to promote action on climate policy—like detailing and emphasizing the enormous magnitude of climate change as a problem—could actually make the problem worse by triggering cognitive and emotional protective mechanisms, such as psychic numbing and denial. The result is something of a catch-22 in climate policy. While the psychological characteristics of climate harm suggest that the scale, type, and moral importance of climate change is likely to be systematically minimized and underresponded to, attempts to heighten attention to the problem may well trigger additional cognitive and emotional protective mechanisms, leading people to further minimize climate change as a concern. The result is a kind of psychological-denial treadmill. Psychology can help illuminate the existence of this treadmill. But to actually address climate change itself, law and policy will have to find a way to address these psychological realities.

Climate Injury as Environmental Injury

We have suggested that climate change presents special psychological challenges to decision makers because of its distinctively high stakes, unprecedented nature, and moral impact. Climate law and policy needs to take note of psychology in part because these characteristics tend to generate a kind of psychological-denial treadmill, where upping the "speed" by emphasizing the overwhelming qualities of climate change may simply result in individuals "running faster" to minimize their own cognitive and emotional responses to a perceived threat. In this section, we suggest that climate change also presents the quintessential trifecta of environmental injury: Its impacts are extraordinarily diffuse through space and time, they are highly complex, and they operate through non-human processes that massively impact nonhuman stakeholders. We discuss each quality in more detail below, noting particularly instances where these characteristics operate in ways distinctive to climate change. But in short, the extreme diffusion of climate impacts through space and time makes them less salient and thus easy to neglect while simultaneously introducing barriers to empathy; the extreme complexity of climate change generates substantial cognitive load and makes thinking about it cognitively costly; and the impact of climate change on nonhuman stakeholders further increases cognitive and emotional load, which still further interferes with caring and contributes even further to denial. Each of these qualities will affect the psychology of climate change *policy*, too, because each substantially affects how people are likely to think about climate change as a problem and thus about potential solutions. All of these challenges also stack on top of the distinctive climate challenges discussed in the prior section. Together they may create significant cognitive incentives to minimize or even reject the challenges posed by climate change.

DIFFUSION

Some of the greatest psychological effects on climate change decision making stem from the extreme diffusion of climate behaviors and impacts across both space and time. Because greenhouse gases contribute to climate change on a global scale (Metz et al., 2007), it is impossible even for trained experts to draw a clear causal link between any particular emissions behavior and a local or particular impact. In a literal and figurative sense, this means that it is impossible for individuals to "see" the effects of their climate behaviors on the global climate. As a result, climate impacts lack salience, and they can seem distant and relatively unimportant in comparison to more immediate and more obvious risks and opportunities (Spence et al., 2012). This may create a kind of "unavailability heuristic" that obscures climate change from individuals' psychological radar (Lazarus, 2009). At a general level, its diffuse nature allows decision makers to detach from the expected effects of climate change. The fact that people may have cognitive and emotional difficulty perceiving or owning up to the harm they cause to future generations and to others living in other parts of the world creates additional difficulty in incentivizing them to change their behavior.

The nonidentifiability of climate victims may play a particularly important role in permitting decision makers to detach. As we have discussed, people are far more concerned about—and far more willing to invest their resources in protecting—identifiable lives than unidentified or statistical ones (Small & Loewenstein, 2003; Slovic et al., 2013). Especially when unidentifiability is combined with a large problem, people can suffer from "pseudoinefficacy," or a "drop in the bucket" effect, which leads people to discount incremental improvements in the belief that their contribution cannot address the larger problem (Bartels & Burnett, 2011; Västfjäll et al., 2015). In a classic illustration of this problem, Paul Slovic and others found that people would give more money to help one little girl in Africa who needed food aid than they would give when they were provided the same information about the little girl plus the information that millions of others in Africa were also at risk of starvation (Small et al., 2007). Research suggests this may happen in part because the negative feelings associated with those not being helped blends with the good feelings about those who can be helped (Västfjäll et al., 2015). Perhaps counterintuitively, as we have discussed, this effect makes people less likely to act the larger they believe a problem to be (Bartels, 2006; Slovic et al., 2002). Combined with the phenomenon of learned helplessness, communications about the overwhelming magnitude of climate impacts may therefore sometimes backfire, by generating a feeling of impotence. Some research suggests this effect may be combated through exercises designed to block intrusion of irrelevant feelings, as by reminding decision makers that their negative feelings in fact follow from the portion of the problem they cannot solve, rather than the portion of the problem over which they have control (Schwarz et al., 2007; Västfjäll et al., 2015).

The cognitive distance engendered by diffuse climate change impacts may further reinforce people's tendency to dismiss the gravity of externalities they generate. The average American emits about 16 metric tons of carbon dioxide equivalent a year—enough, as one scholar has estimated, to cause "the serious suffering and/or deaths of two future people" over an average lifetime of emissions (Nolt, 2011). Yet most Americans will never directly witness any of these deaths; and if they did, would not easily connect their own behaviors to suffering on another continent, in another decade, from the hunger, coastal flooding, or reductions in water supplies that the IPCC estimates are likely to affect hundreds of millions of people.

Other psychological phenomena attach specifically to the geographic and temporal diffusion of climate change impacts, and they may affect how much people care about the impacts they do perceive. On the geographic front, most climate impacts will accrue to distant people and ecosystems—a fact that may matter, given differences in how people think about, and value, foreign and domestic risks (Rowell & Wexler, 2014). Recall that foreign impacts are likely to be cognitively categorized as accruing to the "other," invoking out-group biases that lead people to dismiss—sometimes even gain pleasure from—risks that accrue to outsiders (Cikara, Bruneau & Saxe, 2011). And again, people are generally more interested in and empathetic toward identifiable and relatable victims (Small & Loewenstein, 2003; Small et al., 2007). Insofar as "foreign" harms accrue to outsiders, they may be systematically less likely to trigger empathy and caring. Even where people do not entirely dismiss the value of distant, foreign harms—particularly if they themselves expect one day to travel to an affected area where harm may accrue, such as Venice—their weighting of such harms may be less than if they perceive a risk as accruing domestically (Dana, 2009; Rowell, 2015).

From a temporal perspective, most of the expected impacts of climate change will not accrue for decades—in many cases, long after the individual who is acting has died. The injuries caused by climate change are thus intergenerational as well as intertemporal. In addition to introducing the possibility of intertemporal "othering"—which may be exacerbated when the others affected are not yet born, will never have to be faced, and are thus unidentifiable (Hsu, 2008)—the extreme latency of climate impacts triggers a host of heuristics and phenomena, including present bias, hyperbolic discounting, and failures of hedonic forecasting. In addition, the gradual nature of many of these changes may affect individuals' ability to observe and notice them. These impacts have been discussed in the legal and economic literature primarily through the lens of "discounting," or the process of making monetary amounts comparable through time (Stern, 2007; Nordhaus, 2008; Weisbach & Sunstein, 2008). Because of the long latency periods associated with climate change, small changes in the discount rate used to make regulatory decisions may lead to substantially different policies (Stern, 2007; Nordhaus, 2008; Weisbach & Sunstein, 2008). Psychological processes that affect the choice of discount rate—such as present bias and hyperbolic discounting—may therefore have an outsized impact on climate change policy.

More subtly, one ongoing debate in climate law and policy is whether legal policy should value harms to current people and future generations in the same way (Revesz, 1999; Sunstein & Rowell, 2007). Currently, U.S. legal policy—embedded within regulatory cost-benefit analysis—generally treats environmental harms to present and future generations equally, in the sense that it applies the same valuation and discounting methods to valuing intragenerational and intergenerational risks (Sunstein & Rowell, 2007; Rowell, 2012a). Arguably, this approach is supported by the fact that intertemporal and intergenerational harms are identical from an economic perspective, once they have been monetized (Sunstein & Rowell, 2007). But if people value risks to current and future generations differently—for example, because they view future people as "others"—it may be that the actual monetization practices for risks, which generally rely upon measures of people's willingness to pay to reduce risk, *should* differ based upon the timing of the risk.

Finally, although U.S. legal scholarship has focused on discounting policy when addressing cost-benefit analysis and the temporal aspects of climate change (Rowell, 2014), other psychological phenomena may also be relevant to how people perceive and understand climate impacts through time. For example, so-called "environmental generational amnesia," where people make their own direct experience a baseline for environmental quality (Kahn, 2002; Doherty & Clayton, 2011), may create additional psychological barriers for people in recognizing the extent to which the climate has degraded over time.

COMPLEXITY

Despite the well-established link between greenhouse gas emissions and climate change, its actual pattern—severity, time, scale, scope—is almost overwhelmingly complex. Unfortunately, as we have seen, human psychology often struggles to manage complex risks, and the sheer complexity of the problem of addressing climate change is, on its own, a barrier to meaningfully addressing it (Weber & Stern, 2011).

The complexity of climate change generates significant cognitive and emotional load. On an emotional level, this exacerbates the bad feelings climate change (and thinking about climate change) generates. It may also reinforce temptations toward denial, numbness, and apathy, as well as toward behaviors of learned helplessness. From a cognitive perspective, complexity exacerbates the temptation to adopt simplifying heuristics as a way to lower the cost of thinking about and responding to climate change. We have already discussed various techniques people have for coping with complexity. We will not rehash all these phenomena here, but we will note that the psychological implications of complexity play out in predictable ways in the domain of climate change. For instance, research suggests that people unconsciously use their political ideologies, values, and world-views as guides for what facts to believe (Hornsey et al., 2016).

The consequences of ideologically motivated cognition, sometimes called cultural cognition, can be subtle (Kahan et al., 2006). Because climate change is so complex, individuals are forced to rely at least partially on experts for information about likely impacts and opportunities. Yet as we discussed in Chapter 3, whether people perceive some-one as an "expert," and whether they perceive consensus among those experts, is partially driven by preexisting values. People are more likely to recognize expertise in people whose worldviews they see as consistent with their own (Earle & Cvetkovich, 1995). And people's ideology shapes their individual beliefs about the existence of expert consensus: The more ideologically appealing it is to believe that scientists "agree" on a factual point, the more likely people are to believe such scientific consensus does exist (Kahan et al., 2010). These factors feed upon one another: The more people trust climate scientists and the more they believe scientists agree that climate change is real, the more people report believing in climate change science themselves (Hornsey et al., 2016). They also are deeply influenced by social networks: The more they are surrounded by and connected to others who believe in climate change, the more people seek out information about it and how they can adapt to it (Smith et al., 2012).

While complexity exacerbates many of the psychological challenges associated with dealing with climate change, it is worth noting that it may also offer some opportunities. For instance, beliefs that are held on the basis of socially mediated processes, such as partisan ideology, may be particularly subject to so-called availability cascades. As we have discussed elsewhere, in an availability cascade, the popularity of a belief triggers a chain reaction within a social network (Kuran, 1995; Kuran & Sunstein, 1999). Additional research may be warranted into whether climate change beliefs may be subject to such cascades, and whether policy makers might harness their power to change attitudes.

NONHUMAN CHARACTER

A final important aspect of climate change is how nonhuman processes interact with human behaviors to generate climate injury. Two implications may be particularly worth highlighting in regard to the nonhuman character of many climate change impacts: its relation to debates on whether climate change is anthropogenic and the extraordinary impacts that climate change is expected to have on nonhuman animals and ecosystems.

First, consider the remarkably durable debate about whether climate change is anthropogenic. The notion that nature—as distinct from things produced by humans—is safer or less risky, is deep seated (Rozin et al., 2004). People prefer natural to manmade scenery (Kardan et al., 2015), are more likely to suffer PTSD after a manmade disaster than a natural one (Galea et al., 2005), and prefer natural to processed foods and medicines (Rozin et al., 2004). Perhaps it should be no surprise then that whether or not climate change is "natural" seems to matter to people. Farmers, for instance, who believe climate change is happening but who believe it is not caused by human actions are less concerned about it and more likely to dismiss the need to do anything about it (Arbuckle et al., 2013). Of course, adaptation and other measures may be necessary to respond to climate change, even if—as scientists now emphatically reject—the causes of climate change were nonanthropogenic. Yet for many people, believing that climate change is natural seems to reassure them that it is also not worrisome.

Second, and as we discussed earlier, the degree to which people identify with the nonhuman victims of climate change may make it both easier and harder for regulators to mandate behaviors. The more people feel connected to particular places, the more motivated they are to support environmental policies designed to protect them (Reser et al., 2011). And the more they identify with, and notice, nonhuman animals, the more supportive they will be toward policies that protect *them*. This bodes well for polar bears (Dillahunt et al., 2008; Marseille et al., 2012; Swim & Bloodhart, 2015) but far less well for worms, let alone for fungi, bacteria, and other uncharismatic species.

Other phenomena we have discussed generate a further risk that nonhuman species and ecosystems could suffer from affective neglect. Individually identifiable animals—especially charismatic ones—may trigger empathy and caring, but when large numbers of animals, or whole ecosystems, are under threat, it may counterintuitively make people *less* able to process, understand, and respond to extreme nonhuman impacts. Consider in this light the well-publicized estimate that a billion animals (including kangaroos, koalas, and wallabies) perished in the catastrophic 2019–2020 Australian wildfires (Dickman, 2020)—the type of blaze that scientists say could be three times more common by the end of the century as a result of changing climatic conditions (Gramling, 2020). On the one hand, communication about the staggeringly large nonhuman impacts of these fires helps to highlight the magnitude of climate change risks and thus their importance. On the other, the scale is so large that many people may feel cognitive pressure to minimize their emotional impact through psychic numbing, denial, or related avoidance techniques. And the fix is not simple: Emphasizing the sheer number of animals affected, or attempting to increase empathy and caring by flagging the cuteness and relatability of many of the animals affected, may actually increase the emotional load people feel in considering the magnitude of the disaster.

Psychology of Climate Law and Policy

This part of the chapter outlines key policy and legal responses to the climate change challenges identified above and identifies opportunities for adopting a psychological approach to climate law and policy. Generally, it suggests that psychology can play a significant role in climate change decision making, both by individuals and by institutions, and thus can be helpful in increasing the ability of law and policy to effectively understand, predict, and shape human behavior regarding climate change.

Basic Climate Policy: Strategies for Response

The challenges articulated above have made it extremely difficult for policy makers to develop effective policy responses to climate change. Indeed, proposals about the best policy tools for addressing climate change remain wide and deep, with no single dominant strategy emerging. That said, policy makers generally have three active approaches at their disposal: (1) mitigation, (2) adaptation, and (3) climate engineering. Policy makers also have a fourth option, through choosing none of the above: (4) climate inaction. Many strategies—as with the policy recommendations presented by the IPCC—incorporate aspects of each active approach on the theory that no one approach can successfully address all of the causes and effects of climate change (Masson-Delmotte et al., 2018; Pachauri et al., 2015). We describe each approach a bit further below.

Generally speaking, *mitigation* seeks to limit the magnitude and rate of long-term climate change. Reducing anthropogenic greenhouse gas emissions is the most important method of mitigation. The theory is that reducing the amount of greenhouse gases emitted will (eventually) reduce the concentration of greenhouse gases in the atmosphere. Emissions reduction was the central strategy first proposed in the UNFCCC, and it remains the cornerstone of most climate strategies (Pachauri et al., 2015). There are a number of mechanisms that can be used to achieve mitigation, including carbon taxes, emissions quotas, bans on high-emission behaviors, and incentives for emission-reducing behaviors. Unfortunately, effective mitigation faces a series of psychological barriers (Gifford, 2011). Many of these relate to the general challenges highlighted above, but others are more specific to mitigation. In particular, the extraordinary costs associated with effective mitigation are likely to trigger ideological and motivated reasoning. In some cases, aggressive mitigation strategies have triggered solution aversion, whereby opposition to the proposed mitigation gives rise to a tendency to disbelieve climate science or minimize likely impacts (Campbell & Kay, 2014). For example, in the United States, solution aversion appears to be particularly likely where mitigation strategies attempt to employ climate taxes, promote renewable energy, or are perceived as governmental abuses of power (Jacques & Knox, 2016).

A second fundamental tool in climate policy is *adaptation*, which involves adjusting to expected or experienced changes to reduce the damage they cause. This can incorporate a wide variety of behaviors, including adopting technologies or processes that reduce the harm from increased temperatures, humidity, natural hazards, or mosquito-borne illnesses, as well as investments in infrastructure, such as sea walls and flood drainage, that reduce climate harms. Adaptation strategies can also target either human harm, as by addressing public health, or the health and viability of nonhuman plants, animals, and ecosystems, as through habitat restoration (Pachauri et al., 2015). Generally, adaptation is expensive, and the speed of change matters: Incremental changes in behavior may be less costly, more palatable, and more in line with natural processes such as natural selection than sudden changes. As a result, the overall cost of climate adaptation is likely to vary with the amount of greenhouse gases emitted and the speed of consequent change, leading the IPCC, among others, to recommend mitigation as a strategy for reducing adaptation costs (Pachauri et al., 2015).

From a psychological perspective, adaptation, too, faces both general and specific psychological challenges (Gifford, 2011; van Valkengoed & Steg, 2019). In particular, individuals and households may exhibit substantial variability in their motivation for adopting adapted behaviors (van Valkengoed & Steg, 2019). Furthermore, the very novelty of new adaptations may heighten the perceived risk associated with them (Slovic, 2000), or may even draw attention to existing risks that individuals had otherwise managed to ignore. New sea walls, for example, may be a vivid reminder of the dangers of sea level rise. In addition, the diffusion of climate impacts will sometimes interact with how people perceive adaptation; Americans who believe climate change will primarily affect people from distant places, for example, are less likely to support adaptation policies (Singh et al., 2017).

Research on the plausibility of *climate engineering* (also called geoengineering or negative emissions technologies) is still quite young, though the IPCC relies on projections of negative emissions technologies in its claim that it may be possible to hold overall warming to 1.5° C (Masson-Delmotte et al., 2018). Two main groups of climate-engineering technologies are carbon dioxide removal (CDR) and solar radiation management (SRM). For CDR, the common focus is on carbon capture and storage, as through afforestation and ecosystem restoration. Although the basic function of many biological systems in carbon capturing and storage is well established, experts warn that it remains an open question of how feasible CDR processes are on the massive scales that would be required to substantially alter the global climate (Masson-Delmotte et al., 2018). Moreover, "all are in early stages of development, involve substantial uncertainties and risks, and raise ethical and governance dilemmas" (Lawrence et al., 2018, p. 3734). SRM might be accomplished through several means. One approach involves stratospheric aerosol injection, which would replicate the cooling climate impacts of volcanic eruptions (Masson-Delmotte et al., 2018). This remains an experimental technology, however, and "face[s] large uncertainties and knowledge gaps as well as substantial risks . . . and constraints . . ." (Masson-Delmotte et al., 2018, pp. 14–15). Other SRM approaches, such as installing massive mirror installations to reflect sunlight back into space, remain even more experimental, uncertain, and unprecedented.

Climate engineering, too, faces its own distinctive psychological challenges. Two—often competing—characteristics are particularly worth noting. First, optimism about the promise of geoengineering tends to align with pre-existing normative beliefs about technology (Wibeck et al., 2017). The more optimistic people are about technology, the more promise they see in geoengineering, regardless of the specifics of any particular geoengineering technology (Kahan et al., 2009). By contrast, geoengineering can also be perceived as "unnatural" and therefore risky. Indeed, when people perceive geoengineering as "messing with nature," they also perceive it as riskier and less beneficial (Corner et al., 2013).

Finally, policy makers have the option of *inaction*: continuing business as usual and refusing to take substantial action on climate change. Although this strategy requires ignoring the substantial costs of climate change, by some lights this remains the dominant climate strategy in the United States, if not around the world. From a psychological perspective, inaction offers a number of attractive features, and these features may explain much of the historical inaction on climate change (Rachlinski, 2000b). As we have discussed throughout the book, and expand on further below, a broad constellation of psychological phenomena tend to entrench the status quo, making it cognitively, motivationally, and emotionally difficult to substantively change climate behaviors (Gifford, 2011).

Although much ink has been spilled comparing strategies for reducing the harm of climate change on political, economic, social, and scientific grounds, relatively little attention has been paid to the comparative psychology of each of strategy. This is unfortunate, as each may trigger distinctive cognitive pathways. Indeed, one important puzzle in climate policy is the extent to which these various strategies may be perceived as substitutes for one another. It is often asserted that attempts to promote adaptation may "backfire" by providing a justification for lesser mitigation (Lorenzoni et al., 2007; Shepherd & Kay, 2012). Similar arguments are often made about geoengineering and technology-based solutions (Kahan et al., 2015). The psychology of this is currently unclear. Some research suggests that perceptions of the hopelessness of a problem, or the unpalatability of a solution, may lead people to detach entirely, as we have already noted, but other research suggests that carefully framed solutions can overcome this phenomenon (Kahan et al., 2015). Additional psychological research is urgently needed to guide policy makers in choosing the most effective climate strategies and to accurately predict responses to those strategies. Until then, we have flagged instances where we believe individual and institutional psychology may interact with the choice of climate strategies.

Climate Law and Psychology

It should be no surprise that climate law has become its own subfield within environmental law. This is particularly true outside the United States, where international law plays a central role in climate change policy (Gray et al., 2016). Even within the United States, however, scholars are beginning to specialize in climate law and policy (Farber & Carlarne, 2017). At the same time, research on the psychology of climate change—particularly in regard to individual behaviors—has been blossoming (Swim et al., 2012; Clayton et al., 2015). Yet thus far, treatments of the psychology of climate change *law* have been rare. In fact, the most notable treatment of climate psychology in legal scholarship—Jeff Rachlinski's 20-year-old article on the "Psychology of Global Climate Change"—is remarkable in part because of its dismissal of law as a feasible method for addressing the psychological challenges he sees attaching to climate change. Perhaps hesitant to end his article on such a doomed note, Rachlinski suggests that technological developments of cheap alternatives to fossil fuels might present a solution to climate change, despite social and cognitive limitations to other solutions (Rachlinski, 2000b). Yet law, he warns, will not be a solution.

Whether discouraged by Rachlinski or simply busy with other affairs, legal scholars have yet to fully take up the rich and constantly expanding literature on the psychology of climate change. This may be a missed opportunity. While the psychology of climate change does present special challenges to law, there is no reason to think that ignoring those challenges is more likely to result in effective policy than addressing them considerately. Furthermore, research on individual behavior and on climate change communications may offer new vehicles for potentially shaping human behaviors toward reducing the impacts of climate change. In some cases, those vehicles may help in finding paths around the obstacles presented by the psychological phenomena that make climate change so difficult to process and respond to.

INSTITUTIONAL DECISION MAKING ON CLIMATE CHANGE

Countries vary in how central domestic law is to their climate policy. The United States' climate policy is distinctively domestic (Rowell, 2015; Rowell & van Zeben, 2020), for instance, while countries within the EU are largely driven by international agreements (van Zeben & Rowell, 2020). For jurisdictions where domestic policy is particularly determinative, the psychology of decision making within domestic legal institutions becomes highly relevant to substantive climate policy. For the rest of the world, the psychology of international law and international agreements is more relevant—though as we suggest below, there may be reason to suspect that international agreements could have a theoretical psychological impact even on countries who have chosen not to ratify them.

The Psychology of International Environmental Law

The psychology of international law remains an underdeveloped field (van Aaken & Broude, 2019), and the psychology of international climate law still more so. At least theoretically, however, international climate agreements may create psychological focal points against which future judgments can be formed (Rowell & van Zeben, 2016) as domestic law has been found to do in other contexts (Korobkin, 2000; McAdams, 2000). The terms of negotiated international agreements—as with the terms of negotiated contracts (Korobkin, 2000)—may create a perceived norm, triggering the power of the endowment effect and loss aversion against diversions from the perceived status quo. Notably, as with domestic law, this effect could operate independently of traditional enforcement mechanisms, meaning that highly salient agreements such as the Paris Agreement could influence the perceptions   and thus the behavior—even of individuals and institutions who are not a party to the relevant agreement at all (Rowell & van Zeben, 2016). The psychological effect of international agreements may be heightened through additional contextual factors, including unanimity and the selection of quantifiable measures of success or failure. In this light, the Paris Agreement's decision to adopt a quantified and ambitious goal—of keeping global warming "well below" 2° C, and of aiming to keep it at less than 1.5° C above pre-industrial levels—could in theory generate significant psychological stickiness as a baseline, even without an international police, court, or other entity able to enforce it. That said, these are speculations based upon existing research on the psychological impacts of domestic non-climate law. As the psychology of climate change law continues to develop, the psychological impact of climate change agreements is a particularly ripe area for further research.

Domestic Environmental Legal Institutions

Although international law may have indirect psychological impacts on law and policy, within the United States the psychology of decision making within domestic legal institutions remains particularly relevant. Distinctive aspects of U.S. climate law worth considering might include: (1) the lack of legislative action at the federal level; (2) the outsized role of the executive; (3) the substantial impact of agencies, and particularly their use of monetized cost-benefit analysis, on national policy; and (4) the role of courts in climate law.

First, consider the fact that the U.S. Senate has not ratified any major international mitigation agreement, and that Congress has no overarching legislative strategy for addressing mitigation. This lack of legislative action leaves enormous discretion for the President in setting U.S. policy, as we discuss below, but also exhibits a functional choice to engage in climate *inaction* as a management strategy. Furthermore, the length of time international scientific and political bodies have warned of climate change's dangers, and the United States' consistent choice not to engage in international actions combating climate change, may create a kind of psychological path dependence, where the status quo in the United States seems more and more to be a lack of legislative action regarding climate change. The choice not to act may then become stickier and stickier, making it harder and harder for legislators to act, at least absent some exogenous shock.

In many ways, psychology may help in explaining why the United States—and indeed, by some lights, many other countries—have selected inaction as their dominant approach to climate change (Rachlinski, 2000b). Even where actions are not costly, status quo bias leads people to prefer existing arrangements over changing their behavior. As Jeff Rachlinski (2000b) has noted, legal or regulatory interventions in climate change that ask people to change their ordinary ways of acting, or to give up something they are accustomed to having, thus face special psychological hurdles. Overcoming inertia becomes even more challenging where the perceived costs and benefits of climate action are distorted by perceived "distance," such that the costs of action are borne immediately by present people, while the risks of inaction are borne primarily by future and foreign others; where the complexity and uncertainty of climate predictions present cognitive space for rationalization; and where the nonhuman processes and interests triggered by climate change affect the ability of individuals to connect with climate harms on an emotional level.

Second, consider that the United States, lacking international agreements and meaningful legislative action on climate change, invests extraordinary authority in the executive branch to manage climate policy (Rowell, 2015; Rowell & van Zeben, 2020). In countries that rely on a single person to wield executive power, the psychology and decision-making context of that lone individual can have significant impacts on climate law and policy. Personal psychology, even to the level of personality (Rubenzer & Faschingbauer, 2004), psychopathy (Lilienfeld et al., 2012), or mental health (Davidson et al., 2006), becomes influential on overarching law and policy. In the United States, this may be well illustrated by the example of President Donald Trump (McAdams, 2016), whose decisions to reject the prior administration's powerful climate actions—the Clean Power Plan, the global Social Cost of Carbon, the Climate Action Plan, the acceptance of the Paris Agreement—have single-handedly substantially altered U.S. climate policy. In considering such policy flips, note that the relationship of an executive with the prior executive may also matter significantly to law and policy. Where an executive perceives the prior executive to be part of an "in-group," for example, because she or he shares the same political party, the executive may perceive past actions to be particularly worthy of respect and thus will be less likely to overturn them. The opposite may occur where, as is the case with President Donald Trump following President Barack Obama, the existing executive regards the prior executive as a member of an "out-group" or competitor (Ross & Ward, 1995).

A third distinctive institutional aspect of U.S. climate policy is the central role played by regulatory agencies, particularly in implementing executive orders on cost-benefit analysis (Rowell & van Zeben, 2020). In the United States, again because of the vacuum left by the legislature and international agreements, federal climate policy is substantially implemented by agencies following executive direction (Rowell, 2015).

In recent years, this has largely involved incorporating a monetized estimate of the "social cost of carbon"—the expected harm caused by each ton of carbon dioxide emissions—into regulatory cost-benefit analyses. Though seemingly obscure, such incorporations can substantially change which regulations pass muster and how stringently agencies regulate things like car emissions and power plants (Pizer et al., 2014). One of the most consequential decisions in calculating the social cost of carbon is whether U.S. agencies should be counting the harm caused by U.S. emissions to the entire world, or only those inflicted within U.S. borders (Rowell, 2015). Perhaps unsurprisingly, considering harm to the whole globe leads to more stringent regulations, while focusing only on domestic harm makes the damage of climate change look smaller, and thus can be used to justify less stringency. Agencies have opted for different approaches to calculation under different presidents: Under President Obama, they calculated the harm of U.S. actions on the whole world, while under President Trump, they have focused on domestic impacts.

These choices are complex and multifactorial (Rowell, 2015), but because they have the power to substantially influence the stringency of U.S. climate action, it is worth considering the psychological factors that may play a role in selecting between a policy that addresses the global harm of climate emissions and a policy that minimizes apparent harm by focusing on domestic-only impacts (Rowell & Wexler, 2014). Again, out-group bias and motivated cognition may encourage dismissal of foreign impacts; psychic numbing and the emotional distance of foreign persons may encourage a lack of empathy for widespread global impacts; and the psychology of harming others may engender systematic cognitive incentives to minimize, justify, and rationalize harming global persons with U.S. actions. All of these factors would tend to push regulatory policy toward using the lower, domestic estimates of the harm of climate change emissions—even where there are not good political, scientific, or legal reasons to do so.

Finally, consider the role that courts now play in climate change law as well as the role they could play in future. Judicial approaches to climate law and policy have been gaining global attention in recent years (Dellinger, 2018; Peel & Osofsky, 2019). The *Urgenda* case from 2019 in the Netherlands has been particularly influential. In it, the Dutch court held that because of its extraordinary impacts, climate change violates theories of basic human rights, and the Netherlands therefore has an obligation to act urgently to address its emissions. Similar legislation is pending in the United States, perhaps most notably in the case *Juliana v. United States*, a suit brought by 21 young people claiming to have a Constitutional right to be protected from climate change. The case was filed in 2015 in the federal district court of Oregon and as of this writing, continues to wend its way through the U.S. court system.

Though such cases invite new jurisprudence addressing the distinctive aspects of climate injury—and therefore respond to scholarly calls for jurisprudence distinguishing environmental injury (Lazarus, 2000)—courts have yet to develop any such distinctive approach to climate change or climate injury. As David Markell and J. B. Ruhl concluded after a careful empirical analysis of climate change litigation around the country, "[T]he story of climate change in the courts has not been one of courts forging a new jurisprudence, but rather one of judicial business as usual" (Markell & Ruhl, 2012, p. 15). That said, as climate litigation becomes an increasingly popular strategy for attempting to address climate injury, research on the psychology of judicial decision making (Klein & Mitchell, 2010) will become ever more relevant to the study of climate law and policy. Importantly, the current state of empirical knowledge continues to struggle to distinguish between *judicial* decision making and *individual* decision making. That is, it remains unclear whether judges make decisions *qua* judges that are different than the individual decisions of other decision makers (Schauer, 2010). It is even less clear whether judicial decisions *about climate change* have any distinctive flavor to them; further research on this point would be valuable. Until such research materializes, however, general research on individual decision making on climate change may be our best portal into understanding the psychology of judicial climate decisions. Fortunately, as we discuss below, the psychology of individual climate change decision making is a flourishing field in psychology, about which there is much to say.

INDIVIDUAL DECISION MAKING ON CLIMATE CHANGE

Psychological and behavioral analysis of individual climate decisions is at the forefront of climate policy, and significant opportunities remain to develop new ways to address individual behaviors, both through empirically informed knowledge of people's psychology and through the use of behavioral tools. Individuals' decisions affect climate change law and policy in a number of important ways. These include behaviors that affect legal and policy action (or inaction) directly as well as behaviors that can either substitute for, or be incentivized by, laws regarding mitigation, adaptation, or climate engineering. Importantly, individual decision making may also affect individuals who act in their institutional capacities, such as judges or regulators.

Individual behaviors affect climate change through legal and political processes, as by bringing (or failing to bring) political pressure on elected officials, and/or participating in political and legal processes for addressing climate-related grievances. The psychology of mitigation, adaptation, and climate engineering—each addressed further below—can thus all affect the likelihood of political and legal action through typical political and legal tools. The likelihood and extent of such action is affected, however, by several distinctive cognitive phenomena.

First, consider that there is a line of research on the psychology of political engagement (Boeckmann & Tyler, 2006). Among other things, it finds that people are more likely to engage when they feel like respected members of their communities (Boeckmann & Tyler, 2006). Whether or not people choose to engage politically on climate change—through voting, commenting on proposed regulations, direct contact with legislators, or other forms of political and community action—is thus likely to be mediated by their feelings of trust toward their community and toward the political process, and by whether they feel like they play a part in the political procedures in which climate change decisions are made.

Second, there is also a body of literature on the psychology of individuals engaging in legal action (Dunbar & Sabry, 2007; Macfarlane, 2000; Merry, 1990; Relis, 2006). For instance, one important recent movement in climate change law and policy is the bringing of private lawsuits to address climate change, as in the case of *Juliana v. United States* described above. Such suits offer substantial potential for shaping the future of climate change law and policy. But these suits can only happen if individuals overcome the individual psychological challenges to taking action that climate change creates.

The normative desirability of legal action may be contingent, for some, upon the ability of individuals to effectively manage climate change as a problem. We began this chapter by noting a set of psychological challenges that individuals as well as policy makers are likely to face in perceiving, understanding, and responding to climate change risks. While that research suggests that there are serious reasons to be concerned that climate change injury is peculiarly susceptible to denial and neglect, the lack of research on the institutional psychology of climate change makes it difficult to tell whether that denial and neglect at the institutional level is likely to be greater, lesser, or equal to what it is at the individual level. As a result, it may be helpful to consider what options exist for individuals to engage in climate-relevant behaviors—behaviors that might either substitute for, or be encouraged by, legal policy.

Consider how individual behaviors affect mitigation. Individuals have a direct effect on how many greenhouse gases are emitted. Stopping breathing is off the table, but in the developed world, energy use, transportation, and food choices are responsible for most individual emissions. These individual emissions are affected both by daily choices, such as whether or how to use an automobile or appliance, or whether to eat meat or reduce food waste at a particular meal, as well as more periodic choices, such as whether to purchase a more fuel- or energy-efficient car or appliance, or whether to give up flying altogether, or whether to become a vegan. And these choices are affected by psychological processes and phenomena (Clayton et al., 2015).

Scholars have increasingly called for policies to address individual mitigation behaviors, and advocates are increasingly focused on finding policies that will change people's individual emission behaviors (Vandenbergh et al., 2008; Clayton et al., 2015; Williamson et al., 2018). Models suggest that reducing food waste, adopting a plant-rich diet, and switching out a gasoline car for an electric one represent three of the most cost-efficient and effective individual behaviors for reducing climate emissions (Williamson et al., 2018). Food production alone is responsible for as much as 30% of greenhouse gas emissions (Willett et al., 2019), and food waste generates about 8% of the world's carbon emissions (Hawken, 2017). Indeed, many experts believe that central climate policy goals, such as the Paris Agreement's goal of limiting global warming to well below 2° C, can only be achieved if institutional policies, such as decarbonizing the global energy system, are combined with substantial changes to individual behaviors (Willett et al., 2019).

Thus far, the most expansive attempt at developing individual-based behavioral interventions to reduce emissions is a report by the Center for Behavior & the Environment (2018), which built on strategies identified in *Drawdown: The Most Comprehensive Plan Ever Proposed to Reverse Global Warming*. The report identified 30 behavioral strategies for individuals that, if they were universally adopted, it estimates would mitigate 19.9% to 36.8% of global emissions from 2020–2050 (Williamson et al., 2018). The strategies are categorized into four sectors: food, agricultural and land management, transportation, and energy and materials.

Some of the strategies are well known to those even casually concerned about CO2 emissions, like the value of solar roof panels and electric cars, but some may be more surprising, like the significant effects of planting trees on farmland and pasture, and the impact of plant-based diets. The report estimates that the top six recommendations—reducing food waste, switching to plant-rich diets, adding trees to pastures, driving electric vehicles, adding tree crops, and installing rooftop solar—could each reduce greenhouse gas emissions by the equivalent of as much as 40 gigatons of carbon dioxide between 2020 and 2050. Many of these behavioral strategies are implementable by individuals—and could, of course, also be encouraged through legal policy.

Each of these individual behavioral changes presents an opportunity for psychological and behavioral study, and for crafting policies that effectively shape the targeted behaviors in light of their psychology. Food choices, for example, present distinctive questions regarding people's personal tastes, identities, and time-health-cost trade-offs. As with decisions to consume animal products, food choices can also implicate ethical questions about the appropriate relationship between human and nonhuman animals (Rosenfeld, 2018), and even issues of identity. These issues are already personally, morally, economically, and thus psychologically complex (Shepherd & Raats, 2006) even without introducing their substantial impact on climate emissions. The psychology of tourism, though relatively less studied, is also rich, implicating questions of personal identity and life satisfaction, while triggering questions of adaptive hedonic forecasting, positive psychology, memory, and emotion (Skavronskaya et al., 2017). All of these considerations add to the already complicated question of how the effect of these activities on the climate might motivate changes in people's behavior.

Individuals can also have a direct effect on how much harm climate change causes by choosing (or failing) to engage in adaptive behaviors, which can increase or decrease the harm caused by a changing climate, independent of emissions they generate. As with behaviors affecting mitigation, adaptation-related behaviors can be either habitual—such as adopting good home ventilation habits—or more episodic, as by planting rain gardens to reduce climate-induced flooding risk, or developing emergency plans, or buying insurance to manage higher-likelihood natural disasters. As we have noted, individuals' approach toward adaptive behaviors can vary significantly (van Valkengoed & Steg, 2019). Generally, people seem to exhibit greater motivation to adapt when they perceive their personal risk from climate change to be higher (Osberghaus, Finkel & Pohl, 2010), and less motivation to adapt when they perceive the impacts of climate change to be largely distant (Singh et al., 2017). That said, while adaptation is a recognized strategy for reducing the harm caused by climate change, and is an increasing focus of scientific and scholarly attention (Field et al., 2014), thus far, there has been relatively limited treatment of the psychology of individual climate adaptation behaviors, at least in comparison to individual climate mitigation behaviors. The International Panel on Climate Change's 2014 report on Impacts, Adaptation, and Vulnerability, for instance, devotes only a page to the psychology of decision making about adaptation (Field et al., 2014).

Individuals also have the opportunity to limit the harm from climate change via climate engineering, including through carbon sequestration. Decisions about climate engineering may have a direct effect, as where individuals invent or deploy methods of climate engineering (like planting trees), or indirect, as where individuals affect market demand for climate-engineering products or processes, or where individual appetite (or disgust) for climate engineering informs political and legal pressures.

Common activities such as planting a tree do have carbon sequestration impacts. But some individuals may also have direct opportunities to affect larger projects, including by adopting so-called "regenerative agriculture" practices, such as no-till and low-till methods for crop cultivation (Williamson et al., 2018). Individuals also choose whether, when, and how to invest in climate-engineering technologies. The psychology of investment thus may also matter to the continued development of climate-engineering solutions. Research suggests, among other things, that the psychology of sustainable investment may vary between individual and institutional investors (Jansson & Biel, 2011). As the invention and availability of climate-engineering methods and technologies increases, individual decisions about when to engage in them will become increasingly important.

More frequently, individuals can exercise *indirect* power by making political or market-based decisions about climate-engineering projects. Many individuals already participate in climate engineering through the purchase of carbon credits, which operate as offsets to carbon emissions.

The psychology of these offers a series of difficult psychological questions, such as whether the availability of offsets might actually increase people's emissions elsewhere. "Rebound effects" of this type have been found in other contexts, as where individuals given an opportunity to demonstrate their egalitarianism are more likely to subsequently discriminate against a minority (Monin & Miller, 2001), or where charging parents a small fee when they were late picking up their children led to more late pick-ups than when there was no charge at all (Gneezy & Rustichini, 2000). Of course, such decisions may be highly context dependent, and thus far, there is limited research on the psychology of offsets—despite their potential importance for reaching climate goals (Kotchen, 2009). As a result, this remains an important area for further study.

Finally, the way that individuals perceive climate engineering may have critical implications for the development, investment, and implementation of climate-engineering policies. Here, the psychology of risk perception, which we have already discussed, is likely to play a particularly important role. Perceptions of technology risk may be important; on that front, recall that people's views about the promise of geoengineering tend to align with pre-existing normative beliefs about technology (Wibeck et al., 2017), as well as with their cultural and political priors (Kahan et al., 2009).

ADDRESSING INDIVIDUAL BEHAVIORS

Any policy interventions targeted at individual behaviors—whether addressing mitigation, adaptation, legal and political involvement, or climate engineering—should address common challenges to behavioral change. This might include developing psychologically distinctive strategies for promoting changes in habits and incorporating the social and identity-based effects of individual climate choices, specifically addressing how choices are framed. Recent research in science communication also provides concrete strategies for how best to communicate with individuals about climate-relevant behaviors that policy makers wish to change.

Habitual Versus Episodic Behaviors

Habitual and episodic behaviors operate through different cognitive pathways. Generally speaking, episodic behaviors operate through deliberative processes—through System II reflection. As a result, rational arguments can sometimes work to get people to take single, deliberate actions. But rational arguments are more likely to fail where people's behaviors are driven primarily by routinized, instinctive System I processes. It is the latter that typically inform climate-relevant habits (Kurz et al., 2014).

Habits are formed through repetition (Neal et al., 2006), and they are notoriously resistant to change, even when people have the intent to alter their behavior (Webb & Sheeran, 2006). Changing habits may even require some kind of exogenous shock to disrupt the environmental cues that trigger them (Verplanken & Wood, 2006). For climate behaviors that are habitual—such as many food choices, driving habits, and in-home ventilation habits—interventions that introduce or leverage exogenous shocks may be most effective (Verplanken & Wood, 2006). This might involve what are sometimes called "downstream" interventions, timed at points when contextual cues are already vulnerable (as when changing jobs or moving from one community to another), and/ or "upstream" interventions, timed to occur before habits are formed (as by introducing plant-based dietary choices in primary school) (Verplanken & Wood, 2006).

Social Pressures, Meaning, and Identity
While the behaviors described in this section are individual actions, they do not occur in a vacuum. People decide whether or not to engage in any behavior at least partly as a function of social pressures. It is hard to be the only vegetarian in town, and not just because of the unavailability of veggie burgers in the frozen section of the local grocery store. Social pressures matter too, and people are simply more likely to engage in behaviors they see neighbors and peers performing (Cialdini, 2001; Cialdini et al., 2006).

As a result, it is important that policy makers take care in how they encourage and communicate to citizens that they should engage in pro-environmental behaviors, whether they be mitigation, adaptation, or engineering. Public information campaigns, for instance, that try to highlight a problematic behavior by emphasizing how common it is can backfire. Policy makers should also be careful about triggering concerns about scarcity, which might inspire an antisocial desire to run down the resource. For instance, research shows that calls for lower energy usage in the face of a brown out actually trigger *higher* energy usage (Holladay et al., 2015). Another interesting study showed that in the face of a water crisis where citizens were asked not to take showers, the difference in who still bathed did not depend on general concern for the community or caring about the water crisis, but simply on whether they thought other people were bathing (Monin & Norton, 2003).

Another potentially important factor in understanding individual behavior is the social *meaning* of that behavior. In many cases, people's interest in engaging in mitigation, adaptation, or political action on climate change is affected by their perception of how their behavior will be perceived by those around them. Such perceptions can be complex and extremely context specific. Existing psychological research on food choices, for example, suggests that meat eaters have varying views of vegetarians depending upon the reasons vegetarians give for their choice. Vegetarians who explain their choice on the basis of health are viewed more positively than environmentally driven vegetarians, and both are viewed more positively than those who are vegan or vegetarian on ethical grounds (Rosenfeld, 2018). The landmark report by the EAT-Lancet Commission set out a "planetary health diet" that makes food recommendations based on both individual health and sustainability for the planet, a goal defined in large part by reference to the diet's impact on climate emissions (Willett et al., 2019). The report calls, among other things, for a significant reduction of meat consumption in Western countries, citing the impact of meat production on climate emissions (Willett et al., 2019). Yet the report is careful to also present health-based justifications for moving away from meat. The EAT-Lancet Report's care in framing its dietary recommendations as "healthy"—in addition to justifiable on environmental and climate-change grounds— may thus make a transition to plant-based eating more socially acceptable, and thus more likely to happen.

Communicating with Individuals about Climate Change
A rapidly growing literature on communication and framing of information about climate change suggests that communication strategies can play an important role in changing individual behaviors (Clayton et al., 2015; Bolsen & Shapiro, 2017; Corner et al., 2018). Because of the

psychological challenges created by processing and responding to climate change impacts, adopting psychologically informed best practices in communicating about climate change can lead to more effective policy interventions (Field et al., 2014; Morgan et al., 2009; Pidgeon & Fischhoff, 2011).

In 2018, the IPCC commissioned a handbook to summarize key social science research about climate change communication (Corner et al., 2018). Although the handbook was geared toward scientists writing for the IPCC, it provides a quick, accessible resource for identifying strategies for effectively communicating about climate injury and risk. Strategies the handbook recommends include the following:

- "Talk about the real world, not abstract ideas." To address psychological distancing, and avoid overwhelming people with the magnitude of the problem, the handbook recommends relating climate change to people's day-to-day experiences and backing away from the "big numbers" of climate change. For example, it recommends emphasizing the health benefits of pro-climate behaviors, such as cycling or walking rather than driving. Such benefits appeal to a broad cross section of the public, and create hopeful rather than fearful emotions about climate change (Meyers et al., 2012). This strategy may also avoid the specter of unappealing "moralizing."
- "Connect with what matters to your audience." To address motivated cognition and unavailability, the handbook recommends emphasizing the relationship between people's values and the information being presented. It also suggests connecting information with widely shared public values, or with points of known interest.
- "Tell a human story." Another strategy for addressing apathy, distancing, and numbing is to present information through a narrative structure, rather than relying on numerical information. It suggests that narratives are most effective when they describe a problem, lay out the consequences, and then talk about solutions. The handbook emphasizes the importance of identifying solutions to address the emotionally overwhelming aspects of climate change (Campbell & Kay, 2014).
- "Lead with what you know." To address the complexity and uncertainty of climate impacts, the handbook recommends focusing on "knowns" before "unknowns," and emphasizing areas of strong scientific agreement around a topic, such as on the broad consensus that humans are respon-

sible for climate change. The handbook acknowledges that advocates may struggle to overcome deep-rooted divides that stem from differences in values and political beliefs.

Other strategies may also be helpful (Clayton et al., 2015), such as using sources to communicate about climate change that are trusted by various social and political subgroups (Kahan et al., 2011; Lupia, 2013; Druckman, 2015).

Because of the psychological challenges created by processing and responding to climate change, adopting psychologically informed best practices in communicating about it may help lead to more effective policy interventions, when those interventions depend on changing individual behavior (Field et al., 2014; Morgan et al., 2009; Pidgeon & Fischhoff, 2011). These strategies also provide guidance for lawyers and advocates seeking to communicate effectively with legal decision makers such as judges and regulators.

Conclusion

In this chapter, we have argued that a psychological approach to climate law and policy can help illuminate where, when, and how law and legal institutions can more effectively regulate behaviors, by focusing on people's perceptions, motivations, and cognition regarding climate change. In many cases, common psychological phenomena are likely to create barriers to recognizing, caring about, and acting in response to the risk and harms of climate change. By understanding these psychological barriers, policy makers may eventually be able to find ways to navigate around them.

Key Psychological Challenges Presented by Climate Change
Climate-Specific Challenges
Climate-specific challenges make climate impacts difficult to process and thus tempting to deny.

- Extraordinary magnitude. The extremely large magnitude of potential impacts exacts a high cognitive and emotional load, and may trigger psychic numbing and denial.

- Unprecedented nature. The novelty of climate change undermines many common tools for debiasing, and may make them seem less credible, in a "tragedy of the uncommons."
- Moral impacts. The disturbing moral quagmire presented by climate change may generate motivated cognition and cognitive distortions, and emotional responses may trigger denial.

Environmental Nature of Climate Harms

The environmental nature of climate harms makes them easy to neglect.

- Diffusion. The temporally and spatially diffuse consequences of climate change trigger a number of phenomena that tend to make climate change be perceived as less serious and less salient. These phenomena include nonidentifiability of victims, the "unavailability heuristic," outgroup bias, and present bias.
- Complexity. The extraordinary complexity of climate change generates a high cognitive and emotional load, creating an incentive to rely on simplifying heuristics and triggering motivated cognition.
- Nonhuman character. The nonhuman impacts of climate change create barriers to empathy. Furthermore, even where empathy is overcome, emotional responses to the overwhelming scope of impacts may trigger denial.

Climate law and policy can use psychology to more effectively shape climate behaviors.

- Choosing climate strategies. Mitigation, adaptation, climate engineering, and climate inaction each trigger specific as well as general psychological concerns. More research is needed about the psychology of how these strategies interact with one another.
- Institutional psychology. Climate law may be importantly affected by the psychology of whichever institutions are making and implementing it. In much of the world, the psychology of international law is highly relevant; in the United States, the individual psychology of the President of the United States plays an outsize role.

- <u>Addressing individual behaviors.</u> Policy interventions targeting individual behaviors should address common challenges to behavioral change. In addition, climate interventions can be informed by the psychology of habitual versus episodic behaviors; the psychology of social pressure, social meaning and identity; and by specialized research on the psychology of climate change communication.

Conclusion

Future Directions in the Psychology of Environmental Law

Throughout this book, we have sought to identify the basic building blocks for environmental law and psychology, and for applying a psychological analysis to specific environmental laws. To that end, we have identified key ways that psychological research can help in understanding and predicting why, when, and how people think about and respond to environmental harm. We have also argued that a psychological approach to environmental law and policy, which takes account of this research, can help the law more effectively shape human behavior to desired ends—whatever those ends might be.

In this chapter, we set out to flag a set of questions, projects, and data needs that could help policy makers and attorneys to even better understand and predict the impacts of environmental law, as well as develop more effective (and in some cases cheaper) environmental laws and regulations. There is no way to make such a chapter exhaustive, and we have not even tried. Instead, below, we simply highlight three fascinating, fundamental, and open questions that future research may help to inform, and that may be helpful for future researchers to ponder regardless of the area of environmental law and psychology they are addressing.

Finally, we conclude with a few thoughts on how the psychology of environmental law may interact with the COVID-19 pandemic. This book was written before the emergence of the pandemic, and will be published before the world has been aware of COVID-19 for even a year. Yet it is already clear that the pandemic will have extraordinary consequences for society and for law, including environmental law. As environmental law increasingly seeks to predict and shape people's behavior in light of ever-evolving circumstances, the focus of psychology on context-driven experimental research may prove to be more valuable than ever before.

Debiasing Through Law

How can law most effectively debias, or counteract, the cognitive qualities and distortions of environmental impacts?

One particularly pressing question is the effect of forced consideration of environmental impacts, such as are required by the National Environmental Policy Act (NEPA), and by hundreds of other laws around the world that were patterned on NEPA.

Of course such laws may offer benefits beyond debiasing, for example by increasing the transparency and thus democratic legitimacy of government actions. And the possibility that they might also offer a significant cognitive benefit is both valuable and tantalizing. This makes the relative paucity of directed psychological analysis of NEPA and similar laws frustrating. How effective is forced consideration at counteracting the relatively low salience of environmental impacts? What mechanisms of forced consideration are most effective? Do NEPA-like interventions do better at balancing out the neglect of some environmental impacts versus others? If so, are there effective ways to tailor interventions so that they increase salience (only) of those impacts that are most likely to otherwise run under the cognitive radar? Answering these questions could give practical guidance to regulatory bodies like the Council on Environmental Quality (CEQ). The CEQ is statutorily directed to, and routinely does, issue guidance to try to make NEPA more effective. Guidance on how to make an environmental analysis more effectively serve a debiasing function would fall well within its bailiwick.

Answering these questions may suggest additional and new methods for debiasing through law, including via decision structures targeting public or private decision makers. In the NEPA context, for instance, this might inform calls for extending forced consideration of environmental impacts to private actors such as developers. Such calls would be better supported if there were more research into how forced consideration would operate for such actors.

Alternatively, consider the role that the public plays in selecting species protected by the Endangered Species Act (ESA). We noted in our discussion of ecosystem management that species listed, and thus protected, under the Endangered Species Act are largely determined by private actors filing petitions, and we suggested that the actions of these actors are likely affected by psychological mechanisms including the availability heuristic, biophobia, and biophilia. As a result, mammals are more likely to be protected (regardless of ecosystem impact) than worms, spiders, and snakes, even where the latter groups perform critical ecosystem functions. There is no evidence that Congress intended such disparities, so what mechanisms of debiasing or choice architecture would be most effective at correcting this distortion? How well do mechanisms of biophobia and biophilia, for instance, respond to simple interventions such as informing people that they occur? As we have suggested, it might be possible for policy makers to perform relatively simple interventions—such as an explicit call from the Fish and Wildlife Service requesting petitions for tiny, ugly, or unlikeable species. On the other hand, if no reasonable and effective mechanisms for debiasing the petition process exist, then that, too, would be valuable to know. It suggests that any counterbalance to the neglect of such species would have to occur elsewhere, for instance, by the Fish and Wildlife Service increasing their own attention to species they know to be relatively underappreciated by public petitioners. Studies on the likely effect of either of these solutions are currently lacking.

Another area of potential study is the unintended consequences of attempts to debias through law. Consider again the forced consideration of environmental impacts as required under NEPA. Does forcing consideration ever backfire, for example, by causing frustration that leads policy makers to resist the exercise? Or, does forcing consideration ever lead to overcompensation—to a kind of environmental *over*salience, where decision makers consider (some or all) environmental impacts more frequently, and with greater weight, than lawmakers believe they should? Does it matter if decision makers are being influenced by multiple disclosure or behavioral regimes at once (Rowell, 2017)? These questions, too, should matter to policy makers, both at the stage of creating and of implementing these policies.

Finally, and more philosophically, how can individuals tell if decision makers are thinking "too little," "too much," or "just the right amount" about the environment? Answering Goldilocks questions of this sort is key to calibrating attempts to debias through law. But these are hard questions, and thus far we believe we lack robust and convincing answers to them.

Politics and the Psychology of Environmental Law

How might psychology affect the politics of environmental law? As we have discussed throughout this book, the environmental effects of people's actions are prone to a kind of cognitive disappearing act. What is the political consequence of this?

One possibility is that the low salience of most environmental impacts—a product of their dispersed, complex, and nonhuman nature—tends to push environmental issues lower on people's list of political priorities. Though this may seem like a simplistic observation, if true, it raises serious concerns. It suggests that people's political priorities about the environment may reflect tricks of cognition rather than their all-things-considered preferences. Furthermore, the impacts of those cognitive tricks are likely to be unidirectional, pushing political concern for the environment *down* across people and parties. We worry that exactly this may be happening, and we think that the political and democratic implications of such an effect create ample—even pressing—need for further study.

Another avenue for study would be to explore the reasons that people's perceptions of environmental risk seem so susceptible to motivated cognition (Kahan & Braman, 2006; Slovic, 2000), as well as still further research about *which* environmental risks are most vulnerable to the phenomenon. The relatively low salience of many environmental impacts, combined with the high cognitive load imposed by their consideration, might create the perfect combination of features to generate motivated cognition. If so, then environmental issues may be chronically susceptible to politicization, and further study of debiasing techniques carries particular urgency. It is also possible that people are making other associations—perhaps emotional, perhaps cognitive—between some environmental phenomena and particular political identities, associations that could be affected by norm entrepreneurs, the media, or public interest groups. Right now, we know what happens *when* particular environmental risks get politicized, but we are mostly in the dark about *why* they do. Here, too, further research is very much needed.

Updating Environmental Laws

Law and psychology is a relatively young field, and environmental law and psychology even more so—in fact, so far as we know, this book is the first to discuss "environmental law and psychology" *as* a field. Even environmental law itself is a relatively young area, with most of the major federal environmental statutes tracing to the "Environmental Decade" of the 1970s. As such, most federal environmental statutes predate not only treatments of environmental law and psychology, but also the general law and psychology and empirical legal studies movements. This means that existing environmental law and policy has been developed largely without informed consideration of the impact of psychology on environmental behaviors. Of course legislators, regulators, and activists have always had their own intuitive accounts (also known as "guesses") about how law is likely to affect behavior, but as work in law and behavior has shown, such intuitive accounts are sometimes wrong (Ulen, 2014). In other cases, policy makers may have guessed right about the direction of the impact of law, but have left some opportunities on the table. Even laws that control and predict behaviors reasonably well could often be still-more effective—or still-more efficient—at doing so.

There are a variety of potential psychologically informed approaches to legal updating that are available to multiple legal actors. Congress could pass psychologically informed amendments to existing environmental laws, for example to address diffuse pollution behaviors like nonpoint source water pollution, or to address indoor pollution as well as outdoor. Or they could pass new legislation entirely. For example, right now there is no major federal legislation that directly addresses climate change; Congress could (at least theoretically) fix that hole. Agencies also have significant options, including revisiting their own interpretations of the statutes they implement in light of psychological factors. The EPA, for instance, might reinterpret the Clean Air Act to focus on pollution that endangers people specifically because of cognitive challenges people face in recognizing and understanding it, such as indoor air pollution or pollution that harms because of its interactions with other pollutants in a manner lay people cannot readily perceive. Agencies could also reallocate their internal resources in light of expected cognitive impacts. For instance, the Fish and Wildlife Service could revisit which species it evaluates itself, rather than waiting for a petition under the Endangered Species Act. Or, agencies could rework guidance. The CEQ, for example, could develop guidelines to deal with the cognitive effects of NEPA. OMB and OIRA could update their guidance on valuation to encourage agencies to address the psychological challenges associated with monetizing diffuse, complex, and nonhuman environmental harms, or they could incorporate routine salience-increasing questions into their review of cost-benefit analyses that address environmental impacts. Any or all of these actions, however, would be better supported with additional descriptive and prescriptive work, done in light of expected psychological consequences.

Courts face special psychological challenges in addressing environmental law questions. One such area is in the law of standing, which acts as a gatekeeper for judicial review (Lazarus, 2000). Standing poses a "persistent problem," even a "paradox," in environmental law (Doremus, 2010b; Laitos, 2013). Psychology could further inform how standing in environmental law is evaluated, both by scholars and judges. On this front, consider the familiar formulation of the doctrine, which holds that standing requires that a person bringing suit must show that she or he has suffered (1) an injury in fact, (2) caused by (3) something that is redressable by the court (*Lujan v. Defenders of Wildlife*, 1992). How should such requirements be understood in light of research on diffuse, complex, and nonhuman environmental impacts? The injury-in-fact element, for instance, is commonly held to require that the injury be imminent and that it represent a particularized injury experienced more by the person bringing the suit than by the public at large. The rule requires, in other words, that the injury be *acute* rather than diffuse. It may be sensible for courts to treat diffuse and acute injuries differently, in light of psychological research that people tend to perceive those injuries differently. Yet psychological research on the differential perception of diffuse risks presumably applies to courts as well as to petitioners, and it may suggest—though this deserves further research—that courts' standing doctrine may itself be partially a product of judges' struggles to conceive of dispersed harm. Similar criticisms might be made of the causation requirement, which may be burdened by cognitive complexity, and the redressability requirement, which may face special challenges in circumstances where the affected stakeholders tend to be nonhuman and thus unable to bring suit.

Individuals, too, may have a role to play in a psychologically informed approach to environmental law—at least individuals who are involved in environmental activism. As we have seen, this may play itself out either in political action or through more direct mechanisms, such as commenting on agency actions, bringing petitions under the Endangered Species Act, or filing judicial suit. Just as policy makers should take care about how they regulate, lawyers and activists should take care about how they advocate.

COVID-19 and Environmental Law and Psychology

As we completed this book manuscript, the world was shaken by the emergence of the global COVID-19 pandemic. Although the future trajectory of the pandemic remains uncertain, it has already brought many changes to how people live and engage with their environments, and is likely to bring many more.

We believe the seismic social and behavioral shifts created by the pandemic will have fundamental effects on how environmental law operates in the years and decades to come. As one of us suggests elsewhere, there are at least four types of change that should be expected to be triggered by the pandemic: behavioral change, demographic change, changes in resources, and changes in values (Rowell, 2020c). As environmental law and policy makers develop strategies for managing the environment in light of the pandemic, they will need strategies for dealing with each of these types of change. In many cases, a psychological approach to environmental law and policy may be helpful in understanding, predicting, and shaping future environmental responses to these changes.

The role psychology may play in pandemic-era environmental law may be clearest when we consider pandemic-related behavioral changes, and how those behaviors affect the environment. For example, a mass global shift toward "staying home" led to extraordinary decreases in production and transportation—and thus to significant reductions in pollution associated with those behaviors. At the same time, public health-related shifts have led to increased production of medical waste and increased usage of disinfectants and the attendant emissions of cleaning byproducts. People are now exposed more than ever to their indoor home environments, even as workplace exposure has decreased.

How people see, understand, and respond to new and evolving environmental risks can, we suggest, be foundationally informed by the psychological research we have summarized and commented upon throughout this book. Furthermore, research on the psychology of environmental risk—and perhaps particularly on the psychology of pollution—may also prove to be helpful in analyzing behaviors regarding viral "pollution" and transmission. As with more traditional pollutants, "polluter psychology" may lead people to subconsciously minimize the risks and harms they generate by engaging in behaviors that may spread COVID, and source effects may simultaneously make them minimize risks from familiar sources, like their families and friends.

We have suggested throughout this book that even pre-pandemic, people's environmental behaviors were sometimes poorly predicted and understood, given psychological research on how people see, understand, and respond to environmental risks and harms. In the pandemic, however, an additional "expectation gap" has opened between the behaviors that environmental law and policy anticipates, and how people actually behave, because people's behaviors in so many realms have changed. Regulatory stringency on plastics and disinfectants, for example, was set pre-pandemic without reference to the benefits that disposables and disinfectants have in a global infectious outbreak, or to increased and decentralized use of those materials. International climate agreements like the Paris Agreement set their expectations on the basis of pre-pandemic climate behaviors; many of those behaviors, and the emissions they produce, have changed with widespread shifts in transportation and production. Similarly, State Implementation Plans designed to address the sources and amounts of air pollution under the Clean Air Act were all completed without reference to pandemic-led changes in behavior. For environmental law, much may turn upon whether the environmental impacts of these behavioral changes have created a "new normal," or perhaps instead are treated as a kind of extended exception to the pre-pandemic status quo (Rowell, 2020c).

Furthermore, because the risks and consequences of a global pandemic of this type remain unprecedented in modern memory, observational studies based on pre-pandemic behaviors face a systemic disability in trying to explain and predict pandemic-era behaviors. Experimental research has at least a marginal advantage in such labile and unexpected circumstances, precisely because it depends upon identifying context-specific features that may drive behavior. Psychological research on risk perception, emotion, and motivation may therefore help substantially in describing and predicting pandemic-era behaviors, and therefore in creating behaviorally informed environmental policies in the wake of it.

We also believe that psychological research may guide policy responses to other pandemic-era changes, including those related to shifts in demography and background risk. COVID, for example, may increase survivors' vulnerability to pollution in the future, even as it preys disproportionately on those whose health and resilience has been impacted by pollution in the past. How such shifts in risk levels and distribution are perceived may prove to be partially affected by a number of psychological factors, including in-group and out-group dynamics, status quo bias, and system justification.

Other—though still more speculative—changes may be triggered by COVID, including increasing scarcity in resources that can be allocated toward environmental goals as COVID affects global, national, and local economies; and emerging changes in people's social values that may affect their approach to the environment. The psychology of scarcity may inform both private and public responses to increased resource constraints. Psychological research on salience and prominence may suggest mechanisms through which hyperfocus on pandemic-related risk may crowd out concern for other risks. In some cases, such impacts may be significant enough to affect normative values: It may well prove, for instance, that attention and care spent addressing pandemic-related risks tend to crowd out concern for environmental risks, such as climate change.

Alternatively, it may be that pandemic-related changes will lead to increased appreciation of the psychological amenities provided by access to nature and green spaces; to increased fear and even revulsion from practices, such as those involved in wildlife markets, that involve human/nonhuman interactions that can lead to cross-species infection; and/or to make the mass behavioral changes that aggressive climate change policy might require seem more imaginable, and thus more likely to occur.

All of these possibilities are valuable grounds for future study. As this book has shown, psychology often matters to environmental law, and yet the psychology of environmental law remains understudied. This situation presents challenges and opportunities to policy makers and opportunities to students, scholars, and activists who would like to improve the effectiveness of environmental law and policy.

Because the psychology of environmental law is a neglected field, we have often felt in drafting this book that we are wandering through a ripening orchard, gesturing as quickly as we can at the low-hanging fruit that is ready to be plucked. We hope we have been successful in conveying some of these opportunities, as well as the rich harvest that we hope will increasingly be brought in by scholars, lawyers, and lawmakers working in both law and psychology and in environmental law. We are so excited to see how the field develops from here.

ACKNOWLEDGMENTS

First, we would like to thank Linda J. Demaine for her work organizing
the Psychology and the Law series and for proposing the idea of a book
on the psychology of environmental law to us in the first place. We are
also grateful for her valuable suggestions and support throughout the
process. Second, we would like to thank our ever-patient editor, Jennifer
Hammer, for bringing this book through to completion.

We (and the book!) also benefited from the generosity of many
colleagues and scholars who took time out of their busy schedule to
brainstorm, review, read, comment, criticize, and generally make this
manuscript better. In particular, we would like to thank Vanessa Casado
Pérez, Dan Cole, Heidi Doremus, Rob Glicksman, Paul Heald, Bruce
Huber, Shi-Ling Hsu, Felix Mormann, Jonathan Nash, Mark Nevitt, Jennifer Robbennolt, Josephine van Zeben, Gabriel Weil, and Lesley Wexler
for all their help. We were also greatly benefitted by presenting early
drafts of this work to audiences at the Notre Dame University School
of Law, the Texas A&M School of Law, the University of Luxembourg,
and the annual meeting of the Society for Environmental Law and
Economics.

Students and staff at the University of Illinois College of Law offered
research assistance and help with the manuscript. We particularly thank
Stephanie Davidson for her research and librarianship, Molly Lindsey
for her superb administrative support, Dylan Robinson for his skill as
a research assistant and editor, and Syed Umair for his thoughtful comments on our climate change chapter.

We also want to thank our mentors, friends, and scholars whose work
inspired our interest in law and psychology and in environmental law.
In particular, we thank Holly Doremus, Dan Farber, Dan Kahan, Richard Lazarus, Jeff Rachlinski, and Cass Sunstein for their inspiration. We
would also like to thank John Nagle, who passed away unexpectedly
during the course of writing this book. We were lucky enough to get his

characteristically generous and insightful feedback at the very earliest stages of this project. The field of environmental law greatly misses you, John, but we know your spirit lingers on in the wild interiors of the National Park System you loved so much.

Finally, we want to acknowledge the invaluable support of our families. A special thank you to Dan Bacon, Alec Rowell, Graham Rowell, Laurie Rowell, and Cecelia Wyatt; and to Rebecca Bilz and Dan Jabs.

NOTES

CHAPTER 2. DIFFUSION

1 To get the right answer, remember that the test is "only" 99% (.99) accurate. So 1% (.01) of the time the result is *actually* "common," the test will *claim* it is "rare." That means it will wrongly answer "rare" .01 × .05 (50,000 out of a million, or 5% of the time). True, 99% of the time that the result *is* actually "rare" the test will correctly declare it as "rare"—but given the infrequency of that chemical, this correct call will almost never happen. To be precise, it will happen .000099% of the times the test is run (.99 × 1 ppm, or .000001). So the test will *say* "rare" 5% + .0099% of the time (.050099), but it will only *be* "rare" .0099% of the time. And .0099%/5.0099% is .001976, or about 0.2% of the time.

CHAPTER 6. THE PSYCHOLOGY OF POLLUTION CONTROL

1 Although the EPA does not directly regulate indoor air pollution, it maintains a resource summarizing research on indoor air pollution on its website, and it issued reports to Congress on the dangers of indoor air pollution as early as the late 1980s (Environmental Protection Agency, 1989).

REFERENCES

Abelson, R. P. (1963). Computer simulation of hot cognition. In S. S. Tompkins & S. Messick (Eds.), *Computer Simulation of Personality* (pp. 227–298). Wiley.

Ackerman, B. A. & Stewart, R. B. (1985). Reforming environmental law. *Stanford Law Review, 37*(5), 1333–1365.

Ackerman, F. (2004). *Priceless: On knowing the price of everything and the value of nothing.* The New Press.

Ackerman, F. & Heinzerling, L. (2002). Pricing the priceless: Cost-benefit analysis of environmental protection. *University of Pennsylvania Law Review, 150,* 1553–1584.

Adler, M. D. & Posner, E. A. (1999). Rethinking cost-benefit analysis. *Yale Law Journal, 109,* 165–248.

Ainsworth, C. H., Paris, C. B., Perlin, N., Dornberger, L. N., Patterson, W. F., III, Chancellor, E., Murawski, S., Hollander, D., Daly, K., Romero, I. C., Coleman, F., & Perryman, H. (2018). Impacts of the Deepwater Horizon oil spill evaluated using an end-to-end ecosystem model. *PloS One, 13*(1), e0190840.

Akl, E. A., Oxman, A. D., Herrin, J., Vist, G. E., Terrenato, I., Sperati, F., Costiniuk, C., Blank, D., & Schunemann, H. (2011). Framing of health information messages. *Cochrane Database of Systematic Reviews, 12,* Cd006777.

Anderson, E. (1995). *Value in ethics and economics.* Harvard University Press.

Angeler, D. G., Fried-Petersen, H., Allen, C. R., Garmestani, A., Twidwell, D., Chuang, W-C., Donovan, V. M., Eason, T., Roberts, C. P., Sundstrom, S. M., &Wonkka, C. L. (2019). Adaptive capacity in ecosystems. *Advances in Ecological Research, 60,* 1–24.

Arbuckle, J. G., Jr., Prokopy, L. S., Haigh, T., Hobbs, J., Knoot, T., Knutson, C., Loy, A., Mase, A. S., McGuire, J., Morton, L. W., Tyndall, J., & Widhalm, M. (2013). Climate change beliefs, concerns, and attitudes toward adaptation and mitigation among farmers in the Midwestern United States. *Climatic Change, 117*(4), 943–950.

Arnett, J. J. (2008). The neglected 95%: Why American psychology needs to become less American. *American Psychologist, 63,* 602–614.

Aronson, E. (2011). *The Social Animal* (11th ed.). Worth Publishers.

Aronson, E., & Mills, J. (1959). The effect of severity of initiation on liking for a group. *Journal of Abnormal and Social Psychology, 59*(2), 177–181.

Arrow, K., Solow, R., Portney, P. R., Leamer, E. E., Radner, R., & Schuman, H. (1993). Report of the NOAA panel on contingent valuation. *Federal Register, 58*(10), 4601–4614.

Arthur, W. B. (1994). Inductive reasoning and bounded rationality. *American Economic Review, 84*(2), 406–411.

Asch, S. E. (1946). Forming impressions of personality. *Journal of Abnormal and Social Psychology, 41*(3), 258–290.

Asch, S. E., & Guetzkow, H. (1951). Effects of group pressure upon the modification and distortion of judgments. In H. S. Guetzkow, *Groups, Leadership, and Men* (pp. 222–236). Office of Naval Research.

Ashraf Vaghefi, S., Abbaspour, N., Kamali, B., & Abbaspour, K. C. (2017). A toolkit for climate change analysis and pattern recognition for extreme weather conditions— Case study: California-Baja California Peninsula. *Environmental Modelling & Software, 96*, 181–198.

Atir, S., Rosenzweig, E., & Dunning, D. (2015). When knowledge knows no bounds: Self-expertise predicts claims of impossible knowledge. *Psychological Science, 26*(8), 1295–1303.

Atreya, A., Ferreira, S., & Michel-Kerjan, E. (2015). What drives households to buy flood insurance? New evidence from Georgia. *Ecological Economics, 117*, 153–161.

Baars, B. J., & Gage, N. M. (2010). *Cognition, brain, and consciousness: Introduction to cognitive neuroscience.* Academic Press.

Bach, T. (2014). Protecting human health and stewarding the environment: An essay exploring values in U.S. environmental protection law. *Michigan Journal of Environmental and Administrative Law, 3*, 249–260.

Bahník, Š., Englich, B., & Strack, F. (2017). Anchoring effect. In R. F. Pohl (Ed.), *Cognitive illusions: Intriguing phenomena in thinking, judgment and memory* (p. 223–241). Routledge/Taylor & Francis Group.

Balliet, D., Wu, J., & De Dreu, C. K. (2014). Ingroup favoritism in cooperation: A meta-analysis. *Psychological Bulletin, 140*(6), 1556–1581.

Bandivadekar, A., Bodek, K., Cheah, L., Evans, C., Groode, T., Heywood, J., Kasseris, E., Kromer, M., & Weiss, M. (2008, July). *On the road in 2035: Reducing transportation's petroleum consumption and GHG emissions.* http://web.mit.edu

Bandura, A. (1991). Social cognitive theory of self-regulation. *Organizational Behavior and Human Decision Processes, 50*(2), 248–287.

Bandura, A. (2002). Selective moral disengagement in the exercise of moral agency. *Journal of Moral Education, 31*(2), 101–119.

Bandura A. (2015). *Moral disengagement: How people do harm and live with themselves.* Worth Publishers.

Barbier, E. B., Markandya, A., & Pearce, D. W. (1990). Environmental sustainability and cost-benefit analysis. *Environment and Planning A, 22*(9), 1259–1266.

Bargh, J. A., Gollwitzer, P. M., Lee-Chai, A., Barndollar, K., & Trötschel, R. (2001). The automated will: Nonconscious activation and pursuit of behavioral goals. *Journal of Personality and Social Psychology, 81*(6), 1014–1027.

Baron, J., & Ritov, I. (1994). Reference points and omission bias. *Organizational Behavior and Human Decision Processes, 59*(3), 475–498.

Baron, J., & Ritov, I. (2004). Omission bias, individual differences, and normality. *Organizational Behavior and Human Decision Processes, 94*(2), 74–85.

Bartels, D. M. (2006). Proportion dominance: The generality and variability of favoring relative savings over absolute savings. *Organizational Behavior and Human Decision Processes, 100*(1), 76–95.

Bartels, D. M., & Burnett, R. C. (2011). A group construal account of drop-in-the-bucket thinking in policy preference and moral judgment. *Journal of Experimental Social Psychology, 47*(1), 50–57.

Bartkowski, J. P., & Swearingen, W. S. (1997). God meets Gaia in Austin, Texas: A case study of environmentalism as implicit religion. *Review of Religious Research, 38*(4), 308–324.

Batchelor, M., & Brown, K. (1994). *Buddhism and ecology.* Motilal Banarsidass.

Batson, C. D. (2011). *Altruism in humans.* Oxford University Press.

Batson, C. D., Lishner, D. A., Cook, J., & Sawyer, S. (2005). Similarity and nurturance: Two possible sources of empathy for strangers. *Basic and Applied Social Psychology, 27*(1), 15–25.

Batson, C. D., Sager, K., Garst, E., Kang, M., Rubchinsky, K., & Dawson, K. (1997). Is empathy-induced helping due to self–other merging? *Journal of Personality and Social Psychology, 73*(3), 495–509.

Baum, S. D., & Tonn, B. E. (2015). Confronting future catastrophic threats to humanity. *Futures, 72*, 1–3.

Baumeister, R. F. (2012). Need-to-belong theory. *Handbook of Theories of Social Psychology, 2*, 121–140.

Baumeister, R. F., Brewer, L. E., Tice, D. M., & Twenge, J. M. (2007). Thwarting the need to belong: Understanding the interpersonal and inner effects of social exclusion. *Social and Personality Psychology Compass, 1*(1), 506–520.

Baumeister, R. F., & Leary, M. R. (1995). The need to belong: Desire for interpersonal attachments as a fundamental human motivation. *Psychological Bulletin, 117*(3), 497–529.

Baumol, W. J. (1952). *Welfare economics and the theory of the state.* Harvard University Press.

Baumol, W. J., & Oates, W. E. (1988). *The theory of environmental policy* (2nd ed.). Cambridge University Press.

Baxter, J. (2017). Energy justice: Participation promotes acceptance. *Nature Energy, 2*(17128), 1–2.

Beckman, L. & Uggla, F. (2016). An ombudsman for future generations. In I. Gonzalez-Ricoy & A. Gosseries (Eds.), *Institutions for future generations* (pp. 117–134). Oxford University Press.

Beekman, V. (2004). Sustainable development and future generations. *Journal of Agricultural and Environmental Ethics, 17*(1), 3–22.

Been, V. (1992). What's fairness got to do with it? Environmental justice and the siting of locally undesirable land uses. *Cornell Law Review, 78*, 1001–1085.

Been, V. (1994). Locally undesirable land uses in minority neighborhoods: Disproportionate siting or market dynamics? *Yale Law Journal, 103*, 1383–1422.

Belk, R. W. (1988). Possessions and the extended self. *Journal of Consumer Research, 15*(2), 139–168.

Belmi, P., Neale, M. A., Reiff, D., & Ulfe, R. (2019). The social advantage of miscalibrated individuals: The relationship between social class and overconfidence and its implications for class-based inequality. *Journal of Personality and Social Psychology, 118*(2), 406–406.

Berners-Lee, M. (2011). *How bad are bananas? The carbon footprint of everything.* Greystone Books.

Bernstein, M., & Crosby, F. (1980). An empirical examination of relative deprivation theory. *Journal of Experimental Social Psychology, 16*(5), 442–456.

Biggers, T., & Pryor, B. (1982). Attitude change: A function of emotion-eliciting qualities of environment. *Personality and Social Psychology Bulletin, 8*(1), 94–99.

Bilz, K., & Nadler, J. (2009). Law, psychology, and morality. In D. M. Bartels, C. W. Bauman, L. J. Skitka, & D. L. Medin (Eds.), *Psychology of learning and motivation, 50* (pp. 101–131). Elsevier.

Binger, B. R., Copple, R., & Hoffman, E. (1995). Contingent valuation methodology in the natural resource damage regulatory process: Choice theory and the embedding phenomenon. *Natural Resources Journal, 35*, 443–459.

Bless, H., & Schwarz, N. (2010). Mental construal and the emergence of assimilation and contrast effects: The inclusion/exclusion model. *Advances in Experimental Social Psychology, 42*, 319–373.

Bloom, P. (1996). Intention, history, and artifact concepts. *Cognition, 60*(1), 1–29.

Bloom, P. (2004). *Descartes' baby: How the science of child development explains what makes us human.* NY Basic Books.

Boeckmann, R. J., & Tyler, T. R. (2006). Trust, respect, and the psychology of political engagement. *Journal of Applied Social Psychology, 32*(10), 2067–2088.

Bolsen, T., & Shapiro, M. A. (2017). Strategic framing and persuasive messaging to influence climate change perceptions and decisions. In *Oxford Research Encyclopedia of Climate Science.* https://oxfordre.com/

Bourg, D., & Schlegel, J. (2001). *Parer aux risques de demain: Le principe de precaution.* Editions du Seuil.

Bradshaw, J. W., & Paul, E. S. (2010). Could empathy for animals have been an adaptation in the evolution of Homo sapiens? *Animal Welfare, 19*(1), 107–112.

Bradshaw, K. (2016). Settling for natural resource damages. *Harvard Environmental Law Review, 40*, 211–250.

Bratman, G. N., Hamilton, J. P., & Daily, G. C. (2012). The impacts of nature experience on human cognitive function and mental health. *Annals of the New York Academy of Sciences, 1249*(1), 118–136.

Brehm, J. W. (1956). Postdecision changes in the desirability of alternatives. *Journal of Abnormal and Social Psychology, 52*(3), 384–389.

Brehm, J. W. (1966). *A theory of psychological reactance.* Academic Press.

Brennan, A., & Lo, Y. (2016). Environmental ethics. In E. N. Zalta (Ed.), *The Stanford encyclopedia of philosophy*. Stanford University. https://plato.stanford.edu

Brewer, M. B. (1979). In-group bias in the minimal intergroup situation: A cognitive-motivational analysis. *Psychological Bulletin, 86*(2), 307–324.

Brickman, P., Coates, D., & Janoff-Bulman, R. (1978). Lottery winners and accident victims: Is happiness relative? *Journal of Personality and Social Psychology, 36*(8), 917–927.

Brion, D. J. (1987). An essay on LULU, NIMBY, and the problem of distributive justice. *Environmental Affairs, 15*, 437–503.

Brosnan, S. F., Jones, O. D., Lambeth, S. P., Mareno, M. C., Richardson, A. S., & Schapiro, S. J. (2007). Endowment effects in chimpanzees. *Current Biology, 17*(19), 1704–1707.

Brothers, L. (2002). The social brain: A project for integrating primate behavior and neurophysiology in a new domain. In J. Cacioppo, G. B. Berntson, R. Adophis, C. S. Carter, R. Davidson, M. McClintock, B. S. McEwen, M. Meaney, D. L. Schacter, E. Sternberg, S. Suomi, & S. E. Taylor (Eds.), *Foundations in Social Neuroscience, 367* (pp. 367–386). The MIT Press.

Broude, T. (2015). Behavioral international law. *University of Pennsylvania Law Review, 163*, 1099–1157.

Broughton, E. (2005). The Bhopal disaster and its aftermath: A review. *Environmental Health: A Global Access Science Source, 4*(1), 6. Retrieved February 21, 2020, from https://ehjournal.biomedcentral.com

Brown, J. H., Gupta, V. K., Li, B.-L., Milne, B. T., Restrepo, C., & West, G. B. (2002). The fractal nature of nature: power laws, ecological complexity and biodiversity. *Philosophical Transactions of the Royal Society of London. Series B: Biological Sciences, 357*(1421), 619–626.

Brown, T. C., & Gregory, R. (1999). Why the WTA-WTP disparity matters. *Ecological Economics, 28*(3), 323–335.

Bruner, J. (1990). *Acts of meaning.* Harvard University Press.

Bruner, J. S., & Goodman, C. C. (1947). Value and need as organizing factors in perception. *Journal of Abnormal Psychology, 42*(1), 33–44.

Bonaito, M., Breakwell, G. M., & Cano, I. (1996). Identity processes and environmental threat: The effects of nationalism and local identity upon perception of beach pollution. *Journal of Community & Applied Social Psychology, 6*(3), 157–175.

Bradshaw, K. & Lueck, K. (Eds.) (2012). *Wildfire: Law and Economics Policy Perspectives.* Resources for the Future.

Broome, J. (2012). *Climate matters: Ethics in a warming world.* W.W. Norton & Co.

Brown, J. (2006, February 14). *700 Club anchor touted global warming skeptics' petition reportedly signed by non-scientists, fictitious characters.* Media Matters for America. www.mediamatters.org

Brown, L. M., Bradley, M. M., & Lang, P. J. (2006). Affective reactions to pictures of ingroup and outgroup members. *Biological Psychology, 71*(3), 303–311.

Brown, S.-E. (2004). The human-animal bond and self psychology: Toward a new understanding. *Society & Animals, 12*(1), 67–86.

Brown, S.-E. (2007). Companion animals as selfobjects. *Anthrozoös, 20*(4), 329–343.

Buccafusco, C., & Sprigman, C. J. (2011). The creativity effect. *University of Chicago Law Review, 78*, 31–52.

Buckert, M., Schwieren, C., Kudielka, B. M., and Fiebach, C. J. (2014). Acute stress affects risk taking but not ambiguity aversion. *Frontiers in Neuroscience, 8*(82), 1–11.

Bullard, R. D. (1983). Solid waste sites and the black Houston community. *Sociological Inquiry, 53*(2–3), 273–288.

Bullard, R. D. (1993). Anatomy of environmental racism and the environmental justice movement. In R. D. Bullard (Ed.), *Confronting environmental racism: Voices from the grassroots* (pp. 15–40). South End Press.

Bullard, R. D. (2005). *The quest for environmental justice: Human rights and the politics of pollution.* Sierra Club Books.

Burns, D. (1989). *The feeling good handbook: Using the new mood therapy in everyday life.* Plume.

Butterworth, B. (1999). *The mathematical brain.* Macmillan.

Butts, M. M., Lunt, D. C., Freling, T. L., & Gabriel, A. S. (2019). Helping one or helping many? A theoretical integration and meta-analytic review of the compassion fade literature. *Organizational Behavior and Human Decision Processes, 151*, 16–33.

Butz, D. A. (2009). National symbols as agents of psychological and social change. *Political Psychology, 30*(5), 779–804.

Butz, D. A., Plant, E. A., & Doerr, C. E. (2007). Liberty and justice for all? Implications of exposure to the US flag for intergroup relations. *Personality and Social Psychology Bulletin, 33*(3), 396–408.

Bužeková, T., & Išová, M. (2010). Disgust and intimacy. *Human Affairs, 20*(3), 232–240.

Byerly, H., Balmford, A., Ferraro, P. J., Wagner, C. H., Palchak, E., Polasky, S., Ricketts, T. H., Schwartz, A. J., & Fisher, B. (2018). Nudging pro-environmental behavior: Evidence and opportunities. *Frontiers in Ecology and the Environment, 16*(3), 159–168.

Cadinu, M. and Reggiori, C. (2002). Discrimination of a low-status outgroup: The role of ingroup, threat. *European Journal of Social Psychology, 32*: 501–515.

Calazzo, F., Ashok, A., Waitz, I. A., Yim, S. H. L., & Barrett, S. R. H. (2013). Air pollution and early deaths in the United States. Part I: Quantifying the impact of major sectors in 2005. *Atmospheric Environment, 79*, 198–208.

Campbell, T. & Kay, A. (2014). Solution aversion: On the relation between ideology and motivated disbelief. *Journal of Personality and Social Psychology, 107*(5), 809–824.

Carson, R. T. (2011). *Contingent valuation: A comprehensive bibliography and history.* Edward Elgar Publishing.

Carson, R. T., Flores, N. E., & Meade, N. F. (2001). Contingent valuation: Controversies and evidence. *Environmental and Resource Economics, 19*(2), 173–210.

Carter, T. J., & Dunning, D. (2008). Faulty self-assessment: Why evaluating one's own competence is an intrinsically difficult task. *Social and Personality Psychology Compass, 2*(1), 346–360.

Caruso, E. M., Vohs, K. D., Baxter, B., & Waytz, A. (2013). Mere exposure to money increases endorsement of free-market systems and social inequality. *Journal of Experimental Psychology: General, 142*(2), 301–306.

Case, T. I., Repacholi, B. M., & Stevenson, R. J. (2006). My baby doesn't smell as bad as yours: The plasticity of disgust. *Evolution and Human Behavior, 27*(5), 357–365.

Ceballos, G., Ehrlich, P., & Dirzo, R. (2017). The real sixth mass extinction: Biological annihilation signaled by population losses and declines in vertebrates. *Proceedings of the National Academy of Sciences, 114*(30), E6089–E6096.

Center for Biological Diversity v. National Highway Traffic Safety Administration, 538 F.3d 1172 (9th Cir. 2008).

Chaiken, S. (1980). Heuristic versus systematic information processing and the use of source versus message cues in persuasion. *Journal of Personality and Social Psychology, 39*(5), 752–766.

Chaiken, S., Giner-Sorolla, R., & Chen, S. (1996). Beyond accuracy: Defense and impression motives in heuristic and systematic information processing. In P. M. Gollwitzer & J. A. Bargh (Eds.), *The psychology of action: Linking cognition and motivation to behavior* (pp. 553–578). Guilford Press.

Chapman, G. B., & Johnson, E. J. (1994). The limits of anchoring. *Journal of Behavioral Decision Making, 7*(4), 223–242.

Chelleri, L., Minucci, G., Ruiz, A., & Karmaoui, A. (2014). Responses to drought and desertification in the Moroccan Drâa Valley region: Resilience at the expense of sustainability? *International Journal of Climate Change: Impacts & Responses, 5*(2), 17–33.

Chen, S., Qin, P., Tan-Soo, J.-S., & Wei, C. (2019). Recency and projection biases in air quality valuation by Chinese residents. *Science of the Total Environment, 648*, 618–630.

Chesapeake Bay Foundation. (2014, October 6). *The economic benefits of cleaning up the Chesapeake: A valuation of the natural benefits gained by implementing the Chesapeake Clean Water Blueprint.* www.cbf.org

Chevron U.S.A., Inc. v. Natural Resources Defense Council, Inc., 467 U.S. 837 (1984).

Chilton, S. (2007). Contingent valuation and social choices concerning public goods: An overview of theory, methods, and issues. *Revue D'Economie Politique, 117*(5), 655–674.

Choi, I., Nisbett, R. E., & Norenzayan, A. (1999). Causal attribution across cultures: Variation and universality. *Psychological Bulletin, 125*(1), 47–63.

Christensen, N. (1996) The report of the Ecological Society of America Committee on the Scientific Basis for Ecosystem Management. *Ecological Applications, 6*(3), 665–691.

Cialdini, R. B. (1984). *Influence—How and why people agree to things.* Morrow.

Cialdini, R. B. (2001). *Influence: Science and practice* (4th ed.). Allyn and Bacon.

Cialdini, R. B. (2003). Crafting normative messages to protect the environment. *Current Directions in Psychological Science, 12*(4), 105–109.

Cialdini, R. B., Demaine, L. B., Sagarin, B. J., Barrett, D. W., Rhoads, K., & Winter, P. L. (2006). Managing social norms for persuasive impact. *Social Influence, 1*(1), 3–15.

Cialdini, R. B., Reno, R. R., & Kallgren, C. A. (1990). A focus theory of normative conduct: Recycling the concept of norms to reduce littering in public places. *Journal of Personality and Social Psychology, 58*(6), 1015–1026.

Cialdini, R. B., Trost, M., & Newsom, J. T. (1995). Preference for consistency: The development of a valid measure and the discovery of surprising behavioral implications. *Journal of Personality and Social Psychology, 69*(2), 318–328.

Cikara, M., Botvinick, M. M., & Fiske, S. T. (2011). Us versus them: Social identity shapes neural responses to intergroup competition and harm. *Psychological Science, 22*(3), 306–313.

Cikara, M., Bruneau, E. G., & Saxe, R. (2011). Us and them: Intergroup failures of empathy. *Current Directions in Psychological Science, 20*(3), 149–153.

Clayton, S., Devine-Wright, P., Stern, P., Whitmarsh, L., Carrico, A., Steg, L., Swim, J., & Bonnes, M. (2015). Psychological research and global climate change. *Nature Climate Change, 5*(7), 640–646.

Clean Air Act, 42 U.S.C. § 7602(g) et seq. (1970).

Clean Water Act, 33 U.S.C. § 1362(19) et seq. (1972).

Clements, F. F. (1936). Nature and structure of the climax. *Journal of Ecology, 24,* 252–284.

Coase, R. H. (1960). The problem of social cost. *Journal of Law and Economics, 3,* 1–44.

Cohen, J. R., Asarnow, R. F., Sabb, F. W., Bilder, R. M., Bookheimer, S. Y., Knowlton, B. J., & Poldrack, R. A. (2010). A unique adolescent response to reward prediction errors. *Nature Neuroscience, 13*(6), 669–671.

Cole, D. H., & Ostrom, E. (2012). The variety of property systems and rights in natural resources. In D. H. Cole & E. Ostrom (Eds.), *Property in land and other resources* (pp. 37–64). Lincoln Institute of Land Policy.

Collman, J. P. (2001). *Naturally dangerous: Surprising facts about food, health, and the environment.* University Science Books.

Consolidated Version of the Treaty on the Functioning of the European Union art. 11, 2016 O.J. C 202/53.

Cooper, J., Bennett, E. A., & Sukel, H. L. (1996). Complex scientific testimony: How do jurors make decisions? *Law & Human Behavior, 20*(4), 379–394.

Corner, A., Parkhill, K., Pidgeon, N. & Vaughan, N. E. (2013), Messing with nature? Exploring public perceptions of geoengineering in the UK. *Global Environmental Change, 23,* 938-947.

Corner, A., Shaw, C. & Clarke, J. (2018). *Principles for effective communication and public engagement on climate change: A handbook for IPCC authors.* Climate Outreach.

Corrosion Proof Fittings v. EPA, 947 F.2d 1201 (5th Cir. 1991).

Costanza, R., d'Arge, R., de Groot, R., Farber, S., Grasso, M., Hannon, B., Limburg, K., Naeem, S., O'Neill, R. V., Paruelo, J., Raskin, R. G., Sutton, P., & van den Belt, M. (1997). The value of the world's ecosystem services and natural capital. *Nature, 387*(6630), 253–260.

Costanza, R., de Groot, R., Sutton, P., van der Ploeg, S., Anderson, S. J., Kubiszewski, I., Farber, S., & Turner, R. K. (2014). Changes in the global value of ecosystem services. *Global Environmental Change, 26,* 152–158.

Cremer, D. D., & van Vugt, M. (1999). Social identification effects in social dilemmas: A transformation of motives. *European Journal of Social Psychology, 29,* 871–893.

Cropper, M., Hammitt, J. K., & Robinson, L. A. (2011). Valuing mortality risk reductions: Progress and challenges. *Annual Review of Resource Economics, 3*(1), 313–336.

Crosby, F. (1976). A model of egoistical relative deprivation. *Psychological Review, 83*(2), 85–113.

Croston, J., & Pedersen, A. (2013). 'Tell me what I want to hear': Motivated recall and attributions in media regarding asylum seekers. *Australian Journal of Psychology, 65*(2), 124–133.

Crutzen, P. J., & Stoermer, E. F. (2000). The "Anthropocene." *Global Change Newsletter, 41,* 17–18.

Csikszentmihalyi, M. (1993). Why we need things. In S. Lubar & W. D. Kingery (Eds.), *History from things: Essays on material culture* (pp. 20–29). Smithsonian Books.

Curtis, V., Aunger, R., & Rabie, T. (2004). Evidence that disgust evolved to protect from risk of disease. *Proceedings of the Royal Society of London. Series B: Biological Sciences, 271*(suppl 4), S131–S133.

Dakos, V., Mathews, B., Hendry, A., Levine, J., Loeuille, N., Norberg, J., Nosil, P., Scheffer, M., & de Meester, L. (2019). Ecosystem tipping points in an evolving world. *Nature, Ecology & Evolution. 3*(3), 355–362.

Damon, M., Cole, D. H., Ostrom, E., and Sterner, T. (2019). Grandfathering: Environmental uses and impacts. *Review of Environmental Economics and Policy, 13*(1), 23–42.

Dana, D. (2009). *Valuing foreign lives and civilizations in cost-benefit analysis: The case of the United States and climate change policy.* Northwestern Law & Economics Research Paper No. 09-47. https://scholarlycommons.law.northwestern.edu

D'Andrea, M. A., & Reddy, G. K. (2018). The development of long-term adverse health effects in oil spill cleanup workers of the Deepwater Horizon offshore drilling rig disaster. *Frontiers in Public Health, 6,* 117–117.

Damasio, A. R. (2006). *Descartes' error.* Random House.

Darwin, C. R. (1859). *On the origin of species by means of natural selection, or Preservation of favoured races in the struggle for life.* John Murray.

Davidson, J. R. T., Connor, K. M., & Swartz, M. (2006). Mental illness in U.S. presidents between 1776 and 1974: A review of biographical sources. *Journal of Nervous and Mental Disorders, 194*(1), 47–51.

Dawes, R. M. (1980). Social dilemmas. *Annual Review of Psychology, 31*(1), 169–193.

de Oliveira, S., & Nisbett, R. E. (2017). Culture changes how we think about thinking: From "human inference" to "geography of thought." *Perspectives on Psychological Science, 12,* 782–790.

de Sadeleer, N. (Ed.). (2007). *Implementing the precautionary principle: Approaches from the Nordic countries, EU and A.* Earthscan.

de Sadeleer, N. M. (2010). The precautionary principle in EU law. *Aansprakelijkheid Verzekering En Schade, 5,* 173–184.

Deal, P., & Magyar-Russell, G. (2018). Sanctification theory: Is nontheistic sanctification nontheistic enough? *Psychology of Religion and Spirituality, 10*(3), 244–253.

Decety, J., Yang, C., & Cheng, Y. (2010). Physicians down-regulate their pain empathy response: An event-related brain potential study. *NeuroImage, 50*(4), 1676–1682.

Deci, E. L., Koestner, R., & Ryan, R. M. (1999). A meta-analytic review of experiments examining the effects of extrinsic rewards on intrinsic motivation. *Psychological Bulletin, 125*(6), 627–668.

Deese, J., & Kaufman, R. A. (1957). Serial effects in recall of unorganized and sequentially organized verbal material. *Journal of Experimental Psychology, 54*(3), 180–187.

Dellinger, M. (2018). See you in court: Around the world in eight climate change lawsuits. *William and Mary Environmental Law and Policy Review, 42*, 525–551.

Deloria, P. J. (1998). *Playing Indian.* Yale University Press.

Desvousges, W. H., Johnson, F. R., Dunford, R. W., Boyle, K. J., Hudson, S. P., & Wilson, K. N. (1993). Measuring natural resource damages with contingent valuation: Test of reliability. In J. A. Hausman (Ed.), *Contingent valuation: A critical assessment* (pp. 91–164). Elsevier Science B.V.

Dickman, C. (2020, January 8). *More than one billion animals killed in Australian bushfires.* https://sydney.edu.au

Deutsch, M., & Gerard, H. B. (1955). A study of normative and informational social influences upon individual judgment. *Journal of Abnormal and Social Psychology, 51*(3), 629–636.

Devine-Wright, P., & Batel, S. (2017). My neighbourhood, my country or my planet? The influence of multiple place attachments and climate change concern on social acceptance of energy infrastructure. *Global Environmental Change, 47*, 110–120.

Devlin, A. S. (2018). *Environmental psychology and human well-being: Effects of built and natural settings.* Academic Press.

Diamond, P. A., & Hausman, J. A. (1994). Contingent valuation: Is some number better than no number? *Journal of Economic Perspectives, 8*(4), 45–64.

Dickerson, C. A., Thibodeau, R., Aronson, E., & Miller, D. (1992). Using cognitive dissonance to encourage water conservation. *Journal of Applied Social Psychology, 22*(11), 841–854.

Dieckmann, N. (2008). *Numeracy: A review of the literature.* Decision Research Report No. 8-A. https://scholarsbank.uoregon.edu

Dillahunt, T., Becker, G., Mankoff, J., & Kraut, R. (2008). *Motivating environmentally sustainable behavior changes with a virtual polar bear.* Paper presented at the Pervasive 2008 Workshop Proceedings. www.researchgate.net

Diver, S., Vaughan, M., Baker-Médard, M., & Lukacs, H. (2019). Recognizing "reciprocal relations" to restore community access to land and water. *International Journal of the Commons, 13*(1), 400–429.

Do, A. M., Rupert, A. V., & Wolford, G. (2008). Evaluations of pleasurable experiences: The peak-end rule. *Psychonomic Bulletin & Review, 15*(1), 96–98.

Doherty, T. J., & Clayton, S. (2011). The psychological impacts of global climate change. *American Psychologist, 66*(4), 265–276.

Doremus, H. (2000). The special importance of ordinary places. *Environs: Environmental Law and Policy Journal, 23*, 3–17.

Doremus, H. (2006). Using science in a political world: The importance of transparency in natural resource regulation. In W. Wagner & R. Steinzor (Eds.), *Rescuing science from politics: Regulation and the distortion of scientific research* (pp. 143–164). Cambridge University Press.

Doremus, H. (2010a). The Endangered Species Act: Static law meets dynamic world. *Washington University Journal of Law & Policy, 32*, 175–235.

Doremus, H. (2010b). The persistent problem of standing in environmental law. *Environmental Law Reporter, 40*, 10956–10957.

Doremus, H. & Tarlock, D. (2005). Science, judgement, and controversy in natural resource regulation. *Public Land & Resources Law Review, 26*(1), 1–39.

Douglas, K. M., Sutton, R. M., & Cichocka, A. (2017). The psychology of conspiracy theories. *Current Directions in Psychological Science, 26*(6), 538–542.

Douglas, M. (1966). *Purity and danger: An analysis of concepts of pollution and taboo.* Routledge & Kegan Paul Limited.

Douglas, M., & Wildavsky, A. (1982). *Risk and culture: An essay on the selection of technical and environmental dangers.* University of California Press.

Dovidio, J. F., Piliavin, J. A., Schroeder, D. A. & Penner, L. A. (2006). *The social psychology of prosocial behavior.* Psychology Press.

Driesen, D. (2003). *The economic dynamics of environmental law.* MIT Press.

Druckman, J. N. (2015). Communicating policy-relevant science. *PS: Perspectives on Politics, 48*, 58–69.

Dunbar, F. C., & Sabry, F. (2007). The propensity to sue: Why do people seek legal actions? *Business Economics, 42*(2), 31–42.

Dunbar, R. I. (2016). The social brain hypothesis and human evolution. In *Oxford research encyclopedia of psychology.* https://oxfordre.com

Dunlap, R. E. (2008). A widening gap: Republican and democratic views on climate change. *Environmental Science and Policy for Sustainable Development, 50*(5), 26–35.

Dunlap, R., McCright, A. & Yarosh, J. (2016). The political divide on climate change: Partisan polarization widens in the U.S. *Environment: Science and Policy for Sustainable Development, 58*(5), 4–23.

Dunning, D. (2011). The Dunning–Kruger effect: On being ignorant of one's own ignorance. In J. M. Olson & M. P. Zanna (Eds.), *Advances in experimental social psychology, 44* (pp. 247–296). Academic Press.

Earle, T. C., & Cvetkovich, G. (1995). *Social trust: Toward a cosmopolitan society.* Greenwood Publishing Group.

Eigenbrode, S. D., O'Rourke, M., Wulfhorst, J. D., Althoff, D. M., Goldberg, C. S., Merrill, K., Morse, W., Nielsen-Pincus, M., Stephens, J., Winowiecki, L., & Bosque-Pérez, N. A. (2007). Employing philosophical dialogue in collaborative science. *BioScience, 57*(1), 55–64.

Egan, L. C., Bloom, P., & Santos, L. R. (2010). Choice-induced preferences in the absence of choice: Evidence from a blind two choice paradigm with young children and capuchin monkeys. *Journal of Experimental Social Psychology, 46*(1), 204–207.

Egan, L. C., Santos, L. R., & Bloom, P. (2007). The origins of cognitive dissonance: Evidence from children and monkeys. *Psychological Science, 18*(11), 978–983.

Eitam, B., Miele, D. B., & Higgins, E. T. (2013). Motivated remembering: Remembering as accessibility and accessibility as motivational relevance. In D. Carlston (Ed.), *The Oxford handbook of social cognition* (pp. 463–475). Oxford University Press.

Elliott, R. (1982). Faking nature. *Inquiry: An Interdisciplinary Journal of Philosophy, 25*(1), 81–93.

Elster, J. (1998). *Alchemies of the mind: Rationality and the emotions.* Cambridge University Press.

Emanuel, A. S., Updegraff, J. A., Kalmbach, D. A., & Ciesla, J. A. (2010). The role of mindfulness facets in affective forecasting. *Personality and Individual Differences, 49*(7), 815–818.

Emergency Planning and Community Right-to-Know Act, 42 U.S.C. § 11001 et seq.

Endangered Species Act of 1973, 16 U.S.C. § 1531(a)(2) et seq.

Entergy Corp. v. Riverkeeper, Inc., 556 U.S. 208 (2009).

Engel, K. (2013). Perverse incentives: The case of wildfire smoke regulation. *Ecology Law Quarterly, 40,* 623–672.

Engel, K., & Reeves, A. (2012). When "smoke isn't smoke": Missteps in air quality regulation of wildfire smoke. In K. M. Bradshaw & D. Lueck (Eds.), *Wildfire: Law and economics policy perspectives* (pp. 127–141). Resources for the Future.

Environmental Protection Agency. (n.d.). *Learn about lead.* www.epa.gov

Environmental Protection Agency. (n.d.). *Natural resource damages: A primer.* www.epa.gov

Environmental Protection Agency. (n.d.) *Pollution prevention law and policies.* www.epa.gov

Environmental Protection Agency. (1989). *Report to Congress on indoor air quality.* www.epa.gov

Environmental Protection Agency. (2000). *Giardia: Drinking water fact sheet.* www.epa.gov

Environmental Protection Agency. (2000). *Guidelines for preparing economic analysis.* www.epa.gov

Environmental Protection Agency. (2011). *Benefits and costs of the Clean Air Act 1990–2020, the second prospective study.* www.epa.gov

Environmental Protection Agency. (2015). *National Ecosystem Services Classification System (NESCS): Framework design and policy application* (EPA-800-R-15-002).

Epstein, L., Landes, W. M., & Posner, R. A. (2013). *The behavior of federal judges: A theoretical and empirical study of rational choice.* Harvard University Press.

Evans, G. W., Colome, S. D., & Shearer, D. F. (1988). Psychological reactions to air pollution. *Environmental Research, 45*(1), 1–15.

Evernden, N. (1992). *The social creation of nature.* Johns Hopkins University Press.

Executive Order 12,866 (September 30, 1993).

Farber, D. A. (2003–2004). Probabilities behaving badly: Complexity theory and environmental uncertainty. *U.C. Davis Law Review, 37*, 145–173.

Farber, D. (2010). Uncertainty. *Georgetown Law Journal, 99*, 901–959.

Farber, D., & Carlarne, C. (2017). *Climate change law: Concepts and insights*. Foundation Press.

Farber, D., & Hemmersbaugh, P. (1993). The shadow of the future: Discount rates, later generations, and the environment. *Vanderbilt Law Review, 46*, 267–304.

Farnsworth, E. G., Tidrick, T. H., Jordan, C. F., & Smathers, W. M. (1981). The value of natural ecosystems: an economic and ecological framework. *Environmental Conservation, 8*(4), 275–282.

Farnsworth, W. (1999). Do parties to nuisance cases bargain after judgment? A glimpse inside the cathedral. *University of Chicago Law Review, 68*(2), 373–436.

Fearnside, P. M. (2008). Deforestation in Brazilian Amazonia and global warming. *Annals of Arid Zone, 47*(3&4), 1–20.

Federal Insecticide, Fungicide, and Rodenticide Act (1972), 7 U.S.C. § 136 et seq.

Fernandez, J. R., & Kruglanski, A. W. (2019). The psychology of multiple goal pursuit: Choices, configurations, and commitments. *Journal of the Association for Consumer Research, 4*(1), 5–12.

Fernbach, P. M., Light, N., Scott, S. E., Inbar, Y., & Rozin, P. (2019). Extreme opponents of genetically modified foods know the least but think they know the most. *Nature Human Behaviour, 3*(3), 251–256.

Festinger, L., & Carlsmith, J. M. (1959). Cognitive consequences of forced compliance. *Journal of Abnormal and Social Psychology, 58*(2), 203–210.

Fetherstonhaugh, D., Slovic, P., Johnson, S., & Friedrich, J. (1997). Insensitivity to the value of human life: A study of psychophysical numbing. *Journal of Risk and Uncertainty, 14*(3), 283–300.

Fidler, F., & and Wilcox, J. (Winter 2018). Reproducibility of scientific results. In E. N. Zalta (Ed.), *The Stanford Encyclopedia of Philosophy*. https://plato.stanford.edu

Fiedler, K., & von Sydow, M. (2015). Heuristics and biases: Beyond Tversky and Kahneman's (1974) judgment under uncertainty. In M. W. Eysenck & D. Groome (Eds.), *Cognitive psychology: Revisiting the classic studies* (pp. 146–161). SAGE Publications.

Field, C. B., Barros, V. R., Dokken, D. J., Mach, K. J., Mastrandrea, M. D., Bilir, T. E., Chatterjee, M., Ebi, K. L., Estrada, Y. O., Genova, R. C., Girma, B., Kissel, E. S., Levy, A. N., MacCracken, S., Mastrandrea, P. R., & White, L. L. (Eds.) (2014). *Climate change 2014: Impacts, adaptation, and vulnerability. Part A: Global and sectoral aspects. Contribution of working group II to the fifth assessment report of the Intergovernmental Panel on Climate Change*. Cambridge University Press.

Fielding, K. S., & Hornsey, M. J. (2016). A social identity analysis of climate change and environmental attitudes and behaviors: Insights and opportunities. *Frontiers in Psychology, 7*. www.frontiersin.org

Fischhoff, B., & Beyth, R. (1975). 'I knew it would happen': Remembered probabilities of once-future things. *Organizational Behaviour and Human Performance, 13*, 1–16.

Fischman, R. W. (2007). What is natural resources law? *University of Colorado Law Review, 78,* 717–749.

Fiske, A. P., Kitayama, S., Markus, H. R., & Nisbett, R. E. (1998). The cultural matrix of social psychology. In S. T. Fiske, D. T. Gilbert, & G. Lindzey (Eds.), *The handbook of social psychology, Vols. 1–2, 4th ed.* (pp. 915–981). McGraw-Hill.

Fiske, A. P., & Tetlock, P. E. (1997). Taboo trade-offs: Reactions to transactions that transgress the spheres of justice. *Political Psychology, 18*(2), 255–297.

Fiske, S. T. (2000). Stereotyping, prejudice, and discrimination at the seam between the centuries: Evolution, culture, mind, and brain. *European Journal of Social Psychology, 30*(3), 299–322.

Fiske, S. T., & Dupree, C. (2014). Gaining trust as well as respect in communicating to motivated audiences about science topics. *Proceedings of the National Academy of Sciences, 111,* 13593–13597.

Fiske, S. T., & Taylor, S. E. (1984/1991). *Social cognition.* McGraw-Hill.

Flemming, T. M., Jones, O. D., Mayo, L., Stoinski, T., & Brosnan, S. F. (2012). The endowment effect in orangutans. *International Journal of Comparative Psychology, 25,* 285–298.

Folke, C., Carpenter, S., Elmqvist, T., Gunderson, L., Holling, C. S., & Walker, B. (2002). Resilience and sustainable development: Building adaptive capacity in a world of transformations. *AMBIO: A Journal of the Human Environment, 31*(5), 437–440.

Foot, P. (1967). The problem of abortion and the doctrine of double effect. *Oxford Review, 5,* 5–15.

Ford, B., Val Martin, M., Zelasky, S. E., Fischer, E. V., Anenberg, S. C., Heald, C. L., & Pierce, J. R. (2018). Future fire impacts on smoke concentrations, visibility, and health in the contiguous United States. *GeoHealth, 2,* 229–247.

Frederick, S. (2003). Measuring intergenerational time preference: Are future lives valued less? *Journal of Risk & Uncertainty, 26*(1), 39–53.

Frederick, S., O'Donoghue, T., & Loewenstein, G. (2002). Time discounting and time preference: A critical review. *Journal of Economic Literature, 40,* 351–401.

Frederick, S., Read, D., & LeBoeuf, R. (2008). When I'm 64: Temporal referencing and discount rates. In A. Y. Lee & D. Soman (Eds.), *Advances in consumer research, 35* (pp. 55–58). Association for Consumer Research.

Frederiks, E. R., Stenner, K., & Hobman, E. V. (2015). Household energy use: Applying behavioural economics to understand consumer decision-making and behaviour. *Renewable and Sustainable Energy Reviews, 41,* 1385–1394.

Freedman, B. (1989). *Environmental ecology: The impacts of pollution and other stresses on ecosystem structure and function.* Academic Press.

Frey, B. S., & Meier, S. (2004). Social comparisons and pro-social behavior: Testing "conditional cooperation" in a field experiment. *American Economic Review, 94*(5), 1717–1722.

Frey, B. S., & Oberholzer-Gee, F. (1997). The cost of price incentives: An empirical analysis of motivation crowding-out. *American Economic Review, 87*(4), 746–755.

Frey, B. S., & Stutzer, A. (2008). Environmental morale and motivation. In A. Lewis (Ed.), *The Cambridge handbook of psychology and economic behavior* (pp. 406–428). Cambridge University Press.

Gabaix, X., Gopikrishnan, P., Plerou, V., & Stanley, H. E. (2003). A theory of power-law distributions in financial market fluctuations. *Nature, 423*(6937), 267–270.

Gächter, S. (2006). *Conditional cooperation: Behavioral regularities from the lab and the field and their policy implications* (No. 2006-03). CeDEx Discussion Paper Series. https://ideas.repec.org

Gale, R. P., & Cordray, S. M. (1994). Making sense of sustainability: Nine answers to "What should be sustained?" *Rural Sociology, 59,* 311–332.

Galea, S., Nandi, A., & Vlahov, D. (2005). The epidemiology of post-traumatic stress disorder after disasters. *Epidemiologic Reviews, 27*(1), 78–91.

Ganguly, A., & Tasoff, J. (2017). Fantasy and dread: The demand for information and the consumption utility of the future. *Management Science, 63*(12), 4037–4060.

Garcia, E. (2014, March 21). Why are monk parakeets leaving Hyde Park? *WTTW News: Science and Nature.* https://news.wttw.com

Gardiner, S. M. (2011). *A perfect moral storm: The ethical tragedy of climate change.* Oxford University Press.

Geiger, N., & Swim, J. K. (2016). Climate of silence: Pluralistic ignorance as a barrier to climate change discussion. *Journal of Environmental Psychology, 47,* 79–90.

Gelman, S. A., & Davidson, N. S. (2016). Young children's preference for unique owned objects. *Cognition, 155,* 146–154.

Ghiassi-nejad, M., Mortazavi, S. M., Cameron, J. R., Niroomand-rad, A., & Karam, P. A. (2002). Very high background radiation areas of Ramsar, Iran: Preliminary biological studies. *Health Physics, 82*(1), 87–93.

Gifford, R. (2007). *Environmental psychology: Principles and practice.* Optimal Books.

Gifford, R. (2011). The dragons of inaction: Psychological barriers that limit climate change mitigation and adaptation. *American Psychologist,* 290–302.

Gilbert, D. T., Killingsworth, M. A., Eyre, R. N., & Wilson, T. D. (2009). The surprising power of neighborly advice. *Science, 323*(5921), 1617–1619.

Gilbert, D. T., King, G., Pettigrew, S., & Wilson, T. D. (2016). Comment on "Estimating the reproducibility of psychological science." *Science, 351*(6277), 1037–1037.

Gilbert, D. T., Pinel, E. C., Wilson, T. D., Blumberg, S. J., & Wheatley, T. P. (1998). Immune neglect: A source of durability bias in affective forecasting. *Journal of Personality and Social Psychology, 75*(3), 617–638.

Gini, G. (2006). Social cognition and moral cognition in bullying: What's wrong? *Aggressive Behavior: Official Journal of the International Society for Research on Aggression, 32*(6), 528–539.

Glicksman, R. (2012). The justifications for nondegradation programs in U.S. environmental law. In M. Prieur & G. Sozzo (Eds.), *Le Principe de Non-Regréssion en Droit de L'Environment* (pp. 471–500). Bruylant.

Global Warming Petition Project. (n.d.). www.petitionproject.org

Gneezy, U. & Rustichini, A. (2000). A fine is a price. *Journal of Legal Studies, 29*(1), 1–17.

Goebbert, K., Jenkins-Smith, H. C., Klockow, K., Nowlin, M. C., & Silva, C. L. (2012). Weather, climate, and worldviews: The sources and consequences of public perceptions of changes in local weather patterns. *Weather, Climate, and Society, 4*(2), 132–144.

Golman, R., Hagmann, D., & Loewenstein, G. (2017). Information avoidance. *Journal of Economic Literature, 55*(1), 96–135.

Golman, R., & Loewenstein, G. (2016). Information gaps: A theory of preferences regarding the presence and absence of information. *Decision 5*(3), 143–165.

Goudriaan, H., Wittebrood, K., & Nieuwbeerta, P. (2005). Neighbourhood characteristics and reporting crime: Effects of social cohesion, confidence in police effectiveness and socio-economic disadvantage. *British Journal of Criminology, 46*(4), 719–742.

Gould, R. K., & Kearns, L. (2018). Ecology and religious environmentalism in the United States. In *Oxford Research Encyclopedia of Religion*. https://oxfordre.com

Graham, J., & Wiener, J. (1997). *Risk vs. risk: Tradeoffs in protecting health and the environment.* Harvard University Press.

Gramling, C. (2020, January 9). Here's how climate change may make Australia's wildfires more common: Extreme wildfires down under are linked to a weather pattern that starts in the Indian Ocean. *Science News.* www.sciencenews.org

Gray, K. R., Tarasofsky, R., & Carlarne C. (2016). *The Oxford handbook of international climate change law.* Oxford University Press.

Greenwald, N, Suckling, K. F., Hartl, B., & Mehrhoff, L. A. (2019). Extinction and the U.S. Endangered Species Act. *PeerJ, 7,* e6803.

Greshko, M. (2016, July 25). New Zealand announces plan to wipe out invasive predators. *National Geographic.* www.nationalgeographic.com

Grill-Spector, K., Knouf, N., & Kanwisher, N. (2004). The fusiform face area subserves face perception, not generic within-category identification. *Nature Neuroscience, 7*(5), 555–562.

Gross, K., & D'Ambrosio, L. (2004). Framing emotional response. *Political Psychology, 25*(1), 1–29.

Grote, N. K., & Clark, M. S. (2001). Perceiving unfairness in the family: Cause or consequence of marital distress? *Journal of Personality and Social Psychology, 80*(2), 281–293. doi:10.1037/0022-3514.80.2.281.

Gurmankin, A. D., Baron, J., & Armstrong, K. (2004). The effect of numerical statements of risk on trust and comfort with hypothetical physician risk communication. *Medical Decision Making, 24*(3), 265–271.

Guthrie, C., Rachlinski, J. J., & Wistrich, A. J. (2000). Inside the judicial mind. *Cornell Law Review, 86,* 777–830.

Guthrie, C., Rachlinski, J. J., & Wistrich, A. J. (2007). Blinking on the bench: How judges decide cases. *Cornell Law Review, 93,* 1–44.

Hardin, G. (1968). The tragedy of the commons. *Science, 162,* 1243–1248.

Hardy, P. (2019, April 30). Sinking city: How Venice is managing Europe's worst tourism crisis. *Guardian.* www.theguardian.com

Harmon-Jones, E., & Mills, J. (1999). *Cognitive dissonance: Progress on a pivotal theory in social psychology* (1st ed.). American Psychological Association.

Harris, C., Schaeffer, S., Shenkman, E., & Warner, E. K. (2017). Environmental protection in Indian country: The fundamentals. *Environmental Law Reporter, 47,* 10905–10916.

Hart, P. S. (2011). One or many? The influence of episodic and thematic climate change frames on policy preferences and individual behavior change. *Science Communication, 33*(1), 28–51.

Hart, W., Albarracín, D., Eagly, A. H., Brechan, I., Lindberg, M. J., & Merrill, L. (2009). Feeling validated versus being correct: A meta-analysis of selective exposure to information. *Psychological Bulletin, 135*(4), 555–588.

Hastorf, A. H., & Cantril, H. (1954). They saw a game: A case study. *Journal of Abnormal and Social Psychology, 49*(1), 129–134.

Hawken, P. (Ed.). (2017). *Drawdown: The most comprehensive plan ever proposed to reverse global warming.* Penguin Books.

Harvey, C. (2018, January 30). Warming threatens reptiles more than birds and mammals. *Scientific American.* www.scientificamerican.com

Harvey, N. (1997). Confidence in judgment. *Trends in Cognitive Sciences, 1*(2), 78–82.

Hassin, R. R., Ferguson, M. J., Shidlovski, D., & Gross, T. (2007). Subliminal exposure to national flags affects political thought and behavior. *Proceedings of the National Academy of Sciences, 104*(50), 19757–19761.

Hausman, J. A. (Ed.). (1993). *Contingent valuation: A critical assessment.* Elsevier Science B.V.

Havlíček, F., & Morcinek, M. (2016). Waste and pollution in the ancient Roman empire. *Journal of Landscape Ecology, 9*(3), 33–49.

Heal, G. (1999). *Valuing the future: Economic theory and sustainability.* Columbia University Press.

Heath, C. (1996). Do people prefer to pass along good or bad news? Valence and relevance of news as predictors of transmission propensity. *Organizational Behavior and Human Decision Processes, 68*(2), 79–94.

Helmond, P., Overbeek, G., Brugman, D., & Gibbs, J. C. (2015). A meta-analysis on cognitive distortions and externalizing problem behavior. *Criminal Justice and Behavior, 42*(3), 245–262.

Hendrick, C., & Costantini, A. F. (1970). Number averaging behavior: A primacy effect. *Psychonomic Science, 19*(2), 121–122.

Hennes, E. P., Ruisch, B. C., Feygina, I., Monteiro, C. A., & Jost, J. T. (2016). Motivated recall in the service of the economic system: The case of anthropogenic climate change. *Journal of Experimental Psychology: General, 145*(6), 755–771.

Henrich, J., Heine, S. J., & Norenzayan, A. (2010). Most people are not WEIRD. *Nature, 466*(7302), 29–29.

Herr, P. M. (1986). Consequences of priming: Judgment and behavior. *Journal of Personality and Social Psychology, 51*(6), 1106–1115.

Herskovitz, J. (2014, January 11). Permit to hunt endangered rhino sells for $350,000 despite protests. *Scientific American.* www.scientificamerican.com

Hewstone, M., Rubin, M., & Willis, H. (2002). Intergroup bias. *Annual Review of Psychology, 53*(1), 575–604.

Higgins, E. T. (1996). Activation: Accessibility, and salience. In A. W. Kruglanski & E. T. Higgins (Eds.), *Social psychology: Handbook of basic principles* (pp. 133–168). Guilford Press.

Hobson, J. (2018). *Focusing on the bigger picture: An exploration of the relationship between photography and land conservation in New England.* Master's thesis, Harvard Extension School, https://harvardforest.fas.harvard.edu

Hoehl, S., Hellmer, K., Johansson, M., & Gredeback, G. (2017). Itsy bitsy spider . . . : Infants react with increased arousal to spiders and snakes. *Frontiers in Psychology, 8*(1710), 1–8.

Hogg, M. A. (2000). Subjective uncertainty reduction through self-categorization: A motivational theory of social identity processes. *European Review of Social Psychology, 11*(1), 223–255.

Holladay, J. S., Price, M. K., & Wanamaker, M. (2015). The perverse impact of calling for energy conservation. *Journal of Economic Behavior & Organization, 110*, 1–18.

Holyoak, K. J., & Simon, D. (1999). Bidirectional reasoning in decision making by constraint satisfaction. *Journal of Experimental Psychology: General, 128*(1), 3–31.

Hood, B. M., & Bloom, P. (2008). Children prefer certain individuals over perfect duplicates. *Cognition, 106*(1), 455–462.

Horai, J., Naccari, N., & Fatoullah, E. (1974). The effects of expertise and physical attractiveness upon opinion agreement and liking. *Sociometry, 37*(4), 601–606.

Hornsey, M. J., Harris, E. A., Bain, P. G., & Fielding, K. S. (2016). Meta-analyses of the determinants and outcomes of belief in climate change. *Nature Climate Change, 6*(6), 622–626.

Horowitz, J. K. & McConnell, K. E. (2000). A review of WTA/WTP studies. *Journal of Environmental Economics and Management, 44*, 426–447.

Hovland, C. I., Janis, I. L., & Kelley, H. H. (1953). *Communication and persuasion.* Yale University Press.

Howel, D., Moffatt, S., Bush, J., Dunn, C. E., & Prince, H. (2003). Public views on the links between air pollution and health in Northeast England. *Environmental Research, 91*(3), 163–171.

Hsieh, N. (2016). Incommensurable values. In E. N. Zalta (Ed.), *Stanford encyclopedia of philosophy.* Stanford University. https://stanford.library.sydney.edu

Hsu, S.-L. (2008). The identifiability bias in environmental law. *Florida State University Law Review, 35,* 433–467.

Huber, B. (2018). The US public lands as commons. In B. Hudson, J. Rosenbloom & D. Cole (Eds.), *Routledge Handbook of the Study of the Commons* (pp. 135–143). Routledge.

Hughes, T. P., Anderson, K. D., Connolly, S. R., Heron, S. F., Kerry, J. T., Lough, J. M., Baird, A. H., Baum, J. K., Berumen, M. L., Bridge, T. C., Claar, D. C., Eakin, C. M.,

Gilmour, J. P., Graham, N. A. J., Harrison, H., Hobbs, J.-P. A., Hoey, A. S., Hoogenboom, M., Lowe, R. J., McCulloch, M. T., Padolfi, J. M., Pratchett, M., Schoepf, V., Torda, G., & Wilson, S. K. (2018). Spatial and temporal patterns of mass bleaching of corals in the Anthropocene. *Science, 359*(6371), 80–83.

Inglis, I. R. (2000). Review: The central role of uncertainty reduction in determining behaviour. *Behaviour, 137*(12), 1567–1599.

Intergovernmental Panel on Climate Change (1992). *Climate change: The IPCC 1990 and 1992 assessments.* IPCC.

Jacques, P. J., & Knox, C. C. (2016). Hurricanes and hegemony: A qualitative analysis of micro-level climate change denial discourses. *Environmental Politics, 25*(5), 831–852.

Jain, K., Mukherjee, K., Bearden, J. N., & Gaba, A. (2013). Unpacking the future: A nudge toward wider subjective confidence intervals. *Management Science, 59*(9), 1970–1987.

James, W. (1890). *The principles of psychology.* Henry Holt & Co.

Jameson, A. R., & Kostinski, A. B. (2002). Spurious power-law relations among rainfall and radar parameters. *Quarterly Journal of the Royal Meteorological Society, 128*(584), 2045–2058.

Jansson, M. & Biel, A. (2011). Motives to engage in sustainable investment: A comparison between institutional and private investors. *Sustainable Development, 19,* 135–142.

Jiang, B., Li, D., Larsen, L., & Sullivan, W. C. (2016). A dose-response curve describing the relationship between urban tree cover density and self-reported stress recovery. *Environment and Behavior, 48*(4), 607–629.

Jiang, L.-Q., Carter, B. R., Feely, R. A., Lauvset, S. K., & Olsen, A. (2019). Surface ocean pH and buffer capacity: Past, present and future. *Scientific Reports 9* (18624).

Jolls, C., & Sunstein, C. R. (2006). Debiasing through law. *Journal of Legal Studies, 35*(1), 199–242.

Jolls, C., Thaler, R., & Sunstein, C. R. (1998). A behavioral approach to law and economics. *Stanford Law Review, 50*(5), 1471–1550.

Jones, E. E., & Goethals, G. R. (1987). Order effects in impression formation: Attribution context and the nature of the entity. In E. E. Jones, D. E. Kanouse, H. H. Kelley, R. E. Nisbett, S. Valins, & B. Weiner (Eds.), *Attribution: Perceiving the causes of behavior* (pp. 27–46). Lawrence Erlbaum Associates, Inc.

Jones, H. P., Jones, P. C., Barbier, E. B., Blackburn, R. C., Rey Benayas, J. M., Doll, K. D., McCrackin, M., Meli, P., Montoya, D., & Moreno Mateos, D. (2018). Restoration and repair of Earth's damaged ecosystems. *Proceedings of the Royal Society B: Biological Sciences, 285,* 1–8.

Jost, J. T., Banaji, M. R., & Nosek, B. A. (2004). A decade of system justification theory: Accumulated evidence of conscious and unconscious bolstering of the status quo. *Political Psychology, 25*(6), 881–919.

Juslin, P., Winman, A., & Hansson, P. (2007). The naive intuitive statistician: A naive sampling model of intuitive confidence intervals. *Psychological Review, 114*(3), 678–703.

Justus, J., Colyvan, M., Regan, H., & Maguire, L. (2009). Response to Sagoff. *Trends in Ecology & Evolution, 24*(12), 644.

Jylhä, K. M., Cantal, C., Akrami, N., Milfont, T. L. (2016). Denial of anthropogenic climate change: Social dominance orientation helps explain the conservative mail effect in Brazil and Sweden. *Personality and Individual Differences, 98,* 184–187.

Kahan, D. M. (1997). Social influence, social meaning, and deterrence. *Virginia Law Review,* 349–395.

Kahan, D. M. (2003). The logic of reciprocity: Trust, collective action, and law. *Michigan Law Review, 102,* 71–103.

Kahan, D. M. (2007). The cognitively illiberal state. *Stanford Law Review, 60,* 115–154.

Kahan, D. (2009). Nanotechnology and society: The evolution of risk perceptions. *Nature Nanotechnology, 4,* 705–06.

Kahan, D. M. (2010). Culture, cognition, and consent: Who perceives what, and why, in acquaintance-rape cases. *University of Pennsylvania Law Review 158,* 729–813.

Kahan, D. M. (2015). Climate-science communication and the measurement problem. *Advances in Political Psychology, 36*(S1), 1–43.

Kahan, D. M., & Braman, D. (2006). Cultural cognition and public policy. *Yale Law & Policy Review, 24,* 147–170.

Kahan, D. M., Braman, D., Cohen, G. L., Gastil, J., & Slovic, P. (2010). Who fears the HPV vaccine, who doesn't, and why? An experimental study of the mechanisms of cultural cognition. *Law and Human Behavior, 34*(6), 501–516.

Kahan, D. M., Braman, D., Gastil, J., Slovic, P., & Cohen, G. L. (2007a). The second national risk & culture study: Making sense of—and making progress in—the American culture war of fact. *GW law faculty publications and other works.* https://scholarship.law.gwu.edu

Kahan, D. M., Braman, D., Gastil, J., Slovic, P., & Mertz, C. K. (2007b). Culture and identity-protective cognition: Explaining the white-male effect in risk perception. *Journal of Empirical Legal Studies, 4*(3), 465–505.

Kahan, D. M., Hoffman, D. A., & Braman, D. (2009). Whose eyes are you going to believe? *Scott v. Harris* and the perils of cognitive illiberalism. *Harvard Law Review, 122,* 837–906.

Kahan, D. M., Hoffman, D. A., Braman, D., & Evans, D. (2012). They saw a protest: Cognitive illiberalism and the speech-conduct distinction. *Stanford Law Review, 64,* 851–906.

Kahan, D., Jenkins-Smith, H., & Braman, D. (2011). Cultural cognition of scientific consensus. *Journal of Risk Research, 14*(2), 147–174.

Kahan, D. M., Jenkins-Smith, H., Tarantola, T., Silva, C. L., & Braman, D. (2015). Geoengineering and climate change polarization: Testing a two-channel model of science communication. *ANNALS of the American Academy of Political and Social Science, 658*(1), 192–222.

Kahan, D. M., Peters, E., Dawson, E. C., & Slovic, P. (2017). Motivated numeracy and enlightened self-government. *Behavioural Public Policy, 1*(1), 54–86.

Kahan, D. M., Peters, E., Wittlin, M., Slovic, P., Ouellette, L. L., Braman, D., & Mandel, G. (2012). The polarizing impact of science literacy and numeracy on perceived climate change risks. *Nature Climate Change, 2*(10), 732–735.

Kahan, D. M., Slovic, P., Braman, D., & Gastil, J. (2006). Fear of democracy: A cultural critique of Sunstein on risk. *Harvard Law Review, 119*, 1071–1109.

Kahn, P. H., Jr. (2002). Children's affiliations with nature: Structure, development, and the problem of environmental generational amnesia. In P. H. Kahn, Jr. & S. R. Kellert (Eds.), *Children and nature: Psychological, sociocultural, and evolutionary investigations* (pp. 93–116). MIT Press.

Kahneman, D. (2011). *Thinking, fast and slow.* Macmillan.

Kahneman, D., Knetsch, J. L., & Thaler, R. H. (1990). Experimental tests of the endowment effect and the Coase theorem. *Journal of Political Economy, 98*(6), 1325–1348.

Kahneman, D., Knetsch, J. L., & Thaler, R. H. (1991). Anomalies: The endowment effect, loss aversion, and status quo bias. *Journal of Economic perspectives, 5*(1), 193–206.

Kahneman, D., Knetsch, J. L., & Thaler, R. H. (2008). The endowment effect: Evidence of losses valued more than gains. *Handbook of Experimental Economics Results, 1*, 939–948.

Kahneman, D., Ritov, I., Schkade, D., Sherman, S. J., & Varian, H. R. (1999). Economic preferences or attitude expressions? An analysis of dollar responses to public issues. *Journal of Risk and Uncertainty, 19*(1-3), 203–235.

Kahneman, D., Slovic, P., & Tversky, A. (Eds.). (1982). *Judgment under uncertainty: Heuristics and biases.* Cambridge University Press.

Kahneman, D., & Tversky, A. (1979). Prospect theory: An analysis of decision under risk. *Econometrica, 47*(2), 263–291.

Kahneman, D., & Tversky, A. (1984). Choices, values, and frames. *American Psychologist, 39*, 341–350.

Kahneman, D., & Tversky, A. (Eds.). (2000). *Choices, values, and frames.* Cambridge University Press.

Kamijo, Y., Tomiya, A., Mifune, N., & Saijo, T. (2017). Negotiating with the future: Incorporating imaginary future generations into negotiations. *Sustainability Science, 12*(3), 409–420.

Kamin, K. A., & Rachlinski, J. J. (1995). Ex post≠ ex ante: Determining liability in hindsight. *Law and Human Behavior, 19*(1), 89–104.

Kamm, F. M. (2015). *The trolley problem mysteries.* Oxford University Press.

Kardan, O., Demiralp, E., Hout, M. C., Hunter, M. R., Karimi, H., Hanayik, T., Yourganov, G., Jonides, J., & Berman, M. G. (2015). Is the preference of natural versus man-made scenes driven by bottom-up processing of the visual features of nature? *Frontiers in Psychology, 6*(471), 1–13.

Kareiva, P., Marvier, M., & Silliman, B. (2017). *Effective conservation science: Data not dogma.* Oxford University Press.

Karlsson, N., Loewenstein, G., & Seppi, D. (2009). The ostrich effect: Selective attention to information. *Journal of Risk and Uncertainty, 38*(2), 95–115.

Karol, D. (2018). *Party Polarization on Environmental Issues: Toward Prospects for Change.* Niskanen Center. www.niskanencenter.org

Kates, R. W., Parris, T. M., & Leiserowitz, A. A. (2005). What is sustainable development? Goals, indicators, values, and practice. *Environment: Science and Policy for Sustainable Development, 47*(3), 8–21.

Katz, D., & Allport, F. H. (1931). *Student attitudes.* The Craftsman Press.

Katz, E. (2012). Further adventures in the case against restoration. *Environmental Ethics, 34*(1), 67–97.

Keeley, B. L. (1999). Of conspiracy theories. *Journal of Philosophy, 96*(3), 109–126.

Kelly, H. (2015, November 2). No fireplace? These are the 5 best candles that smell like woodsmoke. *Washingtonian.* www.washingtonian.com

Kelman, M., Rottenstreich, Y., & Tversky, A. (1996). Context-dependence in legal decision making. *Journal of Legal Studies, 25*, 287–318.

Keohane, N., Revesz, R. & Stavins, R. N. (1998). The choice of regulatory instruments in environmental policy. *Harvard Environmental Law Review, 22*, 313–367.

Khare, R. S. (1996). Pollution and purity. In A. Barnard & J. Spencer (Eds.), *Encyclopedia of social and cultural anthropology* (pp. 437–439). Routledge.

Kim, U. E., Triandis, H. C., Kâğitçibaşi, Ç. E., Choi, S.-C. E., & Yoon, G. E. (1994). *Individualism and collectivism: Theory, method, and applications.* SAGE Publications.

Kim, Y., Kling, C. L., & Zhao, J. (2015). Understanding behavioral explanations of the WTP-WTA divergence through a neoclassical lens: Implications for environmental policy. *Annual Review of Resource Economics, 7*(1), 169–187.

Klaassen, C. D. (Ed.). (2008). *Casarett & Doull's toxicology: The basic science of poisons* (7th ed.). McGraw-Hill.

Klaassen, C. D., & Watkins, J. B., III (Eds.). (2010). *Casarett & Doull's essentials of toxicology* (2nd ed.). McGraw-Hill.

Klein, D., & Mitchell, G. (Eds.) (2010). *The psychology of judicial decision making.* Oxford University Press.

Klepeis, N., Nelson, W. C., Ott, W. R., Robinson, J. P., Tsang, A. M., Switzer, P., Behar, J. V., Hern, S. C., & Engelmann, W. H. (2001). The National Human Activity Pattern Survey (NHAPS): A resource for assessing exposure to environmental pollutants. *Journal of Exposure Science & Environmental Epidemiology, 11*(3), 231–252.

Kleres, J., & Wettergren, Å. (2017). Fear, hope, anger, and guilt in climate activism. *Social Movement Studies, 16*(5), 507–519.

Knetsch, J. L. (1989). The endowment effect and evidence of nonreversible indifference curves. *American Economic Review, 79*(5), 1277–1284.

Knetsch, J. L. (1990). Environmental policy implications of disparities between willingness to pay and compensation demanded measures of values. *Journal of Environmental Economics and Management, 18*(3), 227–237.

Knetsch, J. L. (2007). Biased valuations, damage assessments, and policy choices: The choice measure matters. *Ecological Economics, 63*, 684–689.

Knetsch, J. L., & Sinden, J. A. (1984). Willingness to pay and compensation demanded: experimental evidence of an unexpected disparity in measures of value. *Quarterly Journal of Economics, 99*(3), 507–521.

Knight, F. (1921). *Risk, uncertainty, and profit.* Courier Corporation.

Knight, R., & Cole, D. (1995). Factors that influence wildlife responses to recreationists. In R. L. Knight & K. J. Gutzwiller (Eds.), *Wildlife and recreationists: Coexistence through management and research* (pp. 71–80). Island Press.

Kogut, T., & Ritov, I. (2005). The "identified victim" effect: An identified group, or just a single individual? *Journal of Behavioral Decision Making, 18*(3), 157–167.

Korobkin, R. B. (1998). Inertia and preference in contract negotiations: The psychological power of default rules and form terms. *Vanderbilt Law Review, 51*, 1583–1651.

Korobkin, R. (2000). Behavioral economics, contract formation, and contract law. In C. Sunstein (Ed.), *Behavioral law and economics* (pp. 116–143). Cambridge University Press.

Korobkin, R. (2014). Wrestling with the endowment effect, or How to do law and economics without the Coase theorem. In E. Zamir & D. Teichman (Eds.), *The Oxford handbook of behavioral economics and the law* (pp. 300–334). Oxford University Press.

Koshland, D. E., Jr. (1991). Credibility in science and the press. *Science, 254*(5032), 629–630.

Kőszegi, B., & Rabin, M. (2007). Reference-dependent risk attitudes. *American Economic Review, 97*(4), 1047–1073.

Kotchen, M. (2009). Offsetting green guilt. *Stanford Social Innovation Review, 7*(2), 26–31.

Kraus, N., Malmfors, T., & Slovic, P. (2001). Intuitive toxicology: Expert and lay judgments of chemical risks. In P. Slovic (Ed.), *The perception of risk* (pp. 290–291). Routledge.

Krebs, D. (1975). Empathy and altruism. *Journal of Personality and Social Psychology, 32*(6), 1134–1146.

Kruger, J., & Dunning, D. (1999). Unskilled and unaware of it: How difficulties in recognizing one's own incompetence lead to inflated self-assessments. *Journal of Personality and Social Psychology, 77*(6), 1121–1134.

Kruglanski, A. W., Kopetz, C., Belanger, J. J., Chun, W. Y., Orehek, E., & Fishbach, A. (2012). Features of multifinality. *Personality and Social Psychology Review, 17*(1), 22–39.

Kuenzler, A., & Kysar. D. A. (2014). Environmental law. In A. Zamir & D. Teichman (Eds.), *The Oxford handbook of behavioral economics and the law* (pp. 748–782). Oxford University Press.

Kuhn, D. (1989). Children and adults as intuitive scientists. *Psychological Review, 96*(4), 674–689.

Kunda, Z. (1990). The case for motivated reasoning. *Psychological Bulletin, 108*(3), 480–498.

Kuran, T. (1995). The inevitability of future revolutionary surprises. *American Journal of Sociology, 100*(6), 1528–1551.

Kuran, T., & Sunstein, C. (1999). Availability cascades and risk regulation. *Stanford Law Review, 51*, 683–768.

Kurz, T., Gardner, B., Verplanken, B., & Abraham, C. (2014). Habitual behaviors or patterns of practice? Explaining and changing repetitive climate-relevant actions. *WIREs Climate Change, 6*, 113–128.

Kurzban, R., & Neuberg, S. (2005). Managing ingroup and outgroup relationships. In D. M. Buss (Ed.), *Handbook of evolutionary biology* (pp. 653–675). Wiley.

Kysar, D. A. (2010). *Regulating from nowhere: Environmental law and the search for objectivity*. Yale University Press.

Laibson, D. (1997). Golden eggs and hyperbolic discounting. *Quantitative Journal of Economics, 112*(2), 443–478.

Laitos, J. G. (2013). Standing and environmental harm: The double paradox. *Virginia Environmental Law Journal, 31*, 55–101.

Lakshminaryanan, V., Chen, M. K., & Santos, L. R. (2008). Endowment effect in capuchin monkeys. *Philosophical Transactions of the Royal Society of London Series B, Biological Sciences, 363*(1511), 3837–3844.

Landon, V. (2003). *DDT: From miracle chemical to banned pollutant*. www.swissinfo.ch

Landry, N., Gifford, R., Milfont, T. L., Weeks, A., & Arnocky, S. (2018). Learned helplessness moderates the relationship between environmental concern and behavior. *Journal of Environmental Psychology, 55*, 18–22.

Latané, B., & Darley, J. (1969). Bystander "apathy." *American Scientist, 57*(2), 244–268.

Latané, B., & Darley, J. M. (1970). *The unresponsive bystander: Why doesn't he help?* Appleton-Century Crofts.

Latham, G. P. (2016). Goal-setting theory: Causal relationships, mediators, and moderators. *Oxford research encyclopedia of psychology*. https://oxfordre.com

Lawrence, M. G., Schafer, S., Muri, H., Scott, V., Oschlies, A., Vaughan, N. E., Boucher, O., Schmidt, H., Haywood, J., & Scheffran, J. (2018). Evaluating climate geoengineering proposals in the context of the Paris Agreement temperature goals. *Nature Communications, 9*, 3734–3752.

Lazarus, R. J. (2000). Restoring what's environmental about environmental law in the Supreme Court. *U.C.L.A. Law Review, 47*, 703–812.

Lazarus, R. J. (2004). Judging environmental law. *Tulane Environmental Law Journal, 18*(1), 201–218.

Lazarus, R. (2009). Super wicked problems and climate change: Restraining the present to liberate the future. *Cornell Law Review, 94*, 1154–1234.

LeDoux, J. (2002). *Synaptic self: How our brains become who we are*. Viking Penguin.

Lehmler, H. J., Liu, B., Gadogbe, M. & Bao, W. (2018). Exposure to Bisphenol A, Bisphenol F, and Bisphenol S in U.S. adults and children: The National Health and Nutrition Examination Survey 2013–2014. *American Chemical Society Omega, 3*(6), 6523–6532.

Lenzen, M., Sun, Y., Faturay, F., Ting, Y., Geschke, A., & Malik, A. (2018). The carbon footprint of global tourism. *Nature Climate Change, 8,* 522–528.

Leonardelli, G. J., Pickett, C. L., & Brewer, M. B. (2010). Optimal distinctiveness theory: A framework for social identity, social cognition, and intergroup relations. *Advances in Experimental Social Psychology, 43,* 63–113.

Leopold, A. (1949). *A Sand County almanac.* Oxford University Press.

Leovy, J. (2015). *Ghettoside: A true story of murder in America.* Spiegel & Grau.

Lerner, J., & Keltner, D. (2000). Beyond valence: Toward a model of emotion-specific influences on judgment and choice. *Cognition and Emotion, 14*(4), 473–493.

Lessig, L. (1996). Social meaning and social norms. *University of Pennsylvania Law Review, 144*(5), 2181–2189.

Levin, S. A. (1998). Ecosystems and the biosphere as complex adaptive systems. *Ecosystems, 1*(5), 431–436.

Lewandowsky, S. (2014). Conspiracy fascination versus public interest: The case of 'Climategate.' *Environmental Research Letters, 9*(11), 1–4.

Lewandowsky, S., Cook, J., & Lloyd, E. (2018). The 'Alice in Wonderland' mechanics of the rejection of (climate) science: Simulating coherence by conspiracism. *Synthese, 195*(1), 175–196.

Lewandowsky, S., Oreskes, N., Risbey, J. S., Newell, B. R., & Smithson, M. (2015). Seepage: Climate change denial and its effect on the scientific community. *Global Environmental Change, 33,* 1–13.

Lewis, Jack. (1985). The birth of EPA. *EPA Journal, 11,* 6–10.

Liberman, N., & Trope, Y. (1998). The role of feasibility and desirability considerations in near and distant future decisions: A test of temporal construal theory. *Journal of Personality & Social Psychology, 75*(1), 5–18.

Lichtenstein, S., Slovic, P., Fischhoff, B., Layman, M., & Combs, B. (1978). Judged frequency of lethal events. *Journal of Experimental Psychology: Human Learning and Memory, 4*(6), 551–578.

Lichtveld, M., Sherchan, S., Gam, K. B., Kwok, R. K., Mundorf, C., Shankar, A., & Soares, L. (2016). The Deepwater Horizon oil spill through the lens of human health and the ecosystem. *Current Environmental Health Reports, 3*(4), 370–378.

Light, S. E., & Vandenbergh, M. P. (2016). Private environmental governance. In L. Paddock, R. L. Glicksman, & N. S. Bryner (Eds.), *Decision making in environmental law* (pp. 253–267). Edward Elgar Publishing.

Lilienfeld, S. O., Waldman, I. D., Landfield, K., Watts, A. L., Rubenzer, S., & Faschingbauer, T. R. (2012). Fearless dominance and the U.S. presidency: Implications of psychopathic personality traits for successful and unsuccessful political leadership. *Journal of Personality and Social Psychology, 103*(3), 489–505.

Lin, J., Pan, D., Davis, S. J., Zhang, Q., He, K., Wang, C., Streets, D. G., Wuebbles, D. J., Guan, D. (2014). Trade and transport of air pollution. *Proceedings of the National Academy of Sciences, 111*(5), 1736–1741.

Lind, E. A., & Tyler, T. R. (1988). *The social psychology of procedural justice.* Plenum Press.

List, J. A. (2003). Does market experience eliminate market anomalies? *Quarterly Journal of Economics, 118*(1), 41–71.

Liu, J., Li, J., Feng, L., Li, L., Tian, J., & Lee, K. (2014). Seeing Jesus in toast: Neural and behavioral correlates of face pareidolia. *Cortex, 53*, 60–77.

Livermore, M. A. (2015). Patience is an economic virtue: Real options, natural resources, and offshore oil. *University of Colorado Law Review, 84*, 581–649.

Llewellyn, K. N. (1949). Remarks on the theory of appellate decision and the rules or canons about how statutes are to be construed. *Vanderbilt Law Review, 3*, 395–406.

Loewenstein, G. (1994). The psychology of curiosity: A review and reinterpretation. *Psychological Bulletin, 116*(1), 75–98.

Loewenstein, G. (2005). Hot-cold empathy gaps and medical decision making. *Health Psychology, 24*(4s), S49–56.

Loewenstein, G., & Lerner, J. S. (2003). The role of affect in decision making. In R. Davidson, H. Goldsmith, & K. Scherer (Eds.), *Handbook of affective science* (pp. 619–642). Oxford University Press.

Loewenstein, G., Sunstein, C., & Golman, R. (2014). Disclosure: Psychology changes everything. *Annual Review of Economics, 6*(1), 391–419.

Long, E., & Biber, E. (2014). The Wilderness Act and climate change adaptation. *Environmental Law, 44*, 623–694.

Lord, C. G., Ross, L., & Lepper, M. R. (1979). Biased assimilation and attitude polarization: The effects of prior theories on subsequently considered evidence. *Journal of Personality and Social Psychology, 37*(11), 2098–2109.

Lorenz, K. (1943). Die angeborenen formen möglicher erfahrung [The inborn forms of possible experience]. *Zeitschrift für Tierpsychologie [Journal of Animal Psychology], 5*(2), 235–409.

Lorenzoni, I., Nicholson-Cole, S., & Whitmarsh, L. (2007). Barriers perceived to engaging with climate change among the UK public and their policy implications. *Global Environmental Change, 17*(3), 445–459.

Lowenthal, D. (1998). Environment as heritage. In K. Flint & H. Morphy, *Culture, landscape, and the environment: The Linacre lectures 1997* (pp. 197–218). Oxford University Press.

Luginaah, I. N., Taylor, S. M., Elliott, J. S., & Eyles, D. J. (2000). A longitudinal study of the community health impacts of a refinery. *Social Science and Medicine, 50*(7-8), 1155–1166.

Luginaah, I. N., Taylor, S. M., Elliott, S. J., & Eyles, J. D. (2002). Community reappraisal of the perceived health effects of a petroleum refinery. *Social Science & Medicine, 55*(1), 47–61.

Lugo, E. (2006). Insect conservation under the Endangered Species Act. *U.C.L.A. Journal of Environmental Law and Policy, 25*(1), 97–123.

Lujan v. Defenders of Wildlife, 504 U.S. 555 (1992).

Lupia, A. (2013). Communicating science in politicized environments. *Proceedings of the National Academy of Sciences, 110*, 14048–14054.

Lydall, E. S., Gilmour, G., & Dwyer, D. M. (2010). Rats place greater value on rewards produced by high effort: An animal analogue of the "effort justification" effect. *Journal of Experimental Social Psychology, 46*(6), 1134–1137.

MacCoun, R., & Perlmutter, S. (2015). Blind analysis: Hide results to seek the truth. *Nature, 526*(7572), 187–189.

Macfarlane, J. (2000). Why do people settle? *McGill Law Journal, 46*, 663–711.

MacNeil, M. K., & Sherif, M. (1976). Norm change over subject generations as a function of arbitrariness of prescribed norms. *Journal of Personality and Social Psychology, 34*(5), 762–773.

Maier, S. F., & Seligman, M. E. (1976). Learned helplessness: Theory and evidence. *Journal of Experimental Psychology: General, 105*(1), 3–46.

Mandel, G. (2011). To promote the creative process: Intellectual property law and the psychology of creativity. *Notre Dame Law Review, 86*, 1999–2026.

Mandelbrot, B. B., & Hudson, R. L. (2010). *The (mis)behaviour of markets: A fractal view of risk, ruin and reward.* Profile Books.

Mann, C. C., & Plummer, M. L. (1995). *Noah's choice: The future of endangered species.* Alfred A. Knopf.

Maple, T. L., & Morris, M. C. (2018). Behavioral impact of naturalistic and wilderness settings. In A. S. Devlin (Ed.), *Environmental psychology and human well-being: Effects of built and natural Settings* (pp. 253–279). Academic Press.

Markell, D. & Ruhl, J. B. (2012). An empirical assessment of climate change in the courts: A new jurisprudence or business as usual? *Florida Law Review, 60*, 15–86.

Markowitz, E., Slovic, P., Västfjäll, D., & Hodges, S. (2013). Compassion fade and the challenge of environmental conservation. *Judgment and Decision Making, 8*(4), 397–406.

Markus, H. R., & Kitayama, S. (1991). Culture and the self: Implications for cognition, emotion, and motivation. *Psychological Review, 98*(2), 224–253.

Marseille, M. M., Elands, B. H., & van den Brink, M. L. (2012). Experiencing polar bears in the zoo: Feelings and cognitions in relation to a visitor's conservation attitude. *Human Dimensions of Wildlife, 17*(1), 29–43.

Marsh, G. P. (1864). *Man and nature; or, physical geography as modified by human action.* Kessinger Publishing.

Marsh, J. K., & Ahn, W.-K. (2006). Order effects in contingency learning: The role of task complexity. *Memory & Cognition, 34*(3), 568–576.

Martin, C., & Czellar, S. (2017). Where do biospheric values come from? A connectedness to nature perspective. *Journal of Environmental Psychology, 52*, 56–68.

Massachusetts v. EPA, 549 U.S. 497, 529 (2007).

Masson-Delmotte, V., Zhai, P., Pörtner, H. O., Roberts, D., Skea, J., Shukla, P. R., Pirani, A., Moufouma-Okia, C., Pean, R., Pidcock, S., Connors, J. B. R., Chen, Y., Zhou, X., Gomis, M. I., Lonnoy, E., Maycock, T., Tignor, M., & Waterfield, T. (Eds.). (2018). *Global warming of 1.5° C: An IPCC Special Report on the impacts of global warming of 1.5° C above preindustrial levels and related global greenhouse gas emission pathways, in the context of strengthening the global response to the threat of climate change, sustainable development, and efforts to eradicate poverty*. IPCC.

Mather, J. (2019). Ethics and care: For animals, not just mammals. *Animals, 9*(12), 1018.

Mattson, M. P. (2014). Superior pattern processing is the essence of the evolved human brain. *Frontiers in Neuroscience, 8*, 265–265.

McAdams, R. H. (2000). Focal point theory of expressive law. *Virginia Law Review, 86*, 1649–1729.

McAdams, D. P. (2016, June). The mind of Donald Trump: Narcissism, disagreeableness, grandiosity—a psychologist investigates how Trump's extraordinary personality might shape his possible presidency. *Atlantic*. www.theatlantic.com

McCarty, J. A., & Shrum, L. J. (2001). The influence of individualism, collectivism, and locus of control on environmental beliefs and behavior. *Journal of Public Policy & Marketing, 20*(1), 93–104.

McFadden, D., & Train, K. (Eds.). (2017). *Contingent valuation of environmental goods: A comprehensive critique*. Edward Elgar Publishing.

Mead, M. N. (2005). Arsenic: In search of an antidote to a global poison. *Environmental Health Perspectives, 113*(6), A378–A386.

Meares, T. L., & Kahan, D. M. (1998). Law and (norms of) order in the inner city. *Law and Society Review, 32*(4), 805–838.

Mee, L. (2006). Reviving dead zones. *Scientific American, 295*(5), 78–85.

Mellström, C., & Johannesson, M. (2008). Crowding out in blood donation: Was Titmuss right? *Journal of the European Economic Association, 6*(4), 845–863.

Meng, M., Cherian, T., Singal, G., & Sinha, P. (2012). Lateralization of face processing in the human brain. *Proceedings of the Royal Society B: Biological Sciences, 279*(1735), 2052–2061.

Merry, S. E. (1990). *Getting justice and getting even: Legal consciousness among working-class Americans*. University of Chicago Press.

Merwin, I., Pruyne, P. T., Ebel, J. G., Jr., Manzell, K. L., & Lisk, D. J. (1994). Persistence, phytotoxicity, and management of arsenic, lead and mercury residues in old orchard soils of New York State. *Chemosphere, 29*(6), 1361–1367.

Metz, B., Davidson, O. R., Bosch, P. R., Dave, R., & Meyer, L. A. (Eds.). (2007). *Climate change 2007: Mitigation of climate change. Contribution of working group III to the fourth assessment report of the Intergovernmental Panel on Climate Change*. Cambridge University Press.

Meyers, T., Nisbet, M., Maibach, E., & Leiserowitz, A. (2012). A public health frame arouses hopeful emotions about climate change. *Climatic Change, 113*(3–4), 1105–1112.

Michigan v. EPA, 576 U.S. 743 (2015).

Millennium Ecosystem Assessment. (2005). *Ecosystems and human well-being: Synthesis*. Island Press.

Milman, O., & Harvey, F. (2019, May 8). US is hotbed of climate change denial, major global survey finds. *Guardian*. www.theguardian.com

Mittone, L., & Savadori, L. (2009). The scarcity bias. *Applied Psychology, 58*(3), 453–468.

Monin, B., & Miller, D. (2001). Moral credentials and the expression of prejudice. *Journal of Personality and Social Psychology, 81*(1), 33–34.

Monin, B., & Norton, M. I. (2003). Perceptions of a fluid consensus: Uniqueness bias, false consensus, false polarization, and pluralistic ignorance in a water conservation crisis. *Personality and Social Psychology Bulletin, 29*(5), 559–567.

Montreal Protocol on Substances that Deplete the Ozone Layer, Sept. 16, 1987, 1522 U.N.T.S. 3.

Moore, D. A., Carter, A. B., & Yang, H. H. J. (2015). Wide of the mark: Evidence on the underlying causes of overprecision in judgment. *Organizational Behavior and Human Decision Processes, 131*, 110–120.

Moore, M. (1993). *Act and crime: The philosophy of action and its implications for criminal law.* Oxford University Press.

Mora, C., Tittensor, D. P., Adl, S., Simpson, A. G. B., & Worm, B. (2011). How many species are there on Earth and in the ocean? *PLoS Biology, 9*(8), e1001127.

Morales, A. C., & Fitzsimons, G. J. (2007). Product contagion: Changing consumer evaluations through physical contact with "disgusting" products. *Journal of Marketing Research, 44*(2), 272–283.

Morgan, M. G., Dowlatabadi, H., Henrion, M., Keith, D., Lempert, R., McBride, S., Small, M., & Wilbanks, T. (2009). *Best practice approaches for characterizing, communicating and incorporating scientific uncertainty in climate decision making.* CCSP.

Morrison, K. R., & Johnson, C. S. (2011). When what you have is who you are: Self-uncertainty leads individualists to see themselves in their possessions. *Personality and Social Psychology Bulletin, 37*(5), 639–651.

Moser, S. C. (2007). More bad news: The risk of neglecting emotional responses to climate change information. In S. C. Moser & L. Dilling (Eds.), *Creating a climate for change* (pp. 64–80). Cambridge University Press.

Moskowitz, G. B., & Skurnik, I. W. (1999). Contrast effects as determined by the type of prime: Trait versus exemplar primes initiate processing strategies that differ in how accessible constructs are used. *Journal of Personality and Social Psychology, 76*(6), 911–927.

Mullainathan, S., & Shafir, E. (2013). *Scarcity: Why having too little means so much.* Macmillan.

Muthukrishna, M., Henrich, J., Toyokawa, W., Hamamura, T., Kameda, T., & Heine, S. J. (2018). Overconfidence is universal? Elicitation of Genuine Overconfidence (EGO) procedure reveals systematic differences across domain, task knowledge, and incentives in four populations. *PLoS one, 13*(8), e0202288.

Myers, D. G., & Lamm, H. (1976). The group polarization phenomenon. *Psychological Bulletin, 83*(4), 602–627.

Nadler, J. Flouting the law. *Texas Law Review, 83*, 1399–1441.

Nagle, J. C. (1998). Playing Noah. *Minnesota Law Review, 82*, 1171–1260.

Nagle, J. (2009). The idea of pollution. *U.C. Davis Law Review, 43*(1), 1–78.

Nagle, J. (2013). Good pollution: A response to Arden Rowell. *University of Chicago Law Review Dialogue, 79*, 31–43.

Nagle, J. (2015). The legal meaning of wilderness character. *International Journal of Wilderness, 231*(3). Retrieved February 17, 2020, from https://ijw.org

Nagle, J. (2019, February 2). Indiana Dunes a deserving lakeshore, not an undeserving national park. *South Bend Tribune.* www.southbendtribune.com

Nagle, J. C., & Ruhl, J. B. (2007). *The law of biodiversity and ecosystem management (2nd ed.).* Foundation Press.

Narula, S. K. (2014, January 5). Sushinomics: How bluefin tuna became a million-dollar fish. *Atlantic.* www.theatlantic.com

Nash, J. R. (2000). Too much market? Conflict between tradable pollution allowances and the "polluter pays" principle. *Harvard Environmental Law Review, 24,* 465–535.

Nash, J. R. (2006). Framing effects and regulatory choice. *Notre Dame Law Review, 82*(1), 313–372.

Nash, J. R. (2008). Standing and the precautionary principle. *Columbia Law Review, 108*(2), 494–527.

Nash, J. R., & R. L. Revesz. (2007). Grandfathering and environmental regulation: The law and economics of new source review. *Northwestern University Law Review, 101*(4), 1677–1733.

National Center for Environmental Economics (2014). *Guidelines for preparing economic analyses.* U.S. Environmental Protection Agency.

National Science Board (2018). *Science and engineering indicators 2018.* Retrieved February 19, 2020, from www.nsf.gov

National Park Service Organic Act of 1916, 16 U.S.C. §1, et seq.

National Toxicology Program. (2008). *NTP-CERHR monograph on the potential human reproductive and developmental effects of Bisphenol A.* NIH Publication No. 08-5994. https://ntp.niehs.nih.gov

National Wilderness Protection Act, 16 U.S.C. § 1133(c).

Navarrete, C. D., & Fessler, D. M. (2006). Disease avoidance and ethnocentrism: The effects of disease vulnerability and disgust sensitivity on intergroup attitudes. *Evolution and Human Behavior, 27*(4), 270–282.

Neal, D. T., Wood, W., & Quinn, J. M. (2006). Habit—A repeat performance. *Current Directions in Psychological Science, 15*(4), 198–202.

Neil, N., Malmfors, T., & Slovic, P. (1994). Intuitive toxicology: Expert and lay judgments of chemical risks. *Toxicology Pathology, 22,* 198–201.

Nelson, T. D. (2009). *Handbook of prejudice, stereotyping, and discrimination.* Psychology Press.

Nemeroff, C., & Rozin, P. (1994). The contagion concept in adult thinking in the United States: Transmission of germs and of interpersonal influence. *Ethos, 22*(2), 158–186.

Newman, G. E., & Bloom, P. (2014). Physical contact influences how much people pay at celebrity auctions. *Proceedings of the National Academy of Sciences U.S.A., 111*(10), 3705–3708.

Newton, D. (2007). *Chemistry of the environment.* Facts on File.

Nicholls, N. (1999). Cognitive illusions, heuristics, and climate prediction. *Bulletin of the American Meteorological Society, 80*(7), 1385–1398.

Nickerson, R. S. (1998). Confirmation bias: A ubiquitous phenomenon in many guises. *Review of General Psychology, 2*(2), 175–220.

Nisbet, M., & Markowitz, E. (2016). *Strategic science communication on environmental issues.* [Commissioned white paper in support of the Alan Leshner Leadership Institute.] American Association for the Advancement of Science. www.aaas.org

Nisbett, R. E., & Ross, L. (1980). *Human inference: Strategies and shortcomings of social judgment.* Prentice-Hall.

Nolt, J. (2011). How harmful are the average American's greenhouse gas emissions? *Ethics, Policy, and Environment, 14*(1), 3–10.

Nordhaus, W. (2008). *A question of balance: Weighing the options on global warming policies.* Yale University Press.

Nordhaus, W. (2011). The economics of tail events with an application to climate change. *Review of Environmental Economics and Policy, 5*(2), 240–257.

Nordhaus, W. (2015). *The climate casino: Risk, uncertainty, and economics for a warming world.* Yale University Press.

Norgaard, K. M. (2011). Climate denial: Emotion, psychology, culture, and political economy. In J. S. Dryzek, R. B. Norgaard, & D. Schlosberg (Eds.), *Oxford handbook on climate change and society, 18* (pp. 399–413). Oxford University Press.

Norgaard, K. M. (2011). *Living in denial: Climate change, emotions, and everyday life.* MIT Press.

Novemsky, N., & Kahneman, D. (2005). The boundaries of loss aversion. *Journal of Marketing Research, 42*(2), 119–128.

Nussbaum, M. (2008). Who is the happy warrior? Philosophy poses questions to psychology. *Journal of Legal Studies, 27*, 81–113.

Nyborg, K. (2010). Will green taxes undermine moral motivation? *Public Finance & Management, 110*(2), 331–351.

Oates, W. E. (2002). A reconsideration of environmental federalism. In J. A. List and A. de Zeeuw (Eds.), *Recent advances in environmental economics* (pp. 1–32). Edward Elgar.

O'Brien, B. (2009). Prime suspect: An examination of factors that aggravate and counteract confirmation bias in criminal investigations. *Psychology, Public Policy, and Law, 15*(4), 315–334.

O'Connor, R. E., Bord, R. J., Yarnal, B., & Wiefek, N. (2002). Who wants to reduce greenhouse gas emissions? *Social Science Quarterly, 83*(1), 1–17.

O'Donoghue, T., & Rabin, M. (1999). Doing it now or later. *American Economic Review, 89*(1), 103–124.

Olson, M. (1965). *The logic of collective action: Public goods and the theory of groups.* Harvard University Press.

Open Science Collaboration. (2015). Estimating the reproducibility of psychological science. *Science, 349*(6251), aac4716.

Orr, J., Fabry, V. F., Aumont, O., Bopp, L., Doney, S. C., Feely, R. A., Gnanadesikan, A., Gruber, N., Ishida, A., Joos, F., Key, R. M., Lindsay, K., Maier-Reimer, E., Matear, R., Monfray, P., Mouchet, A., Najjar, R. G., Plattner, G.-K., Rodgers, K. B., Sabine, C. J. et al., (2005). Anthropogenic ocean acidification over the twenty-first century and its impact on calcifying organisms. *Nature, 437,* 681–86.

Orru, K., Nordin, S., Harzia, H., & Orru, H. (2018). The role of perceived air pollution and health risk perception in health symptoms and disease: A population-based study combined with modelled levels of PM10. *International Archives of Occupational and Environmental Health, 91*(5), 581–589.

Osman, A. E. G., Anderson, J., Churpek, J. E., Christ, T. N., Curran, E., Godley, L. A., Liu, H., Thirman, M. J., Odenike, T., Stock, W., & Larson, R. A. (2018). Treatment of acute promyelocytic leukemia in adults. *Journal of Oncology Practice, 14*(11), 649–657.

Ostrom, E. (1990). *Governing the commons: The evolution of institutions for collective action.* Cambridge University Press.

Overdevest, C., & Christiansen, L. (2013). Using 'cultural cognition' to predict environmental risk perceptions in a Florida water-supply planning process. *Society and Natural Resources, 26*(9), 987–1007.

Pachauri, R. K., Allen, M. R., Barros, V. R., Broome, J., Cramer, W., Christ, R., Church, J. A., Clarke, L., Dahe, Q., Dasgupta, P., Dubash, N., K., Edenhofer, O., Elgizouli, I., Field, C. B., Forster, P., Friedlingstein, P., Fuglestvedt, J., Gomez-Echeverri, L., Hallegatte, S., & Hegerl, G. et al., (Eds.). (2015). *Climate change 2014: Synthesis report. Contribution of working groups I, II, and III to the fifth assessment report of the Intergovernmental Panel on Climate Change.* IPCC.

Palmer, J. A. (1998). Spiritual ideas, environmental concerns and educational practice. In D. E. Cooper & J. A. Palmer (Eds.), *Spirit of the environment: Religion, value and environmental concern* (pp. 150–171). Routledge.

Pan, Y., Birdsey, R. A., Fang, J., Houghton, R., Kauppi, P. E., Kurz, W. A., Hayes, D. (2011). A large and persistent carbon sink in the world's forests. *Science, 333,* 988–993.

Pargament, K. I., & Mahoney, A. (2005). Sacred matters: Sanctification as a vital topic for the psychology of religion. *International Journal for the Psychology of Religion, 15*(3), 179–198.

Paris Agreement to the United Nations Framework Convention on Climate Change, Dec. 12, 2015, T.I.A.S. No. 16-1104.

Parker, L. (2018, June). We made plastic. We depend on it. Now we're drowning in it. *National Geographic.* www.nationalgeographic.com

Patt, A., & Zeckhauser, R. (2000). Action bias and environmental decisions. *Journal of Risk and Uncertainty, 21*(1), 45–72.

Paulos, J. A. (1988). *Innumeracy: Mathematical illiteracy and its consequences.* Macmillan.

Pearce, D., Atkinson, G., & Mourato, S. (2006). *Cost-benefit analysis and the environment: Recent developments.* Organisation for Economic Co-operation and Development.

Pearshouse, R. (2016, Apr. 6). *Nepotism and neglect: The failing response to arsenic in the drinking water of Bangladesh's rural poor.* Human Rights Watch. www.hrw.org

Peel, J., & Osofsky, H. M. (2019). Litigation as a climate regulatory tool. In C. Voigt (Ed.), *International judicial practice on the environment: Questions of legitimacy* (pp. 311–335). Cambridge University Press.

Peng, M., Chang, L., & Zhou, R. (2013). Physiological and behavioral responses to strangers compared to friends as a source of disgust. *Evolution and Human Behavior, 34*(2), 94–98.

Penner, L. A., Fritzsche, B. A., Craiger, J. P., & Freifeld, T. R. (1995). Measuring the prosocial personality. In J. Butcher & C. D. Spielberger (Eds.), *Advances in personality assessment, 10* (pp. 147–163). LEA.

Perdue, C. W., Dovidio, J. F., Gurtman, M. B., & Tyler, R. B. (1990). Us and them: Social categorization and the process of intergroup bias. *Journal of Personality and Social Psychology, 59*(3), 475–486.

Peters, E., Västfjäll, D., Slovic, P., Mertz, C., Mazzocco, K., & Dickert, S. (2006). Numeracy and decision making. *Psychological Science, 17*(5), 407–413.

Peterson, R. A. (2001). On the use of college students in social science research: Insights from a second-order meta-analysis. *Journal of Consumer Research, 28*(3), 450–461.

Petty, R. E., & Cacioppo, J. T. (1984). The effects of involvement on responses to argument quantity and quality: Central and peripheral routes to persuasion. *Journal of Personality and Social Psychology, 46*(1), 69–81.

Petty, R. E., Cacioppo, J. T., & Goldman, R. (1981). Personal involvement as a determinant of argument-based persuasion. *Journal of Personality and Social Psychology, 41*(5), 847–855.

Phelps, E. A., Ling, S., & Carrasco, M. (2006). Emotion facilitates perception and potentiates the perceptual benefits of attention. *Psychological Science, 17*(4), 292–299.

Phillips, B. J., & Sego, T. (2011). The role of identity in disposal: Lessons from mothers' disposal of children's possessions. *Marketing Theory, 11*(4), 435–454.

Phillips, O. L., Lewis, S. L., Baker, T. R., Chao, K.-J., & Higuchi, N. (2008). The changing Amazon forest. *Philosophical Transactions of the Royal Society B: Biological Sciences, 363*, 1819–1827.

Phoenix, C., & Treder, M. (2008). Nanotechnology as a global catastrophic risk. In N. Bostrom & M. M. Ćirković (Eds.), *Global Catastrophic Risks* (pp. 481–503). Oxford University Press.

Pidgeon, N., & Fischhoff, B. (2011). The role of social and decision sciences in communicating uncertain climate risks. *Nature Climate Change, 1*, 35–41.

Pierotti, R., & Wildcat, D. (2000). Traditional ecological knowledge: The third alternative (commentary). *Ecological Applications, 10*(5), 1333–1340.

Pigou, A. C. (1920). *The economics of welfare.* Macmillan.

Piketty, T. (2014). *Capital in the twenty-first century.* Harvard University Press.

Pindyck, R. (2011). Fat tails, thin tails, and climate change policy. *Review of Environmental Economics and Policy, 5*(2), 258–274.

Pine, W. E., Martell, S. J., Walters, C. J., & Kitchell, J. F. (2009). Counterintuitive responses of fish populations to management actions: Some common causes and implications for predictions based on ecosystem modeling. *Fisheries, 34*(4), 165–180.

Pizer, W., Adler, M., Aldy, J., Anthoff, D., Cropper, M., Gillingham, K., Greenstone, M., Murray, B., Newell, R., Richels, R., Rowell, A., Waldhoff, S., & Wiener, J. (2014). Using and improving the social cost of carbon. *Science, 346* (6214), 1189–90.

Plott, C. R., & Zeiler, K. (2005). The willingness to pay–willingness to accept gap. *American Economic Review, 95*(3), 530–545.

Plott, C. R., & Zeiler, K. (2007). Exchange asymmetries incorrectly interpreted as evidence of endowment effect theory and prospect theory? *American Economic Review, 97*(4), 1449–1466.

Plott, C. R., & Zeiler, K. (2013). Against endowment theory. *UCLA Law Review, 61*, 1-63.

Pollution Prevention Act of 1990, 42 U.S.C. §13101 et seq.

Poon, C., Koehler, D., & Buehler, R. (2014). On the psychology of self-prediction: Consideration of situational barriers to intended actions, *Judgment and Decision Making, 9*(3), 207–225.

Poon, C. S. K., & Koehler, D. J. (2006). Lay personality knowledge and dispositionist thinking: A knowledge-activation framework. *Journal of Experimental Social Psychology, 42*(2), 177–191.

Popper, K. R. (1968). *The logic of scientific discovery* (3rd ed. revised). Hutchinson.

Portney, P., & Weyant, J (Eds.) (2013). *Discounting and intergenerational equity*. Resources for the Future.

Posner, E., & Weisbach, D. (2010). *Climate change justice*. Princeton University Press.

Posner, R. A. (1999). An economic approach to the law of evidence. *Stanford Law Review, 51*, 1477–1546.

Posner, R. A. (2004). *Catastrophe: Risk and response*. Oxford University Press.

Pratto, F., & Glasford, D. E. (2008). Ethnocentrism and the value of a human life. *Journal of Personality and Social Psychology, 95*(6), 1411–1428.

Pretty, J., Peacock, J., Sellens, M., & Griffin, M. (2005). The mental and physical health outcomes of green exercise. *International Journal of Environmental Health Research, 15*(5), 319–337.

Price, H. (1996). *Time's arrow and Archimedes' point: New directions for the physics of time.* Oxford University Press.

Priester, J. R., & Petty, R. E. (1995). Source attributions and persuasion: Perceived honesty as a determinant of message scrutiny. *Personality and Social Psychology Bulletin, 21*(6), 637–654.

Proshansky, H. M., Fabian, A. K., & Kaminoff, R. (1983). Place-identity: Physical world socialization of the self. *Journal of Environmental Psychology, 3*(1), 57–83.

Puckett, E. E., Kesler, D. C., & Greenwald, D. N. (2016). Taxa, petitioning agency, and lawsuits affect time spent awaiting listing under the US Endangered Species Act. *Biological Conservation, 201*, 220–229.

Purdon, E. M., Ma, M.-S., Vandevooren, H., Bam, P., & Gomes, S. (2010). *Analyzing and identifying barriers to recycling attitudes and behaviors of students in the south residence of the University of Guelph.* Report prepared for Sustainability Office of the University of Guelph. www.uoguelph.ca

Purdy, J. (2015). *After nature: A politics for the Anthropocene.* Harvard University Press.

Rachlinski, J. (2000a). On being regulated in foresight versus being judged in hindsight. In R. E. Meiners & A. P. Morriss (Eds.), *The common law and the environment: Rethinking the statutory basis for modern environmental law* (pp. 242–263). Rowman & Littlefield.

Rachlinski, J. (2000b). The psychology of global climate change. *University of Illinois Law Review, 2000,* 299–319.

Rachlinski, J. (2011). The psychological foundations of behavioral law and economics. *University of Illinois Law Review, 2011,* 1675–1696.

Rachlinski, J. J., & Farina, C. R. (2002). Cognitive psychology and optimal government design. *Cornell Law Review, 87,* 549-615.

Rachlinski, J. J., Guthrie, C., & Wistrich, A. J. (2006). Inside the bankruptcy judge's mind. *B.U. Law Review, 86,* 1227–1265.

Radin, M. J. (1993). Compensation and commensurability. *Duke Law Journal, 43,* 56–86.

Raffa, R. B., Pergolizzi, J. V., Jr., Taylor, R., Jr., Kitzen, J. M., & NEMA Research Group. (2019). Sunscreen bans: Coral reefs and skin cancer. *Journal of Clinical Pharmacy and Therapeutics, 44*(1), 134–139.

Raffensperger, C., & Tickner, J. (Eds.). (1999). *Protecting public health and the environment: Implementing the precautionary principle.* Island Press.

Random House unabridged dictionary (4th ed.) (2001). Ballantine Books.

Rapanos v. United States, 547 U.S. 715 (2006).

Rayman, N. (2014, April 17). Portland dumps 38 million gallons of water after man pees in reservoir. *TIME.* https://time.com

Rayner, S. (2006). Wicked problems: Clumsy solutions, diagnoses, and prescriptions for environmental ills. Jack Beale Memorial Lecture on Global Environment.

Redelmeier, D. A., Katz, J., & Kahneman, D. (2003). Memories of colonoscopy: A randomized trial. *Pain, 104*(1–2), 187–194.

Redlawsk, D. P. (2002). Hot cognition or cool consideration? Testing the effects of motivated reasoning on political decision making. *Journal of Politics, 64*(4), 1021–1044.

Reeves, R. (2001). *President Nixon: Alone in the White House.* Simon and Schuster.

Reid, V. M., Dunn, K., Young, R. J., Amu, J., Donovan, T., & Reissland, N. (2017). The human fetus preferentially engages with face-like visual stimuli. *Current Biology, 27*(12), 1825–1828.

Relis, T. (2006). It's not about the money: A theory of misconceptions of plaintiffs' litigation aims. *University of Pittsburgh Law Review, 68,* 701–746.

Reser, J. P., Morrissey, S. A., & Ellul, M. (2011). The threat of climate change: Psychological response, adaptation, and impacts. In I. Weissbecker (Ed.), *Climate change and human well-being* (pp. 19–42). Springer.

Reser, J. P., & Swim, J. K. (2011). Adapting to and coping with the threat and impacts of climate change. *American Psychologist, 66*(4), 277–289.

Reuben, E., Rey-Biel, P., Sapienza, P., & Zingales, L. (2012). The emergence of male leadership in competitive environments. *Journal of Economic Behavior & Organization, 83*(1), 111–117.

Revesz, R. (1999). Environmental regulation, cost-benefit analysis, and the discounting of human lives. *Columbia Law Review, 99*(4), 941–1017.

Revesz, R. (2015). *Environmental law and policy.* Foundation Press.

Revesz, R. L., & Livermore, M. A. (2008). *Retaking rationality: How cost-benefit analysis can better protect the environment and our health.* Oxford University Press.

Revesz, R. & Shahabian, M. (2011). Climate change and future generations. *Southern California Law Review, 84*, 1097–1162.

Reyes-Garcia, V., Zurro, D., Caro, J., & Madella, M. (2017). Small-scale societies and environmental transformations: Coevolutionary dynamics. *Ecology and Society, 22*(1), 15.

Richards, K., & van Zeben, J. (Eds.). (2020). *Policy instruments in environmental law.* Edward Elgar Publishing.

Ritov, I., & Baron, J. (1992). Status-quo and omission biases. *Journal of Risk and Uncertainty, 5*(1), 49–61.

Robbins, K. (2013). An ecosystem management primer: History, perceptions, and modern definition. In K. Robbins (Ed.), *The laws of nature: Reflections on the evolution of ecosystem management law and policy* (pp. 3–19). University of Akron Press.

Robertson v. Methow Valley Citizens Council, 490 U.S. 332 (1989).

Rochman, C. M., Cook, A. M., & Koelmans, A. A. (2016). Plastic debris and policy: Using current scientific understanding to invoke positive change. *Environmental Toxicology and Chemistry, 35*(7), 1617–1626.

Rodeheffer, C. D., Hill, S. E., & Lord, C. G. (2012). Does this recession make me look black? The effect of resource scarcity on the categorization of biracial faces. *Psychological Science, 23*(12), 1476–1478.

Rohrer, D., Pashler, H., & Harris, C. R. (2015). Do subtle reminders of money change people's political views? *Journal of Experimental Psychology: General, 144*(4), e73–e85.

Rolland, J., Silvestro, D., Schluter, D., Guisan, A., Broennimann, O., & Salamin, N. (2018). The impact of endothermy on the climatic niche evolution and the distribution of vertebrate diversity. *Nature Ecology & Evolution, 2*(3), 459–464.

Rome, A. W. (1996). Coming to terms with pollution: The language of environmental reform, 1865–1915. *Environmental History, 1*(3), 6–28.

Rosenbaum, S. (2018, July 17). She recorded that heartbreaking turtle video. Here's what she wants companies like Starbucks to know about plastic straws. *TIME.* www.time.com

Rosenfeld, D. L. (2018). The psychology of vegetarianism: Recent advances and future directions. *Appetite, 131*, 125–138.

Rosenthal, R., & Fode, K. L. (1963). The effect of experimenter bias on the performance of the albino rat. *Behavioral Science, 8*(3), 183–189.

Ross, L. (1977). The intuitive psychologist and his shortcomings: Distortions in the attribution process. *Advances in Experimental Social Psychology, 10*, 173–220.

Ross, L., Greene, D., & House, P. (1977). "The false consensus effect": An egocentric bias in social perception and attribution processes. *Journal of Experimental Social Psychology, 13*(3), 279–301.

Ross, L., & Ward, A. (1995). Psychological barriers to dispute resolution. In M. Zanna (Ed.), *Advances in Experimental Social Psychology, 27* (pp. 255–304). Academic Press.

Ross, L., & Ward, A. (1996). Naive realism in everyday life: Implications for social conflict and misunderstanding. In T. Brown, E. S. Reed, & E. Turiel (Eds.), *Values and Knowledge* (pp. 103–135). Erlbaum.

Rothman, L., & Ronk, L. (2016, August 22). These 1861 photographs helped save America's wilderness. *TIME.* https://time.com

Rots, A. P. (2015). Worldwide Kami, global Shinto: The invention and spread of a 'nature religion.' *Czech and Slovak Journal of Humanities, 3*, 31–48.

Rowell, A. (2010). The cost of time: Haphazard discounting and the undervaluation of regulatory benefits. *Notre Dame Law Review, 85*, 1505–1542.

Rowell, A. (2012a). Allocating pollution. *University of Chicago Law Review, 79*, 985–1049.

Rowell, A. (2012b). Partial valuation in cost-benefit analysis. *Administrative Law Review, 64*, 723–742.

Rowell, A. (2014). Time in cost-benefit analysis. *U.C. Irvine Law Review, 4*, 1215–1240.

Rowell, A. (2015). Foreign impacts and climate change. *Harvard Environmental Law Review, 39*, 371–421.

Rowell, A. (2017). Once and future nudges. *Missouri Law Review, 82*, 1–19.

Rowell, A. (2019). Legal knowledge, belief, and aspiration. *Arizona State Law Journal, 41*, 225–291.

Rowell, A. (2020a, in press). Behavioural instruments in environmental regulation. In K. Richards & J. van Zeben (Eds.), *Policy instruments in environmental law.* Edward Elgar Publishing.

Rowell, A. (2020b, in press). Regulating best case scenarios. *Environmental law, 50.*

Rowell, A. (2020c). COVID-19 and environmental law. University of Illinois College of Law Legal Studies Research Paper No. 20-19. doi: 10.2139/ssrn.3582879

Rowell, A., & Bregant, J. (2014). Numeracy and legal decision making. *Arizona State Law Journal, 46*, 191–230.

Rowell, A., & van Zeben, J. (2016). A new status quo? The psychological impact of the Paris Agreement on climate change. *European Journal of Risk Regulation, 7*(1), 49–53.

Rowell, A., & van Zeben, J. (2020). *Essential environmental law: The United States.* University of California Press.

Rowell, A., & Wexler, L. (2014). Valuing foreign lives. *Georgia Law Review, 48*, 499–578.

Rozin, P., Haidt, J., & McCauley, R. (2008). Disgust. In M. Lewis, J. M. Haviland-Jones, & L. F. Barrett (Eds.), *Handbook of emotions* (3rd ed.) (pp. 767–769). The Guilford Press.

Rozin, P., Lowery, L., Imada, S., & Haidt, J. (1999). The CAD triad hypothesis: A mapping between three moral emotions (contempt, anger, disgust) and three moral codes (community, autonomy, divinity). *Journal of Personality and Social Psychology, 76*(4), 574–586.

Rozin, P., Spranca, M., Krieger, Z., Neuhaus, R., Surillo, D., Swerdlin, A., & Wood, K. (2004). Preference for natural: Instrumental and ideational/moral motivations, and the contrast between foods and medicines. *Appetite, 43*(2), 147–154.

Ruback, R. B., Greenberg, M. S., & Westcott, D. R. (1984). Social influence and crime-victim decision making. *Journal of Social Issues, 40*(1), 51–76.

Rubenzer, S. J., & Faschingbauer, T. R. (2004). *Personality, character & leadership in The White House: Psychologists assess the presidents.* Brassey's.

Ruhl, J. (1997). Thinking of environmental law as a complex adaptive system: How to clean up the environment by making a mess of environmental law. *Houston Law Review, 34*(4), 933–1002.

Russell, D., & Jones, W. H. (1980). When superstition fails: Reactions to disconfirmation of paranormal beliefs. *Personality and Social Psychology Bulletin, 6*(1), 83–88.

Safe Drinking Water Act of 1974, 42 U.S.C. § 300f et. seq.

Sagoff, M. (2009). Intrinsic value: A reply to Justus et al. *Trends in Ecology & Evolution, 24*(12), 643.

Salas, R. N., Shultz, J. M. & Solomon, C. G. (2020, July 15). The climate crisis and Covid-19—A major threat to the pandemic response. *New England Journal of Medicine.* www. NEJM.org

Salkind, N. J. (Ed.) (2010). *Encyclopedia of research design.* Sage Publications.

Salzman, J. (1997). Valuing ecosystem services. *Ecology Law Quarterly, 24*, 887–904.

Sanchez-Bayo, F., & Wyckhuys, K. A. G. (2019). Worldwide decline of the entomofauna: A review of its drivers. *Biological Conservation, 232*, 8–27.

Sanft, C. (2010). Environment and law in early imperial China (third-century BCE–first century CE): Qin and Han statutes concerning natural resources. *Environmental History, 15*(4), 701–721.

Sanitioso, R., Kunda, Z., & Fong, G. T. (1990). Motivated recruitment of autobiographical memories. *Journal of Personality and Social Psychology, 59*(2), 229–241.

Schachter, S., & Singer, J. (1962). Cognitive, social, and physiological determinants of emotional state. *Psychological Review, 69*(5), 379–399.

Schaller, M., Park, J. H., Faulkner, J. (2003). Prehistoric dangers and contemporary prejudices. In W. Stroebe & M. Hewstone (Eds.), *European review of social psychology* (pp. 105–137). Psychology Press.

Schauer, F. (2010). Is there a psychology of judging? In D. Klein & G. Mitchell (Eds.), *The psychology of judicial decision making* (pp. 103–120). Oxford University Press.

Scheffer, M., Carpenter, S., Foley, J. A., Folke, C., & Walker, B. (2001). Catastrophic shifts in ecosystems. *Nature, 413*(6856), 591–596.

Schiffman, R. (2017, April 26). Amazon rainforest under threat as Brazil tears up protections. *New Scientist.* www.newscientist.com

Schlebusch, C. M., Gattepaille, L. M., Engstrom, K., Vahter, M., Jakobsson, M., & Broberg, K. (2015). Human adaptation to arsenic-rich environments. *Molecular Biology and Evolution, 32*(6), 1544–1555.

Schlosberg, D. (2009). *Defining environmental justice: Theories, movements, and nature.* Oxford University Press.

Schmidt, B. (2011, June 16). Portland reservoir urination raises few health or scientific concerns—but it is pee. *Oregonian.* www.oregonlive.com

Schultz, P. W., Oskamp, S., & Mainieri, T. (1995). Who recycles and when? A review of personal and situational factors. *Journal of Environmental Psychology 15,* 105–121.

Schultz, P. W. (1999). Changing behavior with normative feedback interventions: A field experiment on curbside recycling. *Basic and Applied Social Psychology, 21*(1), 25–36.

Schultz, P. W., Nolan, J. M., Cialdini, R. B., Goldstein, N. J., & Griskevicius, V. (2007). The constructive, destructive, and reconstructive power of social norms. *Psychological Science, 18*(5), 429–434.

Schure, M. B., Kile, M. L., Harding, A., Harper, B., Harris, S., Uesugi, S., & R. T. Goins (2013). Perceptions of the environment and health among members of the confederated tribes of the Umatilla Indian Reservation. *Environmental Justice, 6*(3), 115–120.

Schwarz, N. (2000). Emotion, cognition, and decision making. *Cognition and Emotion, 14*(4), 433–440.

Schwarz, N., Sanna, L. J., Skurnik, I., and Yoon, C. (2007). Metacognitive experiences and the intricacies of setting people straight: Implications for debiasing and public information campaigns. *Advances in Experimental Social Psychology, 39,* 127–161.

Sears, D. O. (1986). College sophomores in the laboratory: Influences of a narrow data base on social psychology's view of human nature. *Journal of Personality and Social Psychology, 51*(3), 515–530.

Segall, M. H., Campbell, D. T., & Herskovits, M. J. (1966). *The influence of culture on visual perception.* Bobbs-Merrill.

Seltenrich, N. (2014). Take care in the kitchen: Avoiding cooking-related pollutants. *Environmental Health Perspectives, 122*(6), 154–159.

Senate Committee Report for 1982 Amendments to the Endangered Species Act, S. Rep. No. 97-418, (1982).

Shah, A., Mullainaithan, S., & Shafir, E. (2012). Some consequences of having too little. *Science, 338,* 682–685.

Shallow, C., Iliev, R., & Medin, D. (2011). Trolley problems in context. *Judgment and Decision Making, 6*(7), 593–601.

Shalvi, S., Gino, F., Barkan, R., & Ayal, S. (2015). Self-serving justifications: Doing wrong and feeling moral. *Current Directions in Psychological Science, 24*(2), 125–130.

Shao, W., Xian, S., Lin, N., Kunreuther, H., Jackson, N., & Goidel, K. (2017). Understanding the effects of past flood events and perceived and estimated flood risks on individuals' voluntary flood insurance purchase behavior. *Water Research, 108,* 391–400.

Shepherd, L., O'Carroll, R. E., & Ferguson, E. (2014). An international comparison of deceased and living organ donation/transplant rates in opt-in and opt-out systems: A panel study. *BMC Medicine, 12*(1), 131–144.

Shepherd, R., & Raats, M. (Eds.) (2006). *The psychology of food choice.* CABI.

Shepherd, S., & Kay, A. C. (2012). "On the perpetuation of ignorance: System dependence, system justification, and the motivated avoidance of sociopolitical information": Correction to Shepherd and Kay (2011). *Journal of Personality and Social Psychology, 102*(2), 280–280.

Sherif, M. (1935). A study of some social factors in perception. *Archives of Psychology, 27*(187), 1–60.

Sherif, M., & Hovland, C. I. (1961). *Social judgment: Assimilation and contrast effects in communication and attitude change.* Yale University Press.

Shu, L. L., Gino, F., & Bazerman, M. H. (2011). Dishonest deed, clear conscience: When cheating leads to moral disengagement and motivated forgetting. *Personality and Social Psychology Bulletin, 37*(3), 330–349.

Shultz, C. A., McCaffrey, S. M., & Huber-Stearns, H. R. (2019). Policy barriers and opportunities for prescribed fire application in the western United States. *International Journal of Wildland Fire, 28,* 874–884.

Sibley, C. G., & Barlow, F. K. (Eds.). (2016). *Cambridge handbook of the psychology of prejudice.* Cambridge University Press.

Siegrist, M., & Sutterlin, B. (2014). Human and nature-caused hazards: The affect heuristic causes biased decisions. *Risk Analysis, 34*(8), 1482–1494.

Sierra Club v. Marsh, 872 F.2d 497 (1st Cir. 1989).

Sierra Club v. Morton, 405 U.S. 727 (1972).

Singh, A. S., Zwickle, A., Bruskotter, J. T., & Wilson, R. (2017). The perceived psychological distance of climate change impacts and its influence on support for adaptation policy. *Environmental Science Policy, 73,* 93–99.

Simon, D., Snow, C. J., & Read, S. J. (2004). The redux of cognitive consistency theories: Evidence judgments by constraint satisfaction. *Journal of Personality and Social Psychology, 86*(6), 814–837.

Simmonds, C., McGivney, A., Reilly, P., Maffly, B., Wilkinson, T., Canon, G., Wright, M., & Whaley, M. (2018, November 20). Crisis in our national parks: How tourists are loving nature to death. *Guardian.* www.theguardian.com

Skavronskaya, L., Scott, N., Moyle, B., Le, D., Hadinejad, A., Zhang, R., Gardiner, S., Coghlan, A., & Shakeela, A. (2017). Cognitive psychology and tourism research: State of the art. *Tourism Review, 72*(2), 221–237.

Skibins, J. C., Powell, R., & Hallo, J. C. (2013). Charisma and conservation: Charismatic megafauna's influence on safari and zoo tourists' pro-conservation behaviors. *Biodiversity and Conservation, 22*(4), 959–982.

Slovic, P. (1987). Perception of risk. *Science, 236*(4799), 280–285.

Slovic, P. (2000). *The perception of risk.* Earthscan.

Slovic, P. (2007). "If I look at the mass I will never act": Psychic numbing and genocide. *Judgment and Decision Making, 2*(2), 79–95.

Slovic, P. (2015). When (in)action speaks louder than words: Confronting the collapse of humanitarian values in foreign policy decisions. *University of Illinois Law Review Slip Opinions, 2015,* 24–31.

Slovic, P., Finucane, M. L., Peters, E., & MacGregor, D. G. (2002). The affect heuristic. In T. Gilovich, D. Griffin, & D. Kahneman (Eds.), *Heuristics and biases: The psychology of intuitive judgment* (pp. 397–420). Cambridge University Press.

Slovic, P., Fischhoff, B., & Lichtenstein, S. (1981). Perceived risk. In R. Schwing & W. A. Albers (Eds.), *Societal risk assessment: How safe is safe enough?* (pp. 181–216). Plenum.

Slovic, P., & Zionts, D. (2012). Can international law stop genocide when our moral intutions fail us? In R. Goodman, D. Jinks & A. K. Woods (Eds.), *Understanding social action, promoting human rights* (pp. 100–134). Oxford University Press.

Slovic, P., Zionts, D., Woods, A. K., Goodman, R., & Jinks, D. (2007). Psychic numbing and mass atrocity. *Judgment and Decision Making, 2,* 79–95.

Slovic, P., Zionts, D., Woods, A. K., Goodman, R., & Jinks, D. (2013). Psychic numbing and mass atrocity. In E. Shafir (Ed.), *The behavioral foundations of policy* (pp. 126–142). Princeton University Press.

Small, D. A., & Loewenstein, G. (2003). Helping *a* victim or helping *the* victim: Altruism and identifiability. *Journal of Risk and Uncertainty, 26*(1), 5–16.

Small, D. A., & Loewenstein, G. (2005). The devil you know: The effects of identifiability on punishment. *Journal of Behavioral Decision Making, 18*(5), 311–318.

Small, D. A., Loewenstein, G., & Slovic, P. (2007). Sympathy and callousness: The impact of deliberative thought on donations to identifiable and statistical victims. *Organizational Behavior and Human Decision Processes, 102*(2), 143–153.

Smith, P. A. (2013, July 23). *The kitchen as a pollution hazard.* New York Times. https://well.blogs.nytimes.com

Smith, J. W., Anderson, D. H., & Moore, R. L. (2012). Social capital, place meanings, and perceived resilience to climate change. *Rural Sociology, 77*(3), 380–407.

Sokoloski, R., Markowitz, E. M., & Bidwell, D. (2018). Public estimates of support for offshore wind energy: False consensus, pluralistic ignorance, and partisan effects. *Energy Policy, 112,* 45–55.

Solé, R. V., & Bascompte, J. (2006). *Self-organization in complex ecosystems.* Princeton University Press.

Sonnenwald, D. H. (2007). Scientific collaboration. *Annual Review of Information Science and Technology, 41*(1), 643–681.

Spence, A., Poortinga, W., and Pidgeon, N. (2012). The psychological distance of climate change. *Risk Analysis, 32,* 957–972.

Standish, R. (2008). Concept and definition of complexity. In A. Yang & Y. Shan (Eds.), *Intelligent complex adaptive systems* (pp. 105–124). IGI Global.

Stanovich, K. E., West, R. F., & Toplak, M. E. (2013). Myside bias, rational thinking, and intelligence. *Current Directions in Psychological Science, 22*(4), 259–264.

Stavins, R. N. (Ed.) (2019). *Economics of the environment: Selected readings.* Edward Elgar Publishing.

Stern, N. (2007). *The economics of climate change.* Cambridge University Press.

Stern, S., & Lewinson-Zamir, D. (2020). *The psychology of property law.* NYU Press.

Stevenson, R. J., & Repacholi, B. M. (2005). Does the source of an interpersonal odour affect disgust? A disease risk model and its alternatives. *European Journal of Social Psychology, 35*(3), 375–401.

Stotland, E. (1969). Exploratory investigations of empathy. *Advances in Experimental Social Psychology, 4,* 271–314.

Strycker's Bay Neighborhood Council v. Karlen, 444 U.S. 223 (1980).

Stubbings, R. G., & Carmines, E. G. (1991). Is it irrational to vote? *Polity, 23*(4), 629–640.

Study of Critical Environmental Problems (SCEP) (1970). *Man's impact on the global environment: Assessment and recommendations for action.* MIT Press.

Sturgeon, N. (2009). *Environmentalism in popular culture: Gender, race, sexuality, and the politics of the natural.* University of Arizona Press.

Sunstein, C. R. (2000). Cognition and cost-benefit analysis. *Journal of Legal Studies, 29*(S2), 1059–1103.

Sunstein, C. R. (2002a). The arithmetic of arsenic. *Georgetown Law Journal, 90,* 2255–2309.

Sunstein, C. R. (2002b). *The cost-benefit state: The future of regulatory protection.* American Bar Association.

Sunstein, C. (2002c). *Risk and reason: Safety, law, and the environment.* Cambridge University Press.

Sunstein, C. R. (2003). Beyond the precautionary principle. *University of Pennsylvania Law Review, 151*(3), 1003–1058.

Sunstein, C. R. (2004). Lives, life-years and willingness to pay. *Columbia Law Review, 104,* 205–252.

Sunstein, C. R. (2005a). Cost-benefit analysis and the environment. *Ethics, 115*(2), 351–385.

Sunstein, C. R. (2005b). *Laws of fear: Beyond the precautionary principle.* Cambridge University Press.

Sunstein, C. R. (2006a). Irreversible and catastrophic. *Cornell Law Review, 91,* 841–898.

Sunstein, C. (2006b). Misfearing: A reply. *Harvard Law Review, 119,* 1110–1125.

Sunstein, C. R. (2007). *Worst-case scenarios.* Harvard University Press.

Sunstein C. R. (2014). *Why nudge? The politics of libertarian paternalism.* Yale University Press.

Sunstein, C. R., & Reisch, L. A. (2014). Automatically green: Behavioral economics and environmental protection. *Harvard Environmental Law Review, 38,* 127–158.

Sunstein, C. & Rowell, A. (2007). On discounting regulatory benefits: Risk, money, and intergenerational equity. *University of Chicago Law Review, 74,* 171–208.

Sunstein, C. R., Schkade, D., Ellman, L. M., & Sawicki, A. (2006). *Are judges political? An empirical analysis of the federal judiciary.* Brookings Institution Press.

Sunstein, C., & Vermeule, A. (2009). Conspiracy theories: Causes and cures. *Journal of Political Philosophy, 17*(2), 202–227.

Swim, J. K., & Bloodhart, B. (2015). Portraying the perils to polar bears: The role of empathic and objective perspective-taking toward animals in climate change communication. *Environmental Communication, 9*(4), 446–468.

Swim, J. K., Markowitz, E. M., & Bloodhart, B. (2012). Psychology and climate change: Beliefs, impacts, and human contributions. In S. D. Clayton (Ed.), *Oxford library of psychology. The Oxford handbook of environmental and conservation psychology* (pp. 645–669). Oxford University Press.

Taber, C. S., & Lodge, M. (2006). Motivated skepticism in the evaluation of political beliefs. *American Journal of Political Science, 50*, 755–769.

Tajfel, H. (1970). Experiments in intergroup discrimination. *Scientific American, 223*(5), 96–103.

Tajfel, H., Billig, M. G., Bundy, R. P., & Flament, C. (1971). Social categorization and intergroup behaviour. *European Journal of Social Psychology, 1*(2), 149–178.

Tajfel, H., & Turner, J. C. (1979). An integrative theory of intergroup conflict. In W. G. Austin & S. Worchel (Eds.), *The social psychology of intergroup relations* (pp. 33–48). Brooks-Cole.

Talluri, B. C., Urai, A. E., Tsetsos, K., Usher, M., & Donner, T. H. (2018). Confirmation bias through selective overweighting of choice-consistent evidence. *Current Biology, 28*(19), 3128–3135.

Tanner, C., & Medin, D. L. (2004). Protected values: No omission bias and no framing effects. *Psychonomic Bulletin & Review, 11*(1), 185–191.

Tarakeshwar, N., Swank, A. B., Pargament, K. I., & Mahoney, A. (2001). The sanctification of nature and theological conservatism: A study of opposing religious correlates of environmentalism. *Review of Religious Research, 42*(4), 387–404.

Tarlock, D. (2010). Environmental law: Then and now. *Washington University Journal of Law and Policy, 32*, 1–31.

Taylor, B., Van Wieren, G., & Zaleha, B. (2016). The greening of religion hypothesis (part two): Assessing the data from Lynn White, Jr, to Pope Francis. *Journal for the Study of Religion, Nature and Culture, 10*(3), 306–378.

Taylor, B. R. (2010). *Dark green religion: Nature spirituality and the planetary future.* University of California Press.

Taylor, D. E. (2000). The rise of the environmental justice paradigm: Injustice framing and the social construction of environmental discourses. *American Behavioral Scientist, 43*(4), 508–580.

Taylor, M. L., Gwinnett, C., Robinson, L. F., Woodall, L. C. (2016). Plastic microfibre ingestion by deep-sea organisms. *Science Reporter, 6*, 33997.

Taylor, P. W. (1983). In defense of biocentrism. *Environmental Ethics, 5*(3), 237–243.

Taylor, S. E., Crocker, J., Fiske, S. T., Sprinzen, M., & Winkler, J. D. (1979). The generalizability of salience effects. *Journal of Personality and Social Psychology, 37*(3), 357–368.

Taylor, S. E., & Fiske, S. T. (1978). Salience, attention, and attribution: Top of the head phenomena. In L. Berkowitz (Ed.), *Advances in experimental social psychology, 11* (pp. 249–288). Academic Press.

Tennessee Valley Authority v. Hill, 437 U.S. 153 (1978).

Tetlock, P. E. (2003). Thinking the unthinkable: Sacred values and taboo cognitions. *Trends in Cognitive Sciences, 7*(7), 320–324.

Tetlock, P. E., Kristel, O. V., Elson, S. B., Green, M. C., & Lerner, J. S. (2000). The psychology of the unthinkable: Taboo trade-offs, forbidden base rates, and heretical counterfactuals. *Journal of Personality and Social Psychology, 78*(5), 853–870.

Thaler, R. H. (1991). Some empirical evidence on dynamic inconsistency. *Quasi Rational Economics, 1,* 127–136.

Thaler, R. H., & Benartzi, S. (2004). Save more tomorrow: Using behavioral economics to increase employee saving. *Journal of Political Economy, 112*(S1), S164–S187.

Thaler, R. H., & Johnson, E. J. (1990). Gambling with the house money and trying to break even: The effects of prior outcomes on risky choice. *Management Science, 36*(6), 643–660.

Thaler, R. H., & Sunstein, C. R. (2003). Libertarian paternalism is not an oxymoron. *University of Chicago Law Review, 70*(4), 1159–1202.

Thaler, R. H., & Sunstein, C. R. (2008). *Nudge: Improving decisions about health, wealth, and happiness.* Penguin Books.

Thorsheim, P. (2006). *Inventing pollution: Coal, smoke, and culture in Britain since 1800.* Ohio University Press.

Thunberg, G. (2019). *No one is too small to make a difference.* Penguin Books.

Titmuss, R. (2018). *The gift relationship (reissue): From human blood to social policy.* Policy Press.

Toxic Substances Control Act of 1976, 15 U.S.C. § 2601 et seq.

Trafimow, D., Triandis, H. C., & Goto, S. G. (1991). Some tests of the distinction between the private self and the collective self. *Journal of Personality and Social Psychology, 60*(5), 649–655.

Treaty on European Union art. 130r, 1992 O. J. C 191/29.

Treaty of Neah Bay (1855). 12 Stat. 939.

Triandis, H. C. (1989). The self and social behavior in differing cultural contexts. *Psychological Review, 96*(3), 506–520.

Trinkner, R., & Tyler, T. R. (2016). Legal socialization: Coercion versus consent in an era of mistrust. *Annual Review of Law and Social Science, 12,* 417–439.

Trinkner, R., Tyler, T. R., & Goff, P. A. (2016). Justice from within: The relations between a procedurally just organizational climate and police organizational efficiency, endorsement of democratic policing, and officer well-being. *Psychology, Public Policy, and Law, 22*(2), 158–172.

Trouwborst, A. (2002). *Evolution and status of the precautionary principle in international law.* Kluwer Law International.

Truelove-Hill, M., Erickson, B., Anderson, J., Kossoyan, M., & Kounios, K. (2018). A growth-curve analysis of the effects of future-thought priming on insight and analytical problem-solving. *Frontiers in Psychology, 9* (1311), 1–9.

Turner, J. C., Hogg, M. A., Oakes, P. J., Reicher, S. D., & Wetherell, M. S. (1987). *Rediscovering the social group: A self-categorization theory.* Basil Blackwell.

Tversky, A., & Kahneman, D. (1973). Availability: A heuristic for judging frequency and probability. *Cognitive Psychology, 5*(2), 207–232.

Tversky, A., & Kahneman, D. (1974). Judgment under uncertainty: Heuristics and biases. *Science, 185,* 1124–1131.

Tversky, A., & Kahneman, D. (1981). The framing of decisions and the psychology of choice. *Science, 211*(4481), 453–458.

Tversky, A., & Kahneman, D. (1983). Extensional versus intuitive reasoning: The conjunction fallacy in probability judgment. *Psychological Review, 90*(4), 293–315.

Tversky, A., Sattath, S., & Slovic, P. (1988). Contingent weighting in judgment and choice. *Psychological Review, 95*(3), 371–384.

Tyler, T. R. (1990). *Why people obey the law: Procedural justice, legitimacy, and compliance.* Yale University Press.

Tyler, T. R., & Lind, E. A. (1992). A relational model of authority in groups. *Advances in Experimental Social Psychology, 25,* 115–191.

Tymula, A., Belmaker, L. A. R., Roy, A. K., Ruderman, L., Manson, K., Glimcher, P. W., & Levy, I. (2012). Adolescents' risk-taking behavior is driven by tolerance to ambiguity. *Proceedings of the National Academy of Sciences, 109*(42), 17135–17140.

Ubel, P. A., Loewenstein, G., & Jepson, C. (2005). Disability and sunshine: Can hedonic predictions be improved by drawing attention to focusing illusions or emotional adaptation? *Journal of Experimental Psychology: Applied, 11*(2), 111–123.

Uchiyama, M., Nishio, Y., Yokoi, K., Hosokai, Y., Takeda, A., & Mori, E. (2015). Pareidolia in Parkinson's disease without dementia: A positron emission tomography study. *Parkinsonism & Related Disorders, 21*(6), 603–609.

Uhlmann, D. M. (2014). Environmental law, public health, and the values conundrum. *Michigan Journal of Environmental and Administrative Law, 3,* 231–242.

Ulen, T. S. (2014). The importance of behavioral law. In E. Zamir & D. Teichman (Eds.), *The Oxford handbook of behavioral economics and the law* (pp. 93–124). Oxford University Press.

Ulrich, R. S. (1993). Biophilia, biophobia, and natural landscapes. In S. R. Kellert & E. O. Wilson (Eds.), *The biophilia hypothesis* (pp. 73–137). Island Press.

United Nations Framework Convention on Climate Change, May 9, 1992, 1771 U.N.T.S. 107.

United Nations Scientific Committee on the Effects of Atomic Radiation. (2008). *Sources and effects of ionizing radiation: Report to the general assembly with scientific annexes (Vol. 1).* United Nations Publications.

Urgenda Foundation v. the State of the Netherlands, Rb. Den Haag 24 juni 2015, 2015, 7196 m.nt. (Urgenda Foundation/Kingdom of the Netherlands) at 1 (Neth.). www.urgenda.nl

U.S. Fish and Wildlife Service. (2019). *Listed species summary (boxscore).* https://ecos.fws.gov

U.S. Geological Survey. (n.d.). *Background soil-lead survey: State data.* www.epa.gov

U.S. Geological Survey. (2016). *Comprehensive study finds widespread mercury contamination across western North America.* www.usgs.gov

U.S. Office of Management and Budget. (2003). *OMB Circular A-4 regulatory analysis.* Executive Office of the President.

van den Berg, M., Maas, J., Muller, R., Braun, A., Kaandorp, W., van Lien, R., van Poppel, M. N. M., van Mechelen, W., & van den Berg, A. (2015). Autonomic nervous system responses to viewing green and built settings: differentiating between sympathetic and parasympathetic activity. *International Journal of Environmental Research and Public Health, 12*(12), 15860–15874.

Vandenbergh, M., Barkenbus, J., & Gilligan, J. M. (2008). Individual carbon emissions: The low-hanging fruit. *U.C.L.A. Law Review, 55*, 1701–1758.

van Aaken, A. & Broude, T. (2019). The psychology of international law: An introduction. *European Journal of International Law, 30*, 1225–1236.

van der Kolk, B. A. (1994). The body keeps the score: Memory and the evolving psychobiology of posttraumatic stress. *Harvard Review of Psychiatry, 1*(5), 253–265.

Van Dijck, S. J., Laouina, A., Carvalho, A. V., Loos, S., Schipper, A. M., Van der Kwast, H., Nafaa, R., Antari, M., Rocha, A., Borrego, C., Coen, J., & Ritsema, C. J. (2006). Desertification in northern Morocco due to effects of climate change on groundwater recharge. In W. G. Kepner, J. L. Rubio, D. A. Mouat, & F. Pedrazzini (Eds.), *Desertification in the Mediterranean region: A security issue* (pp. 549–577). Springer.

van Valkengoed, A. M. & Steg, L. (2019). Meta-analyses of factors motivating climate change adaptation behaviour. *Nature Climate Change, 9*, 158–163.

van Zeben, J., & Rowell, A. (2020). *Essential environmental law: The European Union.* University of California Press.

Vandello, J. A., & Cohen, D. (1999). Patterns of individualism and collectivism across the United States. *Journal of Personality and Social Psychology, 77*(2), 279–292.

Varnum, M. E. W., Grossman, I., Kitayama, S., Nisbett, R. E. (2010). The origin of cultural differences in cognition: The social orientation hypothesis. *Current Directions in Psychological Science, 19*, 9–13.

Västfjäll, D., Peters, E., & Slovic, P. (2014). Compassion fatigue: Affect and charity are greatest for a single child in need. *PLoS one 9*(6), e100115.

Västfjäll, D., Slovic, P., & Mayorga, M. (2015). Pseudoinefficacy: Negative feelings from children who cannot be helped reduce warm glow for children who can be helped. *Frontiers in Psychology, 6*, 616–627.

Verplanken, B., & Wood, W. (2006). Interventions to break and create consumer habits. *Journal of Public Policy & Marketing, 25*(1), 90–103.

Vesilind, P., Peirce, J., & Weiner, R. (1998). *Environmental pollution and control* (pp. 241–43). Elsevier.

Vihanto, M. (2003). Tax evasion and the psychology of the social contract. *Journal of Socio-Economics, 32*(2), 111–125.

Viscusi, W. K. (1998). *Rational Risk Policy: The 1996 Arne Ryde Memorial Lectures.* Oxford University Press.

Vohs, K. D. (2015). Money priming can change people's thoughts, feelings, motivations, and behaviors: An update on 10 years of experiments. *Journal of Experimental Psychology: General, 144*(4), e86–e93.

Wade-Benzoni, K. A., Tenbrunsel, A. E., & Bazerman, M. H. (1996). Egocentric interpretations of fairness in asymmetric, environmental social dilemmas: Explaining harvesting behavior and the role of communication. *Organizational Behavior and Human Decision Processes, 67*(2), 111–126.

Walster, E., Aronson, E., & Abrahams, D. (1966). On increasing the persuasiveness of a low prestige communicator. *Journal of Experimental Social Psychology, 2*(4), 325–342.

Wansink, B. (1996). Can package size accelerate usage volume? *Journal of Marketing, 60*(3), 1–14.

Wansink, B. (2002). Changing eating habits on the home front: Lost lessons from World War II research. *Journal of Public Policy & Marketing, 21*(1), 90–99.

Wason, P. C. (1968). Reasoning about a rule. *Quarterly Journal of Experimental Psychology, 20*(3), 273–281.

Wason, P. C., & Shapiro, D. (1971). Natural and contrived experience in a reasoning problem. *Quarterly Journal of Experimental Psychology, 23*(1), 63–71.

Waytz, A., Epley, N., & Cacioppo, J. T. (2010). Social cognition unbound: Insights into anthropomorphism and dehumanization. *Current Directions in Psychological Science, 19*(1), 58–62.

Weary, G., & Edwards, J. A. (1996). Causal-uncertainty beliefs and related goal structures. In R. M. Sorrentino & E. Higgins (Eds.), *Handbook of motivation and cognition, vol. 3: The interpersonal context* (pp. 148–181). Guilford Press.

Webb, T. L., & Sheeran, P. (2006). Does changing behavioral intentions engender behavioral change? A meta-analysis of the experimental evidence. *Psychological Bulletin, 132*(2), 249–268.

Weber, E. U. (2006). Experience-based and description-based perceptions of long-term risk: Why global warming does not scare us (yet). *Climatic Change, 77*, 103–120.

Weber E. U., & Johnson, E. J. (2009). Decisions under uncertainty: Psychological, economic and neuroeconomic explanations of risk preference. In P. W. Glimcher, C. F. Camerer, C. Fehr, & R. A. Poldrack (Eds.), *Neuroeconomics: Decision making and the brain* (pp. 127–144), Academic Press, Elsevier.

Weber, E. U., & Stern, P. C. (2011). Public understanding of climate change in the United States. *American Psychologist, 66*(4), 315–328.

Weisbach, D., & Sunstein, C. R. (2008). Climate change and discounting the future: A guide for the perplexed. *Yale Law & Policy Review, 27*, 433–458.

Weiss, E. B. (2011). The evolution of international environmental law. *Japanese Yearbook of International Law, 54*, 1–27.

Weitzman, M. (2011). Fat-tailed uncertainty in the economics of catastrophic climate change. *Review of Environmental Economics and Policy, 5*(2), 975–292.

Westbury, H. R., & Neumann, D. L. (2008). Empathy-related responses to moving film stimuli depicting human and non-human animal targets in negative circumstances. *Biological Psychology, 78*(1), 66–74.

White, L. (1967). The historical roots of our ecologic crisis. *Science, 155*(3767), 1203–1207.

Whiteside, K. H. (2006). *Precautionary politics: Principle and practice in confronting environmental risk.* MIT Press.

Whitmarsh, L. (2009). Behavioural responses to climate change: asymmetry of intentions and impacts. *Journal of Environmental Psychology, 29*, 13-23.

Whitson, J. A., & Galinsky, A. D. (2008). Lacking control increases illusory pattern perception. *Science, 322*(5898), 115–117.

Wibeck, V., Hansson, A., Anshelm, J., Asayama, S., Dilling, L., Feetham, P. M., Hauser, R., Ishii, A., & Sugiyama, M. (2017). Making sense of climate engineering: A focus group study of lay publics in four countries. *Climatic Change, 145*, 1–14.

Wiener, J. B. (2016). The tragedy of the uncommons: On the politics of apocalypse. *Global Policy, 7*(S1), 67–80.

Wiener, J. B., Rogers, M. D., Hammitt, J. K., & Sand, P. H. (Eds.) (2011). *The reality of precaution: Comparing risk regulation in the United States and Europe.* Earthscan.

Wiesel, E., & Boehm, R. (2015). "Ingroup love" and "outgroup hate" in intergroup conflict between natural groups. *Journal of Experimental Social Psychology, 60*, 110–120.

Wildavsky, A. (1995). *But is it true?* Harvard University Press.

Wildschut, T., Pinter, B., Vevea, J. L., Insko, C. A., & Schopler, J. (2003). Beyond the group mind: A quantitative review of the interindividual-intergroup discontinuity effect. *Psychological Bulletin, 129*(5), 698–722.

Willett, W., Rockström, J., Loken, B., Springmann, M., Lang, T., Vermeulen, S., Garnet, T., Tilman, D., DeClerck, F., Wood, A., Jonell, M., Clark, M., Gordon, L. J., Fanzo, J., Hawkes, C., Zurayk, R., Rivera, J. A., De Vries, W., Sibanda, L. M., Afshin, A., et al. (2019). Food in the Anthropocene: The EAT-*Lancet* Commission on healthy diets from sustainable food systems. *Lancet Commissions, 393*(10170), 447–492.

Williams, D. R., Patterson, M. E., Roggenbuck, J. W., & Watson, A. E. (1992). Beyond the commodity metaphor: Examining emotional and symbolic attachment to place. *Leisure Sciences, 14*(1), 29–46.

Williamson, K., Satre-Meloy, A., Velasco, K., & Green, K. (2018). *Climate change needs behavior change: Making the case for behavioral solutions to reduce global warming.* Rare.

Willis, K. J. (Ed.). (2017). *State of the world's plants 2017.* Royal Botanic Gardens, Kew.

Wilson, E. O. (1986). *Biophilia.* Harvard University Press.

Wilson, T. D., & Gilbert, D. T. (2003). Affective forecasting. *Advances in Experimental Social Psychology, 35*, 345–411.

Wilson, T. D., Wheatley, T., Meyers, J. M., Gilbert, D. T., & Axsom, D. (2000). Focalism: A source of durability bias in affective forecasting. *Journal of Personality and Social Psychology, 78*(5), 821–836.

Wistrich, A. J., Guthrie, C., & Rachlinski, J. J. (2005). Can judges ignore inadmissible information? The difficulty of deliberately disregarding. *University of Pennsylvania Law Review, 153*(2), 1251–1345.

Woerdman, E., Arcuri, A, & Clò, S. (2008). Emissions trading and the polluter-pays principle. *Review of Law and Economics, 4*(2), 565–589.

The World Commission on Environment and Development. (1987). *Our common future.* Oxford University Press.

World Health Organization. (2002). *Arsenic: Mass poisoning on an unprecedented scale.* www.who.int

World Health Organization. (2006). *Indoor residual spraying: Use of indoor residual spraying for scaling up global malaria control and elimination: WHO position statement.* World Health Organization. http://apps.who.int

World Health Organization. (2018). *WHO global ambient air quality database.* World Health Organization. www.who.int

World Trade Organization. (2019). *DS381: United States–Measures concerning the importation, marketing and sale of tuna and tuna products.* World Trade Organization. www.wto.org

World Trade Organization. (2001). *DS58: United States–Import prohibition of certain shrimp and shrimp products.* World Trade Organization. www.wto.org

Wuchty, S., Jones, B. F., & Uzzi, B. (2007). The increasing dominance of teams in production of knowledge. *Science, 316*(5827), 1036–1039.

Wundt, W. M. (1904/1969). *Principles of physiological psychology* (E. B. Titchener, Trans.). The Macmillan Co.

Wyles, K. J., Pahl, S., Thomas, K., & Thompson, R. C. (2016). Factors that can undermine the psychological benefits of coastal environments: Exploring the Effect of tidal state, presence, and type of litter. *Environment and Behavior, 48*(9), 1095–1126.

Yamagishi, T., Mifune, N., Liu, J. H., & Pauling, J. (2008). Exchanges of group-based favours: Ingroup bias in the prisoner's dilemma game with minimal groups in Japan and New Zealand. *Asian Journal of Social Psychology, 11*(3), 196–207.

Zajonc, R. B. (1984). On the primacy of affect. *American Psychologist, 39*(2), 117–123.

Zhang, Q., Xu, E. G., Li, J., Chen, Q., Ma, L., Zeng, E. Y., & Shi, H. (2020). A review of microplastics in table salt, drinking water, and air: Direct human exposure. *Environmental Science & Technology, 54*(7), 3740–3751.

Ziegler, R., Diehl, M., Zigon, R., & Fett, T. (2004). Source consistency, distinctiveness, and consensus: The three dimensions of the Kelley ANOVA model in persuasion. *Personality and Social Psychology Bulletin, 30*(3), 352–364.

Zinck, R. D., & Grimm, V. (2009). Unifying wildfire models from ecology and statistical physics. *American Naturalist, 174*(5), E170–E185.

Zlatevska, N., Dubelaar, C., & Holden, S. S. (2014). Sizing up the effect of portion size on consumption: A meta-analytic review. *Journal of Marketing, 78*(3), 140–154.

INDEX

abundance, perceived, 194

acidification, ocean, 67, 222, 224

actors, public, 21

acts, 73–75, 91

acute injuries, 266

acute pollution, 152–53

adaptation, 66–67; behaviors, 251–52; hedonic, 46–47; local, 153; psychological challenges, 240; source effect, 158–59

administrative agencies, 20, 27–28, 168–69, 265

affect, 45–46; disgust, 149; forecasting, 47–48, 50, 227–28; heuristic, 128, 133–34, 148, 210; neglect, 238; response, 151, 157–59, 177

afforestation, 241

agencies, 27–28, 168–69, 265; *Chevron* doctrine, 86, 169

agriculture, 14, 55; policy, 184; pollution, 186; regenerative, 252; runoff, 57

air pollution, 16, 150, 166, 168–70, 173–74

all or nothing response, 133, 157–58

allocation of harms, 160–61

altruism, 59, 89, 112–13, 120

Amazon rain forest, 55–57

anchoring, 77

Andes mountains, 67

animals: annelid worms, 199, 201; aquatic life, 95–96; environmental statutes, 184; fish, 95–96, 106, 153, 198; habitats, 106, 184; insects,163, 199–201; mammals, 98, 134, 199–200, 202, 263; monk parakeets, 103; reptiles, 199–202; snail

darter, 199, 210; spiders, 201, 263; ugly, 134, 202–4, 263; whale hunting, 144

animism, 109

annelid worms, 199, 201

Anthropocene, 14–15

anthropogenic climate change, 220; denial, 123, 229–30; emissions, 150, 222–23, 237, 239; science, 224. *See also* climate

anthropology, 156

anthropomorphism, 97–98, 114–15, 217

antidegradation, 43–44

antisocial behavior, 33, 228

apophenia, 78–79

aquatic life, 95–96

arachnids, 199, 201

arsenic, 31, 67, 158, 164

artificiality, 159, 164–65

Asch, Solomon, 137

assimilation effects, 77

atmosphere, 221–22, 239; Global Warming Petition Project, 86. *See also* greenhouse gases

attention: barriers, 151, 154–55; bisphenol A, 167–68; differential, 201, 204; legislative, 25; motivated cognition, 28, 122–23, 168–69, 236; psychological process, 18–19; public, 5, 11, 35, 47–48, 86

attitudes: components, 117–18, 122, 125

attribution error, fundamental, 111, 142

Australian wildfires, 238

authority: experts, 119–21, 147; agency, 27–28, 245–46

availability heuristic, 35–38, 76–77, 115, 134; "availability cascades," 38, 166

bandwagon effects, 197
bargaining with future, 51–52
barriers to empathy, 115–16, 154–55, 175
base rate neglect, 38–40, 61
Bayesian analysis, 81–82
behavioral economics, 214–17
behavioral instruments, 19, 131, 175–76, 178
beliefs, strongly motivated, 123–27
best practices: climate communication, 256–57; psychology, 146–47
Bhopal, India, 152–53
bias, 132, 134–35, 204; confirmation, 83–84, 91; Dunning-Kruger, 85–86; group-based, 57–58; hindsight, 132–33, 148; motivational, 71, 122; overprecision, 84–85; peak-end, 77; present, 41, 46, 48–50, 62, 235; recency, 71, 77; status quo, 42, 128–31; studying, 134–36. *See also* cognitive errors: heuristics
biophilia, 98, 202–3, 263
biophobia, 201–2, 263
biota, aquatic, 95–96
biotic community, 74, 183
birds: monk parakeets, 103 bisphenols, 167–68
blinding: double, 83; triple, 146
boundaries, ecosystem, 190–91
BP oil spill, 94, 153
BPA, 167–68
Brazil, 55–57
Buddhist traditions, 109
bystander intervention, 138

canons of construction, 134–35
carbon: capture, 241; credits, 252; sequestration, 252; sink, 55
carbon dioxide (CO2), 234; greenhouse gas emissions, 221–22, 224–25, 246, 250–52; removal (CDR), 241
Carson, Rachel, 16, 163, 167
cascades, availability, 38, 57, 166–68, 197, 237

catastrophes, 45; shifts, 65–67
causality, 64, 68–70
CERCLA, 16, 36, 94
change, environmental, 66–67
charismatic species, 134, 201–2, 238. *See also* cuteness
Chevron doctrine, 86, 169
China: air pollution, 31; culture, 111; imperial, 15
chlorofluorocarbons (CFCs), 221
choice architecture, 19, 128, 131, 175–76, 263
Cialdini, Robert, 118–20, 193–94
citizen suits, 23, 195, 249
Clean Air Act, 16, 150, 166, 168–70, 173–74
Clean Water Act, 43–44, 95–96, 150, 190, 203; wetlands, 184
climate: action *vs.* inaction, 239–42; adaptation, 239–40; cognitive load, 228–29; communication, 257; complexity, 235–37; definition, 221; denial, 229–31, 236; detachment, 226–27; diffusion, 232–35; discomfort, 228–29; emotional load, 228–29; environmental injury, 231–32; ethical challenges, 225, 228; greenhouse gas emissions, 221, 234–36, 239, 246–47, 250–51; inaction, legislative, 230–31, 239, 241–42, 244–46; individual behaviors, 248–56; Industrial Revolution, 14–15, 221; institutional decision making, 243–48; International Panel on Climate Change, 222–24, 239–40, 252, 256; magnitude of harms, 226–28; mitigation, 223–25, 239–40, 248–50; nonhuman environment, 237–38; policy, 224–25; psychic numbing, 226–27, 229, 257–58; psychological challenges, 220, 225–38; scientific challenges, 224–25; special challenges, 226–27; strategies, 239–42, 258; United Nations Framework Convention on Climate Change, 222–24; victims, 233
coal, 15, 67

NAAQS. *See* National Ambient Air Quality Standards
Nagle, John, 183
National Ambient Air Quality Standards (NAAQS), 165
National Environmental Policy Act (NEPA), 16–17, 203–4, 262
National Forest Service, 182
National Institutes of Health (NIH), 167
National Park Service, 16, 192
National Wilderness Preservation System, 184, 191–92
Native Americans, 143–44, 150; land use practices, 144; stereotypes, 141, 144; traditions, 109; tribes, 143; land use practices, 144
natural disasters, 16, 159
Natural Resource Defense Council, 166
natural resources, 190
natural risks, 159
natural systems, 68
nature, 12; human interactions, 64, 101–2; noninterference, 74; spiritual value, 109–11
negative emissions technologies, 240–41 negative externalities, 32–33, 61
negative feelings, 33, 229, 233, 236
Netherlands, the, 247
New Zealand, 103–4, 192
nitrous oxide, 221–22
Nixon, Richard M., 16, 26
nonhuman environment: effects, 115; emotional benefits, 101–2; impacts, 93–116, 154–55, 174, 179, 189–90, 237–38; preferences, 99–100; psychology, 29; salience, 98–99; valuing, 96–97, 113
nonidentifiability, 233
noninterference, 73–74, 91
nonpoint source pollution, 151–52
nonprofit institutions, 21–22, 196–97
Norgaard, Kari, 230–31
normal curve, 65–66

normativity, 18–19, 174–75, 177; conformity, 136–37; goals, 19; values, 10, 14
Norway, 230–31
not in my backyard (NIMBY), 177 nudges, 19, 128, 131, 175
numbing, psychic, 45, 59–60, 226–27, 229, 247

Obama, Barack H., 17, 216, 223, 246–47
obligations, 41, 51
observed changes, 222
Occupational Safety and Health Act (OSHA), 16, 173
oceans, 37, 153, 222; acidification, 67, 223–24
Office of Management and Budget (OMB), 213
oil spills, 153
omissions, 73–75, 91
Open Science Collaboration, 145
optical illusions, 143
OSHA. *See* Occupational Safety and Health Act
Ostrom, Elinor, 12
othering, 160–61, 234
out of sight, 36
out-group dynamics, 25, 53–58, 144; bias, 234; effects, 62; perception, 246
overdetection, 79
overestimation, 85–86, 122; effects, 39; impacts, 40
overfamiliarity, 172
overperception, 79
overprecision bias, 84–85
oversalience, 166, 263
overtourism, 105–6, 194
overvaluation, 215
ownership, 42–43, 130, 191

palliative comparisons, 33, 228
pandemic, COVID-19, 44, 261, 267–69
Paris Agreement, 24, 223, 244, 250; commitments, 223; goals, 223
particulate matter, 31, 165–66

psychological effects (*cont.*)
regulators, 162–78; response, 152; risk perception, 159–62, 253; scarcity, 104–5, 192–95, 218, 269; sustainability, 205–9; tourism, 251; uniqueness, 192–95, 218
psychopathy, 26, 246
public actors, 21
public goods, 32–33, 56–58, 120
public information campaigns, 254–55
public lands, 180, 182, 184, 192
punitive behavior, 60

quantification, 28, 210–14
quantitative analysis, 69; risk, 158

Rachlinski, Jeff, 27, 132, 134, 243–45
radiation, 164
rareness, 39, 45, 70, 105–6; risks, 45
reactance, 105
Reagan, Ronald, 17, 213
reasoning, 70–71, 123
rebound effects, 253
recency, 70–71; bias, 77
reciprocity, 119–20, 147; norms, 120
recoil, 156–59, 176–77
recycling, 39–40, 127
redressability, 266
reference points, 43, 122
regenerative agriculture, 252
regulation, 54, 163, 246; agencies, 246; impacts, 213–14; regulatory impact analysis (RIA), 213; regulators, 163, 168; stages, 162; tools, 19; valuations, 94
religion, 96, 106, 109–10, 115–16
replication crisis, 118, 145–46, 148
representativeness heuristic, 35–36, 38–40, 61, 76–77, 91, 133
reptiles, 199–202
research, 141, 146, 148, 261
Resource Conservation and Recovery Act, 16, 150, 176–77
resource extraction, 186, 190
revealed preference, 214

Rio Declaration on Environment and Development, 205–6, 208
risk, 39, 61, 209; assessment, 74; estimation, 132–33; intergenerational, 235; management, 268; overwhelming, 207; perception, 80–82, 153–56, 159, 161, 170–71, 196, 241, 264, 269; precautionary principle, 208–9; prioritization, 155; technology, 253
Roman law, 15
Romantic movement, 181
Ruhl, J. B., 183, 248
runoff, 54–55, 57, 151–52, 186

Safe Drinking Water Act, 16, 150
salience, 24, 44–45, 69–70, 166, 176, 195, 198–202, 208, 211–12, 228, 263; effects, 70; increasing, 52, 116, 144, 193, 262; oversalience, 166, 263; psychological research, 198, 228, 269; undersalience, 186, 202, 264; uniqueness, 193
Santa Barbara oil spill, 16, 25, 36
scarcity, 54, 104, 116, 119–20, 147, 255, 269; mindset, 104–5, 193–94; perception, 190, 193–94; psychology of, 192–94; thinking, 194
science, 236; climate change, 71–72, 222–25; communication, 70; ecology, 182–83; open science collaboration, 145–46
sea levels, 222–24
self-justification, 56
self-serving justification, 160–61
Sherif, Muzafer, 136–37
Shinto religion, 109
shortcuts, 35–36, 38, 69–70, 76, 81, 135, 143
Silent Spring, 16, 163, 167
similarity, 108, 147
skepticism, 80, 230
snail darter, 199, 210
snakes, 201
social cost of carbon, 246–47
social identity, 102–4, 122, 136–37, 144, 148, 192, 254–55

Arden Rowell is Professor of Law at the University of Illinois. She has also taught at Harvard, Duke, and the University of Chicago Law Schools. Her research focuses on risk regulation and on building bridges between environmental law and other disciplines.

Kenworthey Bilz is Professor of Law in the College of Law at the University of Illinois. She has also taught at Northwestern, Duke, Notre Dame, and KU-Leuven. She teaches courses in criminal law, evidence, negotiations, and psychology. She conducts empirical research in the moral psychology of the law.